AF691589

THE MORAL LIMITS OF LAW

The Moral Limits of Law

Obedience, Respect, and Legitimacy

RUTH C. A. HIGGINS

OXFORD
UNIVERSITY PRESS

This book has been printed digitally and produced in a standard specification in order to ensure its continuing availability

OXFORD
UNIVERSITY PRESS

Great Clarendon Street, Oxford OX2 6DP

Oxford University Press is a department of the University of Oxford. It furthers the University's objective of excellence in research, scholarship, and education by publishing worldwide in

Oxford New York

Auckland Cape Town Dar es Salaam Hong Kong Karachi Kuala Lumpur Madrid Melbourne Mexico City Nairobi New Delhi Shanghai Taipei Toronto

With offices in

Argentina Austria Brazil Chile Czech Republic France Greece Guatemala Hungary Italy Japan South Korea Poland Portugal Singapore Switzerland Thailand Turkey Ukraine Vietnam

Oxford is a registered trade mark of Oxford University Press in the UK and in certain other countries

Published in the United States by Oxford University Press Inc., New York

Oxford is a registered trade mark of Oxford University Press in the UK and in certain other countries

Published in the United States by Oxford University Press Inc., New York

© R. Higgins, 2004

The moral rights of the author have been asserted

Database right Oxford University Press (maker)

Reprinted 2005

All rights reserved. No part of this publication may be reproduced, stored in a retrieval system, or transmitted, in any form or by any means, without the prior permission in writing of Oxford University Press, or as expressly permitted by law, or under terms agreed with the appropriate reprographics rights organization. Enquiries concerning reproduction outside the scope of the above should be sent to the Rights Department, Oxford University Press, at the address above

You must not circulate this book in any other binding or cover And you must impose this same condition on any acquirer

ISBN 0-19-926567-4

In order to exist, man must rebel, but rebellion must respect the limits that it discovers in itself—limits where minds meet, and, in meeting, begin to exist.

(A. Camus)

for Amber

Preface

Modern societies are drawn in a tension between the centripetal pull of the local and the centrifugal stress of the global. Boundaries that once appeared permanent are now permeable. Transnational legal, economic, and trade institutions, and multinational corporate actors increasingly erode the autonomy of states. None the less, it is typically through national law that transnational principles find expression.

For law's subjects, this tension brings into focus the interaction of legal and moral obligations. The ethical, 'what ought I do?' of the private realm, in the public realm becomes, 'what am I morally obligated to do on account of legal obligation?' or more broadly, 'how do my moral and legal obligations interact?' Throughout this work, I will refer to the problem articulated by these questions—the problem of reconciling inconsistent legal and moral demands that is traditionally subsumed within the idea of political obligation—as the problem of conscientious obedience.

Discussions concerning conscientious obedience betray two contradictory signs of their pedigree. Their persistence signals their continuing importance but sometimes makes them seem tired. This tiredness largely consists in a fixed methodological armature built around by several standard concepts and a discussion that typically neglects questions beyond obligation and full-blooded membership. In addition, the debate moves in and out of fashion in response to historical events. The turbulence that defined both North America and Central Europe during the 1960s provoked a rush of interest in the topic. The increasing peace and stability of the Western world during the 1990s gave the enquiry an abstruse air.

This work began as a D. Phil. thesis, undertaken between 1996 and 2000 at Balliol College, Oxford. In completing my thesis in November 2000, I began the conclusion by observing that, in times of peace and governmental equilibrium, questions of obedience and legitimacy seem pleasantly odd. The authority of law is a queen pawned by more mundane dilemmas. But, that, at all times, law exercises a peculiarly deep influence on all domains of our lives.

Political and economic events over the last three years have once again crowned the issues of obligation and legitimacy. The question is not only more urgent, but demands a response that breaks free from the methodological and substantive constraints that have ossified traditional discussion.

In *The Death of Ivan Ilyich*, Tolstoy writes of a magistrate re-evaluating life as he confronts death. He is struck by the paradox of legal propriety: '"Maybe I did not live as I ought to have done... But how could that be, when I did everything properly?"... and he remembered all the legality, correctitude and propriety of his life.'[1]

This book is an attempt to investigate this paradox as a living concern. It provides a comprehensive analysis of existing discussions of the problem of conscientious obedience and proposes a reframing of the issue through a theory of respect for law, which situates obligation within the increasingly global nature of moral concerns. In Chapter 2, I begin with the ineliminable and minimal enquiry, attempting to discover that which is universally valuable in law—that which might merit the respect even of sceptic, outsider, and visitor. I derive an obligatory attitude of respect for law, entailing duties not to harm and damage law's proper functioning, from the duty of respect for the capacity of persons. The argument from respect provides an understanding of the intrinsic value of persons and the instrumental value of reasonably just and efficient law, while drafting a normative sketch of the appropriate attitude of any individual towards reasonably just law. It also facilitates a theory of conscientious obedience that accommodates circumstances of interdependence. Respect acknowledges persons *qua* persons and not *qua* citizens. It ascribes no prevailing moral weight to national boundaries. States are necessarily territorial. Boundaries necessarily delimit their extent. But this fact has no necessary implications for the moral significance ascribed to these boundaries. Any such moral weight cannot be assumed and must be argued for. I suspect that this inclusiveness is now a necessary condition of any such theory, and that theories of conscientious obedience that assume a bounded conception of the polity are no longer tenable.

However, the argument from respect does not support an obligation to obey. The final section of the Chapter 2 therefore considers whether respect enjoys the conceptual resources necessary to underwrite obligation. By evaluating the recent works of Philip Soper, I attempt to show that his arguments distort the nature of respect, which does not extend to a comprehensive obligation to obey: Respect is already awake to the magistrate's paradox

In the following chapters, I analyse the most articulate defences of the core concepts that have been deployed in discussions of conscientious obedience—consent, community, fairness, and gratitude. Chapter 3 is critical of the forms and objectives of consent theory, and suggests that Raz's theory of respect for law, which trades on the same justificatory factors as consent theory to reach quite different conclusions, appropriately frames the ideas at play in consent. Razian respect, however, is a permissible but non-obligatory attitude which concedes the non-universality of obligation. Respect and scepticism again embrace. Chapters 4 to 7 therefore attempt to analyse whether any other theory supplies the defects of respect. I conclude that the absence of an obligation to obey is no defect, and that a bifurcated attitude of respect for law best captures

[1] Quoted in Zinn 'Law, Justice and Disobedience' 920. This is a theme to which Tolstoy returns in *The Slavery of Our Times*, where having suggested that that no man, in his one life, should act contrary to the voice of conscience, he concludes: 'And what will come of this—I do not know. Only, I think that no harm can result from acting as my conscience demands' (*The Slavery of Our Times* 124).

the citizen's appropriate moral posture towards reasonably just law. The theory of respect also attempts to rehabilitate discussion by emphasizing the primacy of duty, both logically and psychologically, within the political lives of individuals, by accommodating cosmopolitan thinking about ethics in the context of political obligation, and by demonstrating that theories of conscientious obedience should be sensitive to their historical context.

As I noted above, this work began as a D. Phil. thesis. That work was supervised by Professor Joseph Raz. His influence should be manifest throughout. What will be less apparent is that his intellectual and personal generosity, his precision, and analytic vigour made that process not only possible, but unexpectedly rewarding. I am grateful, in turn, to my lecturers at Glasgow University Law School for encouraging me to study with Joseph.

For funding assistance throughout my time at Balliol, I am grateful to the Student Awards Agency of Scotland and the Snell fund of Balliol College and the University of Glasgow.

I spent the first term of my second year at Balliol as a visiting scholar at Columbia University, New York. For funding which facilitated this visit, I am grateful to Columbia and Oxford Universities. For the initial opportunity, I owe further thanks to Joseph Raz. I owe thanks also to Dr Lucia Zedner and Professor Henry McQuay (and Maureen Woodford) for appointing me during the last year of my thesis, respectively, to a law lectureship at Corpus Christi College and a decanal position within Balliol. Both of these greatly facilitated completion of the D.Phil.

For emotional and financial support throughout my academic career, I owe deep gratitude to my parents. My father died between my graduation and the writing of this book. Much of what I learned emotionally about obligation and responsibility I learned from him. For their friendship and support, I would like to thank Roisin, Aidan, Denise Boyle, David Morgan, Ian MacPhail, Nick Kemp, Shepley Orr, Tony Abrahams, and Ron and Lola Sharp. I owe special thanks to Matthew Glossop and Liora Lazarus for their empathy, insight, and wit (then and since).

Impersonal, though no less explicit, thanks are owed to the writings of A. John Simmons and Leslie Green. Their influence, again, should be manifest throughout this work. I hope that my discussion reflects the clarity and lucidity of the works that influenced and shaped my thinking on this topic.

I would like to thank the partners of Gilbert + Tobin, Sydney, particularly Liza Carver and Gina Cass-Gottlieb, for facilitating the writing up of this book by reducing my workload during the six-month period in which its conversion from thesis to book occurred.

For comments on the work, I am grateful to Dr Timothy Endicott of Balliol College, Oxford and Dr Nigel E. Simmonds of Corpus Christi College, Cambridge, who examined my thesis in February 2001, and to two anonymous referees for Oxford University Press, who provided invaluable structural and substantive suggestions for improvements. This work is unquestionably better as a result. The book remains largely unchanged from the original thesis save for incorporation of supervening scholarship, the changes that have been suggested by referees, and the correction of some errors. At Oxford University Press, I am grateful to John Louth, Dr Gwen Booth, Louise Kavanagh, and Virginia Williams for their efficient and helpful oversight of the publication process.

My deepest thanks are owed to Amber. She has accompanied this work, and me, through every little crisis and every unexpected excitement, providing invaluable comments and unquestioning support. Amber is the light by which I see everything else, and, like everything else, this book is dedicated to her.

Sydney, 2003 R. C. A. H.

Contents

1

The Problem of Conscientious Obedience

> 'Obey the law.' That is a powerful teaching, often powerful enough to overcome deep feelings of right and wrong, even to override the fundamental instinct for personal survival.
>
> (Zinn)[1]

Obedience is an education as basic as language. Children learn the force of commands as they learn to comprehend. Obedience is also as pervasive as language; relations of authority accompany individuals throughout their lives. Among these relations, none is as pervasive as the authority of law. Prohibitions, prescriptions, and permissions litter the lives of every subject of any state. Through the mechanism of law, states claim a supreme and comprehensive authority to regulate and bind the activities of many individuals within potentially any domain. Every end of our earth echoes to the claims of some state. It is therefore unsurprising that among relations of authority and obedience, none is as problematic as that mediated by law.

John Dunn has recently stated this point with some force, observing that:

> there is no part of the world today in which a human being can confidently expect to escape from the presumption of political subordination. The state of nature may subsist, for some purposes, between the jurisdictions of particular modern states; but nowhere, not even in the unpopulated polar territories or the far recesses of the great common of the oceans, is there habitable space on earth which lies simply beyond the jurisdiction of state power. Virtually everyone in the modern world, accordingly, is claimed as subject to political obligation.[2]

'Political obligation' is a sometimes ambiguous technical term. Construed broadly, the term identifies the idea of the good citizen, encompassing the broad ethical bonds between an individual and her community and incorporating ideas such as active participation in public life, volunteering for public service in times of national crisis, paying taxes, and obedience to laws. Construed narrowly, political obligation is synonymous with the enquiry into the obligation to obey the law. This enquiry seeks to determine whether, *inter alia*, the mere fact of legal validity confers a prima-facie or more categorical obligatory character upon each legal directive. Where this is the case, there is a moral

[1] 'Law, Justice and Disobedience' 900.
[2] Dunn 'Political Obligation' 66.

obligation to obey each valid legal directive, and each violation of a valid law may be doubly wrongful. Violation of theft laws sounds in the immorality of the wrongful appropriation of another's property, and in the morally wrong quality of breaching a valid law.[3] This obligation can be interpreted as transcending a single community. On this interpretation, the obligation to obey is wider than political obligation since it possesses a universal nature. It is not yet jurisdictionally restricted. We look for the value inherent in law *qua* law in any place at any time. Within one community, however, the obligation to obey the law is narrower than the complex obligation of good citizenship, concerning fidelity only to law and ignoring wider questions of participation and membership.

Obedience is often treated as constituting the core of political obligation. Typically, this juxtaposition is harmonious. Law can only secure its intended aims on the condition of general compliance. This is the aspect of the doctrine of the rule of law that directly involves the actions of citizens.[4] The necessary minimum for sustaining the rule of law and the values law is designed to protect (security, stability, coordination, and so on) is widespread conformity among those governed. Where law is functioning well, moral membership will normally require obedience. However, law may be deployed towards ends destructive of moral membership or it may be thought mistaken. Here, membership and the injunctions of autonomy may seem to require resistance. From this confrontation arises the problem of conscientious obedience—the belief that there exist good moral reasons to breach a valid law.

This book analyses both the enquiry into whether there exists a moral obligation to obey the law and broader questions of conscientious citizenship. It focuses specifically on the obligations of citizens and not of officials. Officials voluntarily enter into the stations they occupy. Oaths, ceremonies, and undertakings constitute the commitments they undertake. Membership (and thereafter citizenship) within a community flows from the simple fact of birth. This absence of volition renders the obligations of ordinary individuals more problematic and interesting.

The claims of law and political phenomenology motivate the problem of obligation. Law addresses us in normative language—as subjects we have duties, obligations, and rights—and as subjects we have a genuine sense of the normative nexus these claims create. Margaret Gilbert begins her most recent writings on the topic with an observation coupled with a question: 'many people take themselves to have certain *obligations* by virtue of the fact that a certain country is *their* country... Is their sense of things justified?'[5] Similar comments punctuate the literature. Simmons observes that 'many people feel, I think, that they are tied in a special way to their government, not just by "bonds of affection" but by

[3] For a similar conceptualization, see Himma 'Positivism, Naturalism, and the Obligation to Obey Law' 153–4. See generally, Smith 'Is There a Prima Facie Obligation to Obey the Law?' and Simmons *Moral Principles and Political Obligations* 1–6 (hereafter, *Simmons Moral Principles*).

[4] Raz *The Authority of Law* 212 (hereafter, Raz *Authority*).

[5] Gilbert *Sociality and Responsibility* 97–8. See also Nielsen 'Why is there A Problem about Political Obligation?' 236.

moral bonds'. The difficulty arises in trying to 'give any substance to this feeling of a special moral bond'.[6]

The arguments I consider in this work assume that individuals have, or at least believe themselves to have, some extra-legal obligation to obey the law. The supporting argument includes as a non-redundant premise the fact that the law requires a certain action, and issues in the conclusion that there exists a moral obligation to obey the law.[7] The arguments typically advance an obligating reason or principle—consent, fairness, community, gratitude—and seek to demonstrate that the conditions under which the reason or principle binds extend to the case of political obligation.[8]

Enquiries into the obligation to obey the law have exercised legal and political thinkers from Socrates to Simmons. A tradition of relatively settled belief in obligation met consistent challenge throughout the last century.[9] The political events of the 1960s—of anti-war civil disobedience, and civil rights demonstrations—prompted decades of discussion of the legitimacy of the claims of states, the conditions under which there exists an obligation to obey, and of the conditions of justified civil disobedience.[10] Throughout this period scepticism gained ground. Recent debates on each topic have, however, been characterized by a retreat from scepticism. Apologists for the state and advocates of the value of law have proposed new accounts of obligation. Discussion of these recent accounts occupies much of this work.

FRAMING AND PHRASING THE ENQUIRY

A theory of obligation might be advanced within various projects, in support of various ends. The existence of a general obligation to obey the law might be taken to be expressive of communal bonds—what we owe to those with whom we interact on account of our shared belonging in some political community. These reciprocal obligations would then constitute a horizontal matrix of membership.[11] The obligation to obey is here a mutual obligation to sustain common institutions and practices, in so far as these are mediated by the mechanism of law. Burton Zweibach locates obligation along a horizontal axis:

[6] Simmons *Moral Principles* 3. Gilbert describes Simmons's quandary as a 'skeptical paradox': 'He starts with an entrenched common belief: he then shows that this belief has no basis'. The problem with such paradoxes, she suggests, 'is that they call into question beliefs that seemed firm'. Gilbert 'Group Membership and Political Obligation' 119.

[7] Raz *Authority* 234.

[8] Wolff 'Political Obligation, Fairness, and Independence' 89.

[9] Simmons's *Moral Principles* and Robert Paul Wolff's *In Defense of Anarchism* are the classic sceptical works. Dunn's *Political Obligation in its Historical Context* provides a detailed analysis of the history of the problem.

[10] On civil disobedience, see generally Bedau (ed) *Civil Disobedience in Focus*.

[11] For the genesis of the distinction between horizontal and vertical bonds, see Walzer *Obligations* 207.

[O]ur primary obligations are to a set of ideals and values, to a way of life we share with those with whom we are engaged in a common undertaking ... To realize a common life we must understand that our primary obligation must be to those with whom we are engaged in a common undertaking ... We are obligated to obey the law to the extent that it is a formalisation of the values of the common life.[12]

An alternative, or additional, argument understands obligation as a vertical bond. This bond, between the individual and her government, governors or state, legitimates the relationship of subordination between the two. The individual's obligation to obey correlates to the ruler's right to command.

Discussion of horizontal and vertical bonds presupposes some sense of related notions such as state, government, and community. I will broadly follow Raz's definition in *The Morality of Freedom*. Herein, the state is characterized as the political organization of a society; the government as the agent through which the state acts; and law as the vehicle through which much of government power is exercised.[13] I will understand an individual's legal-political community as the territorial and moral unit defined and constituted by the laws and directives of the state. Legal-political community may be a significantly fluid notion and need not coincide with geographical, national, or ethnic groupings. Political membership can be a plural phenomenon. Great Britain, with its devolved legislatures and membership of the European Union, vividly exemplifies this point. In speaking of community, I intend some idea of a legally defined membership shared by those subject to the same body of laws, beyond mere propinquity, entailing a mutuality of restrictions and interactions.

Political authority is typically exercised through the making of laws and binding directives. Many theorists indirectly approach the question of the legitimacy of authority by considering whether there is an obligation to obey the law.[14] To do so is to presuppose that *de facto* (and hence *de jure*) authority claims a moral right to rule, including a right to command, which correlates to an obligation to obey these commands. It is to presuppose certain facts about the claims of law, and some version of the correlativity thesis.[15] A correlativity thesis may make one of several claims as to content; that to (every or specific) rights there correlate certain duties; that to (every or specific) duties there correlate certain rights, or that to (every or specific) rights there correlate certain obligations. Different types of claim might be made. One might make a strong conceptual claim: That the relationship between a right and an obligation is as tight as the relationship that obtains where knowing that *X* stands to the south of *Y* entails that *Y* stands to the north of *X*. Alternatively, one might make a logical

[12] Zweibach *Civility and Disobedience* 75–6.

[13] Raz *The Morality of Freedom* 70 (hereafter, Raz *Freedom*).

[14] e.g. Raphael *Problems of Political Philosophy* 69; Simmons *Moral Principles* 14–15, 195–6, and Nielsen 'Why is there a problem about Political Obligation?' 240.

[15] See generally, Feinberg 'The Nature and Value of Rights' and 'Duties, Rights and Claims'; Hohfeld *Fundamental Legal Conceptions*; Ross *The Right and The Good* 48–64; Brandt *Ethical Theory* 433–41; Hart 'Are There Any Natural Rights?', and Lyons 'The Correlativity of Rights and Duties'.

claim concerning the formal relationship between certain rights and obligations: That a certain right in *X* entails a certain obligation on *Y*.

In the present context, the relevant notion is that a legitimate government's right to rule is the ground of a citizen's obligation to obey. It is a substantive and not a conceptual/analytic enquiry. Authority centrally involves a right to rule, which is understood as correlated with an obligation to obey. The fact that authorities claim a moral right to rule, to impose duties and rights, implies the existence of an obligation to obey. In exercising its right to rule, an authority seeks to operate through its subjects' practical reasoning (distinguishing authority from bald power) and appeals to its subjects' compliance.[16] This invokes the obligation to obey.

Within this approach, if we can prove the existence of an obligation to obey, we can indirectly establish the legitimacy of political authority, just as observing a mirror's reflection lets us know of the existence of the obverse object. The right to command grounds the obligation to obey. Below I outline this type of position as it features in accounts of the claims of law, and illustrate the conditions under which the problem of conscientious obedience is relevant to the problem of legitimacy.

THE CLAIMS OF LAW

To question the legitimacy of political authority is to question whether we should accept law's claims as justified. Questions concerning the claims of law are thus logically prior to questions concerning legitimacy. We must establish what the law claims when it claims authority. The theorist's conception of the nature and extent of law's demands will circumscribe her theory of obligation, since *X*'s obligation to *obey* *Y* will, at most, only be coextensive with *Y*'s own demands.[17] I will outline three conceptions of the claims of law: a stringent version provided by Joseph Raz; Philip Soper's recent re-conceptualization of law's claims, and Kent Greenawalt's more moderate model of law as an authority operating within a limited domain.

Methodological preliminaries

In speaking of 'law' as an entity that makes claims, I intend a polyphonic conception in which law is the product of the activities and intentions of a continuous tradition of inter-related individuals and institutions. The claims of law are the claims made by these many representatives of the legal system over time. This notion of the claims of law: may seem abstruse. What is the nature of these claims? More specifically, consider the peculiarly sophisticated nature of the claim that this discussion presupposes: A claim that the fact that the law

[16] See Raz 'Authority and Justification' 116.

[17] See also Greenawalt *Conflicts of Law and Morality* 6–7 (hereafter Greenawalt *Conflicts*). Note that actions and attitudes beyond obedience—allegiance, loyalty, supererogation—will not be similarly circumscribed.

requires a certain action is a non-redundant premise in an argument that issues in the conclusion that there exists a moral obligation to obey the law.

This claim, if it exists, has several necessary structural features.[18] It must be an extra-legal (moral) claim and not simply a meta-legal claim. It must be a generic claim, preferably with propositional content, and not simply the aggregate of the moral contents of individual legal norms. That is, law must claim the existence of a *content-independent* moral obligation to obey.[19] Content-independence concerns the way legal directives bind: The fact that a command has been issued, and not its substance, is intended to provide the subject with a reason for obedience. Although ostensibly obscure, such a claim seems an axiomatic presumption of citizenship rendered explicit in certain contexts. Consider the undertakings that punctuate descending levels of a legal system, from a President's oath of office, to oaths undertaken by members of the judiciary and other members of the legal profession, to naturalization vows. Such vows vary among states, but typically contain explicit reference to obedience to laws:

> From this time forward I pledge my loyalty to Australia and its people whose democratic beliefs I share, whose rights and liberties I respect, and whose laws I will uphold and obey.[20]

> that I will support and defend the Constitution and laws of the United States against all enemies, foreign and domestic.[21]

Where a legal system requires individuals to undertake such a commitment, it implicitly claims an entitlement to loyalty in its terms. Both logic and language suggest that such undertakings are moral in nature. They pivot around the normative language of respect, obedience, and loyalty. Moreover, a meta-legal norm entailing commitment to a generic legal obligation to obey the law would be otiose; it would generate no additional normative force beyond the aggregate of first-order legal norms and no secondary motivation from any sanction that might be imposed for breach of this meta-legal norm. Perhaps more significantly, there would be no symbolic or expressive value in such an undertaking. It might be objected that these claims attach either to the few citizens who assume legal roles or the few aliens who naturalize, and therefore omit much of the population. However, the implication is clear. The commitment that is an explicit condition of assuming citizenship is an implicit assumption of those who enjoy ascriptive citizenship. Whether or not such an assumption is warranted, and whether or not such a claim might be justified, is the normative enquiry that occupies this work.

[18] This section benefits from, and draws on, the discussion in Himma 'Law's Claim of Legitimate Authority'.

[19] Hart *Essays on Bentham* 256.

[20] Australian Pledge of Commitment pursuant to the Australian Citizenship Amendment Act 1993 (Cth).

[21] Naturalization Oath of Allegiance to the United States of America.

The enquiry into whether law claims authority may comprise several subsidiary investigations.[22] First, a conceptual investigation into what it means to claim authority. This is not a linguistic analysis, but an analysis of the forms and content of our social practices. Secondly, (in Raz's phrase) an 'explanatory-normative' investigation as to whether law does in fact claim authority. Here, the theorist, having determined the content of the claim to authority assesses whether this is a claim that the law, speaking through its institutions, in fact makes. This may also be accompanied by a conceptual enquiry as to whether law or legal systems conceptually *must* claim authority in order to constitute law or legal systems.[23] Finally, a normative investigation into whether law is justified in claiming authority.

The arguments concerning the claims of law I will consider below are in most part explanatory-normative theories about a central social practice. They are explanatory in so far as they attempt to give meaning to a concept familiar and significant within our cultures, to account for the experiences of individuals within these practices, and hence, as Raz observes, 'to make explicit elements of our common traditions'.[24] They are normative in so far as theory-construction is an intrinsically normative act,[25] and in the minimally normative sense that all description presupposes evaluative considerations that guide choices as to which aspects of a practice are essential to its analysis.[26] There may also be an analytical interplay between normative and explanatory considerations. For example, if you were required to discriminate between two ostensibly feasible conceptions of the claims of law, one of which none the less seemed not to underwrite the *practices* of law, you might reject this explanation as normatively wanting because its adoption would lack descriptive fidelity.

The simple criterion of success of an explanatory-normative account of the claims of law is whether it displays an illuminating fidelity to the forms and conceptions of our practices. As Jonathan Dancy has observed, philosophers should 'give an account of our practices rather than . . . tell us that we all ought to be doing something else. To the extent that this cannot be done, it is normally a fault in the philosophy rather than in the practice.'[27]

Raz and law's self-perception

Several commitments underpin Raz's conception of the claims of law and the nature of its authority. First, political-legal authority is a species of practical

[22] See also Soper *The Ethics of Deference* 28–34 (hereafter, Soper *Deference*) and Bogg 'In Defence of Correlativity: Authority, Autonomy and Mistaken Legal Directives'.

[23] e.g. Raz 'Authority, Law and Morality' in *Ethics in the Public Domain* 210 (hereafter Raz *Ethics*).

[24] Raz *Freedom* 63.

[25] ibid.

[26] See Green 'Law and Obligations' 521 and Waldron 'Legal and Political Philosophy' 357.

[27] Dancy *Moral Reasons* 67, quoted in Bogg 'In Defence of Correlativity: Authority, Autonomy and Mistaken Legal Directives' 85–6. Charles Larmore makes a similar point in *The Morals of*

authority, which purports to provide reasons for action.[28] Theoretical authority, by contrast, provides only reasons for belief. Only if we conceive of political authority as a species of practical authority that purports to provide reasons for action can there be an obligation to obey and, hence, a problem of obligation. This problem is motivated by the anarchist's challenge. We accept and obey authority only by according it the status it claims for itself, when we do as commanded *because we have been so commanded*. But to accept authority on these terms is to forfeit autonomy; the right and responsibility to judge, for oneself, what reason requires. Acceptance of authority is then variously characterized as irrational or immoral. I will return to this challenge below.

Having understood political authority as a species of practical authority, Raz suggests that we must understand law's claims 'at face value'[29] as legal authority itself understands them. Adopting the self-perception of the state has several implications. First, law claims to possess moral force: 'That means that it claims that legal requirements are morally binding, that is that legal obligations are real (moral) obligations arising out of the law'.[30] The legitimacy of law rests on justifying the imposition of obligations on its subjects. This seems correct. Law trivially claims a legal right to rule, but the myriad areas it regulates, and the conclusions it issues—the imposition of duties and ascription of rights, the loss of liberties and affording of privileges—are ineliminably moral. Law addresses its subjects both in the language, and with the implications, of moral authority.

Law also claims unlimited power to obligate. It claims to be comprehensive and supreme.[31] Comprehensiveness entails that legal systems 'claim authority to regulate any type of behaviour'.[32] The law recognizes no limits to the spheres of conduct it regulates. No other secular normative system claims such powers. Legal systems necessarily claim this power, though they do not necessarily legitimately possess it. Again, legal systems do not necessarily actually regulate all forms of behaviour. They claim to be able potentially to regulate them in some way(s).[33] Regulation need not take the form of prohibition. Explicit permission testifies to the comprehensiveness of law, where the decision to allow implies the capacity to forbid. 'In just about all states there are legal means to change any law, and to pass any conceivable or inconceivable law.'[34]

Modernity 15: 'common opinion cannot be dismissed as but the repository of error, which a heroic philosophy must transcend. Without the bearings it provides, we lose any sense of what it is for our own thinking to go wrong. This does not mean that philosophy must be complacent and simply defer to existing views. On the contrary, only by heeding this ideal of clarity can philosophy be argumentative, for only thus do we open ourselves to criticism by others.'

[28] For a detailed criticism of Raz, see Hurd 'Challenging Authority'.

[29] Raz 'Hart on Moral Rights and Legal Duties' 131.

[30] ibid.

[31] Raz *Authority* 116–21 and *Practical Reason and Norms* 149–54, and Gans *Philosophical Anarchism and Political Disobedience* 24–6 (hereafter Gans *Anarchism*).

[32] Raz *Practical Reason and Norms* 150–1 and *Authority* 116–20.

[33] Raz *Practical Reason and Norms* 151.

[34] Raz 'Government by Consent' in *Ethics* at 363.

A legal system also claims to be supreme as regards other institutionalized systems. 'In other words it claims authority to prohibit, permit or impose conditions on the institution and operation of all the normative organizations to which members of its subject-community belong'.[35]

Law is a content-independent, normative system. Content-independence concerns the way legal directives bind. The fact that a command has been issued, as opposed to its substance, is intended to provide the subject with a reason for obedience.[36] Content typically bridges between reason and action: We eat because we are hungry; we attend concerts because listening to music is intrinsically enjoyable; we do not harm others because wrongful infliction of harm is immoral. Content-independence severs the link between a reason for action and the action for which it provides reason. Truly to obey the law entails that one does λ because one has been commanded to do λ. One may also do λ because it is the morally correct course of action. But this reason for action is not obedience. Robert Paul Wolff stresses: 'Obedience is not a matter of doing what someone tells you to do. It is a matter of doing what he tells you to do *because he tells you to do it*. Legitimate, or *de jure*, authority thus concerns the grounds and sources of moral obligation.'[37] The reason-giving nature of commands resides in its authoritative legal source. This obtains whether X commands Y to B or to not-B.

That law is a normative system entails that it purports to provide reasons for action and to guide conduct. Where citizens' conduct simply coincides with legal directives, law fails in its normative role. Commands claim to be complete reasons for action, and not mere signposts on the road to such reasons.

The final distinctive aspect of Raz's conception of the authority of law is the suggestion that authoritative commands provide peremptory, exclusionary reasons for action.[38] On this conception, practical reasoning has a layered and not a unilinear structure. The first level of reasoning features first-order reasons—contingent desires, interests, and needs. Conflicts among such reasons are resolved by a comparison of relative weight. This is the simple calculus of ordinary decision-making. On the second level of reasoning, second-order reasons operate. These are reasons for or against acting on other reasons for action. Conflicts amongst second-order reasons are resolved by one reason outweighing another. The picture is more complex in resolving conflicts between the two levels of reasoning. Where a second order reason and a first-order reason come into tension, the former defeats the latter by *kind* and not by weight. It is an exclusionary reason. It excludes decision on the balance of

[35] Raz *Practical Reason and Norms* 151.

[36] Hart *Essays on Bentham* 256.

[37] Wolff *In Defense of Anarchism* 9.

[38] Raz *Freedom* 57–69; *Practical Reason and Norms* 37–45, 47–8. For critical discussions of this conception, see: Gans *Anarchism* 36–41 and 'Mandatory Rules and Exclusionary Reasons'; Perry 'Second Order Reasons, Uncertainty and Legal Theory' and 'Judicial Precedent and the Common Law'; Shapiro 'Authority' and articles cited therein.

the available first-order reasons. For example, you face a difficult decision while feeling ill. Your capacity to decide is temporarily diminished. You decide to do nothing. The fact of illness is not a reason for acting or not acting. It is a reason for deciding not to decide (though not to decide is necessarily not to act). Raz attributes this practical force to commands and obligations.[39]

Characterized fully, commands and obligations are categorical protected reasons. They provide both first-order reasons for ϕ-ing and exclusionary reasons against acting on (some of the) reasons for not ϕ-ing.[40] Categorical protected reasons have a peculiar stringency. They are categorical because they exclude and do not simply override first-order reasons. But they are neither conclusive nor absolute. A reason (α) is a conclusive reason for X to ϕ, only if (α) is an uncancelled reason for X to ϕ, and there is no reason (β) that overrides or outweighs (α). A categorical protected reason need not be conclusive. Other second-order reasons may outweigh it, and there may be non-excluded first-order reasons that, in the final balance, are conclusive. An obligation (ϕ) may exclude action on whimsical wants, but not exclude action on deeply held personal goals. Similarly, a categorical reason is not necessarily an absolute reason. A reason is absolute only if there is no reason that could conceivably override it. Categorical protected reasons are, therefore, both categorical and yet prima-facie. The final force of any such reason will be a product of the weight of first-order reasons provided for ϕ-ing, and the scope of the reasons against ϕ-ing that are excluded.[41]

This deontic sketch constitutes one aspect of Raz's defence of the possibility of legitimate practical and political authority. It allows him to dissolve the anarchist's challenge. Within this layered picture of practical reasoning one can act contrary to the balance of first-order reasons without necessarily acting unreasonably. To complete the defence, Raz must explicate the conditions under which it is not irrational, and may actually promote rationality, to accept authority. These conditions are established through the *service conception of authority*. This is a fundamentally instrumental justification of authority, in which the basis of legitimacy is comparative success in enabling people to conform to reason.[42] Much of the potency of the anarchist's challenge derives from the idea that in accepting authority one may be forced to act contrary to

[39] Raz's full account characterizes the formal aspect of obligation as consisting in exclusionary reasons alongside a first-order reason for action, and the material aspect as deriving from values that operate independently of an agent's goals: 'Promises and Obligations' 224.

[40] Raz *Practical Reason and Norms* 37 and Green *The Authority of the State* 37–40 (hereafter, Green *Authority*).

[41] Raz *Practical Reason and Norms* 27–8.

[42] The scheme is instrumental because it justifies authority not by reference to any intrinsic value it possesses (e.g. the intrinsic values of identification) but by reference to its ability to facilitate rational conduct by promoting better compliance with independently applicable reasons. The account is not necessarily consequentialist because authority may be justified by its ability to promote compliance with independently applicable deontological constraints. For related observations, see Christiano 'Justice and Disagreement at the Foundations of Political Authority' 179 n. 13.

reason. To demonstrate that authority can facilitate, and improve, conformity with right reason neuters this challenge.[43]

The service conception of authority consists in three theses. The first (the normal justification thesis) outlines the type of argument required to justify the claim that an authority is legitimate; that authority can enable us to act better on reasons that independently apply to us in any event. Authority is relational. It may apply differently to different individuals and may apply only selectively to an individual's deliberations. A related moral thesis (the dependence thesis) sets out the types of considerations that should guide the actions of government, reasons that already independently apply to the subjects of authority in the circumstances within a directive's ambit.[44] The final thesis (the pre-emptive thesis) describes the way in which binding authoritative directives affect the reasoning of authority's subjects. An authority's demand is a reason that does not supplement the first-order metric of reasons for and against acting. Rather, it excludes and supplants some of them. If a directive is meant to reflect reasons that already apply to one, then the reasons for the directive cannot be added to the directive itself in weighing the overall balance of reasons. To do so is to count the dependent reasons (those that already apply to the subject) twice, and to forfeit the advantages of accepting authority.[45]

Legitimate authoritative directives are, therefore, peremptory. While they do not necessarily preclude deliberation on the merits of a course of action, they do preclude action contingent on such deliberation. To the extent that subjects surrender obedience conditional on their personal judgment, they have surrendered judgment in the manner authority requires. This surrender of judgment is not absolute, and does not entail action contrary to reason. The pre-emptive thesis operates only once the malleable normal justification thesis has circumscribed legitimate authority. There must, therefore, exist sufficient good reasons for accepting authority. The threshold of normal justification must first be passed.[46]

Raz's account takes seriously the constraint of fidelity to the forms of our social practices. Though there is no unanimous agreement on the nature and implications of the concept of political authority, there is a large measure of agreement. 'Societies we know about are invariably subject to institutions claiming a right to bind their subjects'.[47] This is a mainly empirical argument;

[43] An alternative strategy for defeating the anarchist is to suggest that some inherent value resides in conforming to communal authority, for example, that one realizes the good of community or recognizes the duty one owes to one's community or rulers. Examples of such strategies will be discussed below in Chapters 4, 5, and 6. For full discussion of the service conception of authority, see Raz *Freedom* 38–69. On abortive attempts to dissolve the anarchist's paradox, see Raz *Ethics* 357–8.

[44] The dependence thesis states that authorities ought to act only on such reasons and not that they necessarily always do: Raz *Freedom* 47.

[45] Raz *Freedom* 46.

[46] ibid. 37–69.

[47] ibid. 27. I here follow Soper 'Legal Theory and the Claim of Authority' 220.

this happens to be the concept of authority used by every political society we know of, so this is the concept we must explain and justify.

Raz also adopts the systemic perspective. This is how legal authorities understand the nature of legal authority. His conception of the nature and claims of law therefore assumes law's own self-perception. It takes law literally. Its vision of law's demands is consequently stringent. Having adopted this perspective, 'any conditional or qualified recognition of legitimacy will deny the law the authority it claims for itself'.[48] Law's normative pretensions are impressive, and so too should be our demands for its justification. We can look for evidence of such justification in the search for an obligation to obey. For, as Raz observes, the justification of political authority and of the obligation to obey the law are one and the same question if we understand the obligation to obey as the obligation to obey the law as it requires to be obeyed. We might, however, also understand the obligation as a mere prima-facie reason to obey. This may be based on reasons other than the authority of law (for example, the value of community) and need not import any recognition of authority.[49]

Soper's paradox

I noted above the various descriptive and normative questions that comprise enquiries into the claims of law. The orthodox resolution of these questions suggests that law both claims a right to command correlated to an obligation to obey ('strong authority'), and that it possesses this authority. The paradoxical resolution—that of the philosophical anarchist—issues in asymmetry: Law claims strong authority but this claim is not justified.

In his recent writings,[50] Philip Soper has inverted this paradox, arguing that law does not claim—but does possess—strong authority. Soper suggests that:

1. Law does not claim a right to command correlating to a content-independent obligation to obey;
2. Law does claim:
   (*a*) a content-dependent right to decide matters in good faith; and
   (*b*) a content-independent right to enforce its decisions in the event of violation; and
3. Law is the object of a content-independent obligation to obey (a 'duty of deference').[51]

Soper argues that law's minimal claim to justice is that its actions in establishing legal norms (the right to decide) and the enforcement of these norms (the right to enforce) are morally justified. Consequently, the only reasons law claims

[48] ibid. 76. [49] ibid. 100–1.

[50] *Deference* and 'Law's Normative Claims'. This position marks a departure from his earlier writings, in which Soper endorses Raz in observing: 'a view that denies the correlation between the assertion of authority and the assertion of a duty to obey is simply "not faithful to the main features of the notion of political authority prevalent in our culture"'. 'Legal Theory and the Claim of Authority' 220.

[51] *Deference* ch. 3.

citizens have for following the law are content-dependent ones (obey the law because in good faith we believe the law to be just) or coercive ones (obey the law because we will impose sanctions if you do not). The latter claim presupposes the former. Law claims the right to enforce alongside certain claims regarding the perceived correctness of the decision it enforces. Moreover, the claimed right to decide comprises two subsidiary claims:

(*a*) *content claims*: where the substantive objectives of legal rules are fundamental to their normative defence, law claims that it has made its best judgment as to these objectives;

(*b*) *procedural claims*: law addresses the possibility that the content of law's decision may be mistaken by reference to the fair procedures by which law has sought to determine the truth of the substantive dispute. 'The law... claims only to act in good faith as respects both content and process. It believes the laws to be just, even though citizens and [law's] agents may not.'[52]

This strange troika prompts three questions, the third of which I will defer until Chapter 2. First, whether Soper's account of the claims of law is faithful to the forms of our social practices, and to his methodological commitments. Secondly, whether the paradox these claims create be meaningfully dissolved or whether it signifies a departure from our common conception of these practices. Finally, whether Soper's argument for obligation substantiates law's actual, unclaimed authority.

Before I turn to the first two of these questions, two preliminaries merit mention. First, the conception of authority as a right to command correlated to an obligation to obey instantiates a claim-right: claim rights correlate to duties, entailing performances or forbearances to which the right-holder is entitled. Claim rights consequently presuppose institutional structures that prescribe this interaction of agents, claims, and duties.[53] Soper's account of the claims of law relies not on the notion of a claim right, but on a justification right, and in this regard is Hobbesian in spirit. Governmental authority consists only in a justification right, arising in a context in which the authority and power claimed by government demands justification. Government must justify this arrogation of power to coerce those who deviate from the standards it prescribes. On Soper's account, a legal system is justified because it provides values of security and stability that anyone will acknowledge make the state preferable to anarchy.[54] Secondly, a central methodological commitment of Soper's in constructing his theory is that conceptual analysis of law should illuminate elements of the practice of law that are 'essential' to that practice by explicating them in a manner that avoids inconsistency with other existing concepts and

[52] Soper *Deference* 60–1 and 75.

[53] See Feinberg 'The Nature and Value of Rights' and Ladenson 'In Defense of a Hobbesian Conception of Law'.

[54] Soper *Deference* 165.

practices.[55] This explains why the philosophical anarchist's paradox troubles Soper: Legal theory presents political theory with a challenge it cannot meet. It is against this methodological standard that I will evaluate Soper's claims.

Soper suggests that law claims a content-dependent right to decide in good faith. Consequently, in addressing its subjects, law makes only an ordinary moral claim that citizens have reasons to follow a legal norm because the content of the norm is believed to be, from the law's perspective, correct. The requirement of good faith is a substantive constraint upon the range of eligible reasons upon which to base decisions, as is the need to decide on the basis of reasons that the authority believes relevantly apply to law's subjects[56]. The use in this context of the language of 'content-dependent' is ambivalent. Essentially, content-dependence flows from the requirement of good faith. Law must try to decide correctly and can therefore purport to represent the contents of its norms as correct. However, we should note that each legal decision, though content-dependently correct from law's perspective, has a relational aspect, and will, in the process of translation to the subject's perspective, become a content-independent decision. For Soper, this content-independence relates not to a norm providing content-independent reasons to *obey*, but to *comply* for fear of sanction, since law will enforce its decisions irrespective of correctness. This is the essence of Soper's 'leader' conception of authority. Decisions regarding the best action in any case are often deeply controversial, and we cannot avoid giving some persons in society the power authoritatively to resolve these disputes.

As Soper notes,[57] we must distinguish between reasons that *justify* the existence of the state in the first place (justification), and reasons for *following authority* in any particular case (legitimacy). On Soper's account, the notion of an authoritative socio-legal entity is both necessary and justified because in circumstances of pervasive disagreement on substantive social issues, someone must decide, and that decision must be dispositive of the matter. Different grounds are required to justify why *this person* is the legitimate occupant of this justified and necessary role or why *this conception* of the institutional form of this necessary solution is justified. It is important, therefore, to stress that between justification and legitimacy, law should make and meet a claim to a kind of authority that might sensibly explain subjects' willing submission, and issue in legitimacy.

Soper's argument for legitimacy is that law's agents must decide in good faith; the same kind of ordinary moral claim made by a friend or colleague in giving me advice in good faith. Consider, however, the analogy to a friend or colleague. I would not take crucial emotional advice from someone who merely indicated that she would advise me in good faith. I would seek additional indicia of eligibility; for example, that this person understands the key facts of my life

[55] ibid. 30 and 67.

[56] Note that the reasons that relevantly apply to Y need not appeal solely to Y's self-interest. Many moral reasons may relevantly apply to Y as a member of a moral community. Note also that Soper's conception of the reasons that must inform a decision is more subjective than Raz's dependence thesis.

[57] Soper *Deference* 50, and, generally, Simmons 'Justification and Legitimacy'.

and my character or that she has a professional expertise that will enable her quickly to assimilate and comprehend these facts.

A requirement of good faith seems too thin to underwrite the practice of law. Good faith claims, let us assume, are claims sincerely made, in the belief of their accuracy, and in the belief of their relevance to the life circumstances of the addressee. Can a citizen safely assume without further enquiry that law's claims will be made in good faith? Consider Elster's rendering of a Habermasian point, that 'implicit norms of propositional truth, normative rightness, and truthfulness are always presupposed in discussion'.[58] These norms may compel self-interested agents to address issues in terms of a wider public interest, even if concern for this public interest does not motivate the agent's approach to the issue (felicitously described by Elster as 'the civilising force of hypocrisy').[59] Consequently, a government's perceived good faith may largely issue from the logic of discursive conduct. Its genuine motives may hide behind the mask of socially constrained discursive practices enabling us to know very little about its laws' objectives. This point underscores a normative concern about the kinds of claim subjects of law believe that law *should* make in reaching for legitimacy. The kind of claim we expect here is something of the strength of an instrumental claim that law will coordinate our action and guide us, epistemically and morally, better than we might do if we decided and acted alone. Soper's conception of law's claims seems unable to underwrite law's pretensions. This normative point has descriptive implications. This conception of law's claims does not fit with our understanding and expectations of this central social practice. This normative aspect does not accelerate substantive assessment into the analysis of law's claims. The substantive legitimacy of an authority will not (necessarily) hinge directly on what it claims. As Soper also acknowledges, whether law is legitimate is a substantive question of moral theory. None the less in describing law's claims there is, as noted above, an analytical interplay between normative and explanatory considerations. A conception of the claims of law that seems not to underwrite the *practices* of law is normatively wanting because its adoption will lack descriptive fidelity.

Our second question asks whether the paradox these claims create can be meaningfully dissolved, or whether it reflects a deeper inconsistency between the theory and our social practices. That is, is it possible to speak of one who does not claim authority but does possess it?[60] Soper suggests that this seems plausible of a theoretical authority. Whether one is a theoretical authority is a matter of fact relating to one's expertise irrespective of one's subjective estimation. For Soper, there is no reason why a practical authority need be any different. What makes one a practical authority is a complex matter of moral and political theory: 'One can have authority (or be an authority), in short, without knowing it, and thus, *a fortiori*, without claiming it'.[61]

[58] Elster 'Introduction' at 12. [59] ibid. [60] Soper *Deference* 86.

[61] ibid. Soper notes two final features of law's posture. If law did not at least expect voluntary compliance it is unlikely that it could have authority and though law does not claim that there is an obligation to obey the law, it likely hopes that there is.

A theoretical authority may be an authority even though she does not consider herself to be, for various reasons including humility and insecurity. Her status as an authority will operate relatively independently of her own perceptions, being in large part a product of her objective excellence and the inter-subjective recognition of her peers. To the extent that she authoritatively influences theoretical beliefs, she will be a theoretical authority. There may be some point at which subjective blindness to this fact may either harm her authority or slip into coyness. There is, however, nothing strange in imagining that she does not claim a recognition to which she is entitled.

Practical authority, however, may be significantly affected by an equally humble posture. This is both an empirical point concerning efficacy and a conceptual point concerning the role of a legal authority within our practical reasoning.[62] The existence of practical authority presupposes a necessary minimal salience and efficacy. This requirement is aggravated for a practical authority that seeks to coerce: X cannot command Y to ϕ if X is unable to compel $A \ldots W$ to ϕ. That is, *de facto* (and hence *de jure*) practical authority is parasitic on efficacy, which derives from recognition as a practical authority. Some cases of practical authority may be spontaneous. For example, the person who issues the first and sensible instructions when a boat starts sinking. However, isolated instances of Weberian 'charismatic authority'[63] of this type are relevantly distinguished from systematic legal authority sustained over time. The paradox of unclaimed authority increases if law in fact has strong authority. This empirical point has a conceptual counterpart. The Razian argument for the nature of the claims of law rests in part on the idea that if law is to serve a mediating role between law's subjects and the reasons that apply to them, it must be possible to identify an authoritative directive without resorting to the reasons informing the directive. Only if this condition is satisfied can law make a difference to our practical reasoning. Law must at least be the sort of thing that is capable of claiming authority, in the sense that 'it claims that legal requirements are morally binding, that is, that legal obligations are real (moral) obligations arising out of the law.'[64] If law speaks to us only as a friend, in the language of first-order reasons that are added to the balance of our considerations, we are continually on the brink of being thrown back into the detail of any dispute.

Finally, consider the methodological concern motivating Soper's characterization of the claims of law, that conceptual analysis of law should illuminate elements of the practice of law that are 'essential' to that practice by explicating them in a manner avoiding inconsistency with other existing concepts and practices. In the present context this is a concern about philosophical anarchism—that legal theory will warrant claims that political theory cannot substantiate.

[62] See also Marmor *Positive Law and Objective Value* 54 and Soper *Deference* 32 n. 25.

[63] Weber's thesis is helpfully summarized by Ken Morrison in *Marx, Durkheim, Weber* 284–8.

[64] Raz 'Hart on Moral Rights and Legal Duties' 131.

However, this strategy seems doubly flawed. We should analyse and interpret our existing social practices as we find them, and not shape them to foreclose anticipated consequences of analysis. It is a mistake to sacrifice certain apparent characteristics of law in pursuit of the goal of theoretical tidiness. Consider the following two comments: 'How could it be that the practice of law, in the claims it makes, is so out of step (and presumably has always been out of step as long as states have existed) with the conclusions of moral philosophy?'[65] and: 'law may simply "hope" that it will turn out that political theory will demonstrate that there are content-independent reasons to obey'.[66] I suspect that law has less regard for political theory than Soper does. Possibly only Kelsen among history's constitutional framers will have considered his work's future treatment by political theory. We should not reformulate the claims of law to accommodate the failings of political theory.[67]

Secondly, Soper presents a false dichotomy, whereby to escape the philosophical anarchist's paradox we must choose either 'a revision of currently popular political theory to make it coincide with law's strong claim or a revision of current legal theory to reduce law's claims to the status of ordinary moral claims'.[68] This dichotomy suffers twin errors. Many political philosophers (including Soper!) believe they can substantiate law's strong claims. Chapters 3 to 7 below are largely occupied by discussion of these theories. There is also a *tertium non datur.* Law may overstate its claims but this overstatement may itself be justified, for example by a normative-instrumental thesis from the need for an over-determination of duty; for acculturation as a means of securing social stability; from the need to foster a sense of legal community, or from the excessive social costs of enforcing legal norms through sanctions.

Consider the difference between: '*X*'s claim to being ϕ is justified (where *X* is ϕ)' and 'X is justified in claiming to be ϕ (where *X* is not ϕ)'. This difference traces the distinction between justifying the legitimacy of a claim and justifying an exaggerated claim to legitimacy. The distinction is this. I can be justified in making a claim, despite the fact that the claim I make is not justified. Consider a concerned father. His 10-year-old son becomes increasingly hypochondriac. He frequently has psychosomatic symptoms, and reads medical Web pages to allay his fears, only ever aggravating his anxiety. His father tells him that the Web is an unreliable source, and that he is a medical expert, so the boy should come to him when he is worried. Now the father is not an expert. He does know enough about common medical problems that should his son come to him with a non-blanching rash, aching joints, and a temperature of 100 degrees, he will know to take his son to hospital. The claim he makes is therefore not justified. But it is not

[65] Soper *Deference* 78. [66] ibid. 87.

[67] Frederick Schauer makes a similar error in 'Positivism as Pariah' at 34: 'the definition of law is a matter of choice rather than discovery'. See the helpful discussion of Schauer in Dickson *Evaluation and Legal Theory* ch. 5.

[68] Soper *Deference* 12–13.

reckless. Moreover, he is justified in making the claim. It is important for him to intercede between his son and neurosis.

In light of this distinction, consider one possible normative-instrumental justification for an exaggerated claim to legitimacy. Where I believe that law is content-independently justified only in coercing but not in commanding me, violation becomes a strategic lottery. If I am found out I will be sanctioned, but I will do all I can to avoid this and, if successful, I will not, simply by violating the norm, have done anything morally wrong (which may exhaust much of the wrongfulness of offences *mala prohibita*). Questions of the normativity of law aside, it makes sense that law would wish to extend its claims to pre-empt this kind of reasoning, and moreover that this extension might be instrumentally justified. Therefore, even were a gap to arise between law's strong claims and its weaker justifications, this gap can still be sensibly and non-paradoxically bridged by political theory, and the urgency of the problem is again lost.

Greenawalt and law's limited domain

Consider one final attempt, by Kent Greenawalt, to dilute the claims of law and undermine the correlativity thesis. Greenawalt sets himself the task of exploring the preliminary assumption that law truly claims obedience.[69] He suggests that the assumption fails to illuminate various senses in which law may proscribe or prescribe conduct, and the more complex significations of the demands of a system of rules. Demands may, he suggests, be less exacting than they seem. Power-conferring rules genuinely limited to prescribing how a person must engage law's help do not relevantly demand obedience. Certain prohibitive formulations, beyond the criminal paradigm, can properly be considered as presenting people with a choice between rendering compliance or compensation. While the bulk of criminal and tort rules require compliance and not submission to penalty, the voluntary obligations of contract law may sometimes equally well be discharged by compliance or compensation.[70] The law's demand for compliance varies significantly between different areas of law.

Greenawalt questions the scope of law's true claims and whether it genuinely seeks to displace other competing reasons for action. He notes that 'most individuals will not concede the law ultimate authority with respect to their own choices'.[71] His scepticism is informed by adopting the perspective of the subject and not the authority. He questions authority's claims not from the perspective of autonomy, but from that of political phenomenology. People simply do not regard legal authority in this way.

[69] Greenawalt *Conflicts* 6–18.

[70] Holmes 'The Path of the Law'. See also Calabresi and Melamed 'Property Rules, Liability Rules, and Inalienability: One View of the Cathedral'; Schroeder 'Causation, Compensation, and Moral Responsibility'; and Weinrib *The Idea of Private Law* 3, 4, 38–46, 121–4 and 212–13.

[71] Greenawalt *Conflicts* 18.

A distinction between a claim to unqualified ultimate authority, and a claim to ultimate authority within a certain domain, sets up Greenawalt's enquiry. An analogy to the running of a tennis tournament illustrates the idea of ultimacy within a specific domain. The director informs a finalist of the date of the final, which clashes with visiting hours in the hospital in which the finalist's sister is dying. Any failure to play leads to forfeit. The director does not, however, recommend or condone prioritizing participation over family duties. The director holds ultimate authority only within his own domain. Greenawalt concedes that the analogy breaks down at certain points. Law regulates the lives of those to whom it applies in a uniquely pervasive manner, and more clearly makes judgments concerning matters of moral rightness. He suggests only that a similar idea of ultimate authority in one domain could exist for secular state authority. Such a picture is 'conceivable' and any 'further claim to ultimacy as the final arbiter, overall, of the reasons for performing actions is not a logical corollary of state law'.[72]

If these observations are warranted, the search for an obligation to obey can be relaxed to asking whether 'citizens should always attach *some moral weight* in favour of obedience'.[73] Consequently, any duty to comply must apply only to behaviour law really demands, as opposed to everything formally designated a legal duty.

However, law simply is the supreme secular normative system practised within any modern community. This is a pre-theoretical fact of our experience. Law is more comprehensive in its claims than Greenawalt suggests. Clearly much of civil law is permissive and operates to facilitate citizens' independent goals. Tort and criminal law bear the onus of proscription. None the less, when the law renders immoral contracts void *ab initio*, executes compulsory purchase orders, and issues tax demands (particularly in relation to citizens living abroad), it is ultimate beyond its own domain. Law's normative pretensions are boldest in cases of moral controversy. Where moral views diverge on the issues of euthanasia, genetic engineering and abortion, law is the arbiter of the permitted. Having established rules, law does not leave discretion in the individual. It threatens penalties in event of breach. Any residual discretion is typically devolved to subordinate authority figures (for example, doctors). Neither law's claims nor its actions are as modest as Greenawalt's comments suggest.[74]

Greenawalt's primary focus in Chapter Four of *Conflicts of Law and Morality* is the claim that the concept of political authority includes the notion that those subject to authority have a duty to obey. It is, he submits, either wrong or correct in an unhelpful way, yielding an unsatisfactory approach to determining the scope of a duty to obey. The link is not logical, but rests on empirical premises and a normative approach deriving duties from 'what is needed for effective legitimate government'.[75] The argument he is criticizing proceeds through the

72 ibid. 19–20. 73 ibid. 20–1. 74 See also Gans *Anarchism* 31–3.
75 Greenawalt *Conflicts* 56.

following premises. Government is necessary for social life; a sense of the duty to obey (and not mere conformity) is necessary for legitimate government to work effectively; morality articulates standards that allow humans to coexist. Therefore, individuals have some moral duty to obey the law.

Greenawalt questions this thesis. If legitimate governments in stable societies can survive without a wide sense of the duty to obey, the obedient attitude is not always essential to the continued existence of government.[76] Where a legitimate government is effective, society is viable even if citizens do not recognize any moral duty to comply.

It is immediately paradoxical that in such a society, where efficacy and legitimacy are presupposed, Greenawalt should consider the moral duty most superfluous. The citizens of the state will have considerable reason for trusting and respecting those in authority. Consider the scenario of an inefficient, unjust society. It would appear from Greenawalt's account that this authority would need—but surely not merit—a higher degree of the sense of a duty to obey. Greenawalt might simply be saying that a sense of the duty to obey is either redundant or undeserved. The assumption he attacks holds that, in order to be legitimate, government must be successful, and to be successful, needs its subjects to have a sense of the duty to obey. Legitimacy demands success, which demands a sense of duty. But, Greenawalt argues, if government is already successful, we dispense with the need for the sense of duty. However, the argument he criticizes is more deeply flawed. In suggesting that legitimacy presupposes or in some sense rests on a sense of the duty to obey, it inverts the correct conceptual order. A sense of a duty to obey flows from a belief in the legitimacy of an authority, where legitimacy will rest partly upon *de facto* efficacy and partly upon claims made (and realized) by the authority.

As a coda, it is important to note that different vertical justifications will imply different justifications of correlativity. Consent theory bases legitimacy in voluntary undertakings in the history of the individual, whereas Raz's account bases legitimacy in success in facilitating better conformity with right reason. Both are means of showing that law's claims, and the correlativity thesis, are justified. Further, where legitimate authority is understood as a right to command, the failure to ground an obligation to obey will frustrate this model of legitimate authority and vice versa. However, it need not frustrate all models of legitimacy. Even in the absence of an obligation to obey strictly understood, a state may be a largely justified type of institution and this instantiation of the state may be largely legitimate as measured against other indices. Here, an asymmetry obtains. For while the legitimacy of the state may in some respects survive scepticism regarding obligation, the converse is more difficult to imagine. If a state is simply not legitimate, not even a weakened obligation to obey the law *qua* law will survive. What may survive in such a case are horizontal obligations of community or solidarity. *X* may owe Y, as a fellow subject of an authoritarian

[76] ibid. 53.

regime, certain performances that cluster around laws, even though each owes the law no fidelity.[77]

Correlativity and stability

Greenawalt suggests that the correlativity thesis masks the empirical point that the exigencies of social order are sufficient to ground an obligation to obey the law. The argument is simple. Without obedience there is chaos. If each individual, even in good faith, exercises personal discretion, anarchy beckons. There is a moral obligation to obey, grounded in our moral obligation to avoid the inevitable harm that lawlessness entails.

There are various law-abiding attitudes, falling short of a belief in obligation, which citizens might display. Three broad types of attitude can be distinguished.

1. *Habitual conformity*: Unreflecting conformity, where the fact that λ is a law simply triggers habitual obedience;
2. *Conscientious watchfulness*: Compliance with a law, where the fact that λ is a law is secondary to the individual's approval of its specific content; and
3. *Obligation to obey*: A belief in obligation, where the fact that λ is a law is content-independently sufficient to guide an agent's action.[78]

The argument from stability does not discriminate among these possible affirmative attitudes. While only the third is sufficient to warrant talk of obligation, the widespread existence of either the first or second attitudes (within a just state) will be sufficient for stability. As Zweibach observes: 'It is pointless to speak of obligation as required by the survival of society. If it is undeniable, it is also not very helpful . . . If the only thing relevant to the obligation is the necessity for social survival, then any form of obligation, however oppressive, is justified so long as it reasonably guarantees survival.'[79]

The problem of obligation concerns a very specific ground of compliance; the citizens' belief that the state or government can create moral duties. Where habitual conformity and not obedience is involved, we have no evidence of the acceptance of the state's authority, nor does this unreflective conformity constitute any authority the state possesses.[80] One can conform one's conduct to the

[77] For example, imagine that an authoritarian ruler passes an edict requiring that all the adult males in a village must build a wall around that village within three days from the date of the ruling. A rota of activities is instated. Departure by anyone from his duties will result in the random execution of one of the group. *X* will have an obligation to obey this edict that is grounded not in the edict itself but in the interests in survival of the others. (He will also have self-interested reasons to conform—making the villagers' crisis more a coordination than a cooperation problem.) This obligation therefore has as its object, but is not grounded in, the ruler's edict. (For a similar example see Greenawalt *Conflicts* 131 illustration 7–5.)

[78] For a related taxonomy see Green 'Who Believes in Political Obligation?' 9–10.

[79] Zweibach *Civility and Disobedience* 29.

[80] Green *Authority* 87. Soper (*Deference* 17) does not sufficiently discriminate amongst these various practical attitudes towards law in his observation that: 'If most people do submit to law in ways that seem inconsistent with the contemporary philosopher's claim that law does not have

law without being guided by law.[81] The argument also tacitly assumes that many or all violations of law are a threat to order. However, arguments from the importance of stability or of systemic features are adequate only against disobedience threatening at the systemic level.[82] And, as Walzer notes, 'there is very little evidence which suggests that carefully limited, morally serious civil disobedience undermines the legal system or endangers physical security'.[83] While stability may be a minimal and necessary condition of legitimacy, stability and legitimacy are not equivalent. A government could be both perfectly stable and quite unjust.[84] Governments also employ means other than authority—advice, sanctions, and advertising—to quell citizen initiative. Obligation is not a precondition of stability.

Methodological implications

The discussion in this chapter implies a rejection of the methodology of robust normativism. Ronald Dworkin has most prominently advanced this position in recent legal theory.[85] His position derives from a Galliean notion of law as an essentially contested concept, the analysis of which is plurally contested and necessarily deeply normative, requiring commitment to a substantive moral/political theory.[86] For Dworkin, all jurisprudence is necessarily interpretative and all interpretations involve not simply evaluative aspects, but value judgments.

Dworkin suggests that a proper characterization of law requires that we ascribe a purpose or function to law, that we reach conclusions about the values law serves. For Dworkin, this purpose is 'to guide and constrain the power of government in the following way. Law insists that force not be used or withheld, no matter how useful that would be to ends in view, no matter how beneficial or noble these ends, except as licensed or required by individual rights and responsibilities flowing from past political decisions about when collective force is justified.'[87] An adequate description of law requires moral evaluation of law. This is true of law at all levels of abstraction and of participants in the system at all levels of involvement. Dworkin advocates a functionally undifferentiated (and deeply democratic) conception of law in which the

authority, it is possible that the moral theory that underlies the philosopher's claim is not the morality of most people'.

[81] Raz *Practical Reason and Norms* 124–5.

[82] Raz *Authority* 240.

[83] Walzer *Obligations* 17.

[84] Nagel *Equality and Partiality* 35.

[85] For a cognate position in political philosophy, see Walzer *Spheres of Justice* p. xiv.

[86] Gallie 'Essentially Contested Concepts'. Dworkin suggests that 'legal practice is an exercise in interpretation not only when lawyers interpret particular documents or statutes but generally. Law so conceived is deeply and thoroughly political. Lawyers and judges cannot avoid politics in the broad sense of political theory.' *A Matter of Principle* 146. For critiques of Dworkin, see Dickson *Evaluation and Legal Theory* ch. 5 and 6 and Marmor *Positive Law and Objective Values* 153–7.

[87] Dworkin *Law's Empire* 93.

theorist articulating the concept of law, and the judge and citizen confronting a discrete legal norm, seek answers to essentially the same questions. And all such questions are correctly interpreted and answered according to a particular conception of constructive interpretation. Law is an argumentative social practice. To interpret that practice the individual, whoever she might be, must engage in it.

Constructive interpretation involves imposing a purpose on an object or practice to render it the best possible example of its ascribed genre.[88] The relevant interpretative purposes are those of the interpreter and not the author, although the history and mould of the practice circumscribe eligible interpretations. The interpreter proposes a purpose for a practice by stipulating certain interests, goals, and principles the practice can be taken to express. The two essential criteria of constructive interpretation are descriptive fit (requiring that interpretation be a reasonably accurate reflection of existing practices and of the point or purpose of law) and normative justification (requiring that interpretation impute some defensible normative purpose to the practice). The correct interpretation of law will be that which shows it as the best item of its genre, and essentially moral criteria will determine which interpretation meets this test. Translated into the context of political obligation, the project of constructive interpretation entails that: 'Political obligation is then not just a matter of obeying the discrete political decisions of the community one by one, as political philosophers usually represent it. It becomes a more protestant idea: fidelity to a scheme of principle each citizen has a responsibility to identify, ultimately for himself, as his community's scheme.'[89] The subject should therefore understand law through a process of discovering his 'own intention in maintaining and participating in that practice... in the sense of finding a purposeful account of his behavior he is comfortable in ascribing to himself'.[90]

Let us weight heavily the significance of an interpreter, Jim's, interpretative perspective on his world. Assume that there is first-person authority;[91] that Jim possesses privileged understanding of present-tense claims he makes in respect of his propositional attitudes (desires, beliefs, intentions). Assume also that Jim can most authentically interpret his experiences of, and interactions within, the world.[92] These interactions comprise an interwoven thread in the complex fabric of his life. This does not, however, entail that his interpretative purposes have legitimate priority in his interpretation of the legal system in his country. First, he may simply lack any intelligible sense of what is meant by his 'intentions in maintaining and participating in the practice of law'. It is likely that many citizens conceive of themselves not as participants in, but as spectators of, the

88 ibid. 52. 89 ibid. 190.

90 ibid 58. Leslie Green discusses related topics in 'Law and Obligations' 521–2.

91 See Davidson *Subjective, Intersubjective, Objective* ch. 1.

92 Some might dispute this idea. See e.g. Davidson's discussion of Agassi in *Subjective, Intersubjective, Objective* 6–7. See, generally, Moran *Authority and Estrangement*.

legal system. Permissive and facultative laws may to a greater extent engage a citizen's sense of participation (where *X* can contract with *Y*, *X* feels involved in a legal process) than do proscriptive laws. However, many citizens may still fall short of any sense of participation.

Secondly, consider the distinction between, 'the meaning of *X*', 'an interpretation of (the nature of) *X*', and 'what does X mean *to me*?' These enquiries might be separated by a distinction between meaning and interpretation and a conviction that these concepts are not coextensive.[93] Where I know the meaning of an expression (within any given model of meaning) I do not need to interpret it, because I *understand it*. Interpretation mediates between unclear meaning and understanding: I interpret that which is ambiguous, complex, or foreign (for example, a language).[94] This explains the fact and expectation of plural and competing interpretations of objects. These three enquiries also mark off points in the continuum of interpretation along which objective and subjective judgments lie.[95] An enquiry into 'an interpretation of *X*' presupposes that there exists an *X* that may be interpreted, and involves Jim's analysis of *X* independently of his own interaction with, participation in, or evaluation of, *X*. Jim abstracts from *X* to describe it, and this is simple in so far as *X* is something that is relatively independent of Jim, that enjoys a continuity independent of him (or that now lacks any continuity, for example, defunct social practices). Consequently, a descriptive enquiry into the nature of law ('what legal norms apply to my present situation?') is distinct from an interpretation of the nature of law (a theory of jurisprudence) and from an enquiry into what law means to Jim (or, Jim's intentions in maintaining the practice of law). The first enquiry involves an attempt to remain descriptively faithful to the nature of legal systems; to read off law's content. Interpreting the nature of the legal system and providing a theory of law will necessarily involve evaluative considerations. These might include evaluative decisions as to which features of legal systems are essential to our understanding of such systems and meta-theoretical evaluative criteria such as simplicity, explanatory power, or comprehensiveness. However, where analysis suggests that some moral principle is pivotal to the point of a social practice—for example, justice in the law—an interpretation that includes this observation may remain agnostic as to the value of either the concept of justice or the conception of justice instantiated in the relevant social practice. As Waluchow notes, 'we should distinguish between seeking value in an interpretation (i.e. trying to make

[93] See Wittgenstein *Philosophical Investigations* II. xi. 212[e]: 'Do I really see something different each time, or do I only interpret what I see in a different way? I am inclined to say the former. But why?—To interpret is to think, to do something; seeing is a state.' See also Raz 'Interpretation without Retrieval' 163: 'Meaning and interpretation are reciprocal notions. Interpretation is the elucidation of a meaning, and what has meaning which is not trivially obvious can be interpreted.' For a criticism of this type of position, see Frazer *The Problems of Communitarian Politics* ch. 3.

[94] These comments are perfunctory. For an excellent and detailed discussion, see Marmor *Positive Law and Objective Values* ch. 4 (esp. 73).

[95] Again, these concepts are complex and receive fuller treatment at Marmor *Positive Law and Objective Values* ch. 6–8 and Raz *Engaging Reason* ch. 6.

our interpretation a good one) and seeking value (e.g. a justification for coercion) in the object of the interpretation'.[96] I can grasp the morally relevant aspects of a proper understanding of a legal system without reaching any value judgments concerning them. Moral principles will, however, feature in a final critical evaluation of law or the legal system.

Dworkin's methodology risks a conflation of these different stages of analysis. If I am analysing something with a view to evaluating it I must first accurately describe what I am analysing. I must be careful not to ascribe to it a point or purpose that is too stipulative, and that might preclude meaningful analysis. Where this object exists independently of my intentions, beliefs, and preferences about it, these seem immaterial to my description and interpretation.[97] My analysis can select moral values as central to the object I am interpreting without requiring that I evaluate or endorse these values.

Similarly, in providing an analysis of the claims of law, we must keep distinct, and not shift too loosely between, the different perspectives of authority and subject. We can only understand the nature of law's claims by adopting law's own perspective, the internal perspective of participants—judges, legislators—within the system. We then move to the separate enquiry into whether these claims are justified. Here we evaluate whether law's claims are or ought to be acceptable to law's subjects. These are extra-legal questions, bringing substantive empirical or moral issues to bear on jurisprudential findings. We may fail at this stage to provide a cogent account of legitimacy or obligation. But we cease to analyse our actual institutions if we let fear of failure in the second enquiry pollute the data analysed in the first enquiry. If the subject's and the authority's perceptions rightly differ, then, while law's claims are not self-contradictory, they may be unjustified.[98]

PHRASING THE ENQUIRY

This work seeks to provide answers to three questions. First, a question of Razian stringency: Whether there is an obligation to obey the law, as it requires to be obeyed, subject only to exceptions it permits, and accepting its directives as peremptory, content-independent, exclusionary reasons for action. Secondly, the more relaxed question that maps onto Greenawalt's enquiry: Whether we have a good moral reason for complying with a directive because it is a valid law of a community. Finally, what constitutes the proper moral attitude of the conscientious agent towards the directives of her reasonably just legal system, that is, what do we owe the law? All three enquiries concern the actual lives of citizens of actual states.

[96] Waluchow *Inclusive Legal Positivism* 26.

[97] Raz *Ethics* ch. 13. It is important to note that the arguments of these paragraph are arguments from and not for a certain conception of theoretical analysis. In this regard, see generally, Jackson *From Metaphysics to Ethics: A Defence of Conceptual Analysis* and Dickson *Evaluation and Legal Theory.*

[98] See also Gans *Anarchism* 24–33.

Throughout, I will make no distinction between the terms 'obligation' and 'duty'.[99] Though these do have different paradigmatic usages, 'duties' seeming more natural in the context of role-requirements, and 'obligations' in the context of commitments an agent voluntarily undertakes,[100] I do not wish to be stipulative in setting out the problem. Semantic and etymological digressions obfuscate the basic enquiry into whether any type of moral bond exists between an individual and her community or state. Throughout, where required, I will refer to certain peculiar features of obligations, duties and responsibilities. For present purposes, it is sufficient to note the general character of these types of reason, and to make one distinction between all three and the notion of 'ought' judgments.

In considering the fundamental ethical question 'what ought I to do?' we question what conduct our conclusive, all-things-considered reasons dictate. It is a question that seeks to resolve deliberation and issue in action. Typically, we use 'ought' to signify conclusive reasons for action.[101] Equally, 'ought' can signify a narrower perspective on judgment—'ought' may be moral, prudential, legal, and so on.[102] However, the perspective from which judgment is taken is not part of the meaning of the word,[103] and specific 'ought' judgments typically signify the conclusion of deliberation or advice.[104] The promiscuous perspectives from which 'ought' judgments may be delivered does, however, make a formulation of the present enquiry in terms of 'why *should* one obey the law' insufficiently precise.[105] Prudential arguments from the undesirability of sanctions could adequately meet this challenge. It is important to phrase our enquiry in the language of obligation.

As discussed above, however, judgments of obligation, though categorical, are neither absolute nor conclusive. Consequently, the enquiry into whether there exists an obligation to obey is one important, but inconclusive, factor in the political agent's 'what ought I to do?' It is not decisive, but if such an obligation exists, it should be sufficiently important to bear upon his decision in every relevant case. Moreover, being a categorical reason, it may conflict with an agent's immediate self-interest; her wants, desires and goals.[106]

[99] For a similar position, see Horton *Political Obligation* 14.

[100] Brandt 'The Concepts of Obligation and Duty'.

[101] Simmons *Moral Principles* 9.

[102] See generally, Williams *Moral Luck* ch. 6.

[103] Simmons *Moral Principles* 9; Beran 'Ought, Obligation and Duty'; Mish'Alani '"Duty", "Obligation" and "Ought"'.

[104] For different considerations that might be brought to bear on general 'ought' judgments such as 'one ought to keep one's promises', see Beran 'Ought, Obligation and Duty' 219–20.

[105] This formulation is used in McPherson *Political Obligation* 4 and Singer *Democracy and Disobedience* v. It is criticized in Newey 'Reason beyond Reason? "Political Obligation" Reconsidered'.

[106] For supplementary general material: Dagger 'What is Political Obligation?'; Pateman *The Problem of Political Obligation* ch. 2; Whitely 'On Duties'; Williams 'Ought and Moral Obligation' and 'Practical Necessity' in *Moral Luck*.

The possibility of conflicts of obligation is entailed by the non-conclusive nature of obligation.[107] Special obligations may have plural subjects or plural grounds, and will coexist with general obligations. The permutations of conflict are considerable. Such conflicts seem inevitable within the structures of modern societies—particularly liberal democratic societies which support citizens holding different comprehensive conceptions of the good life.[108] Conflict will often be the litmus test of the obligation to obey.

CRITERIA FOR A SUCCESSFUL ACCOUNT

In this section I will evaluate various suggestions for criteria necessary for a successful account of obligation against two tests. First, whether they are made necessary by the logic of the enquiry, and, secondly, whether they are made desirable by the purpose of the enquiry.[109]

UNIVERSALITY

Raz's explication of the obligation to obey captures the possibility of a tripartite universality. 'The obligation to obey the law is a general obligation applying to all the law's subjects and to all the laws on all the occasions to which they apply.'[110] Is universality strictly necessary along each axis, and where, if at all, is compromise to *generality* permissible?

Act-token universality

The idea of having an obligation to obey the law *qua* law entails that the reason to do what law requires is the fact that law requires it. The fact that a law requires one to ϕ must be at least part of one's reason for obedience. This distinguishes obedience from conformity. It distinguishes the fact of doing ϕ because it is legally commanded, from doing it because it is the morally right, morally optimific, prudential, or sanction-avoiding thing to do. Gans refers to this as the 'constraint of non-contingency', and observes: 'In order to show that there is a moral duty to obey the law we must show that the characteristic of

[107] Martha Nussbaum provides an excellent discussion of the complex nature of conflicting obligations in Part 1 of *The Fragility of Goodness*. As she notes, certain traditions in moral philosophy reject the possibility of conflict among obligations. Conflict is understood as a shortcoming and inconsistency in practical reasoning that should be eliminated. See also Raz *Practical Reason and Norms* 25–8 and Stocker 'Moral Conflicts: What They Are and What They Show'.

[108] On peculiarly liberal dimensions of the problem of political obligation, see DeLue *Political Obligation in a Liberal State*.

[109] Simmons's equivalent conditions are set out at *Moral Principles* 29—38. They are: (*a*) that an account need not provide an answer as to our all-things-considered correct action; (*b*) the constraint of 'particularity'; (*c*) there need be no requirement of singularity of ground; (*d*) no strict requirement of universality of subjects.

[110] Raz *Authority* 234.

being ordered by a law is one which renders them dutiful'.[111] The idea is that all duty-act-tokens of the duty-act-type 'obey the law' are obligatory *just by* being tokens of this type.

What, then, are the implications of the constraint of non-contingency for act-token universality? Leslie Green links the ideas of content-independence, non-contingency, and the universality of act-tokens requirement:

> [I]f law has content-independent force, then it has it *qua* law, and that will underwrite the obligation to obey all the laws. Is this too demanding? Aren't there cases of necessity, of infractions *de minimis*, in which one is entitled not to obey certain valid laws? Indeed there are, but the state purports to regulate these exceptions as well. Like a universal law of nature, the thesis of political obligation cannot withstand a single counterexample.[112]

But this conclusion, Gans believes, backs us into a cul-de-sac of questioning. If this is the case, how can some act-tokens with the character 'ordered by law' not be dutiful? The wealth of apparent counter-examples to universality seems to expose the poverty of political obligation. There seems to be no argument showing that every single act-token falling under the act-type 'obey the law' is required by peremptory practical force, and thus, no general moral obligation to obey the law. Gans wants to avoid this conclusion and suggests that we understand the constraint of non-contingency in a way not entailing universality.

The core idea is that, if there is a duty to obey, we must show that there is a non-contingent link between act-tokens belonging to this category and their becoming obligatory. We are presently assuming that non-contingency means that belonging to this act-type is a characteristic *necessarily* rendering act-tokens obligatory. Gans proposes an alternative construction. The characteristic(s) that makes this act-type obligatory *typically* belongs to act-tokens in this category.[113] Non-contingency now concerns a *non-accidental* and not a *necessary* link.

Any discussion of the obligation to obey law presupposes a legal theory stating criteria for the identification of laws. Gans adopts a positivist legal theory, within which, 'norms and rules need not meet any moral criteria whatsoever in order to count as laws in the legal sense'.[114] The criteria of identity are purely factual. Membership of the system is not a function of moral argument. Legal positivist criteria of identification preclude considering a norm invalid since immoral. Once a positivist commits to the existence of an obligation to obey, what deficiency in a legally valid obligation might entail failure to bear some moral obligation *qua* law? It seems necessary that the idea of an obligation to obey must mean one of the following: There is some feature intrinsic to legal validity, which, in itself, imports obligatory force; there is some consequence of legal validity, which, in itself, imports obligatory force; there is some principle which when applied to law entails an obligation to obey; or that the obligation to obey is a pragmatic or Kelsenian transcendental presupposition of the existence of law.[115]

[111] Gans 'The Obligation to Obey the Law: Comment' 184.
[112] Green *Authority* 229.
[113] Gans 'The Obligation to Obey the Law: Comment' 186.
[114] Gans *Anarchism* 5.
[115] This suggestion was made by an anonymous referee for Oxford University Press.

Consider an analogy to the doctrine of respect for persons *qua* human beings. This doctrine strives to guarantee a minimal dignity to individuals. Status simply *qua* person merits respect. This respect entails duties not to humiliate or harm. These are categorical, though limited, constraints. Once we have determined criteria for the identification of personhood, all persons satisfying these criteria deserve this respect. They may deserve a lot more respect than this. But they necessarily deserve at least this. In certain circumstances this respect may be overridden by other considerations. But our presumption is of respect, and it is universal.

Imagine the criterion for respect is the capacity to re-evaluate one's life-plan.[116] It would seem strange to say: 'James is cognitively intact, and capable of re-evaluating his life-plan, but I know that he is amoral and unreflective. So really, despite his ostensible membership in our relevant class, we should omit him *ab initio*. Most people will not be like this so there is no great loss to generality.' This seems simply to miss the point that he meets the criteria of respect. Respect for persons creates a presumption of minimally proper treatment of all persons. Similarly, the idea of a general obligation to obey creates a presumption of obedience to every law. There is a difference between relaxing the meaning of non-contingency and specifying different levels of reasoning at which this universality must obtain. The obligation to obey does not purport to be absolute or conclusive, but it does purport to be universal and of peremptory categorical force. *All things equal*, the obligation to obey expresses universal and categorical demands. *All things considered*, it will, almost necessarily, lose this universality.[117] All that need be shown is universality all equal, and not all considered, just as all persons, all equal, deserve basic respect, but all considered, may not. But if, all equal, certain laws seem absent any categorical force, it is problematic. Gans's solution quickly dissolves, and counter-examples to the thesis must count against it.

The nature of law's claims also supports a strict interpretation here. Law does not *typically* claim to impose moral obligations. It is a universal claim. Legal systems do not claim that every law passed imposes a discrete moral obligation, but they do claim that every law possesses some morally obligatory force simply *qua* law. If the law assigned discretion to any but its own agents, we might be able to relax our requirements. Given it does not, we cannot.

Duty-subject universality

John Ladd suggested in an early article that political obligation must be a 'universal moral requirement binding on everyone in the society'.[118] Simmons submits that he can see no obvious objection to a theory which allows that some have political obligations, while others, even in the same state, do not. The desire

[116] Margalit *The Decent Society* 70.

[117] Gans makes a similar suggestion at 'The Obligation to Obey the Law: Comment' 180, 188. It is a less confused approach than the idea of non-accidental non-contingency.

[118] Ladd 'Legal and Political Obligation' 27. Similar comments are found in McPherson *Political Obligation* and Tussman *Obligation and the Body Politic*.

for universality here, he suggests, arises from the idea that no government is legitimate to which every citizen is not obligated, and that no citizen can be obligated to an illegitimate government. But, Simmons suggests, this is mistaken.[119] Generality short of universality will suffice.

The logic of the problem will not guide our enquiries here. We must look to the nature of the state and the scope of its claims to understand duty-subject universality.

Law is the primary mechanism through which a state's government exercises authority. All states are territorial. Many coincide with the borders of specific nations. So territory is at least one factor in the equation of scope. But some laws reach beyond territorial borders—tax laws taxing citizens for earnings abroad; conscription laws calling a non-resident citizen back to his state to fight. Laws also apply differentially to different individuals within their borders, depending on legally defined status. Types and degrees of membership are also relevant. The burdens and benefits of the citizen differ from those of the permanent resident, the guest worker, and the tourist. Territory and membership circumscribe this axis of universality. Still, legal authorities claim the authority to bind and sanction all those within the area they govern, to the extent appropriate to their (legally defined) status. Despite this, I will suggest one principled argument for greater tolerance of non-universal generality here.

Membership of norms within a legal system is a question of legal theory, which determines criteria of identification. Membership within a state is a question of legal rules. Membership details are often complicated and plural. Ambiguity need not arise only from plurality. Governments may not regard nomads and Romany as full members of their territory, and may exempt them from certain laws. The internal or external alien is, however, not quite equivalent to the *ultra vires* law. The margins of membership are more fluid than those of validity. There might be some—hermits, nomads, Romany, those systematically neglected or disadvantaged by the law—whom we believe lack full membership in some technical or moral way.

Consider an objection. Legal systems claim to apply within their territory in a comprehensive, supreme, and open manner. If we take them at their word as regards the stringency of their claims, we should take them at their word as regards their scope. If the morality of laws does not alter their validity and bindingness, nor should the systematic immorality of a government's treatment of a social group exclude them from membership.

An important distinction arises here, with different implications for accounts operating on the horizontal and vertical axes. I am not suggesting that one lacking full membership should be exempted from the need to obey many or most laws. Every morally worthy law ought to be obeyed, for independent reasons, in its own right. Instead, I am suggesting that there may be categories of people whom we do not naturally consider liable *to a moral obligation to obey*

[119] Simmons *Moral Principles* 35–7.

the law qua *law* of their community. Their relationship to the state or community may not warrant this. Should they break the law, they will be punished. But the violation may not be aggravated by also breaching an obligation to obey. On a vertical account, we may only exempt those whom it seems the state also exempts. On a horizontal account, we have more latitude. Those whom a community exempts *or excludes* seem to inhabit a limbo of belonging.[120] There may, therefore, be categories of people who do not seem, even all things equal, subject to an obligation to obey. Or there may be different groups who seem to be subject to obligations to obey of different scope. So we can, here, imagine a generality short of universality.

These observations suggest a caveat. Non-universal membership does not remove the need for generality. The theorist cannot argue that membership is coincident with obligation and that whatever group she shows to be obligated is sufficient to show that all members of the community are obligated. There must be some accommodation between the comprehensive claims of the state and possible shortfall in terms of membership. Reasonable generality must be demonstrated in order to provide a successful account of obligation.

Universality of application

The obligation to obey must apply universally to all laws, all things equal, and universally to all *genuine* members of a state. Does the obligation therefore bind on each occasion to which a law applies? This point must not be taken too literally. On a rural ramble I skip over a stile into a field to see the view from the hillside. In doing so I trespass. Obligation obtains objectively but not subjectively to this situation (where objective obligation is the obligation which attaches were I to know all relevant facts, and subjective obligation is my obligation based upon the facts which I actually know). For purposes of prosecution, *ignorantia lex neminem excusit* obtains, and my ignorance will not save me. For purposes of the obligation to obey, the relevant factor is the agent's reaction to laws of which she is aware. For one to *obey* the law the fact that a directive is a law must figure at least partially within one's practical reasoning.

Given our conclusions above, universality applies here as regards the application of all laws of which the agent is aware. Two provisos are suggested. A good citizen should know the important laws of her country and, where in significant doubt, should seek clarification. Further, I exempt instances of settled practices of non-enforcement under prosecutorial discretion. In Scotland in the 1980s, the law forbidding sodomy between consenting adult males was consistently not prosecuted, for principled reasons. Someone engaging in such acts while aware

[120] As noted by an anonymous referee for Oxford University Press, the notion of a 'limbo of belonging' can be fruitfully compared to distinctions within Locke relating to full and qualified membership within a political community. This limbo is one that community imposes upon individuals as opposed to one chosen by individuals (ostracization as opposed to alienation). On Locke, see Simmons '"Denisons" and "Aliens": Locke's Problem of Political Consent'.

of this prosecution pattern may technically have broken the law but he did not betray his political obligation (should it exist).

PARTICULARITY

'Particularity' is a criterion first made explicit by A. John Simmons and now generally accepted, by which the obligation is relativized to the relationship between an individual and her community.[121] The motivation for the requirement was to avoid an individual being morally bound to different governments, and to account for why a government's being *ours* is morally significant. It conveys the necessity of some sense of membership, and not mere propinquity. Political commitments tie us to particular states and should not be as light as our luggage.

Particularity informs the status of political obligation as a special obligation. A particularized relational component is introduced into the debate by making this requirement necessary. The natural loci of obligations are now transactions, relationships, and other morally important aspects of identity.

Phillip Soper suggests that 'to make specificity into an independent constraint seems at best unnecessary and at worst misleading'. The problem of political obligation begins with a confrontation of force. This may typically be the force of one's community or of countries in which one is travelling. 'But there is no need to prejudge the issue in advance of the attempt to distinguish those situations of effective force that are legitimate from those that are not.'[122] This *is* a limiting criterion. Certain theories—Rawls's Natural Duty of Justice, utilitarianism—may fail simply due to its inclusion. At the level of general theory, it might be wiser to retain a wide lens, only later to narrow one's focus. Membership duties could then be presented as an independent solution to political obligation, as opposed to being a constraint on its solution. To argue against this widening of the enquiry, one must argue that omission of this criterion misses something crucial. To aid discussion I will suggest an alternative account of particularity, which leaves the general enquiry agnostic as to the importance of membership.

Above, when discussing duty-subject universality, I noted that membership status could affect the scope of law's application to an individual. Full citizens pay taxes, vote, serve on juries, and run for political office. Temporary residents pay taxes but cannot vote. As regards non-members, law has jurisdictional limits. It can only sanction visitors for acts within its borders. As regards members it has a wider reach. It can issue extradition orders for crimes committed within its borders, tax for earnings abroad, and so on. This picture is one of *pragmatic particularity*. Membership, itself a creature of law, invests particular-

[121] Simmons *Moral Principles* 30–5; Raz *Authority of Law* 260; Horton *Political Obligation* 13, 14; Morris *An Essay on the Modern State* 214–15, and Smith *Liberalism and Affirmative Obligation* 177–9; 199–200.

[122] Soper 'The Obligation to Obey the Law' 132–3 at n. 12.

ity in certain laws; a particularity that is not conditioned on perfect justice or good sense. I have no alternative but to pay UK taxes. I may think Swedish taxes more just, but I cannot pay them. I can make voluntary contributions to the Swedish budget or make additional contributions to the UK budget, if I think the tax rates too low. But this is quite different. Certain laws are partial. That does not mean the obligation to obey must be. The practical necessity of spatial limits on law's jurisdiction need not have moral implications. Certain laws will create special subjects. Aside from this, we are all equal in the eyes of the law. The particularity which laws themselves create is all the particularity we need.[123]

Having sketched this picture of pragmatic particularity, we can consider again whether there is an obligation to obey. Law is a social means, a mechanism for bringing about certain social ends. It is an instrument, and has no obvious intrinsic value. Imagine, now, the question put to an individual: 'Do you have a moral obligation to obey law ϕ, just because it is a law?' The addressee would almost certainly ask for further information. The questioner might concede that, since all law functions only in some community, it is a law of a determinate community. The addressee might be hoping for a response making reference either to the morally good nature of law ϕ, the generally just legal system of the relevant community, or the fact that ϕ is a law of her own community. Many, though not all, accounts of the obligation to obey assume the second of these points. The first point clearly cannot feature in the criteria for an obligation to obey. But it would seem as though one of these points is required to relativize the question in a way that makes sense of, and gives value to, the enquiry. Each of these additions to the original question hints at something of intrinsic value to the achievement of which law might work—morally good laws; a generally just legal system; a united, coordinated community. Phenomenology suggests the priority of particularity as a criterial feature of the enquiry. Individuals may not be able to obey a just legal system, but they may be required to participate in an unjust or barely just system. This may be the reality of many individuals' encounter with law.

The obligation to obey the law is an obligation owed primarily, but not solely, to the law of one's community. Most of the principles I will discuss below will most frequently feature in the relationship between member and community. None the less, similar kinds of considerations should be applicable to all legal systems and their relations with their members. I will, in the next chapter, argue for an attitude of respect for law which accommodates a pragmatically restricted parochial perspective which is capable of translation into a more cosmopolitan ethics. This point is crucial. Our communities are now informed by multiple sources of law, transnational regulations, and internationally applicable norms. The national autonomy of law has been corroded by globalization. And while laws must often ultimately be translated into national application by a domestic

[123] Christiano makes a related point to reach a slightly different conclusion in 'Justice and Disagreement at the Foundations of Political Authority' 177–8.

legislature, the forces that compel incorporation are external. The limits of our legal world are therefore pragmatic, linked contingently to the ambit of the sources of law and the consequences of our actions. The borders of our legal and moral responsibilities have lost some of their territorial and jurisdictional aspect.[124]

Believing the criterion of particularity to be pragmatically relevant does not diminish the extent to which it limits the enquiry. Two particular implications require full explication. First, the relation between particularity and political obligation as a special obligation, and, secondly, the relationship between consequentialist accounts and particularized obligation.

Special obligations

Certain moral requirements are wholly general—the prohibition on unjustified killing of individuals; the duty to aid those in grave danger without risk to oneself. In each of these obligations, every individual (potentially) owes the obligation in question to every other individual. It may never arise, other obligations may override it, or extrinsic circumstances may cancel it. But it remains general in scope. General obligations may apply universally to all agents ('all people should respect all others') or to all moral agents within a particular role ('all parents should care for their children').[125]

Special obligations, in contrast, correlate to special rights, a right held by *A* against *B*. The existence of the obligation entails the existence of the correlative right.[126] The grounds of special obligations reside in significant facts within the history of an individual; in relationships, transactions, contracts, agreements, roles, and other morally significant aspects of identity. Special obligations are rendered obligatory by the relationship or transaction grounding them, and not by the substance of the obligatory acts. A promise obligates as a consequence of the promissory transaction and not the content of the promise.[127] Special obligations are necessarily particular, but they may be plural. I can owe friendship obligations to several persons.

Such obligations seem to be amongst the most basic moral data of daily life. As Parfit observes: 'Most of us believe that there are certain people to whom we have special obligations. These are the people to whom we stand in certain relations—such as our children, parents, friends, benefactors, pupils, patients, clients, colleagues, members of our own trade union, those whom we represent, or our fellow-citizens.'[128]

[124] See generally Sassen *Losing Control: Sovereignty in an Age of Globalization*; Holton *Globalization and the Nation-State*; Stiglitz *Globalization and its Discontents*; Elfstrom *New Challenges for Political Philosophy*; and Booth *et al. How Might We Live? Global Ethics in the New Century*.

[125] On general duties, see Fishkin *The Limits of Obligation* ch. 5. And, on special obligations generally, see Kagan *Normative Ethics* 125–37.

[126] See n. 15 above.

[127] Although the promise may ultimately fail to bind on account of its content.

[128] Parfit *Reasons and Persons* 95.

Despite their ubiquity and intuitive appeal, however, such bonds are the source of several philosophical debates. One of these concerns the foundation of special obligations. Morality as traditionally conceived consists in universal and impartial moral rules. The particularism of special duties sits awkwardly on such foundations. Various suggestions try to accommodate this incongruity: the Kantian and Utilitarian contention that special obligations derive from more general moral laws; that general and special obligations are founded in distinct principles;[129] that ethical particularism maps the psychological limits of human morality.[130] But such foundational questions need not concern us here.[131] An argument for the obligation to obey presupposes both a justification and a foundation for special obligations and seeks instead a justification for *this particular* special obligation.

Special obligations are vulnerable to two polarized substantive attacks. One might argue that they create moral competition; requiring one to prefer one's own, even where imposing an unfair or disproportionate cost on others. Special obligations may unfairly privilege their incumbents and may produce sub-optimal results and unfair distributions of value, inferior to those possible within a more impartial scheme.[132] Alternatively, one might argue that such obligations are an important source of self-expression or personal identity. Often, the bonds we choose reveal us to ourselves. Given that special obligations are onerous and deeply personal, only voluntarism ensures that they are borne fairly and responsibly. Amongst theorists, this voluntarism will admit of degrees. Still, the voluntarist maintains that all genuine special obligations must be based on consent or some other voluntary act.

A theorist might make the strong voluntarist claim that *all* special obligations must be undertaken voluntarily. She may alternatively make the weaker claim that, although certain special obligations should only be capable of being generated by voluntary actions, other special obligations may arise without the consent or voluntary action of the agent. The claim from voluntarism would apply at the particular, and not the foundational, level and would require justification. The stronger claim seems difficult to defend. Nothing in the logic of special obligations suggests that they must be voluntarily undertaken.

Phenomenology supports this idea.[133] Filial, fraternal, and professional obligations may not be strongly voluntary. Few of our general moral obligations and duties are voluntary, and many of our special obligations may instantiate aspects

[129] Smith *Liberalism and Affirmative Obligation* 18–23.

[130] Dagger 'Rights, Boundaries and the Bonds of Community: A Qualified Defence of Moral Parochialism' 441.

[131] For consideration of these issues, see Gewirth 'Ethical Universalism and Particularism'; Cottingham 'Partiality, Favouritism and Morality'; Kekes 'Morality and Partiality'; Mason 'Special Obligations to Compatriots'; Goodin 'What is so Special about our Fellow Countrymen?' and Jeske 'Associative Obligations, Voluntarism, and Equality'.

[132] Pettit and Goodin 'The Possibility of Special Duties' (critically discussed by Mason 'Special Obligations to Compatriots') and Scheffler 'Relationships and Responsibilities'.

[133] Nagel *Mortal Questions* 129.

of these general obligations. One may believe that general and special obligations arise by different means. But if one concedes their joint existence, and that they both function as categorical reasons for action, then terminology does not betray substantive moral significance.

To insist upon general foundational voluntariness excludes certain putative special obligations by fiat. It is better to advance substantive criticism of unmediated moral bonds than to exclude them by definition. This is why I have spoken above of special obligations as being *moral requirements that arise from significant facts within the history of an individual.* This understanding is as inclusive as possible. It does not definitionally preclude non-voluntary theories from the enquiry. Nor does it preclude theories holding that special obligations may be generated within immoral associations. The merits of each of these theories will be examined substantively.

The sceptic concerning obligation might therefore seek to attack it at the deepest level, by arguing that the notion of special obligations is incoherent or morally objectionable; or, that while such obligations may exist, their scope is limited by a criterion of voluntariness. I have suggested an understanding of special obligation that tries to leave the most relevant of these questions open. In seeking to justify or in presupposing a justification for special obligations, we leave many important enquiries unanswered: The circumstances in which, and degree to which, an agent may legitimately prioritize her particularistic bonds over her general obligations; the weight to be assigned to such bonds, both all things equal, and all things considered;[134] and 'value-dependent' constraints on obligation.[135] To acknowledge the possibility of special obligations is not to assert their necessary priority.

Green suggests a further difficulty attending the criterion of particularity. Alongside the criterion of universality, it places a 'deep normative tension' within the attempt successfully to account for obligation. The criteria, though not contradictory, are unstable. The sorts of consideration sufficiently general to cover all persons as citizens are unlikely to ground special obligations[136] and, although special obligations may be universal among *some* social groups, this is more likely to be in groupings less diverse and vast than political society. Certainly, the idea of a special political obligation is more recondite than that of parental duties. Special obligations are owed in virtue of some special transaction or relationship between determinate parties. In political community it may not always be clear who owes obligations or to whom they are owed, since membership status or interpersonal histories may sometimes be vague. This will generate practical problems. But it does not create logical problems. The juxtaposition of universality and particularity remains plausible where the object of

[134] Scheffler 'Relationships and Responsibilities' 206–7.
[135] I owe 'value-dependent' to Simon Caney 'Individuals, Nations and Obligations' 120.
[136] Green *Authority* 233.

obligation is some determinate unit or group, and the ground, content, and limits of obligation are sufficiently clear.

Consequentialism

The juxtaposition of consequentialist accounts and particularity is also awkward. Consequentialist moral theories consist in two theses. First, a theory of value, proposing a value we ought to realize in our actions and, secondly, a theory of the right, proposing a view on *how* agents should realize this value. Consequentialist theories are here distinguished by the thesis that agents ought always to act so as to maximize this value, and that the rightness or wrongness of an action is determined by the totality formed by the act and its consequences.[137] The value of these consequences is aggregated impersonally across all relevant individuals. The relationship between action and value is instrumental for the consequentialist: She always and only acts to promote a certain value. The non-consequentialist allows the possibility of non-instrumental realization of value: I can exemplify the value of friendship in my life, even if doing so produces inferior quantities of this value.[138]

Utilitarian theories provide theories of value that make out the first leg of a consequentialist theory. An act-utilitarian theory accepts an action as right if, and only if, it produces a state of affairs containing at least an equal measure of the stipulated value as would any alternative action. Rule-utilitarian theories argue that 'the rightness or wrongness of an action is to be judged by the goodness or badness of the consequences of a rule that everyone should perform the action in like circumstances'.[139] This distinction can alternatively be construed as the distinction between the 'direct' and 'indirect' utilitarian theory.[140]

Certain features of consequentialist theories sit uncomfortably with definitive aspects of the present enquiry into the binding nature of the relationship between an individual and the law of the community to which she belongs. Particularity is the prime difficulty. It can be accommodated by consequentialist theories by a process of arguing back from the universal to the particular. Scheffler observes that such a process of 'arguing back' provides a schematic strategy for attaching political significance to less-than-universal groups of any size.[141] The individual society can become a unit of peculiar justificatory force if we argue that the interests of all are best served by partitioning the world into discrete communities, each possessing its own political institutions, to protect the well-being of that community. But the strategy is doubly flawed. Indirect accommodation of

[137] Pettit 'Consequentialism' 230; Kagan *Normative Ethics* 60, and Foot 'Utilitarianism and the Virtues' 224.

[138] For a discussion of utility and friendship, see Powers 'Rule Consequentialism and the Value of Friendship'.

[139] Smart 'An Outline of a System of Utilitarian Ethics' 9.

[140] Williams 'A Critique of Utilitarianism' 81.

[141] Scheffler 'Individual Responsibility in a Global Age' 221–2.

particularist concerns cannot afford them the moral primacy the terms of the debate imply. The attachments are instrumental to the goal of maximized utility, and are stripped of intrinsic value. As Gewirth notes, when 'the utilitarian says that overall utility is maximised if one gives particularistic preference to the interests of oneself and one's family, this justification of particularism is extrinsic, not intrinsic'.[142] Additionally, the strategy could only be engaged where global goals will actually be better promoted by their organization along local lines.

The consequentialist might deploy a more pragmatic strategy, arguing from the greater impact of one's actions on one's immediate environment. However, globalization in all its guises undermines this argument, and the strategy only contingently protects particularist concerns. Ultimately 'consequentialism still remains committed to denying what any particularist is most concerned to affirm: the unmediated moral significance of those special ties which bind members of a community to each other, but which, in doing so, also serve to set them apart from people outside the community'.[143]

The obligatoriness and universality of obedience also proves problematic to the consequentialist. The distinction between the praiseworthy (or morally permissible acts) and the obligatory often grows dim within utilitarian accounts.[144] The absolute priority consequentialist theories assign to maximizing the good clashes with the bindingness and content-independence of obligation claims. There will be an imperfect coincidence of optimific and commanded action. Many laws are rendered crude for their tasks by necessary simplifications of scale, and cannot anticipate all eventualities. The utilitarian determines the correct action by a calculus of the consequences of available alternatives. However, for the state, it is never the case that duty is in the eye of the beholder. And, on occasions where individuals do follow law's directives, they will obey the law not *qua* law, but *qua* contingently accurate articulation of the optimific action.

An obvious way to try to circumvent many of these obstacles is to pursue rule-utilitarian strategies. I will not discuss this methodology in any detail here. David Lyons has famously contended that act- and rule-utilitarian thinking can be shown to be extensionally equivalent, and would thus always mandate the same actions.[145] In accounting for obligation and authority, a rule-utilitarian account must not only justify acting on some set of rules in preference to individual judgment as a morally superior course of action, but must also show that acting on specifically legal rules will always be superior.[146] A series of obstacles bars its path to obligation.

[142] Gewirth 'Ethical Universalism and Particularism' 288–9.

[143] Scheffler 'Individual Responsibility in a Global Age' 221–2.

[144] Quinton *Utilitarian Ethics* 2–3.

[145] Lyons *Forms and Limits of Utilitarianism* and Hare *Freedom and Reason* 131–6 for similar considerations. For agreement with Lyons's position, see Smart 'An Outline of a System of Utilitarian Ethics' 9–12 and Simmons *Moral Principles* 45 and 52.

[146] Green 'Law, Legitimacy, and Consent' 807.

This digression has illustrated features of consequentialist accounts incongruous in the context of the present problem. My impressionistic exposition is intended as partial explanation for the fact that consequentialist and utilitarian theories do not receive chapter-length discussion within this book (although at points throughout I will evaluate the merit of arguments from the adverse consequences of disobedience).

Two important observations remain. First, the incongruity of consequentialist tenets within the present problem may ultimately reflect an inadequacy in either. Failure to account for particularity could be viewed as a failure to reflect what is most meaningful in daily relations. It could, alternatively, be viewed as the moral capacity to stretch beyond the parochial. Secondly, a clear solution to the problem has eluded more compatible theories. If our ultimate conclusions are sceptical, we might conclude that utilitarian thinking sees more clearly what other theories confuse. It may also be the case that considerations of utility and, for example, consent, play complementary roles. Both Simmons and Beran argue in favour of a theoretical division of labour, assigning to utilitarian thinking the justification of the state—the justification for having this kind of enterprise at all—and assigning to voluntaristic principles the legitimation of the relationship of obligation between *this* state and *this* individual.[147]

Weight of obligation

Considerations of weight might feature amongst criteria for a successful account in several ways. First, it might be suggested that theories must account for an invariant obligation or one capable of variation;[148] that adequate theories should be able to explain how obligations to obey different laws vary in force;[149] or that every token of the duty-act-type 'obey the law' must be weighty in order for the obligation to be serious.[150] I will consider these proposals in turn.

Invariant general obligations

Several distinct ideas cluster around the idea of the 'weight' of an obligation to obey. First, there is the idea of the legally invariant weight or force of *legal* obligation. Donald Regan observes that 'illegality is not like harm; illegality does not come in degrees. We normally think that an act is either illegal, or it is not. We may not be certain which it is; but degrees of certainty are not the same as degrees of illegality.'[151]

[147] Simmons 'Justification and Legitimacy' 124–6; Beran *The Consent Theory of Political Obligation* 12–13, and Feinberg *Harm to Others* 6–7.

[148] Regan 'Law's Halo' 24–5.

[149] Klosko *The Principle of Fairness and Political Obligation* ch. 1 (hereafter Klosko *Principle of Fairness*), and 'The Moral Force of Political Obligations'.

[150] Smith 'Is there a Prima Facie Obligation to Obey the Law?' 973.

[151] Regan 'Law's Halo' 24. Finnis makes a similar point at *Natural Law and Natural Rights* 314–20.

Secondly, there is the variable moral stringency of discrete obligations law creates. In this regard, George Klosko has suggested that intuitions concerning political obligation support the idea that the obligation to obey different laws varies significantly in moral force.[152] Therefore, an adequate theory of political obligation should be able to present obligations of varying intensities.

It is obviously true that the obligation to obey different laws differs in moral force. But these individual obligations are distinct from the general obligation to obey, and if such an obligation exists, it is not merely an aggregate of all the independent obligations law creates, concretizes, or formalizes.[153] Analysis of the moral force of individual legal obligations is only interesting in this enquiry if there are classes of law which present themselves as clear counter-examples in which there is no obligation at all to obey. The relevant question at the stage of general enquiry is simply whether illegality alone testifies to the moral wrong of violation. Consideration of factors extrinsic to law *qua* law—the moral importance of a provision in terms of content, social significance, relationship to security, stability—is an enquiry one stage beyond the enquiry into the existence of a general obligation.

This suggests a two-stage understanding of obligation. At the first stage, we look to the content-independent force of law *qua* law. This is equivalent to an all things equal enquiry, and is the principal subject of enquiry. At the second stage we look also to the *content*-dependent force of obligation (independent moral and social considerations) and to the *context*-dependent force of obligation (including the circumstances and implications of actions). Whichever principles are used to support the enquiry at stage one may suggest factors to be given particular weight at stage two. We may be able to confirm the appeal of a theory by illustrating that the principle it invokes at stage one, to support a general obligation to obey, renders judgments concerning particular weights which cohere with, and are sensitive to, our intuitions at stage two. But the primary enquiry occurs at stage one.

Finally, there is the idea of an obligation to obey the law *qua* law. I suggest that as regards the general obligation to obey, stringency is constant though 'weight' is empty. The above discussion on authority and obligation suggested that authoritative directives and the obligations they create are intended to be content-independent, peremptory, and categorical reasons for action. That obligations are categorical does not necessarily mean they are weighty reasons. This reflects our experience of obligations as being reasons capable of being both categorical and trivial. But all these obligations will necessarily exclude or override certain considerations militating against performance of the obligation. What should be constant is this structure of categorical but non-absolute stringency. The simple fact that ϕ is a law should have categorical significance. Until we know content- and context-dependent facts concerning

[152] Klosko *Principle of Fairness* 16 and 'The Moral Force of Political Obligations' 1237.

[153] Raz *Ethics* 341; Regan 'Law's Halo' 24–5.

obligations we cannot assign weight as such. In the preliminary stages, 'weight' is an empty enquiry, but stringency is constant. This is the minimal moral bindingness guaranteed to a law by the mere fact of its status. Content- and context-dependent weight will vary but this has no implications for the core of content-independent stringency.

If there exists an obligation to obey, then the discrete moral obligations of individual laws should be minimally as stringent as this obligation. Overall weight will vary from law to law—some obligations will be conclusive, others overridden. The legally invariant force of legal obligations is unrelated to the constant stringency of the obligation to obey. If it were argued that the presence of prosecutorial discretion or the variability of sanctions among different laws reflected degrees of legality, it would have no implications for the logic of the argument concerning the obligation to obey. Nor need there be any link between the weight of the legal and the moral obligation (generic or particular) to obey a law. The fact that not all immoralities are illegal entails a related point. Law does not always trace morality in the significance it attributes to acts (and vice versa).

What, however, is the relationship between an ostensibly trivial obligation to obey law λ and the idea of a minimally stringent and constant moral obligation to obey?

Counter-examples from trivial weight

M. B. E. Smith has famously suggested that, even 'if there is a prima-facie obligation to obey the law, it is at most of trifling weight'.[154] Smith measures the stringency of prima-facie obligations on a two-part scale: 'First, that a prima-facie obligation is a serious one, if and only if, an act which violates that obligation and fulfils no other is seriously wrong; and second, that a prima-facie obligation is a serious one if, and only if, violation of it will make considerably worse an act which on other grounds is already wrong'.[155]

Arguments from examples lead Smith to conclude that the obligation to obey cannot be serious. Driving through a red light in a deserted 2 a.m. street does not instantiate moral wrongdoing. But in the absence of possible harm or adverse examples, the only potential residue of obligation is the general obligation to obey. Similarly, gravely immoral acts are not aggravated by illegality. We do not frown on the murderer's lawlessness; we are shocked by his cruelty. Examples from both morally neutral and morally crucial laws undermine a serious duty to obey.

Chaim Gans suggests that this test of seriousness is inadequate.[156] The 'anomalous' traffic light example illuminates only the fact that some cases of the obligation are trivial. It does not show that the whole range of the duty's application is trivial.[157] It is, he suggests, a mistake to draw conclusions about

[154] Smith 'Is there a Prima Facie Obligation to Obey the Law?' 973. [155] ibid. 970.
[156] Gans *Anarchism* 89–93. [157] ibid. 91.

the value of the general duty to obey from the triviality of specific applications of it. If we can undermine the duty to obey in this manner, then other general duties (for example, to keep promises), seem equally vulnerable. From the perspective of the value of the duty to obey, some and possibly many legal duties are trivial. They do not place at risk the values protected by the duty to obey, or else the extent to which they do so depends on empirical probabilities that vary among norms. Equally, many promises have a fragile relation to the values protected by the preservation of a system of interpersonal reliance.

It is correct to observe that importance attaches to types of obligations and not to tokens of a type.[158] Experience corroborates this. Life is littered with trivial promises and stuffy laws. The fact that some legal obligations are, all things considered, morally trivial does not *per se* entail that a general obligation to obey is trivial. We need to analyse this at the level of all things equal enquiry. If a general obligation to obey is thought to exist, then it is likely that different tokens will engage and threaten the values the obligation promotes to different degrees.

However, *it is not the triviality of the obligation but the triviality of the breach that matters.* The fact of breach must in itself render an action morally wrong. A promise may be substantively trivial while its breach is deeply disappointing. The promise to pick up a loved one from the station may not be morally serious. But failure to perform may be. Disappointment, a loss of trust, and sadness may follow. Similarly with laws, if the subject-matter is trivial, but the breach is serious, the universality of duty is not undermined. Should the breach seem entirely neutral, however, a threat is posed to the universality of the duty. There is an important distinction between the triviality of a token and the triviality of its breach. Only the latter has implications for the obligation to obey.

Consider now a sceptical gambit: 'I concede the moves that establish that the obligation to obey is of constant stringency, and that it purports to be universal. Law ϕ and law λ thus share a common core of stringency that represents this obligation. But what of a law, α, that seems to exert no force *at all*? If this is the constant core of stringency, the 2 a.m. traffic light is checkmate. There is no universal obligation to obey the law *qua* law.'

What moves are possible? One might deny universality. However, for the theorist of political obligation, this is to tip the king before play even begins. If we are forced to concede that there are pockets of trivial breach or of non-application of the principles of duty, we might say that there is no general duty to obey at all, since it is not universal. Alternatively, we might say that there are classes of law that, because they are laws, *and because they are members of this class* (or these classes) exert additional moral force over us. Now, however, we must establish the relevant classes, the reasons for their relevance, and the implications of non-universality for community and authority. A new enquiry begins. However, it is defences of the traditional enquiry, subject to the strict standards of success, which concern me here.

[158] For related comments: Green 'Law, Legitimacy, and Consent' 799.

Singularity of ground

Singularity of ground can be construed in two ways. Within the broad conception of political obligation we might ask whether all duties of good citizenship rest upon the same ground. Do the same reasons justify the obligation to obey and duties to assist in times of war? There is no obvious reason to believe that one single set of reasons should have such extensive explanatory power. Alternatively, we might ask whether there must be only one ground of the obligation to obey. This notion is dismissed almost without exception in the literature. Simmons and Klosko both encourage plurality;[159] and Rawls's idea of layered natural duties and fairness obligations implicitly embraces it.[160] Only Ladd amongst recent writers has supported the criterion.[161] Meta-theoretical considerations such as theoretical tidiness or simplicity might support singularity of ground.[162] Alternatively, one might suggest that given we are all, theoretically, equal before the law, it generates obligations sharing a ground, and possibly also content. However, as discussed above, people receive different classification and treatment by law. Some individuals may be clothed in a complex skin of obligations (members of the judiciary), while others have no such obligations (hermits) or obligations with different sources.

Uniformity of content for all duty-subjects

The criterion of uniformity concerns the content of obligation. Must all subjects have obligations of identical content? Practical arguments might support this criterion. Governments may struggle to govern those with variable moral commitments.[163] But in systems invoking prudential motives and applying sanctions, this cannot be compelling. It might be a concern relevant to the broad conception of political obligation, since it creates the possibility of some citizens with more extensive obligations than others. But it does not seem to be a concern relevant to the obligation to obey. The content of this duty-act-type is simply 'obey the law'. The relevant qualifications and fluctuations will concern not content but weight, scope, and stringency. Differentially benefited parties may not be bound to the same degree, or may be exempted as regards certain laws. The content of the obligation ('obey the law') remains the same. There seems to be little persuasive argument for including this criterion.

The morality of obligation

I will treat the obligation to obey as a moral requirement, as do the vast majority of writers on the topic.[164] Amongst all the writers considered, only

[159] Simmons *Moral Principles* 35–6 and Klosko *Principle of Fairness* 4.
[160] Rawls *A Theory of Justice*.
[161] Ladd 'Legal and Moral Obligation'.
[162] See also Wolff 'Pluralistic Models of Political Obligation' 13–15.
[163] ibid. 16–17.
[164] Greenawalt *Conflicts* 47 and Klosko *Principle of Fairness* 2.

Margaret Gilbert rejects this criterion.[165] I discuss her account fully in Chapter 4 below.

Within the literature, moral reasons are typically depicted in terms of one material and certain formal features. The material component is that moral reasons derive their validity from considerations relating to the well-being of *other* individuals. It might relate to others' interests, rights, or goals, or generally to what is owed to them.[166] As Klosko notes, the formal component consists in the following notion: 'Moral principles should apply similarly to individuals who are similar or similarly situated; the moral individual judges the conduct of others according to the same principles that he applies to himself'.[167] Such a perspective forecloses the possibility of duties to oneself. We can accommodate the possibility of duties to oneself by defining morality as encompassing 'all categorical reasons, that is, all the reasons whose validity does not derive from the contingent desires of the people to whom they apply'.[168] Though duties to oneself could only ever peripherally impinge upon this topic, I will substitute this formulation for the material component. My preferred interpretation of a categorical reason is in terms of Raz's characterization of exclusionary reasons. For the purposes of evaluating the work of writers who do not assume a similar sense, it will be sufficient for an obligation to be a reason capable of overriding or excluding certain other reasons for action.

THE IMPLICATIONS OF POLITICAL AND LEGAL THEORY

Arguments advanced by both political and legal theorists will be considered in the following chapters. Just as affiliations to liberal and communitarian thinking will divide the former, allegiances to legal positivism and natural law will segregate the latter. Theoretical commitments and their presuppositions can influence both the kind of answer a theory provides and the importance to that theory of providing an answer.

For the communitarian thinker, who holds to the idea of an individual committed to her social roles and duties, not as an extrinsic imposition, but as a constitutive aspect of identity, the problem of obligation dissolves. As Dunn observes, the problem 'of political obligation, accordingly, loses both its starkness and its relative urgency. It becomes hard to distinguish human individuals from their social or cultural obligations; and political obligation is either a logical extension of, or an impertinent competitor with, these other more central and deeply insinuating bonds.'[169] Dunn, however, provides a useful caveat. It is optimistic complacency to look for a simple solution to the problem of obliga-

[165] 'Agreement, Coercion and Obligation'; 'Group Membership and Political Obligation'.
[166] Greenawalt *Conflicts* 27 and Raz *Ethics* 29 and 40.
[167] Klosko *Principle of Fairness* 2.
[168] Raz *Ethics* 40.
[169] Dunn *The History of Political Theory and other Essays* 71.

tion in social and religious solidarity and community groupings. Such groupings can be just as much the enemy of political stability as its ally.

On the other hand, for the individualist, a certain urgency infects the problem of obligation. The individual is confronted with comprehensive commands that constitute an external threat to individual freedom. Their legitimacy must be justified or denied. Both the communitarian and the individualist, it would seem, must defend the claim to obligation.

Similarly, crude interpretations of legal positivism and natural law thinking can suggest that the problem of obligation is insoluble to the former and trivial to the latter.[170] This point merits attention. Is fidelity to positivist doctrines incompatible or inconsistent with the existence of an obligation to obey and similarly, does denial of these doctrines by natural law accounts entail or imply the existence of such an obligation?

A theory of law can address three different questions. First, what is the nature of law? This enquiry seeks criteria for the identification of law and legal systems. Secondly, there are questions concerning the normativity of law, either of the form 'how are we to account for the use of normative language in describing law and legal institutions?' or, 'how is it that law can (claim to) be an action-guiding institution?'[171] The question here concerns *how* law binds. Finally, there are questions concerning the moral force of law: 'does the mere fact that something is a law impose a moral obligation to obey it?' This enquiry tries to discover *why* law binds morally. Different theories will express conflicting positions as to the independence or interconnectedness of these questions.

The doctrine central to this debate is the positivist sources thesis. This thesis is relevant to the first of our three enquiries—the search for criteria which identify the existence and content of law. It concerns validity and neither normativity nor moral force. The sources thesis states that what is and what is not law is a matter—either exclusively (strong social thesis/exclusive legal positivism)[172] or ultimately (weak social thesis/inclusive legal positivism)[173]—of social fact. The latter position allows that what is law may depend partly on moral criteria, but only where such criteria are made relevant by social facts—for example, rules whose existence is a matter of social fact. Both positions agree, however, that the ultimate criteria for identifying the existence and content of law or legal systems do not necessarily require reliance on moral argument. There are, therefore, no *necessary* moral filters on legal validity and substance. Nothing precludes the possibility of a legal system imposing moral filters on the content of law. Equally, nothing requires it. The identification of law and morality are conceptually distinct.

[170] Coleman 'On the Relationship Between Law and Morality' 66.

[171] Green *Authority* 117.

[172] Raz *Ethics* 210 and Marmor *Positive Law and Objective Values* 49.

[173] Waluchow *Inclusive Legal Positivism*; Coleman 'Negative and Positive Positivism' 160–2 and *The Practice of Principle: In Defence of a Pragmatist Approach to Legal Theory* 103; Lyons 'Moral Aspects of Legal Theory' and Hart *The Concept of Law* ch. 9.

Does this conclusion as to the nature of law have ramifications for answers regarding the moral force of law? The positivist clearly believes in the possibility of immoral laws. But this does not preclude an argument supporting an obligation to obey. The positivist could, as Green has suggested, argue from properties that, though essential to the existence of law, are not linked to its identification. Once a legal system is effective within a jurisdiction, we may have an obligation to obey the law *just because it is the law*, not because of necessary moral properties of the content of laws, but on account of moral considerations necessarily flowing from the consequences of having such laws. It is only a conceptual truth that there is a moral obligation to obey the law *qua* law in every possible legal system, if the factor which gives rise to the existence of the obligation to obey is also a conceptually necessary condition for the existence of a legal system at all.[174] Prizing a gap between the enquiries into whether society *X* has a legal system, and whether society *X*'s legal system is morally legitimate allows the theorist to hold consistently to the sources thesis and a theory of obligation. Green continues that to hold that there are morally neutral tests for law does not entail that obedience to law is morally neutral.[175] Even where law can be identified by reference to social tests alone, law Ψ (being a just law), may require obedience, and the system of which Ψ forms part may generically require obedience through moral considerations extrinsic to the law itself (for example of fairness). Similarly, to hold that facts alone determine the existence and content of law leaves open the question as to whether these facts guarantee any moral value to law (just as the factual practice of promising generates moral obligations). An affirmative answer to this last question leaves open whether this moral value is sufficient to underwrite an obligation to obey. Alternatively, as Waldron notes, the theorist who argues for the separation of law and morality may pitch her argument at the level of the moral content of individual laws. This construction leaves open the possibility that law *as a form* might be understood in a way that explains its claims. Adopting the sources thesis is not necessarily inconsistent with a belief in obligation.[176]

Natural law theories, which deny the sources thesis, hold that the criteria for identifying the existence and content of laws rely on moral argument. There is a conceptually necessary relation between law and morality. Does this position imply the existence of an obligation to obey?

The moral criteria involved and the value they confer may fall short of the obligatory. Criteria that ensure that a law is not immoral do not necessarily guarantee that it is morally binding. The criteria of identification must avoid

[174] Green *Authority* 223–34 and 'Law, Legitimacy, and Consent' 796–7.

[175] Green 'Law, Legitimacy, and Consent' 796.

[176] Waldron 'Legal and Political Philosophy' 373. As an anonymous referee for Oxford University Press also brought to my attention, the converse proposition—for example Fuller's suggestion (in 'Positivism and Fidelity to Law: A Reply to Professor Hart') that positivism presupposes or entails a very strict obligation to obey—also does not hold. As the referee notes, this did not even hold for Hobbes, who considered that the limits of obedience were reached where government failed to maintain order. See also Hart 'Positivism and the Separation of Law and Morals'.

crude reductionism. For example, the suggestion that only morally obligatory standards should qualify as law solves the problem of obligation tautologically, while dissolving questions of validity. The moral obligation to obey is superfluous alongside obligations to perform discrete morally obligatory acts. As noted above, the idea of such an obligation entails that the violation of any legal norm is doubly wrongful—the immorality of the wrongful act and the immorality of the violation of a legal norm. The reason for compliance should be a norm's content-independent status as law, and not its content-dependent status as morally valid.[177]

There are many denials of the Sources Thesis that do not entail an obligation to obey. Himma notes that a natural lawyer might hold simply that negation of the sources thesis implies that every law is consistent with the set of morally obligatory standards. But this would not imply that the content of each standard is morally obligatory.[178] Where the natural lawyer ascribes necessary moral value to law, this value need not underwrite an obligation to obey all the laws of this or any possible legal system. Many possible connections between law and morality will fail to generate general obligations.[179] Simply to assume a position within legal theory will neither necessarily preclude, nor present, solutions to the problem of obligation.

Substantive enquiry is necessary to resolve the problem of conscientious obedience.

[177] See generally, Himma 'Positivism, Naturalism and the Obligation to Obey Law'.

[178] ibid. 156.

[179] Green *Authority* 240 and 'Law, Legitimacy, and Consent' 797; Raz 'Authority, Law and Morality' 323.

2

Respect for Persons and Law

> Establishing respect for the law does not automatically ensure a better life, for that, after all, is a job for people and not for laws and institutions . . . The most important thing is always the quality of that life and whether or not the laws enhance life or repress it, not merely whether they are upheld or not. (Often strict observance of the law could have a disastrous impact on human dignity.)
>
> (Havel)[1]

Traditional theories of conscientious obedience often seek to illuminate for insiders—those who identify with and value their communities as governed by law—the grounds and content of their obligations. But a theory should first address the sceptic. The theory of respect sketched in this chapter is therefore directed primarily at persuasion of the outsider.[2] The outsiders of modern societies are characteristically the alienated—those who nominally belong but are disaffected from their community—and aliens—those who seek to belong but are ostracized from their adopted communities. Each of these types is significant within, and to some extent definitive of, life in modern political communities. These margins of membership are the crucial focus of a moral theory of legal obligation because it is here that law is most despairingly viewed and often most significantly fails its subjects. In summary, I argue that, where law is a morally worthy object of respect, and is instrumental in facilitating the realization of human capacity, our basic duty of respect for the capacity of persons extends to a duty of respect for law. This duty requires that we refrain from damaging or diminishing what is of value. The injunctions of respect are minimal but categorical and seek to address outsider and insider alike. Other principles beyond respect, principles applicable only to insiders, may also validly arise. These will be considered below. However, the theory of respect, I will suggest, constitutes the ineliminable core of a theory of conscientious obedience.

That the duty is grounded in respect for persons also entails that the theory does not ascribe moral significance to physical boundaries. This significance must be argued for and not assumed. Consequently, it accommodates a cosmo-

[1] Havel *Open Letters* 191.

[2] Camus's exposition resonates: '[H]e is an outsider to the society in which he lives, wandering on the fringe, on the outskirts of life . . . he refuses to lie . . . Lying is not only saying what isn't true. It is also, in fact especially, saying more than is true . . . he refuses to hide his feelings and society immediately feels threatened.' *The Outsider* 118–19.

politan ethics[3] suited to circumstances of increasing interdependence, but remains susceptible to an accretion of reasons building to accommodate local normative concerns. Finally, the theory of respect looks beyond obedience and allegiance to the notion of the conscientious citizen. Law and authority do not merely figure in our lives as commands or prohibitions; they also guide, inform, and educate. The respectful citizen must also be self-respecting, and must seek to engage with law in a way that mitigates as far as possible the affront to autonomy entailed by the confrontation with authority. This aspect of the theory echoes in part Kant's call to enlightenment—'*sapere aude!* Have the courage to use your *own* understanding!'[4]

ATTITUDES OF RESPECT[5]

To respect someone or something is to value it. But to value something is not necessarily to respect it. Not all valuable states of affairs or characteristics are appropriate objects of respect. There have been many attempts to make the notion of respect more determinate; Darwall notably suggesting that there exist two *kinds* of attitude of respect: 'recognition' and 'appraisal' respect.[6] Recognition respect consists in a disposition to weigh some feature of a thing appropriately in one's deliberations and to react accordingly. The object of recognition respect is, Darwall suggests, strictly, a fact. The restriction on behaviour—which may be moral or prudential—arises out of the fact itself. To have recognition respect for something is to regard that fact as placing restrictions on one's permissible actions. Appropriate objects of recognition respect are the 'law, someone's feelings, and social institutions with their positions and roles'.[7] Further, 'to have recognition respect for a person as such is not necessarily to give him *credit* for anything in particular, for in having recognition respect for a person as such we are not appraising him or her as a person at all'.[8] Appraisal respect reacts to excellence. It 'is a positive appraisal... made with regard to those features which are excellences of persons'.[9] Appraisal respect is the positive appraisal itself, and does not essentially involve any conception of restrictions on one's behaviour arising out of the object of respect. Thomas Hill Jr. employs a similar distinction amongst his writings on respect, distinguishing,

[3] Thomas Pogge articulates the features of a cosmopolitan position at *World Poverty and Human Rights* 169.

[4] Kant 'What is Enlightenment?' in *Political Writings* 54.

[5] As Christopher Morris notes (*An Essay on the Modern State* 102), discussions of legitimacy can involve reference to attitudes and beliefs in different ways. Sociological accounts, most definitively that of Weber, attempt to understand state legitimacy in terms of the attitudes of citizens, and are descriptive in nature. Such accounts merely defer the point at which the notion of legitimacy becomes problematic. The focus here is the normative variant of the enquiry.

[6] Darwall 'Two Kinds of Respect'. Generally, Downie and Telfer *Respect for Persons*.

[7] ibid. 183.

[8] ibid. 192.

[9] ibid. 191.

'respecting persons for their merits and respecting persons for their social positions'.[10]

Following the tenor of this discussion will clarify certain points obscured by the terms in which it is expressed. I will distinguish three different 'senses' of respect, more accurately understood as related objects and grounds of respect, to identify the nature of these differences, and their implications for the appropriateness of certain attitudes of respect. These three different, commonly employed, senses of respect connote slightly different grounds of respect, and associated affective and practical dispositions. I will (crudely) distinguish these as, respect for capacities, respect *qua* tolerance, and respect *qua* estimation.

Respect for capacities encompasses discussions of respect for the intrinsic dignity of persons. The ground of respect sought in this enquiry is minimal and universal; from Kant's idea of agents having the capacity to be moral,[11] to Williams's notion of each individual being 'owed an effort at identification'.[12] The focus here is basic value and a respect to which all humans *qua* humans are equally entitled. This is an egalitarian attitude of respect and is linked to practical dispositions not to harm, humiliate, or degrade; to allow individuals an opportunity to realize their capacities. Respect *qua* tolerance operates primarily within the realm of rights. We speak of respecting *X*'s right to freedom of expression or belief, though we may consider *X*'s expressed opinions odious. It is *X*'s possession of the intermediate right, its justifying grounds and its implications, that we respect. The value of the intermediate right overrides the perceived harm of the expression it ultimately protects. Beyond the circumference of this attitude of respect lie cases where the potential harm of exercising the right outweighs the values it protects.[13] This attitude of respect will be universalizable and is attended by practical dispositions not to interfere with or frustrate. Finally, there is respect *qua* estimation. This is not egalitarian. It is an attitude that reacts to that which is distinctive, and on this ground, singles out its object for favourable treatment. However, the attitude remains universalizable across the object of respect. If *X* respects *Y* for honesty in (circumstances) *C*, *X* will respect all *Y*s for honesty in *C*, and will think that all *Y*s ought to show honesty in *C*. The practical attitudes and dispositions linked to such an attitude of respect are inchoate and may vary. *X* will possibly behave likewise, or encourage honesty in others. This attitude of respect is more obviously measured on a scalar metric.[14]

We could, consequently, say: *X* (capacity) respects *Y* as having human dignity, and (tolerance) respects *Y*'s right to freedom of religious belief, but *X* does not

[10] Hill *Respect, Pluralism and Justice: Kantian Perspectives* 89; emphasis in original omitted. See also, Hill *Autonomy and Self-Respect* chs. 1 and 11.

[11] Kant *Groundwork of the Metaphysics of Morals* ch. II, sect. 436 (at 97) (hereafter, Kant *Groundwork*).

[12] Williams 'The Idea of Equality' 159. See also Margalit *The Decent Society* 57–75.

[13] See e.g. Warren J in *United States v Progressive, Inc* 467 F Supp 990 (WD Wis) (28 March 1979).

[14] For a similar comment about responsibilities as contrasted with duties, see Goodin 'Responsibilities' 53.

(estimation) respect *Y*'s chosen creed and the life this entails. This is instructive. The attitude (respect) does not change. Nor does the object of respect (*Y*). What alters is the *ground* on which the object of respect is respected. An attitude of respect will, therefore, involve fine measurements of appropriateness concerning the interaction of agent, object, ground, and reactive response.[15]

All three senses of respect should be distinguished from behaving respectfully and showing respect. Neither of these practical attitudes necessarily presupposes a genuine cognitive attitude of respect. I may 'respect' the dead by never speaking ill of them, and show 'respect' for nature by staying inside during gale-force storms. I can behave respectfully to those for whom I feel contempt, for example, the local gang leader who can do my family great harm.[16] The reasons for such respectful conduct are both prudential and instrumental.

The primary focus of this chapter is the third sense of (estimation) respect and objects respected on the ground of realized as opposed to potential value. I will attempt to identify features of law that can ground an attitude of (estimation) respect for law, and trace the relationship between this attitude and the duty of (capacity) respect for persons.[17]

The other grounds of respect are inappropriate for a member scrutinizing her political community. Tolerance respect is manifestly misplaced in a discussion of the obligation to obey. The ground of obligation cannot be (tolerance) respect of the right to govern. This ground of respect for the authority of law begs the question.[18] The argument must establish and not presuppose this right. What of capacity respect? Darwall suggests that law deserves recognition respect—that just because something is law we should have a disposition to weigh it appropriately in our deliberations and act accordingly.[19] This is equivalent to some sense of capacity respect for law, for, as noted above, we do not credit the object of recognition respect with anything, nor do we appraise it in any way.[20] In order to grasp the inappropriateness of an attitude of (capacity) respect for law, it is necessary to consider the ways in which we value various objects, and the rough correspondence between these ways of valuing and the categories of respect.

An attitude of respect will be appropriately directed at certain objects only where grounded in specific types of consideration and subject to certain conditions.[21] We value persons as ends-in-themselves. Following Raz, we can note that the final value of an end-in-itself exists where there are things that are good

[15] See also Cranor 'Toward a Theory of Respect for Persons' 314.

[16] ibid. 314.

[17] The grounding of the theory in a duty of respect for the capacity of persons entails that the argument, though directed at the sceptic about law and the state, is not directed at the radical sceptic about value.

[18] A different point applies when one is a tourist or temporary resident in a state not one's own. Then it may be appropriate to (tolerance) respect the regime by recognizing its right to rule, in the manner that states in international relations recognize each other's right to rule.

[19] Darwall 'Two Kinds of Respect' 183.

[20] ibid. 192.

[21] See also Cranor 'Toward a Theory of Respect for Persons' 314.

for that end-in-itself and their being good for it does not derive from that end contributing to some further good.[22] The existence of final value is a logical presupposition of the practice of value.[23] If anything has value, there must exist things that are of value in themselves. The good of conditional value must ultimately derive from unconditioned value. And unconditioned value, though possibly not actual, must actually be possible for value to be possible. Further, as Raz notes, 'We assume that what is of value in itself must have a life, or a history, that is, that it is capable of interacting in meaningful ways with others or with other things, through which it thrives or declines'.[24]

Intrinsic value[25] is value that something has in virtue of its non-relational properties, and independently of its consequences; whereas instrumental value is value that something possesses in virtue of being a means to a valuable end. Extrinsic value is value that something has in virtue of its relational properties, something that derives its value from that which is intrinsically valuable or an end-in-itself. Instrumental value is therefore a species of extrinsic value.[26]

One entity may instantiate complex interrelationships among these different kinds of value. A person may possess final, intrinsic, and instrumental value, although her status as a person will impose certain constraints on the kind of instrumental value she may properly be thought to possess. People can be means to others' ends, in wholly innocent ways that do not undermine their status as ends-in-themselves. A student may consider his teacher a vital means to wisdom or learning. The status of the teacher as an end-in-itself, however, imposes constraints upon her instrumental value. A person must not simply be used.

As well as being ends-in-themselves, people are also appropriate objects of respect grounded in *capacity*. To see this, consider the outlines of a hybrid Kantian/Razian position.[27] Kant considers people to be of value in themselves

[22] See Raz's exposition in *Value, Respect and Attachment* 140–51.

[23] Aristotle *Nicomachean Ethics* Book I. 2. 1094 ᵃ19: 'If, then, there is some end of the things we do, which we desire for its own sake (everything else being desired for the sake of this), and if we do not choose everything for the sake of something else (for at that rate the process would go on to infinity, so that our desire would be empty and vain), clearly this must be the good and the chief good'.

[24] See Raz *Value, Respect and Attachment* at 147 and also Kant *Groundwork* chapter II, 428:66 (at 91).

[25] Raz in *Engaging Reason: On the Theory of Value and Action* and Marmor in *Positive Law and Objective Values* provide related and appealing accounts of the relational nature of value that avoid reliance upon metaphysically suspicious conceptions of value as qualities of objects, aspects of the world, or properties of objects and so on. Marmor notes: 'The attribution of intrinsic value is a complex relational idea, meaning that the object has certain qualities which warrant the attribution of a certain value to it by the kind of creatures confronting it... that given the situation and the creatures confronting it, they would be mistaken if they failed to recognize the value in question'. *Positive Law and Objective Values* 165–6.

[26] Thus extrinsic value need not be instrumental value. Some kinds of relational value are valuable other than as means to a valuable end. See Korsgaard 'Two Distinctions in Goodness' at 116–17 and Zimmerman 'Intrinsic vs. Extrinsic Value'. In 'Rethinking Intrinsic Value', Shelly Kagan argues that it is not merely the case that certain objects may be valued both intrinsically and instrumentally, but that in some instances intrinsic value may be partially *grounded* in relational properties and that intrinsic value may sometimes partially *depend* upon instrumental value.

[27] For Raz's detailed position, see *Value, Respect and Attachment* 151–8.

because they are valuers. That there are things that are good for valuers arises from the mutual but asymmetric dependence of intrinsic goods and ends-in-themselves. Recognition of value is a crucial aspect of appropriately engaging with intrinsic value. Those able to recognize this value are capable of engaging with it appropriately and these values are thereby good for them. Further, the value of persons is not a merely instrumental value. Considering those things with which people engage—artistic and literary works, physical exertion—reveals that the value of engaging with these things is not parasitic on some further value. In their role as valuers people constitute what is of value in itself and also constitute the final postulate of value. Just this status as an end of value in itself marks a certain *capacity* in a person—to engage with and be enhanced by value in appropriate and meaningful ways. It is this capacity—even when not realized—that characterizes people as ends-in-themselves (though people may not be the only ends-in-themselves). Respect for this capacity does not preclude a complementary respect for those who live exemplary lives. Such respect is deserved by a proven achievement as opposed to a potential. Nor does respect for capacity exclude a consequent criticism of those who fail to engage with value.

Law is instrumentally valuable; it is good only because it can be good for people, who possess final value. It lacks the intrinsic value that other goods not ends-in-themselves may possess.[28] Great artistic achievements are intrinsically good though not ends-in-themselves. Law and legal systems are instruments, capable of realizing both great good and great harm. The procedural aspects of the rule of law are law's internal check on this ambivalent potential.

Only an end-in-itself will be an appropriate object of respect grounded in capacity. It alone has a value that is not contingent on realization, but which inheres in potential engagement with value. Contrast this with something intrinsically valuable but not an end-in-itself, like a beautiful painting. This painting has a worth beyond instrumental value. It is not valuable simply as a means to our aesthetic appreciation; its goodness makes such appreciation possible. As Raz notes 'It is good for us because it is good, not because it is good for us. Yet it would not be good if it could not be good for us'[29] (or for other ends-in-themselves). However, this intrinsic value must first be realized in order to be valuable. This realization proceeds in stages. First, it is not the blank canvas that we value but the work as realized upon the canvas (unlike the person whom we respect for the life she might live as opposed to a life lived well). Secondly, although the value of a great painting is realized upon its completion, it is not

[28] For discussion of the futility of ascribing intrinsic value to law, see Gans *Anarchism* 27. See also Coleman 'On the Relationship Between Law and Morality' 67. Paul Kahn offers an interesting counter-poise in *The Reign of Law: Marbury v Madison and the Construction of America* at 41 and 45: 'Lawyers trained in the modern law school have a deep belief that law should be approached as if it were instrumental . . . We must instead approach the rule of law as a set of beliefs by which members of the American culture understand themselves and their world. The rule of law is a structure of the political imagination before it is a structure of political events.'

[29] Raz *Value, Respect and Attachment* 149.

engaged with until viewed and appreciated for the qualities it holds. Consider a painting which, upon completion, is forever locked away in a neglected attic. Its value, though initially realized, is subsequently wasted; the condition under which the painting's value can be realized never crystallizes.[30] Intrinsic value is therefore typically an appropriate object of estimation respect. Consequently, in-so-far as persons are valued *qua* intrinsically valuable objects, they too will relevantly be subject to estimation respect.

The structure of tolerance respect differs from that of capacity or estimation respect. In both capacity and estimation respect, the relationship between object and ground is internal. In tolerance respect the link between object and ground has an external element. The logic of tolerance is that X suppresses a desire to condemn Y in respect of ϕ where X believes that his desire to condemn Y is justified and ϕ is, from X's perspective, wrongful or deficient in some way. X suppresses his desire to condemn Y because he believes there are overriding reasons not to act on this inclination.[31] These reasons derive from the value of tolerance itself, and the reasons for which this practice is valuable. Belief in the value of pluralism may in turn derive from some notion of respect for persons, from the worth of the individual pursuit of value through ends autonomously selected. None the less, in (tolerance) respect the relationship between object and ground of respect is complex. The very point of tolerance is that X does not, to some extent, (estimation) respect the ultimate beneficiary of his attitude. The ground of respect is either external to the object of respect (for example, a belief in the negative value of tolerance as a means of purifying the political realm of deep and irresolvable conflicts whose inclusion within that realm would have adverse consequences)[32] or is internal and derives ultimately from the duty of (capacity) respect. The objects at which tolerance respect will typically be directed are therefore ends-in-themselves, or, by extension, the associations or cultures such ends-in-themselves together constitute.

Estimation respect is clearly the most flexible attitude and may be directed at an end-in-itself ('she is a good and kind person'); intrinsically valuable objects ('it is a profoundly emotive piece of music'), and extrinsically valuable objects ('the fine hairs of this paintbrush facilitate subtle expression').

As noted above, law is instrumentally good and not an end-in-itself. Law and legal systems are instruments, with a potential ambivalent between good and evil. Respect for law is conditional and must be grounded in the realization and protection of valuable ends. Law is a normatively and coercively impressive creature. It must, to some degree, live up to its claims and merit the respect it demands. This conclusion has implications for the universality of any theory that respect can underwrite. Estimation respect for law cannot ground a content-independent duty to obey the law. Estimation respect is a *substantively*

[30] See also Korsgaard 'Two Distinctions in Goodness' 121–2.
[31] See also Raz *Freedom* 401–4.
[32] Geuss *History and Illusion in Politics* 78. See also Nagel *Equality and Partiality* 154.

self-limiting principle: Respect will always be conditional upon an object actually realizing values relevant to its kind (for example, paintings are valuable as measured against aesthetic and emotive criteria; law is valuable as measured against our basic duty of respect for persons).[33] Such a principle maps onto an idea of content-dependence.[34] By contrast, capacity respect for persons is a *scope self-limiting principle*. Once we have adequately determined the scope of the definition of 'person', all members of this class are appropriate objects of capacity respect. Such a principle could map onto an idea of content-independence.

In the discussion below, I first conceptually analyse the idea of an attitude of respect. This analysis draws on, but significantly modifies, the works of Carl Cranor.[35] I then suggest grounds of (estimation) respect for law, and look to the link between this attitude and the duty of (capacity) respect for persons.

A WAY OF SEEING

To respect something is to value it. Respect is, as Dillon notes, 'always a way of *seeing*, a presumed disclosure; what is disclosed is the worth or worthiness of the object'. Respect reacts to value immanent in the object: 'This gives respect an objective logic: to respect something is to regard it as also worthy of the respect of others'.[36] The value of valuable things is not constituted by or conditional upon recognition of that value; values we neglect we may sometimes be mistaken about.[37] Such mistakes about value instantiate a kind of 'aspect blindness'[38]—we lack the moral imagination to grasp the essence of a situation, to make connections among morally relevant facts.[39] This imaginative faculty is as

[33] It might still be argued that the simple fact of being a law merits estimation respect; that this mere fact testifies to a particular achievement. Consider Waldron's comment that 'this, for the time being, is what the community has come up with and... it should not be ignored or disregarded simply because some of us propose, when we can, to repeal it'. *Law and Disagreement* 100. We might expand this point within a democracy to say that law as passed must deserve some minimal estimation respect as the product of respect-worthy, fair decision procedures. However, this assumes the crucial normative point that must be proved and upon which estimation respect is conditional.

[34] See also Hill *Respect, Pluralism, and Justice: Kantian Perspectives* 8.

[35] Cranor 'Toward a Theory of Respect for Persons'; 'Respect for the Law: An Evaluation'; 'Justice, Respect and Self-Respect'.

[36] Dillon 'Introduction' 18.

[37] Although as Marmor notes, something may not be valuable for creatures incapable of recognizing certain aspects of the relevant situation: *Positive Law and Objective Values* 168.

[38] Wittgenstein *Philosophical Investigations* II.xi.214[e].

[39] In *Moral Imagination: Implications of Cognitive Science for Ethics* Mark Johnson argues that imagination has a central role in our ethical deliberation; that both moral universalism and relativism are falsified by empirical studies in cognitive science and crucially neglect the fact that human beings are essentially imaginative moral animals. In talking of moral imagination in the text I am referring only to ways in which we recognize the value in others; the ways in which we can escape cultural context and bias through including and imagining 'the other' (be this a human, organic, or animal other) in her/its own terms in our moral thinking. See also Kekes *Moral Wisdom and Good Lives* chapter 5; Nussbaum *Love's Knowledge: Essays on Philosophy and Literature* ch. 5; Warnock *Imagination* and Murdoch *Metaphysics as a Guide to Morals* 308–48.

relevant in the political domain as elsewhere. As Martha Nussbaum notes, 'We should demand political leaders who display the abilities involved in a reasonable and appropriate compassion—who show not just mastery of pertinent facts about their society and its history, but also the ability to take on in imagination the lives of the various diverse groups whom they propose to lead'.[40]

An attitude of respect involves a quadripartite relationship among the following features:

1. *The respecter*: a person who respects (X);
2. *The object of respect*: an object/person/entity respected (Y);
3. *The ground of respect*:
   (*a*) a quality[41] or characteristic (ϕ) the respecter believes the object possesses, and which the respecter believes provides a reason for an attitude of respect to be directed towards the object (*internally required respect*); or
   (*b*) a fact or value (Ψ) external to the object of respect which the respecter believes provides a reason for an attitude of respect to be directed towards the object, irrespective of, or despite, certain qualities or characteristics the respecter believes the object possesses (*respect external to its object*);
4. *The respect role or perspective*: occupied by the respecter (X):
   (*a*) that renders the reason provided in 3 relevant to her evaluations; and
   (*b*) from which:
      (i) the quality or characteristic (ϕ) internal to the object of respect; or
      (ii) the fact or value (Ψ) external to the object of respect,
      possesses value.

The distinct conditions 3(*a*) and 3(*b*) (and accompanying conditions 4(*b*)(i) and (ii)) mark out different grounds for an attitude of respect. I will refer to these respectively as internally required respect and respect external to its object, and distinguish them through consideration of circumstances in which an attitude of respect is justified as the attitude facilitating compliance with a pre-existing duty.

40 Nussbaum *Upheavals of Thought: The Intelligence of Emotions* 435.

41 Cranor's equivalent condition involves 'some ability or character-trait': 'Toward a Theory of Respect for Persons' 310–11. This weights his analysis towards some sense of estimation respect and makes it less susceptible to ideas of capacity respect. It is important for the analysis here that our understanding of respect captures all three 'senses' and is able to distinguish respect for capacity alone and respect for realized capacity. For similar remarks see, Frankena 'The Ethics of Respect for Persons' 156. Cranor's full picture of respect is: '*R* E-respects *P*'s having *F* (where *F* refers to some ability or character-trait of *P* and *E* refers to some evaluative point of view), if and only if, (1) *R* believes *P* has *F* and that *P*'s having *F* is an *E*-good thing; (2) *R* appreciates (has knowledge and understanding of) why *P*'s having *F* is an *E*-good thing; (3) *R* is disposed to rely upon and have confidence in *P*'s having *F* and *P*'s doing what is appropriate to his having *F*, and (4) *R* is disposed to acknowledge and recognize the value of *P*'s having *F* in ways appropriate to the *F* in question'. 'Toward a Theory of Respect for Persons' 310–11.

INTERNALLY REQUIRED RESPECT

Consider the idea of a duty to promote a healthy work environment. A work environment is healthy if people respect each other. The duty is to promote such an environment, and respect is the attitude necessary to fulfil this duty. The ground of the obligatory attitude of respect itself renders the attitude of respect obligatory. Moreover, the duty arises out of the very same grounds as does respect for persons. The attitude of respect is internally required.

Within this first justification for respect, the third condition (*ground of respect*) places certain constraints on the attitude of the respecter. First, there are cognitive constraints. *X* must have knowledge of the existence of characteristic ϕ. *X* must understand why this is a good characteristic for *Y* to possess and why possessing this quality provides a reason for *X* to respect *Y*. *X* must also have reasonable grounds or evidence for holding this series of beliefs.[42]

X's description of the reason that grounds respect explains, but need not justify, her attitude of respect.[43] Two different kinds of mistake could negate justified respect. *X* could be mistaken as to *Y*'s possession of this quality. Here, though *X* believes *Y* to be scrupulously honest, he is actually mendacious. Alternatively, *X* might be mistaken as to the relationship between the characteristic possessed and the object possessing it. Here, *X* respects *Y* for her stoicism, but it is destructive for *Y* always to be stoic. In this particular case, *X* misunderstands the relationship between the trait and *Y*'s good and misunderstands the reasons this relationship might generate. For the attitude of respect to be appropriate, therefore, there is a *condition of veracity*. What *X* believes to be the case must significantly correspond with what is actually the case (as supported by evidence and experience).

The relationship between the second (*the object of respect*) and the third conditions (*the ground of respect*) places certain constraints on the characteristic in the object that provides reason for respect. It must be relatively permanent and pervasive.[44] We must believe that the characteristic respected will be reasonably enduring and that the entity or person will continue to act in ways, and produce states of affairs, consistent with this quality.

The characteristic must also be subject to some degree of volitional control.[45] We (capacity) respect people for their potential to *engage* with value; to form and pursue conceptions of a worthwhile life; to transcend their own subjectivity by feeling love for, and prioritizing the welfare of, others.[46] We (estimation) respect that which might have been otherwise, and which is made deserving by being as it is. We do not respect a woman's beauty; we admire or wonder at it (although

[42] See also Cranor 'Toward a Theory of Respect for Persons' 313 and 314. [43] ibid. 311.
[44] ibid. 312. [45] ibid.
[46] And hence, despite its universality as a human characteristic we would not respect persons for basic non-moral physical capacities; for example, for possessing a complex respiratory system.

we may respect her fitness). This fundamentally distinguishes capacities and realized characteristics as objects of respect.

The fourth condition (*the respect role or perspective*) also places certain constraints on justification. For example, *X*, a white supremacist, respects the South African regime of the 1980s for its apartheid policy. *X* makes no factual mistakes. The regime was flagrantly racist and, as a racist regime, its policies of discrimination served its ends well.

An individual may occupy many perspectives narrower than the moral. The condition of veracity requires that the beliefs upon which an attitude of respect is based correspond with what is actually the case. Here we have an equivalent *condition of value*. An attitude of respect must be morally justified. In this case, *X* has a factually justified but morally unjustified attitude of respect. It is wrong to discriminate against people on the basis of irrelevant criteria. While *X* may value her attitude of respect, it is not a morally valuable attitude to have. Some writers exclude such attitudes from the category of respect, phrasing them instead as 'being impressed by' or as 'admiring' a certain characteristic. Margalit holds to this position: 'I consider respecting a trait to mean valuing the trait as a morally positive one'.[47] Respect connotes not agent-relative value, but moral value. In such an account the fourth condition would stipulate the moral perspective. Respect is, therefore, either by definition a moral attitude, or its ultimate justification is subject to the condition of value.

RESPECT EXTERNAL TO ITS OBJECT

Condition 3(b) generates a duty of respect that is external to the ground of respect. Consider again an attitude of respect that is justified as the attitude facilitating compliance with a pre-existing duty.[48] *X* promises his partner, *Y*, that he will respect her mother, although *X* does not and cannot like her. Though *X* does not like *Y*'s mother, *X* should respect her, both because she minimally deserves this and because it is important to *Y* that *X* does so. *X*'s duty is grounded in promise and respect is its content. This is, in metaphorical terms, a duty of (tolerance) respect arising out of external facts. As regards such pre-existing duties, attitudes other than respect—love, gratitude, civility, fairness—may be eligible to facilitate action on duty. Respect is not a *necessary* attitude. In cases of this latter kind, even were one to exemplify a pre-existing duty facilitated by an attitude of respect, one would need to consider the following. First, if a variety of attitudes allow fulfilment of duty, it does not automatically follow

[47] Margalit *The Decent Society* 64. See also Cranor 'Toward a Theory of Respect for Persons' 316.

[48] There is potential here for respect to be defended as the attitude appropriate for action on Rawls's natural duty of justice to support and comply with just institutions: *A Theory of Justice* 334. It would render a duty of more restricted content and attend only to the first leg of Rawls's duty since the second requires establishing just systems where these do not exist. See also Cranor, 'Respect for Law: An Evaluation' 539.

that it is obligatory for one to adopt an attitude of respect—even if this is the best means of fulfilling the duty. Acquisition of this duty and what it entails may be merely supererogatory. In arguing for this attitude, one will have to marshal reasons as to whether it does more to promote the duty in question, or whether its adoption leads to advantageous consequences.[49] Respect external to its object need not occupy us further. The focus of the following discussion is internally required respect.

COGNITIVE LINKS BETWEEN RESPECT AND TRUST

Respect is an evaluative reason-based attitude. Loyalty[50] and love can be unconditional. Many actions that would empty out respect may leave love diminished but extant. We cannot respect without believed reason. We wonder at things we do not understand. Respect is similarly distinguished from faith.[51] Faith occupies a space beyond reason, and is undermined by the search for evidence. The demand for proof made Thomas doubting.

We respect mistakenly if we do not understand the value of the ground of respect, or its relationship to the excellence of the object respected. We respect immorally if we respect on the basis of iniquitous characteristics. Respect does not require equality between *X* and *Y*.[52] Indeed, much respect presupposes some inferiority in the respecter, and may involve a relationship in which the idea of equality is inert. Respect, subject to the conditions of veracity and value, merely requires adequate cognitive capacity in *X* to grasp the relationships involved.

Respect depends upon beliefs, knowledge, and understanding, as supported by evidence. There are therefore epistemological issues concerning what *X* must know if she is intelligently to respect *Y*. *X* can only respect an object on the basis of a characteristic she believes to be relatively permanent and pervasive. That is, she must either strategically or normatively trust that person or entity and, in the case of government, must believe that it will act having considered her interests and in accordance with right reason. Trust in government, however, introduces difficulties inherent in the generic notion of trust in institutions as opposed to individuals. These difficulties flow from a belief that complex modern societies preclude a unifying social trust generated purely by interpersonal, affective trust relations, with trust in institutions a possible substitute.[53]

[49] Cranor 'Toward a Theory of Respect for Persons' 318 and 'Respect for the Law: An Evaluation' 540.

[50] See generally, Fletcher *Loyalty: An Essay on the Morality of Relationships* and Oldenquist 'Loyalties'.

[51] See also Cranor 'Toward a Theory of Respect for Persons' 314 and 'Respect for the Law: An Evaluation' 531.

[52] Cranor disagrees: 'Toward a Theory of Respect for Persons' 313.

[53] Habermas observes: 'Complex societies cannot be held together solely by feelings like sympathy and trust, which are geared to the local sphere. Moral conduct towards strangers calls for "artificial virtues", above all a disposition to justice.' Habermas *The Inclusion of the Other: Studies in Political Theory* 14.

Hardin, amongst others, maintains that citizens typically lack the knowledge to hold an attitude of trust or distrust and are typically left with the absence of both.[54] The relationship of citizens to government is not one of trust but one of 'inductive expectations'. The sun will rise tomorrow, and those who govern us are unlikely to perpetrate egregious injustices. Credible responses to this scepticism have been advanced.[55] Mark Warren suggests that one reason we can (or ought to be able to) trust many large-scale institutions 'is that (a) we know the normative idea of the law and thus the normative expectations it places on officials; and (b) the law creates incentives over and beyond the normative incentive for officials to act in accordance with the shared expectations of law, thus reducing the risks of trust'.[56] This account illustrates how respect for law could feed into trust for government. To trust in an institution depends on 'shared knowledge and legitimacy of the (legal) rules that establish institutions'. This cannot be assumed or taken for granted, and in this regard Warren stresses the importance of the 'role of democratic discourse in mediating institutions by constantly testing, revising, invigorating, and communicating norms'.[57] Luhmann similarly notes that: 'law may protect civil rights, freedom, and property even in the face of political opposition. Thereby, it may create a confidence in the legal system, and in positions of security which then makes it easier to place trust in other relations'.[58]

There is a prolific literature on the topic of trust.[59] For our discussion, it is sufficient to distinguish, and trace the relationship between, affective and systemic trust. Affective trust arises in direct interpersonal contexts, and may be of various kinds and degrees. Partners entrust to each other their most intimate selves and expect an altruistic trust in return, a willingness to prioritize the loved one's interests over one's own;[60] individuals invest a trust '*in loco*' in those with whom they leave young children; we sometimes trust for expressive reasons, as a first step in forming a relationship, to generate reciprocal trust, or in an attempt to create a felt sense of obligation in another. Such trust mediates and structures relations between determinate individuals.

Systemic trust arises primarily from procedural and structural dimensions of public institutions.[61] These include: 'agencies of accountability' (Sztompka)

[54] Hardin 'Do We Want Trust in Government?' 23 and 39.

[55] Offe 'How Can We Trust Our Fellow Citizens?' 44. Patterson 'Liberty Against the Democratic State: On the Historical and Contemporary Sources of American Distrust'.

[56] Warren 'Conclusion' 349.

[57] ibid. 350.

[58] Quoted in Sztompka *Trust: A Sociological Theory* 142 (hereafter, Sztompka *Trust*).

[59] Seligman *The Problem of Trust*; Hollis *Trust within Reason*; Uslaner *The Moral Foundations of Trust*; Sztompka *Trust* and O'Neill *A Question of Trust*. John Dunn suggests that we understand trust both affectively and strategically: 'Trust is both a passion (an affective condition, linked to expectations of others' future actions) and a policy (a method of dealing with the fact that most important human interests depend profoundly on the future free actions of other human beings)'. Dunn 'Trust' 95.

[60] See the discussion of Barber's cognate notion of 'fiduciary trust' at Sztompka *Trust* 54.

[61] Sztompka discusses a similar notion of 'procedural' trust at *Trust* 44.

(Ombudsmen, committees of enquiry, Royal Commissions); institutionalized transparency (freedom of information laws, recording of cabinet discussions); external incentive-altering mechanisms (sanctions, rewards, social censure), and entrenched rights against government. Individuals require information, and genuine evidence of good faith, if they are to have the ability to respect, trust, or have confidence in individuals or institutions.[62] In grounding respect for law, an individual can look to regularities of just procedures and outcomes in law and legal systems, to reliable epistemic and coordinative authority. Law *ex facie* allows only justifications based on its own created exceptions. This grounds the formal claims of law. However, as Waldron notes, while law presents itself as supreme, comprehensive, and exclusionary, discretion also pervades legal systems: the relatively non-transparent discretion of the police from street to the station; prosecutorial and judicial discretion; appeal structures; constitutional amendment; legislative reversal; judicial review; periodic elections; and occasionally, the revisiting of issues even by the highest courts within a jurisdiction.[63] This increases the possibilities for respect, trust, and confidence and for individuals to observe the workings of institutions. It is the fact that 'multiple opportunities for testing the validity of distrust (e.g., periodic contested elections, freedom of expression, freedom of the press) are institutionalised and being used from which the trust derives that political elites enjoy'.[64]

The circumstances of modernity create an inverse relationship between the need for affective trust and the circumstances conducive to it. Proliferating divisions of labour and narrowing specializations, the blurring of traditional boundaries and the opening up of opportunities introduce a need to rely upon indefinite, anonymous others. This centrifugal stress simultaneously precludes reliance grounded in affective trust and requires secondary forms of systemic, institutional trust. These secondary forms of trust provide sufficient resources for our theory of respect for law. There is, however, a residual issue. In this transformation of incentives, is something of value lost? Accountability substitutes for trust. We can reasonably believe not in the trustworthiness of individuals' motives but in our ability to rely upon their ultimate decisions.[65] We are set free to 'trust' by the formalization of suspicion. We may still be *deceived*—people may do the right thing for compromised reasons—but we are less likely to be *disappointed*—it is in people's own best long-term interest to act decently. This loss may be a necessary consequence of scale within social relationships. Sztompka captures this tension in his 'two paradoxes of democracy'. First, the emphasis on accountability and pre-commitment in democratic states means

[62] As Mill notes: 'In the case of any person whose judgment is really deserving of confidence, how has it become so? Because he has kept his mind open to criticism on his opinions and conduct. Because it has been his practice to listen to all that could be said against him'. Mill *On Liberty and Other Essays* 25.

[63] Waldron *Law and Disagreement* 88.

[64] Offe 'How Can We Trust Our Fellow Citizens?' 56.

[65] e.g. O'Neill *A Question of Trust* 14: 'Perhaps the fact of the matter is that we simply have to *rely* on institutions and institutions although we *don't really trust them*' (emphasis in original).

that trust is due precisely to the institutionalization of distrust in the architecture of democracy. The more we institutionalize distrust, the greater play we give to spontaneous trust. Secondly, the extensive potential availability of democratic checks must be mirrored by their very limited use. The frequent actualization of these protections suggests that suspicion is warranted.[66] Hence, these systemic mechanisms need not frustrate, and may facilitate, affective trust. In a world in which accountability largely protects us from betrayal, we may be more likely to develop a trusting disposition, which in an interpersonal context may manifest as affective trust.

DIRECT AND DERIVATIVE RESPECT

Thus far I have discussed respect mediated directly by reasons and understanding. There is also a more derivative attitude of respect that is mediated by parasitic reasons. For example, *X* respects *Y*, her tutor, because he consistently demonstrates an exceptional level of analytic rigour (*direct respect*). *Z* respects *Y* because he is a Professor at an esteemed university (*derivative respect*). Both *X* and *Z* have reasons and evidence for their attitudes. In the first case, the reasons for respect are direct and first-hand. *X* fully understands the qualities and talents that distinguish *Y*. *X* is not *Y*'s equal. But she understands the reasons for, and the distance of, the gap between the two. In the second case, *Z* relies on extrinsic indicia of *Y*'s qualities. *Z* takes respect on trust. Assumptions rather than understanding ground her beliefs. This derivative respect can be seen in many attitudes. Many people simply respect and trust firemen. It is quite clear, however, that derivative respect is a much more complacent attitude than direct respect. For example, estimation respect, being founded on achievement, can be forfeited by failure. Greater understanding makes failure less opaque. Both attitudes, however, may lead to similar practical dispositions. The same is also true of one who merely shows respect or behaves respectfully, either unreflectively, or on the basis of instrumental and self-serving reasons.

In different individuals, a cognitive attitude of respect may be generically undergirded or undermined by a genealogical predisposition towards or against deference.[67] People sit along a spectrum of overarching attitudes to authority. Some crave external guidance. Some willingly listen to, but do not seek, advice. Some have an obstinate independence. And finally, there is the rebel, who 'from his very first step, refuses to allow anyone to touch what he is ... He will even accept pain provided that his integrity is respected.'[68] This genealogical aspect complicates the relational nature of an attitude of respect: *X* respects *Y qua* ϕ,

[66] *Trust* 140–6.

[67] On genealogical aspects of trust see Sztompka *Trust* at 97–101.

[68] Camus *The Rebel* 23–4.

but *X*'s attitude may reflect both his genuine opinion of *Y* and his general disposition to those who hold the position *Y* occupies.

THE REACTIVE RESPONSE

A cognitive attitude of respect will necessarily entail certain dispositions (though not necessarily, in conflict situations, action upon these dispositions).[69] One with a practical attitude of respect reacts with conduct appropriate to having respect for the characteristic that is the basis of the attitude of respect. If I respect my tutor's intelligence, I might try to learn from his methods and win his respect in turn. If I respect *X* as a wise woman, I may seek her opinion on delicate matters. Many of these affective and practical dispositions are founded on or involve trust. These attitudes again require that the characteristic respected is relatively enduring and pervasive.

One's reaction must be appropriate not simply to the object respected, but to the characteristic on account of which that object is respected. One may have no general, or only sceptical, attitudes with regard to other aspects of the object. If I respect my friend's kindness and selflessness, but think that she is emotionally erratic, I will not seek her advice on all matters.[70] Few individuals or entities deserve unqualified respect. The syntax of respect betrays this: *X* respects *Y qua* ϕ. Other attitudes, such as loyalty, seem less qualified. The reactive return of respect is appropriate to the ground of respect and not indiscriminately to the object of respect.

Respect always minimally requires certain cognitive and practical dispositions. Cognitively, one must recognize and acknowledge the value of the object respected.[71] Practically, it requires that one not damage or demean the object.[72] This may sometimes be consistent with respect involving obedience to commands. Whether this is appropriate will depend upon the interaction among the object of respect, the characteristic respected, and the respecter. I may respect *X*'s expertise, but believe my own to be superior. Respecting *Y* because he is kind bears no relation to obedience at all. A specific kind of respect-worthiness appropriately links to obedience. It must be appropriate both that obedience to commands flows from the object and ground of respect, and that *this* 'respecter' should obey such commands.

Respect fundamentally requires that one preserve what is valuable.[73] One need not, however, proliferate what is valuable; though this will be morally permissible and often praiseworthy. Respect for persons does not demand that one procreate, nor would respect for just legal systems entail that one should *create* just legal systems. Both do, however, require that we preserve the worth of persons and just legal systems we encounter. Though these requirements are

[69] See also Cranor 'Toward a Theory of Respect for Persons' 314 n. 15. [70] ibid. 314.
[71] ibid. 310. [72] ibid. 314–15. [73] Cranor 'Respect for the Law: An Evaluation' 532.

minimal they are compelling, and have a certain objective quality—they apply to all who ought to respect this value. Respect preserves the future possible realization of and engagement with that which is of value. These then are the basic duties that constitute an attitude of respect. If one has an attitude of respect, it will entail these duties. It will not, however, always be a moral duty to have an attitude of respect.[74]

RESPECT FOR LAW

Our focus is internally required respect, where the duty of (estimation) respect arises out of the same grounds as respect for persons and this ground renders the attitude obligatory. I will suggest that an attitude of (estimation) respect, as *directly* mediated by reasons as possible, is a healthy and obligatory attitude for individuals to have towards law, and for law to inculcate in its subjects. Where it can be said that law is genuinely deserving of respect, one morally should refrain from undermining any respect-worthy traits, and should adopt the practical dispositions appropriate to respect-worthy objects. One has a duty not to damage law's proper functioning deriving from the duty of respect for persons.

One final ambiguity remains. Different practical conclusions might be reached through discussion of the duties entailed by an attitude of respect. It might be concluded that it is justified or obligatory to behave respectfully (practical respect); to acquire an attitude of respect; or to engage in acts helpful in acquiring an attitude of respect.[75] Mere practical respect will incorporate respectful treatment of law without any necessarily significant cognitive component. An attitude comprising both cognitive and practical respect will represent a deeper valuing of law. The third option promises little. Acts helpful in acquiring an attitude of respect are likely to cover a limited range between obedience and participation. The focus here will fall upon an attitude that comprises both cognitive and practical respect, since the latter is necessarily parasitic on, and will often be required by, the former.

The argument is set against three background considerations. First, there is a duty of (capacity) respect for persons. This is a duty not to harm, degrade, or diminish people, and to allow them a reasonable effort at fulfilling their capacity.

[74] ibid. 318 for cognate comments.

[75] ibid. 318 at n. 23. See also the discussion of Kant and Sidgwick in Blum's *Friendship, Altruism and Morality* 195. Here Blum sketches the idea in both thinkers' works that it is possible for us to have a greater amount of a certain feeling or attitude (relevantly, altruistic feeling) than we might otherwise have, by placing ourselves in circumstances we know to be causally related to producing such states in ourselves. Both thinkers consider that there is some kind of moral requirement to do so. For a related point, see Aristotle *Nicomachean Ethics* Book II.1, at 1103 $^{a}33$–$^{b}25$: 'we become just by doing just acts, temperate by doing temperate acts, brave by doing brave acts... This is why the activities we exhibit must be of a certain kind; it is because the states of character correspond to the differences between these.'

Secondly, some form of social order is necessary because the possibility of moral relations between individuals presupposes a context of minimally peaceful relations, in which universal moral norms are given a determinate (customary, conventional, or legal etc.) form.[76] In the absence of unanimity on matters of social importance (in fact, in a world marked by pervasive and deep conflict on many matters of social importance)[77] or of the possibility of Axelrodian spontaneous cooperation, we live in a world in which such order must be externally imposed. Thirdly, we live in societies governed by law. Ours is not 'the problem of beginning'.[78] We do not face the dilemma of whether or not to be original contractors. Our simple dilemma is how to conduct a moral life within societies in which law, as mediated by the state and transnational institutions, is the supreme and comprehensive normative system.

In this context, I suggest the following:

1. Respect for law is necessary to fulfilling the duty of respect for persons, where the following conditions are satisfied:
   (*a*) Law is a morally appropriate object of respect;
   (*b*) Law proves itself as an instrument presently necessary for, or vitally important to, preventing harm, and preserving the well-being of members of the community, and is integral in creating conditions in which human capacity can be realized;
2. Only if law merits our (estimation) respect can our duty of respect for persons extend to respect for law. Law is only instrumentally valuable. We can only respect law's realized capacity for facilitating good, and not its bare potential;
3. One must provide evidence of features of law and legal systems meriting (estimation) respect[79] that are centrally linked to the idea of honouring the dignity of persons and their capacity for realized potential. Four aspects of law recommend themselves.
   (*a*) Law as an epistemic authority;
   (*b*) Law as a coordinative authority;

[76] For an elegant elaboration of this point, see Lomasky 'Toward a Liberal Theory of National Boundaries' 64.

[77] Stuart Hampshire observes: 'Within any nation, there will always be contests arising not only from conflicting interests, particularly economic interests, but also from competing moral outlooks and entrenched beliefs'. *Justice is Conflict* 77. Waldron characterizes disagreement as part of 'the circumstances of politics' and understands it as a peculiarly pervasive feature of modern societies: 'In modern societies, disagreement (including disagreement about principles) is one of the most basic circumstances of political life, in roughly the way that moderate scarcity is one of the circumstances of justice'. *Law and Disagreement* 246–7. Marmor has questioned whether the disagreement that exists is as profound as Waldron believes: 'Waldron is probably right to maintain that even under ideal modes of deliberation rational people may still end up with reasonable disagreements about justice. His mistake lies, however, in the assumption that most of the functions of law in our society concern such deeply disputed matters of principle. In fact they do not.' *Positive Law and Objective Values* 95.

[78] Arendt *On Revolution* 21.

[79] See also Cranor 'Respect for Law: An Evaluation' 535.

(*c*) Law as an authority fostering self-respect; and
(*d*) Law as a reasonably just institutional system;

4. Only if we can reasonably hold an attitude of (estimation) respect for law can we know that our duty of respect for persons is advanced by respect for law. But, if law does merit our respect in this way, we have a duty of respect, derived from the duty of respect for persons, which entails that we ought not to damage or diminish law with regard to these respect-worthy traits. The instrument of law derives its value from facilitating the good of its subjects. The rule of law (assuming the satisfaction of certain conditions) creates a climate in which human capacities can develop, identities can be understood, justice can be done, and self-respect can blossom.

Where law is an instrument presently necessary for, or vital to, preventing harm, and preserving the well-being of members of a community, and is integral in creating opportunities for the realization of human capacity, our duty of respect for persons extends to a duty of respect for law. Respectful behaviour towards law, or an attitude of respect, is necessary to respect for persons because, where law functions well, and given its supremity and comprehensiveness, people organize their expectations around legal directives. They construct their daily lives around the scaffolding of laws. Disrespect for law destabilizes this structure. It undermines individuals' ability to trust their fellows to abide by proper standards of conduct; it erodes confidence in the effectiveness of laws, and it reduces people's ability to perform ordinary acts unafraid of extraordinary threats. Disrespect for law may not actually harm 'Law'. No legal institutions may be weakened. The court buildings will still stand, and judges still sit. Legal officials, *qua* officials, may neither know, nor grow unduly concerned, about isolated acts of disrespect.[80] But the rule of law is undermined. Disrespect for law does impact upon the ordinary citizen. Fear and suspicion infect ordinary activities, and unnecessary caution cauterizes human capacities.

A duty to behave respectfully towards law is entailed by our duty of respect for persons. The latter duty requires that we respect the humanity and capacity of individuals. By implication, it requires that we conditionally respect those instruments centrally linked to the realization of human capacity. The attitude of respect is necessarily required by the grounds of the duty and is obligatory. Since it is directed at an instrument, that instrument must first satisfy the demands of (estimation) respect and demonstrate its centrality to the realization of human value. But this obligatory respect, given the substantively self-limiting nature of an attitude of (estimation) respect, does not lead to an obligation to obey. The distinctive virtue of an account from respect is that it distinguishes the object of respect from the characteristic in virtue of which it is respected. Our duty is to respect legal *justice*, legal *coordination*, and legal *guidance* and not the demands of a legal system willy-nilly. We respect these features because of their ultimate

[80] Phillip Soper's early theory of the obligation to obey, as set out in *A Theory of Law*, rested on notions of the actual disappointment caused to officials by acts of disobedience.

contribution to human value. The adjectival status of 'legal' mirrors the distinction between object and grounds and the contingency of the link. We should equally respect customary coordination. But the link, though contingent, is real and pervasive. When one knowingly undermines law, one knowingly undermines the most comprehensive normative system in a society, and confidence therein. The requirements of respect are less extensive than an obligation to obey but remain categorical. We must refrain from damaging or diminishing what is of value.

The theory of respect provides two kinds of reason for action which correspond to the two layers of the duty. The duty of (estimation) respect for law generates reasons for action directly related to laws. We must not damage or undermine what is of proven value in realizing individuals' capacity. These reasons are consequentialist, and are therefore contingent on empirical analysis as to whether breach of a law actually damages the functioning of law and thereby undermines respect for persons. The foundational duty of respect for persons provides deontological reasons for respect. Deontological reasons relate to the duty not to demean or exploit individuals who deserve respect and are not, unlike consequentialist reasons, empirically fragile. These reasons interact as follows. Imagine Jane cheats on her taxes and no one discovers. At the consequentialist level, her violation may diminish law's functioning by reducing the overall pool of public funds. But this reduction is *de minimis* and no additional consequentialist concerns—for example, the setting of a bad example to others—will be invoked. At the deontological level, however, consumption without contribution flaunts respect for persons as ends in themselves, quite independently of discovery.

The duty of respect may generate conflicts. Imagine the following case. Law *X* is agreed upon by the legislature of ϕ which has a reasonably respect-worthy legal system. Jim considers that law *X* undermines women's freedom of choice and thereby their ability, in certain circumstances, to realize their capacity. What should Jim do? The tension that exists here arises between levels of specificity in a system. Jim believes that the legal system as a whole typically promotes the circumstances of realized capacity, but that this law does not. This raises questions regarding how one evaluates the respect-worthiness of law, whether it is at the level of the system or at the level of the norms that comprise the system. Consider the deep tension that arises where Jim believes that one way in which his legal system is particularly just is in its procedures. In enjoying the right to vote, each person enjoys a single and formally equal unit of influence as to how the country is run. Once the government is elected accordingly, each legislator enjoys a single and equal vote on issues of social importance. These procedures extend to each participant the only formally equal distribution of influence. Depending upon facts within his personal history, Jim may consider that this is a point about the moral implications of voluntary commitment to a decision mechanism or a point about the rational implications of a morally necessary decision mechanism.[81] If Jim acts against the resolution of these procedures, he risks undermining a respect-worthy and respect-enhancing legal procedure and arrogating to himself the status of an exception to this procedure.[82] None the less, Jim believes that law *X* is deeply wrong. It appears, none the less, that Jim is constrained as to the action he can take to seek review of law *X*. He must, typically, act within these procedures and this system and not outside it.[83] The attitude of respect at play here is more akin to tolerance, consequential on an established right. Jim is reticent to behave in a manner that would undermine a system he believes to be generally just. He should concede to a decision he considers wrong for reasons he believes to be right (the justice of the procedures that yield this decision) and seek to remedy this wrong through those same procedures. However, this 'tolerance' is necessarily predicated on an existing attitude of estimation respect for law and may not be warranted in the case of egregious moral wrongs.

THE BOUNDARIES OF RESPECT

Before proceeding to analysis of aspects of law that might ground an attitude of (estimation) respect, it is useful to mark out the boundaries of respect. To do so, consider two polar arguments that might be raised against my theory, one of which suggests that it achieves too little, the other, that it achieves too much.

First, it might be argued as follows. The duty of respect for law derives from the duty of respect for persons. This latter duty requires that we not damage or demean persons and allow them a reasonable opportunity to realize their capacity by engaging with value. But refraining from harm is distinct from actively improving something, and a requirement to afford a person a reasonable opportunity to realize her capacity may require only non-interference in her life. Therefore, the duty of respect for law has the cast of a negative duty not to interfere with the enforcement of law and not actively to damage law, as opposed to a sometimes positive and onerous duty to obey the law. Certain laws that require active obedience and contribution—compliance with revenue laws that require payment of taxes—may not be accommodated by the theory.

[81] Arendt *On Revolution* 164.

[82] Waldron suggests that majority decision-making doubly respects the individuals whose votes it aggregates. First, it 'respects their differences of opinion about justice'. Secondly, 'it embodies a principle of respect for each person in the processes by which we settle on a view to be adopted as *ours* even in the face of disagreement'. Waldron correctly notes that this minimal procedural respect, and not substantive respect as crystallized in outcomes, is the relevant respect. In circumstances of dissensus, someone has to lose, but each party may hope to win another dispute, or keep discourse open on a debate initially lost: *Law and Disagreement* 109–16. To the extent that some either *de jure* or *de facto* lack the equality of influence the method promises, the argument is correspondingly diluted.

[83] This situation would be different were the system as a whole inconsistent with the realization of human capacity.

Three responses are available. First, a duty of respect requires that we preserve what is valuable. The object of respect in the objector's example is a valuable tax law. The value of this law resides in first-order principles of political morality including principles of distributive justice. The duty of respect is consequential on these principles. Therefore, not to comply with this law, by making payment, is to damage and undermine the values it instantiates.

Secondly, only an emaciated notion of respect—a restricted Kantian notion of respect as non-interference, 'the idea that we show our respect for others by leaving them alone to pursue ends and goals they have chosen for themselves'[84]—would prevent respect for persons from featuring amongst the first-order principles of political morality that inform such laws. A more expansive notion of respect for persons can be sensitive to relations of social dependence, to the need to correct the arbitrary circumstances of birth where these are likely to inhibit the ability to realize one's potential, and to create 'a society which would allow each of us to choose our needs as we see fit, while providing us with the necessary means to make these choices'.[85]

Finally, the distinction between non-interference and obedience is not always clearly discernible. Consider an example from William Edmundson's writings.[86] You are standing in a wartime forest. A fleeing convict runs past you. Three people pass you asking about his whereabouts—an Allied MP, a Nazi policeman, and a civilian. Edmundson suggests that there is 'a prima-facie duty not to mislead the MP, but no prima-facie duty not to mislead the German policeman or the civilian'.[87] This is because only the MP acts on behalf of a legitimate state. There is a duty not to mislead that is assimilated to a duty not to interfere. But Edmundson actually provides an example of *assisting in* the fulfilment of an administrative prerogative. In this regard, 'non-interference' goes beyond mere obedience to law. In *Rice v Connolly*[88] LCJ Parker observed that: 'It seems to me quite clear that though every citizen has a moral duty, or, if you like, a social duty to assist the police, there is no legal duty to that effect'.[89] The individual may have a moral duty to assist, but it is not a moral obligation to obey the law, since there is no such law. The duty not to interfere is, here, more exacting than the

84 Seidler *Kant, Respect and Injustice: The Limits of Liberal Moral Theory* 56. See Kant *The Metaphysics of Morals* part II: 'Metaphysical First Principles of the Doctrine of Virtue' sect. 44, 6: 467 (at 213): 'But this is already implicit in the concept of the respect we are bound to show other human beings, which is only a *negative* duty. I am not bound to *revere* others (regarded merely as human beings), that is, to show them *positive* high esteem.'

85 Ignatieff *The Needs of Strangers* 136. Sen notes: 'Political rights are important not only for the fulfilment of needs, they are crucial also for the formulation of needs. And this idea relates, in the end, to the respect that we owe each other as fellow human beings.' (Quoted in Nussbaum 'Capabilities and Human Rights' 134.)

86 Edmundson *Three Anarchical Fallacies* 55–6. See also Christiano 'Justice and Disagreement at the Foundations of Political Authority' 170 where he makes related comments about Christopher Morris's distinction between failing to obey and interference in his *An Essay on the Modern State*.

87 ibid. 55.

88 [1966] 2 QB 414.

89 Quoted and discussed at Oliver and Heater *The Foundations of Citizenship* 83.

duty to obey. But elsewhere, it is clearly conceived as a less exacting standard both of legitimacy and citizen compliance. There is the danger that duties to obey, not to interfere, not to frustrate, not to mislead, and to assist might be conflated. In certain circumstances, the inaction that would elsewhere be non-interference, and possibly obedience, will frustrate good faith efforts, or mislead officials. The intuitive idea of the distinction between a duty not to interfere and a duty to obey is that many acts of disobedience will not be acts of interference. But the edges of this distinction can blur. Obedience and non-interference are not coextensive, but much disobedience may constitute interference.

The second objection expresses anxiety that the theory of respect achieves too much. Our duty of respect for law derives from a duty of respect for persons that requires that we allow them an opportunity to realize their potential by autonomously pursuing valuable ends. How does this theory accommodate laws that protect individuals' rights to free expression exercised to propagate hate speech, which, according to their own subjective values, are integral to their identities and human potential?

It should be clear that the conditional nature of estimation respect (directed at intrinsically and instrumentally valuable objects) and the fact that it is a substantively self-limiting principle, requires that such objects actually enhance respect for persons. It requires that the objects be valuable and not merely valued and that only upon satisfaction of these conditions will such objects derivatively deserve our respect.

But what if it were suggested that it is not estimation respect but respect for capacities that requires that we permit individuals this free expression of their identities? To see how the theory of respect accommodates these concerns consider an argument that arises within Neil MacCormick's writings in support of mild nationalism.[90] The argument builds from the idea that within the shared history and consciousness of a nation there 'inheres the sense of a common identity which is what we signify by ideas like nationhood'.[91] Consequently, 'for each of us, our sense of individual personality and identity is derivative from a social context'.[92] 'What is more, respecting other people entails respecting the things they value.'[93] Finally:

> The Kantian ideal of respect for persons implies . . . an obligation in each of us to respect that which in others constitutes any part of their sense of their own identity. For many people, though quite probably not for all, a sense of belonging to some nation is an element in this precious fabric of identity. This comprises . . . not merely a consciousness of a continuity with the past, but also a will or hope for continuity into the future; and also

[90] This argument appears in various forms in the following discussions: *Legal Rights and Social Democracy* 247; 'Of Self-determination and Other Things'; 'Is Nationalism Philosophically Credible?'; 'What Place for Nationalism in the Modern World?', and *Questioning Sovereignty* 157–92. MacCormick's theory is ably discussed in Vincent *Nationalism and Particularity* ch. 4.

[91] *Legal Rights and Social Democracy* 251.

[92] ibid.

[93] ibid. 253.

consciousness of a form of cultural community which requires protection and expression in appropriate institutional forms.[94]

The argument proceeds: *X* (personal identity) deserves respect; *Y* (national culture) is partially constitutive of *X* and therefore deserves respect; *A*...*C* (national institutional structures) embody and foster *Y*; therefore, *A*...*C* deserve respect.

Two possible, unobjectionable implications of MacCormick's account should be noted. First, the choices facilitated by autonomy arise and acquire meaning within a social context. As Margalit and Raz observe: 'Individual well-being depends on the successful pursuit of worthwhile goals and relationships... Familiarity with a culture determines the boundaries of the imaginable.'[95] Some cultural context is a precondition both of the formation of identity and the realization of one's capacity. Secondly, the need to 'respect that which in others constitutes any part of their sense of their own identity' may capture a rich sense of respect for persons analysed by Elizabeth Spelman through the notion of respecting a person for the person she is.[96] That is, we truly respect persons not when we respect them as the abstract bearers of universal and minimal capacities, but when we attend to them in all their subjective particularity, by reference to that which they value in themselves.

In respecting a person we must acknowledge the foundational nature of identity in any exercise of capacity. We cannot imagine a person (other than one subject to temporary or permanent cognitive impairment) without a sense of himself, of his own identity (even if this is only a sense of being lost, of lacking identity). Indeed, just this identity will be formed by, and orient us towards, the pursuit of value. Similarly, genuine respect should involve an effort at subjective understanding.[97] However, MacCormick's undifferentiated use of respect may leave us uneasy. As Vincent notes, 'Because something constitutes "part" of basic human identity surely does not entail automatic respect of that part'.[98] On the account offered here, depending on the constitutive elements of an individual's identity, we may be able to conclude: I (capacity) respect *X*'s potential to engage with value and thereby to form and nurture an identity, and I (tolerance) respect his chosen identity (and therefore believe, subject to certain limits, that the manifestations of that identity should be preserved), but I do not (estimation) respect his chosen life and sense of himself. This tolerance will be subject to limits. There will come a point where we should not tolerate immoral, hateful identities and the institutional structures that support them. As Moellendorf

[94] ibid. 261.

[95] Margalit and Raz 'National Self-Determination' 133–4. For similar comments see MacCormick *Questioning Sovereignty* 175.

[96] Spelman 'On Treating Persons as Persons' 152.

[97] As Kierkegaard observes: 'The majority of all men are subjective towards themselves and objective towards all others—terribly objective sometimes—but the real task is in fact to be objective towards oneself and subjective towards all others'. Auden (ed) *The Living Thoughts of Kierkegaard* 4.

[98] Vincent *Nationalism and Particularity* 103.

observes: 'Tolerance is a political virtue requiring the acceptance of, and non-discrimination toward, ways of life that respect the demands of justice... Permission of unjust acts is not tolerance. It is either regrettable as an all-things-considered necessity, or it is a moral failure.'[99] To argue that *X* is constitutive of individual identity and therefore deserves respect transforms a descriptive fact into a normative claim. *X*'s basic value need not entail *Y*'s value which may be conditional on the inner logic of respect (*Y* can only be respected in so far as it is consistent with and facilitates respect for persons) and a criterion of value-dependence (respect-worthy objects must be not merely valued but valuable). There are limits to the ability of final value to lend its value to other objects. The exercise of a valuable capacity may be both absent any value and destructive of the present or future exercise of that capacity (or of other sources or objects of value). In evaluating aspects of, or practices within, any national culture as a constitutive aspect of identity, we should extend Taylor's 'presumption of equal value': 'a starting hypothesis with which we ought to approach the study of any other culture'.[100] The validity of the claim to equal value, however, is contingent on an informed appraisal of the culture. This method bears twin rewards. First, we are required to engage with a culture, to understand its constitutive practices from the inside, instead of watching it from beyond, in order to evaluate it. Secondly, respect, if forthcoming, is merited and thereby meaningful. The value and significance of respect for the capacities of ends-in-themselves lies in its universality. Respect for other objects derives its value from being conditional. Were (estimation) respect understood as either entitlement or expectation it would be emptied of meaning. We would respect everything and nothing. Respect for national institutions cannot occur through an unconditional process of derivation from the final value of persons. These institutions are instruments that must facilitate the ends they are justified in preserving.[101]

[99] *Cosmopolitan Justice* 111. See also Amy Gutmann's comments in 'Introduction' in Gutmann and Taylor *Multiculturalism: Examining the Politics of Recognition* 21: 'not every aspect of cultural diversity is worthy of respect. Some differences—racism and anti-Semitism are obvious examples—ought not to be *respected*, even if expressions of racist and anti-Semitic views must be *tolerated*.'

[100] Taylor 'The Politics of Recognition' 66–7. In criticizing Taylor, Seyla Benhabib notes in *The Claims of Culture: Equality and Diversity in the Global Era* 58–60 that, 'I see the idea of "a culture as a whole" as an analytical error... it makes no sense to pass such value judgments on the totality of a culture... Any complex human society, at any point in time, is composed of multiple material and symbolic practices with a history... there cannot be such a single principle of societal culture'. It is crucial to note that estimation respect need not be univocal. We might understand certain aspects of a particular national culture as, on balance, intrinsically valuable loci of meaning, identification and belonging for those who live within it, while also believing that the culture could, by our own standards, afford more rights and better protections to its members. There may come a point at which the second of these voices drowns out the first. A sufficiently oppressive community may, on balance, be a destructive locus of identification.

[101] For additional criticisms of theories from respect, see Dan-Cohen in 'In Defense of Defiance' 42–4, addressed by Soper at *Deference* 166–7 n. 6.

ESTIMATING LAW

The theory of respect for law is conditional. Law must be a morally appropriate object of respect and we must detail the respect-worthy traits in virtue of which it is respected and which the duties of respect require us to preserve. Respect is also deeply cognitive. It must be grounded in reason and understanding. The discussion below addresses the interaction of these two aspects of respect in analysing each of the traits identified above as contributing to the respect-worthiness of law. The discussion aims to illustrate that the duty of respect has implications for law's aspiration to legitimacy and to citizens' aspirations to self-respect.

Law as an epistemic and coordinative authority

In many areas, a government's access to superior epistemic and theoretical knowledge and its ability both to access and control information, yield potentially great advantages in terms of education, coordination, and peaceful relations. The traffic light choreographing safe travel is a microcosm of this most basic governmental function.

Even were an authority not wholly legitimate, we might still respect its capacity to direct us in certain matters so that we better comply with reasons that apply to us independently. The authority's *proven* epistemic and coordinative superiority grounds our respect and gives us reason to comply. In the case of epistemic deficit, rationality provides our reason to comply. In the case of an effective coordinative directive, to respect and to follow the directive may allow us better to perform a pre-existing duty—the redistribution of money within society by taxes; the protection of the environment under governmental directives, or the preservation of others' safety while driving by rules of the road.

Analysis in terms of respect again keeps separate our understanding of the law (object) and the grounds of our attitude of respect. We respect law as a coordinative authority when and because it achieves just and efficient coordination, because these are morally desirable ends. Where it fails to achieve this, our respect and reasons run out. The ground and the object are not necessarily linked. And even where they are, it is the ground that justifies our respect, and provides reason to conform. This analysis perhaps best explains the anomalous traffic light example. We approach it, theoretically and practically, respecting both the authority issuing the command to stop at red lights, and the rationale behind the directive. But the directive just does not seem authoritative here. The object of respect has not altered but it has been robbed of its immediate ground. Not to comply is in accordance with, and not destructive of, respect. We do not expect respect-worthy authorities to require acts that patently serve no purpose. Disregard for the law neither damages law's functioning nor does it diminish or exploit others since they too might disregard the law in the same circumstances.

In discussing epistemic authority we must directly address the deeply cognitive nature of respect. The possibility of respect is predicated on the possibility of understanding. To what extent is talk of understanding in the modern state, with its plural sources of law, and its proliferation of experts, inert or anachronistic? I address this question below through consideration of a topic that reveals both a deep challenge to state legitimacy posed by the circumstances of modernity and the limits of the cognitive capacities of even a watchful citizenry.

Epistemic risk

> Use your head . . . you're on earth, there's no cure for that.
>
> (Samuel Beckett)[102]

As Cass Sunstein has recently noted, 'the diminution of social risks has been the most novel and important task of the national government since the late 1960s'.[103] During recent decades, the topic of risk has increasingly occupied public space, notably in the writings of Ulrich Beck and through his notion of '(global) risk society'.[104]

Risks are not natural dangers. Risks are hazards to which we are consciously exposed; the adverse chances that arise from our choices.[105] Technology limits or eliminates many natural risks only to generate new and unpredictable ones. Risk society marks a disjuncture between industrial society and 'reflexive modernization'. In industrial society, where innovation implied risk, insurance generated a measure of trust in institutions and allowed citizens to conceive of risks as a determinate externality of modernization. Recent modernity, however, lies outside the norms of industrial society and the risks it creates lie beyond insurability: 'it makes no sense to insure oneself against a global recession'.[106] The failure of the old categories is a measure of the enormity of the new dangers: 'since the middle of the twentieth century the social institutions of industrial society have been confronted with the historically unprecedented possibility of the destruction through decision-making of all life on this planet'.[107] Risk society also subverts our traditional categories through its subjunctive language and proleptic logic: 'The past loses its power to determine the present . . . We are discussing and arguing about something which is *not* the case, but *could* happen, if we continue to steer the same course as we have been.'[108] We enter upon risk society when the decisions we reach generate risks that cannot be accommodated within

[102] Beckett *Endgame* 53.

[103] Sunstein 'Health-Health Trade-offs' 233. Sunstein advances his analysis of these topics in his recent *Risk and Reason: Safety, Law and the Environment*. He touches upon related issues in Part III of *Free Markets and Social Justice*.

[104] Beck *Risk Society: Towards a New Modernity*; *World Risk Society*. See also Beck et al. *Reflexive Modernisation: Politics, Tradition and Aesthetics in the Modern Social Order*.

[105] See also Giddens *The Runaway World* ch. 2.

[106] *World Risk Society* 8.

[107] ibid. 53.

[108] ibid. 137.

existing paradigms of risk prevention and control. Risk society in turn leads to reflexive modernization, where modernity focuses upon its *own* unintended consequences and the impact of these upon its foundations.

Risk society poses a multifaceted challenge to state legitimacy. First, as Beck observes, risks are not treated as natural events; they are regarded as man-made dangers that man can and should control. Fewer limitations are placed upon the sphere of collective control, and government, as the holder of collective power, is expected to limit or eliminate these risks. Secondly, the global nature of risk further erodes national boundaries. Risks, like rights, affect individuals *qua* persons and not *qua* citizens. They do not respect boundaries. As Bosanquet observes in another context, 'By the very indifference of space we are liable to the direct impact of all possible factors'.[109] If universal rights are unable to unite mankind, universal risks may do so. Global risks require individuals to unlearn differences and recognize the shared and fragile nature of existence.[110] However, just as universal rights require transnational legal treatment, so too do universal risks. The sovereignty of national politics is correspondingly diluted. Thirdly, questions arise as to the value of a legal system 'that regulates and pursues every detail of the technically manageable risks, but legalizes the mega-hazards by virtue of its authority... and burdens everyone with them, including those who resist'.[111] Nor does government typically adjudicate these risks. It is increasingly reliant upon expert advice, which dilutes democracy and creates challenges of delegation and communication: 'Industrial society has produced a "truncated democracy", in which questions of the technological change of society remain beyond the reach of political-parliamentary decision-making'.[112] Experts articulate risks in a language of statistics, facts, and predictions. But the cultural acceptance of risk is contingent upon assimilation in a lay language that evaluates risk in more intuitive and particularistic terms. Voluntarily accepted risks are thought more palatable than risks arbitrarily allocated; some forms of illness and death are considered more terrifying than others.[113] This in turn creates problems of trust which are aggravated by the fact that increased knowledge generates increased uncertainty—'new knowledge can turn normality into hazards

[109] Quoted in Walzer *Spheres of Justice: A Defense of Pluralism and Equality* 37.

[110] This point raises interesting questions concerning the psychological implications of a 'global risk society'. In *Risk and 'the Other'* Hélène Joffe analyses human responses to risk and danger as explored in anthropology, cultural theory, history, and psychology: 'One common finding arises: people respond "not me", "not my group", "others are to blame" when initially faced with risks... people tend to attain a sense of personal invulnerability to risk by externalising the threat' (1). She observes that: 'The psychological theory of "optimistic bias" points to conclusive findings concerning how people interpret knowledge about risks. Most people imagine that they are less likely than their peers to be affected by a large array of risks' (6). It is possible that with an increasingly global risk society, these defensive psychological mechanisms will come under assault from reality; that the borders segregating the self and the other will blur.

[111] *World Risk Society* 58.

[112] ibid. 70. Emphasis in original omitted.

[113] Beck *World Risk Society* 42 and Powell and Leiss *Mad Cows and Mother's Milk: The Perils of Poor Risk Communication* 27.

overnight'[114]—and that the isolated revisions and successes of experts can erode the holistic credibility of expertise.

For Beck, this public acknowledgment of uncertainty opens a space for more and better democratization. Two interlocking principles undergird this conception: 'first, carrying out a division of powers, and, second, the creation of a public sphere... The public would have the role of an "open upper chamber". It would be charged to apply the standard, "How do we wish to live?" to scientific plans, results and hazards.'[115]

This notion of bottom-up democratic reform brings into focus certain epistemological constraints on holding a deeply cognitive attitude of respect in the political sphere. The modern individual educating herself within the public domain faces constraints of scarcity of time and cognitive capacity; complexity; opportunity costs and credible sources.[116] We can only react to finite stimuli; there are stimuli the significance of which will elude us and, as Beck notes, 'We are children lost in a "forest of symbols" (Baudelaire)... we have to rely on the symbolic politics of the media'.[117] We may typically not only lack crucial knowledge; we may also lack a kind of Socratic ignorance (we know that and what we do not know), being left instead to simple ignorance (we are quite unaware of what we should know).[118] These concerns link to a deeper anxiety within democratic theory that those who are called upon to make reasoned choices may be incapable of doing so, or may be incapable of successfully monitoring agents to whom such choices are delegated. Citizens can only choose or decide on the basis of what they are enabled to know or on what they enable themselves to know.[119] This presupposes that citizens will *be able* to learn what they need to know to reach intelligent decisions, a hurdle heightened by the globalization of rights and risks: The individual is confronted with ever-proliferating sources of potentially relevant information.

Lupia and McCubbins[120] have recently addressed these issues, by asking, 'when ignorance of details prevents reasoned choice, how people choose among potential heuristics, and when these heuristics provide effective substi-

[114] ibid. 58. Havel *Open Letters* 63: 'What yesterday we declared impossible, or at least averred we would never get accustomed to, today we accept, without astonishment, as a fact of life. And, conversely, things that a little while ago we took for granted we now treat as exceptional'.

[115] *World Risk Society* 70. The position echoes Kant: '*Immaturity* is the inability to use one's own understanding without the guidance of another'. 'What is Enlightenment?' in *Political Writings* 54.

[116] In *Law, Pragmatism and Democracy* 204, Richard Posner observes: 'Both the ability and the incentive to overcome one's cognitive deficiencies are weaker in political markets than economic ones because the voter has a smaller stake and less information in choosing between candidates than the consumer has in choosing between sellers of goods and services'. However, although each individual's stake in (influence over) political decisions is nugatory, the stakes are often infinitely higher. It is important to meet Posner's descriptive claim with a normative response, which argues that addressing cognitive political deficits is crucial.

[117] *World Risk Society* 44.

[118] ibid. 127 for a related distinction.

[119] See Stokes 'What Do Policy Switches Tell Us About Democracy?'

[120] *The Democratic Dilemma: Can Citizens Learn What They Need To know?*

tutes for the detailed information people lack'.[121] They provide a model of successful delegation grounded in knowledge (an 'ability to predict the consequences of actions'), trust (common interests), and the heuristics that can substitute for these where direct knowledge or a direct basis for affective trust are absent. They suggest that certain 'incentive-altering external forces' can substitute for knowledge and trust. These include verification (the possibility of a speaker's statements being verified as true or false before the principal chooses), penalties for lying (which directly affect a speaker's utility), and observable costly effort (a cost that 'the speaker must pay to send any signal'). By altering and clarifying a speaker's incentives, these external forces can reduce the extent to which the principal requires direct evidence of either knowledge or trustworthiness. Reasoned choice can therefore be facilitated by an institutional design that nests these incentive-altering external forces, providing speakers with incentives to reveal what they know and principals with the ability to perceive speaker incentives accurately.

This discussion has a twofold relevance to the theory of respect. First, agents must be able to acquire relevant information to be able to hold an intelligent attitude of respect. Without this, talk of respect is otiose. Secondly, in this 'forest of symbols' an individual's ability to maintain healthy self-respect demands that she seek to maintain as much control over her choices and decisions as is possible and appropriate. An 'aristocracy of experts'[122] requires both an active technical branch and a passive citizenry. The affront to autonomy of receiving commands and guidance can be diluted by the subject's efforts at understanding. However, the requirement that we not abrogate responsibility for crucial decisions in our lives stands in tension with the genuine scarcity of resources and cognitive capacity that afflicts individuals in the modern state. Citizens cannot, and should not have to, become global experts.[123]

The primary epistemic anxiety is that citizens will not gain access to relevant and necessary information in reaching decisions. This is most acute in relation to recondite risk issues, which are often characterized by uncertainty and closure. In these circumstances, and drawing on language used earlier in describing the stages of attitudes of respect, citizens cannot typically rely upon *direct* sources of information (personal experience or independent research) to inform attitudes of respect or to reach independent choices. Similarly, both government closure and uncertainty will undermine the possibility of derivative respect. Citizens will therefore be required to rely on *derivative indicia of compromised expertise*. Such indicia might include the state of expertise in an area. The fact of deep

[121] ibid. 13.

[122] Robert Dahl, quoted in Lupia and McCubbins *The Democratic Dilemma: Can Citizens Learn What they Need to Know?* 2.

[123] See also Dryzek *Deliberative Democracy and Beyond: Liberals, Critics, Contestations* 164–5 and Walzer *Spheres of Justice* 289: 'it is undoubtedly true that educated and experienced men and women are partially shielded from lay criticism. The more recondite and mysterious their knowledge... the more effective the shield—a powerful argument for democratic education, whose purpose is not however, to make all citizens experts, but to mark off the boundaries of expertise.'

uncertainty, quite aside from the nature of this uncertainty, cautions scepticism in the face of anodyne government advice.[124] Further indicia of compromised expertise may be found in experts' institutional affiliations and funding sources; for example there should be strict structural and institutional separation of potentially inconsistent interest groups (one organization should not be responsible for potentially conflicting portfolios).[125] Again, one need not understand the substance of an issue to grasp the fact of compromised institutional forms. Official closure may also indicate compromised expertise. Openness may take several forms. It may manifest not only in communicative honesty about the nature of risks, but in openness to independent assessment of risks; for example, whether independent agencies are allowed to review the materials, conclusions, and research of government agencies or government-approved experts.

These observations suggest steps that governments and experts should take to inculcate and justify respect among a populace confronted with escalating risks. Institutional designs that nest incentive-altering external forces increase the likelihood that government agents will address the public honestly and openly. Institutional and regulatory bodies should not be assigned mutually incompatible responsibilities in addressing a risk issue; a strict separation of functions should be observed. It is instrumentally and intrinsically crucial that citizens are offered honest explanations of risks, and of the state of knowledge and uncertainty surrounding them. Intrinsically, this practice acknowledges the rationality of law's subjects, and thereby enhances state legitimacy. As Coleman notes: 'Anyone who offers reasons designed to convince or persuade others makes it clear that he treats others as autonomous and equal in the same way that one regards oneself, as worthy of the respect a practice of offering reasons presupposes and as capable of being moved by reasons as only autonomous agents can be'.[126] Instrumentally, government representatives are more likely to be believed if they address all aspects of a risk. As the UK Phillips Report into Bovine Spongiform Encephalopathy noted: 'If doubts are openly expressed and publicly explored, the public are capable of responding rationally and are more likely to accept reassurance and advice if and when it comes'. Government credibility is fostered by respecting individuals' capacity to assimilate, and respond to, a range of hypotheticals in circumstances of uncertainty. Open and honest communi-

[124] The Phillips Report commissioned by the British government in December 1997 to investigate the BSE crisis finally concluded that uncertainty can, in certain circumstances, provide sufficient reason for prophylactic action. See Phillips Report ch. 14: 'Although likelihood of a risk to human life may appear remote, where there is uncertainty all reasonably practicable precautions should be taken. Precautionary measures should be strictly enforced even if the risk that they address appears to be remote.' http://www.bseinquiry.gov.uk/report/volume1/chapt142.htm#648931.

[125] A further point, which I do not have room to discuss, arises here. The crisis originated in the conversion of herbivores into cannibals; through the recycling of animal protein in ruminant feed. This prompts the question of whether and to what extent we should extend the bases of respect to other species, and how we might evaluate law's success in doing so.

[126] Coleman 'Authority and Reason' 312.

cation cultivates trust and is likely both to prevent irrational public responses and preclude a lasting *ex post facto* sense of betrayal.[127]

Law as an authority fostering self-respect

Self-respect is the measure of a person's own sense of dignity, worth, and accomplishment as the sculptor of her life. It is both a psychological and moral notion.[128] A person's standing in her own eyes frames her ability to function and flourish in the world. Self-respect is in part a product of an agent's autonomous choices. It is forfeited where she acts in a manner unbefitting of the person she believes she should be (either holistically or in relation to a specific role). An action lacking integrity, acquiescence in demeaning treatment by others, creates a cleavage between the life she believes she should live and the reality of the life she is living. In this gap, a loss of self-respect occurs. Awareness of this loss, of course, bridges back to self-respect. Denial or ignorance of the loss signifies an already diminished self-respect. However, we can only forfeit what we first possess, and self-respect is also in part a product of an individual's opportunities, of the choices available to her. A society can undermine the possibility of self-respect by establishing segregations of worth, through class, racist, sexist, or sectarian practices. The sense of self formed in interaction with others amidst these practices is likely to be defined by an awareness of absence, of all that one lacks. And while such practices tacitly imply the equal value they explicitly deny (I only seek to deprive you of that which I believe you have);[129] they none the less shrink their subjects' moral and psychological possibilities.

Clearly, a political community cannot guarantee self-respect to each of its members. Robust and stable self-respect is secured for each individual through the myriad interactions of each day of her life—by formation of, and fidelity to, a valuable life-plan. However, a political community must not undermine, and should do all that is feasible to preserve, the possibility of self-respect for its members. If an authority treats its subjects with the respect persons deserve (for example by extending equal rights and protections to all), thereby facilitating self-respect, it merits a correlative respect—that its subjects not ignore or dismiss its attempts at ruling. But this is a minimal respect. Respectful treatment is what the subjects of authority deserve. Their reactive respect should be to listen in like manner, to treat law with similar respect. Two caveats. Many community members will neither feel, nor in reality, be, respected by their laws and societies in this manner. Members of these classes will have porous grounds for respect.

[127] For discussion of why a government may deliberately render its actions more visible to voters, see Ferejohn 'Accountability and Authority: Toward a Theory of Political Accountability'. For discussion of intra-governmental incentives towards, and costs of, institutional secrecy, see Stiglitz 'On Liberty, the Right to Know, and Public Discourse: The Role of Transparency in Public Life'.

[128] Massey 'Is Self-Respect a Moral or a Psychological Concept?'.

[129] This is essentially Primo Levi's observation about the Nazi regime. The desire to humiliate already concedes the humanity it purports to deny.

Secondly, even those who are treated with respect may not be so in every arena. The attitude of respect is therefore likely to be qualified.

A people without place

> Looking is such a marvellous thing, of which we know but little; through it we are turned absolutely toward the outside... Suddenly, in the shadow of the street, a face is held out to you, and you see, under the influence of the contrast, its essence with such clarity.
>
> Rilke[130]

A government, can, through its actions, affect its members' self-respect in at least three ways:

- it may treat individual members in a manner that prevents these individuals from maintaining healthy self-respect;
- it may treat some of its members in a manner that prevents the remaining members from maintaining healthy self-respect, through making them party to this treatment; and
- it may treat non-members in a manner that prevents members from maintaining healthy self-respect as party to this treatment.

Traditional discussions of self-respect and government[131] focus on the first of these indices. Law must directly facilitate the self-respect of those it governs, or risk the collapse into injustice. However, a focus on the basic respect that all persons deserve simply *qua* persons, unfolds the importance of the second and third indices. My ability to feel healthy and justified self-respect is a function not only of the respect which others show me, but of the respect which I, and those who act on my behalf, show to others. The notion of equal respect for persons argues both that we must respect the capacity of each individual equally, and that the respect a government merits will in part be a function of its role in facilitating this. Similarly, the way in which a government treats non-nationals, seeking entrance to, and within, its borders, will impact upon the capacity of its members to maintain either respect for government or healthy self-respect. I want to suggest that respect for law, and the implications of liberal democratic principles, create a link between a government's treatment of non-nationals and its legitimacy.

People are the exception to increasing globalization. Boundaries that are permeable to global capital, investment, technologies, and communications are patrolled to protect against human mobility.[132] We live in a world of bounded

[130] Quoted in Murdoch *Existentialists and Mystics: Writings on Philosophy and Literature* 56.

[131] Rawls *A Theory of Justice* 440–6 and Thomas 'Self-Respect: Theory and Practice'. See also, Dworkin *Taking Rights Seriously* 272: 'Government must treat those whom it governs with concern, that is, as human beings who are capable of suffering and frustration, and with respect, that is, as human beings who are capable of forming and acting on intelligent conceptions of how their lives should be lived'.

[132] See generally Sassen *Losing Control: Sovereignty in an Age of Globalization* and Holton *Globalization and the Nation-State*. Michael Dummett notes a similar asymmetry in *On Immigration and Refugees* 130.

communities whose boundaries allocate membership, opportunities, identities, and delimited sovereignty; designating states, territories, and peoples. These boundaries are rendered morally troubling in circumstances of gross global inequality of opportunities, resources, and political freedoms.[133] The legal and moral autonomy of states is qualified by transnational regulations, multinational corporate actors, and global trade institutions. The primary incursion consists in human rights norms that attach to persons *qua* persons and not *qua* citizens with the result that rights and citizenship bifurcate. However, the implementation and recognition of rights must ultimately occur within the context of some nation state.

Practices surrounding immigration and the treatment of refugees crystallize issues concerning the legal and moral legitimacy of boundaries in a world of deep inequality. Legally, issues arise as to how states translate and implement transnational legal norms into their domestic law. Morally, issues arise as to how states respond to the imperatives of human need and desperation. The significance of these issues is compounded within a liberal democracy. Commitment to liberal principles involves a belief in the equal moral worth of all persons and the notion that individuals should have rights as against government (civic rights of participation; rights of exit and political freedom, and so on). Commitment to democratic principles involves a belief that the people should rule and that all those subject to law should enjoy equal influence over the way in which they are governed.

Many reasons speak directly to a state's national interest in orienting treatment of non-nationals. Achieving security for others is often necessary to ensuring national security. Immigrant labour is a possible corrective for increasingly aging populations within Western liberal democracies. Once individuals actually settle within a territory internal stability is more likely to be maintained if non-citizens are accorded adequate rights, which facilitate an integrated, stable life, than if state practices create an isolated and disenfranchised enclave of resident aliens.[134] Similarly, breach of, or bad faith in respect of, international treaty obligations correlates to a loss of respect within the global community. These are not the reasons that concern us here, which instead focus on consistency to the commitments of a liberal democracy, and the requirements of respect for persons as a ground of respect for law.

We should begin by paying explicit attention to a series of often assumed preliminaries. A liberal democratic theory, particularly one that stresses respect for persons, must justify the existence and moral implications of national

[133] Thomas Pogge quotes various sources that demonstrate the extent of this inequality in his recent 'Human Rights and Human Responsibilities' 151–2. See, generally, Rubio-Marin's excellent *Immigration as a Democratic Challenge: Citizenship and Inclusion in Germany and the United States* and Kymlika 'Territorial Boundaries: A Liberal Egalitarian Perspective'.

[134] Aristotle *The Politics* III. xi. 1281^{b}21 (203) *et passim*: 'there is a risk in not giving them a share, and in their nonparticipation, for when there are many who have no property and no honours they inevitably constitute a huge hostile element in the state'.

boundaries. If these borders effect injustices, if exclusion creates imparities, these stand in need of justification. As Kymlika notes:

> In a world marked by massive global inequalities, the idea that one's freedoms and opportunities are limited to the state in which one is born means that some people are born into a legal status which guarantees them personal security, ample opportunities, and a decent standard of living, while others (through no fault of their own) are born into a legal status that condemns them to poverty and insecurity.[135]

This justification should flow from liberal democratic premises[136] and not, without further justification, from notions such as the nation or tribe.[137] Once boundaries are drawn, certain special, associative ties may follow; members are co-citizens, they may also be co-nationals. But this initial determination of membership need not define without exception the circumference of all subsequent distributive decisions.[138] Questions arise as to the nature and scope of the obligations we owe individuals beyond the borders of our state who live amidst poverty and political suppression. Even were some special obligations towards fellow citizens justifiable, we would be required to ascertain their nature, scope, weight, defeasibility, and also the types of claim over which they might prevail in the event of conflict. There are good reasons to suppose that our obligations to strangers extend beyond vague positive duties or duties of charity or mutual aid. These reasons may derive from events within the histories of nations that create direct moral bonds between a state and another nation: colonial practices; protectionist trade policies; contribution to the economic links between the emigration state and the home state, or participation in conflict within emigrant states.[139] Thomas Pogge has also persuasively argued that direct and indirect contribution to global inequality through participation in a deeply unjust global economic and political order imposes a determinate negative duty upon states to correct these inequalities.[140]

I will proceed on the basis that national boundaries do not delimit moral obligations and that any moral significance they possess is susceptible to qualification. What are the implications of this premise for the manner in which a liberal democratic state should treat refugees and immigrants?

For a theory resting in respect for persons, and similarly for one that holds to liberal democratic principles, individual freedom of movement is a compelling

[135] Kymlika 'Territorial Boundaries: A Liberal Egalitarian Perspective'.

[136] In 'Cosmopolitan Respect and Patriotic Concern' Richard Miller argues that full and equal respect for all individuals dictates a priority of attention grounded in two arguments: (*a*) from 'the excessive costs in lost social trust'; and (*b*) 'from the need to provide compatriots with adequate incentives to obey the laws one helps to create'. Will Kymlika argues inductively for the legitimacy of national boundaries, analysing the practices that have developed over time in liberal democracies with regard to boundaries, and then attempting to identify normative rationales for the practices, in 'Territorial Boundaries: A Liberal Egalitarian Perspective'.

[137] O'Neill *Bounds of Justice* 178.

[138] Cf. Walzer *Spheres of Justice: A Defense of Pluralism and Equality* 31.

[139] Sassen *Losing Control: Sovereignty in an Age of Globalization* 84.

[140] Pogge *World Poverty and Human Rights* 133.

moral principle. As Michael Dummett notes, in determining whether outsiders have a defeasible right of entry into states or whether states have a defeasible right of sovereignty, 'The presumption for individuals is always in favour of freedom: there must be a particular ground why any state is entitled to curtail that freedom, if indeed it is'.[141] Dummett canvasses certain reasons that are, and may legitimately be, advanced in this regard. These include issues relating to overpopulation and territorial scope; the economic and political conditions in the receiving state (for instance, a fledgling democracy may be disproportionately threatened by an influx of refugees); the right of a people that their national culture not be submerged and that cultural stability be maintained. These latter two reasons exemplify ways in which the individual aspects of the complex of the nation state may bifurcate and interact: The institutions of the state take measures to maintain the integrity of the cultural dimension of the nation, as a, possibly 'imagined'[142], political entity, with a continuity in space and time.[143] These principles are limited by context. National cultures are only likely to be threatened by a significant volume of aliens entering simultaneously, originating from culturally divergent states. In such circumstances, there may be a compelling reason to limit the intake, both through concern for the survival of a national culture and through concerns about the resources of any state responsibly to assimilate refugees into domestic culture in such circumstances. However, this argues only for a reduced intake. Moreover, the flow of refugees is seldom this vast. Arguments to this effect are typically deeply disingenuous and are all the more so in already multicultural states where cultural heterogeneity negates many of these concerns. A state may also refuse entry to individuals considered a criminal or political threat. Though a legitimate ground for refusal where justified, this basis for exclusion clearly generates the greatest possibility of abuse in the circumstances of modernity.

Current international law leaves a space in the centre of refugee policy. Individuals have the right to inhabit their nation of birth, freely to enter and return to that nation, and to leave it at any time.[144] Under the Geneva Convention of 1951 (and its 1966 Protocol) each person with a 'well-founded fear of being persecuted for reasons of race, religion, nationality, membership of a particular social group or political opinion', and who is outside her country of nationality or residence, and unable or unwilling to return to this place, has a right to refuge from persecution. However, this right to refuge (which in its terms

[141] Dummett *On Immigration and Refugees* 57.

[142] Anderson *Imagined Communities.*

[143] Robert Holton notes that 'culture is far harder to globalize than is the economy... the attraction of national cultures is thus bounded to those who claim the reality of a common experience that others do not and cannot directly share... What is not so clear is whether contemporary nationalism is necessarily to be seen as a reaction against globalization per se and whether the global and the national should be seen as warring principles.' Holton *Globalization and the Nation-State* 155–7. See also Helton's discussion at 85.

[144] See, *inter alia*, Article 13.1 and 13.2 of the Universal Declaration of Human Rights and Article 2 of the Fourth Protocol to the European Convention on Human Rights.

admits of many exceptions) nowhere correlates to a duty upon states to accept refugees; persons have no right to enter another state. States are obligated not to penalize illegal entry by those who seek refuge, and not to return persons to the place in which they fear such persecution or to a place from which they will be returned to that place. Only in the absence of any other eligible receiving state is a state in which refuge is sought required to accept applicants. This legal lacuna creates a moral opportunity. Simone Weil observed that, 'At the bottom of the heart of every human being, from earliest infancy, until the tomb, there is something that goes on indomitably expecting, in the teeth of all experience of crimes committed, suffered and witnessed, that good and not evil will be done to him'.[145] The moral opportunity afforded to each state and its citizens is to do good and not evil to refugees; to surprise them with compassion. A state that takes respect for persons seriously might maximally extend the bases of admission (subject to legitimate qualifications) to all circumstances that prevent an individual from enjoying the conditions necessary to engage in valuable and meaningful activities that facilitate the realization of his capacity (for example, severe poverty and economic depravity).[146]

However, this legal gap is also a margin in which moral legitimacy may be forfeited. As Arthur Helton has recently observed: 'Refugees are drenched in human values'.[147] They are the terrible, deracinated face of our new century. But this does not always provoke sympathy: 'the arrival of uninvited people in need can also exacerbate fear of difference and cultural confrontations'.[148] I noted earlier that failure to recognize value may evidence a lack of moral imagination. The inability to help a refugee, to see in him the tragedy of a life lived in the moment between hope and disappointment, is a terrible failing in this regard.[149] But there is more than a failure of imagination in the conduct of governments of liberal democracies, where refusal of asylum is accompanied by active propaganda against refugees[150] and the detention of refugees in circumstances akin to imprisonment.[151] The symbolic significance of this latter point should not be ignored. Detention of refugees results in a country treating those already the victims of cruelty, who are also potential citizens, in the manner of those who

[145] Quoted in Gaita *A Common Humanity: Thinking About Love & Truth & Justice* 51.

[146] For similar comments see Dummett *On Immigration and Refugees* 37.

[147] Helton *The Price of Indifference: Refugees and Humanitarian Action in the New Century* 8.

[148] ibid. 13.

[149] Raymond Gaita's discussion of racism in *A Common Humanity: Thinking About Love & Truth & Justice* (at 59) captures one sense of this failing: 'Her sense of difference centres on how she conceives what suffering may *mean* to the Vietnamese. She fails to see that it could mean anything deep and she takes this attitude to their entire inner life, to all their hopes, fears and joys whatever these may centre on... She responds to them as being *outside of the space of possibilities* which gives sense to judgments of depth and shallowness.'

[150] Michael Dummett observes: 'Poisoning the mind of the public at large against a group of people who ask our help and deserve our pity—or indeed against any whole group—is a worse crime than simply treating its members unjustly'. *On Immigration and Refugees* 45.

[151] Walzer suggests in *Spheres of Justice*, at 51, that one reason compelling states to grant asylum to refugees is that its denial requires the use of force against the helpless. And yet this is a commonplace in Western liberal democratic states.

have, by their own actions, forfeited citizenship. Margalit has noted that a society's treatment of prisoners is eloquent of the sincerity of its respect for persons: 'We have a simple formula which claims that a society is a decent one if it punishes its criminals—even the worst of them—without humiliating them'.[152] To treat those who are victims in a manner similar to criminals, and to humiliate them, is a sign not only of a society that lacks decency, but of government practices that lack moral legitimacy. Where citizens sanction such practices, their ability to hold an attitude of justified self-respect is similarly undermined.[153] Such practices also visit illiberal limitations upon citizens who disapprove of them, by restricting their freedom of association: 'restraint of entry, in denying insiders the option of (for example) housing or employing outsiders, thereby similarly replaces insider's commitment with coercion'.[154]

Slightly different concerns animate the treatment of immigrant residents within a state. The challenge here is a democratic one. Democratic principles require that those subject to state authority have an equal unit of influence over their governance, in order to be able to exercise restraint over government practices. To the extent that this influence is denied to (as opposed to forfeited by) law's subjects, there is a loss of democratic legitimacy: 'Deficits in democratic legitimacy arise whenever the set of those involved in making democratic decisions fails to coincide with the set of those affected by them'.[155] However, the right to vote is almost everywhere reserved only to citizens and not extended to resident aliens who work, live, and participate within a community. Again, certain restrictions are placed upon a state that genuinely seeks to realize respect for persons in its institutional practices, and is committed to the implications of democratic principles.[156] Where individuals contribute financially and emotionally to the life of a community; where the bonds that bring significance and meaning to their lives nest within that community; where they are subject to the authority of the state and reliant upon its institutions for protection and for the preservation of the conditions of their autonomy, they should enjoy civic equality. This issue has many dimensions which I can only touch upon here in a cursory manner. Where participation is predicated on citizenship, the processes and conditions of naturalization should be liberalized. This can occur by reducing the sphere of non-transparent discretionary rejection of applications; by permitting dual citizenship; by facilitating education and integration where some minimal knowledge of local laws and institutions and so on is a requirement of naturalization; and by permitting future citizenship on the basis of *ius soli* as opposed to *ius sanguinis*, to prevent the occurrence of second- and third-

[152] Margalit *The Decent Society* 262.

[153] This comment presupposes that self-respect has an objective dimension; that individuals may mistakenly hold an attitude of self-respect. This objectivity is of two possible types. First, evaluation by an objective self, and secondly, evaluation by others.

[154] Steiner 'Hard Boundaries, Compensation, and Classical Liberalism' 79.

[155] Habermas 'The European Nation State and the Pressures of Globalisation' 220.

[156] For a detailed and excellent discussion of these and cognate issues, see Rubio-Marin *Immigration as a Democratic Challenge: Citizenship and Inclusion in Germany and the United States.*

generation resident aliens. Naturalization need not, then, entail formal renunciation of former ties. These ties may be given meaningful play within individuals' lives by instituting practices of assimilation that leave space for the retention of aspects of national identity.

The theory of respect for law does not, therefore, directly accommodate particularity. Only the practical restraint provided by condition 4 of an attitude of respect will confine the objects of respect. The attitude is pragmatically and contingently relativized to the particular and is at all times susceptible of extension. In this regard, the theory descriptively accommodates the increasingly transnational sources of law and culture. It is also normatively suited to the circumstances of modern states. It ascribes no prevailing moral weight to national boundaries. If there are states there are necessarily boundaries that delimit their extent, but this fact has no necessary implications for the moral weight ascribed to these boundaries, or to the extent to which these boundaries exclude or include individuals. Any such moral weight cannot be assumed and must be argued for.

It might be suggested that this inclusiveness is misplaced. Citizenship, it may seem, simply *is* the centripetal normative force in enquiries into political obligation. However, while possibly true of some political obligations (military service), this should not be as relevant to the question of the moral obligation to obey. Mere citizenship does not presuppose loyalty or commitment, nor does it testify to it. As Lardy has recently commented, communities 'coalesce for reasons far more varied and complex than the fact that all its members happen to have in common a formal legal title'.[157] Her discussion centres upon the restriction of voting rights to citizens. It is, she suggests, insidious to have a society that venerates the practices of citizenship and community without demonstrating a corresponding concern for those excluded from such practices; and such exclusion operates to 'weaken the democratic legitimacy of the political communities'.[158]

The narrow scope of arguments predicated on citizenship, therefore, actually undermines the legitimacy of the state making claims to obedience. Communities increasingly consist in concentric circles of membership and not in the single status of citizenship. People occupying different perspectives can value and support the same entity for different reasons. Both still value it. Respect for persons as a ground of respect for law requires that rights and obligations should be distributed according to *de facto* membership and residence and not formal legal citizenship.

Law as a reasonably just institution

Respect is also merited by a reasonably just legal system. This will have procedural and substantive dimensions. The rule of law will be largely observed.

157 Lardy 'Citizenship and the Right to Vote' 93.

158 ibid. 95. See also Narayan 'Towards a Feminist Vision of Citizenship: Rethinking the Implications of Dignity, Political Participation and Nationality' 61.

Directives will be open, promulgated, based on dependent reasons, and prospective. There will be an equitable distribution of societal goods. Individuals will be able to rely upon the expectations law engenders and will have security, and access to adequate resources, in pursuing their reasonable plans. There will be due process and fairness within judicial procedures. Civil and political rights—to freedom of conscience, expression, and association—will be respected. The basic institutional structure of society will be just, and will treat individuals in a manner consistent with self-respect. Beyond this core, there may be additional goods, such as established and plural voluntary associations in which individuals can pursue worthwhile activities in community with others.

This ground of respect introduces an important distinction between holistic and selective respect. In an overall just system, which also functions well as an epistemic and coordinative authority, and which promotes self-respect among its subjects, one will intelligibly hold an attitude of respect for the total system. It will be rational for one to respect law's directives, advice, and guidance. This may lead to a partial or complete acceptance of the authority of law. It may lead only to conscientious watchfulness. This attitude of respect is separate from the injunction to behave respectfully grounded in the duty to respect persons. However, in a less just, less efficient system, while one may not rationally be able to adopt an attitude of holistic respect for law, the duty of respect for persons still enjoins respect for law where it does function morally and efficiently, and acts as the focus for community expectations and aspirations. The two attitudes are separate but may coexist.

In substantiating law's claims for respect, two evaluations are important. First, law must possess a certain *quality* of the trait in virtue of which it is respected. It must be reasonably just, reliable in epistemic matters, successful in coordinating towards the common good. There must also be sufficient *quantity* or *pervasiveness* of this characteristic, and in the case of law a quantity proportionate to its claims. Law must be largely just, broadly reliable, and widely successful in coordination problems.

Where law merits our respect, our duty of respect for persons requires that we show respect, or acquire an attitude of respect, for law. This flows from the fact that law is contingently but pervasively linked to the realization of human capacity and the quality and security of human lives. This duty requires that we do not damage or demean law. It does not require exhaustive obedience. A respectful attitude is protestant before it is permissive. If we take seriously the duty to respect persons then we will take seriously law's duty to respect us, and its need to live up to its uniquely ubiquitous claims. But, where it comes reasonably close to this standard, and stabilizes and structures human lives, it too deserves respect; both on its own merits, and flowing from our duty of respect for persons. This may create a presumption in favour of the law—where we proceed on the assumption that laws are generally just but stay awake to the possibility of a morally discordant law.

RESPECT FOR LAW: AN INTERIM CONCLUSION

This attitude of respect for law does not generate a universal obligation to obey. This is the point at which respect for persons sketches a circumference around the conscientious citizen's proper attitude towards law. Respect for persons requires respect for law where law merits (estimation) respect and proves itself instrumentally vital in protecting and promoting human capacity. But it does not require that all individuals, in identical manner, are subject to an obligation to obey. Consider Williams's point that what respect involves is 'that each man is owed an effort at identification, that he should not be regarded as the surface to which a certain label can be applied, but one should try to see the world (including the label) from his point of view'.[159] Social labels sometimes ill describe their subjects. Some ostensible members, for any number of reasons, inhabit a penumbra of belonging. Some citizens never know the equality and dignity the tag promises. Respect for persons requires respect for law under the conditions noted above. But it also requires a more subtle understanding of social life than that all membership is equal or that there is an obligation to obey all laws.

The theory of respect can be extended to account for the proper attitude of one who travels to another legal system. This is the attitude Anscombe describes as the secondary correlative of authority.[160] The account also leaves obvious logical space for the justification of conscientious disobedience.[161] Where the object of respect neglects or undermines the ground of respect, the attitude may mandate disobedience.

THE LIMITS OF RESPECT

Before leaving the concept of respect, it is necessary to assess whether I have underestimated its resources; whether it can in fact underwrite a prima-facie obligation to obey the law. Phillip Soper has twice suggested that it can: first, in his theory of respect for the good faith efforts of governing officials[162] and very recently in his theory of a duty to defer to good faith government.[163] Given that

[159] Williams 'The Idea of Equality' 159.

[160] Anscombe 'On the Source of the Authority of the State' 6.

[161] That it requires justification entails that there is no legal right to civil disobedience *per se*: Raz *Authority* ch. 14. For discussion of a moral right to civil disobedience, see Dworkin *Taking Rights Seriously* ch. 8. The rhetoric of respect is often more characteristic of the discourse of civil disobedience than of allegiance. In his 'Letter from Birmingham City Jail' Martin Luther King Jr. counterpoises a moral respect for what is right against a subservient respect for law: 'An individual who breaks a law that conscience tells him is unjust, and willingly accepts the penalty by staying in jail to arouse the conscience of the community over the injustice, is in reality expressing the very highest respect for the law'. In Bedau (ed) *Civil Disobedience in Focus* 74. See also Martin 'Wolff's Defence of Philosophical Anarchism'.

[162] Soper *A Theory of Law* 75–90; Soper 'The Obligation To Obey The Law'.

[163] Soper *Deference*.

the latter theory essentially revises the former, I will focus on the more recent thesis.

KANTIAN DEFERENCE

In *The Ethics of Deference*, Soper advances a theory of conscientious obedience based in a duty of deference, structural and methodological aspects of which were touched upon in Chapter 1. It is a theory that intends to demonstrate that citizens have reasons to defer to the legal norms of a state and that deference to (even mistaken) legal norms may evince respect for the values of the legal community, thereby strengthening political bonds. The theory has a simple structure. Respect through deference in the political context is required due to the intrinsic requirements of consistency in moral principles. The duty to respect legal norms reflects the duty to respect the values one acknowledges in understanding the nature of a legal system.[164] The subjects of law recognize the *necessity* of an enterprise that requires that designated authorities impose norms in good faith on the community at large:[165] 'Consistency in understanding what a state is requires one to concede that the enterprise that leads to the creation and enforcement of norms is a valuable one'.[166] This argument from consistency is supplemented by an argument from empathy: 'I, who could do no different were I in charge, have a prima-facie reason to do as I would expect others in my situation to do'.[167] If one admits that there are good reasons for the state to expect voluntary compliance from its subjects, the argument for a universal prima-facie obligation to obey is essentially complete. One will always have an intrinsic reason (and will often have instrumental reasons) to defer to the state's normative judgments.[168]

Soper articulates the idea of deference in the context of friendship:

> Persons in a close relationship may sometimes conclude that one ought to defer to the opinion of one's partner even though one's partner's opinion is morally wrong. Such examples seem acceptable illustrations of the possibility that moral truth may sometimes require action in accordance with the (erroneous) moral views of another because we can recast this example as a case of competing moral goods: We weigh the prima-facie value of

[164] *Deference* 164.

[165] See Kant 'The Metaphysics of Morals' in *Political Writings* 137: 'The first decision the individual is obliged to make, if he does not want to renounce all concepts of right, will be to adopt the principle that one must abandon the state of nature in which everyone follows his own desires, and unite with everyone else (with whom he cannot avoid having intercourse) in order to submit to external, public and lawful coercion... In other words, he should at all costs enter into a state of civil society.'

[166] *Deference* 166.

[167] ibid. 167. See also 164: 'the law's expectation of voluntary compliance corresponds to what I would also expect if I were the legislator'.

[168] ibid. 167. This expectation of voluntary compliance on the part of the state is crucial. Only if the state expects such compliance (and note that Soper cannot hold that it *claims* such compliance) can a failure to comply manifest disrespect for law.

maintaining the relationship against the prima-facie dis-value of acting incorrectly and discover that sometimes the correct action (in the ultimate sense) requires a compromise of our own (correct) views about what to do.[169]

Reasons for deference have a distinctive structure and substance. Structurally, deference is justified by reasons that outweigh or override the normal reasons that bear on action and involves acting contrary to one's normal view of what is required in a situation. Substantively, deference provides both instrumental and intrinsic reasons for considering another's views as 'more important than I actually think they are'. Soper again illustrates two theoretically distinct kinds of instrumental reason in the context of a relationship: 'I must take into account not only my partner's disappointment if I do not defer, but also the potential impact on the relationship'.[170] Intrinsic reasons are of two kinds: (*a*) objective (where deference serves as a sign of respect for a relationship that is in fact valuable) and (*b*) subjective (where one sincerely, but wrongly, believes that deference is an appropriate sign of respect in a particular relationship, failure to defer would be inconsistent with one's own values).[171]

The reasons one has for deferring to law are therefore twofold in character. First, there are instrumental reasons to obey. Deference to even mistaken legal norms may show respect for the values of law in a way that strengthens political bonds. Failure to defer, we can assume, may lead to disappointment or may undermine the relationship between subject and state. These reasons, however, are subject to two independently sufficient conditions under which they fail. They only hold for one who prefers a cooperative to a competitive society,[172] and an agent's reasons run out where violation does not jeopardize the cooperative arrangement. The second, and deeper, kind of reasons for deference, are intrinsic reasons. These derive either from the agent's own values or from the respect due to oneself or others based on these values. Self-respect mandates deference where not to defer would create inconsistency between one's actions and one's admitted norms, and there is a duty to respect others and the value of the relationship such respect acknowledges. 'The primary value that underlies the theory is respect for persons'[173] as this is instantiated in showing deference to others, in assigning weight to their normative judgments even against one's own judgment of the correct action to take.

Soper's argument therefore proceeds:

- One must acknowledge the necessity of an enterprise requiring that designated authorities impose norms in good faith on the community at large;
- The enterprise that leads to the creation and enforcement of norms (the state) is a valuable one;

[169] ibid. 19. [170] ibid. 24. [171] ibid. 26.

[172] 161: 'a subject who chooses the competitive relationship over the more fraternal cooperative arrangement will not have instrumental reasons to defer'.

[173] ibid. 181.

- There are good reasons for the state to expect voluntary compliance with its norms;
- Self-respect (consistency) or respect for others (deference) will always provide intrinsic reasons to defer to law; therefore
- There is a prima-facie obligation to obey the law.

In order to evaluate Soper's theory I will address three issues. First, is deference a desirable attitude to hold generally, and specifically towards law. Secondly, is Soper's duty of deference universal and, finally, what are the implications of consistency on Soper's account and the account of respect offered in this chapter?

DEFORMATIONS OF DEFERENCE

Consider again, in abbreviated form, Soper's example of deference: 'Persons in a close relationship may sometimes conclude that one ought to defer to the opinion of one's partner even though one's partner's opinion is *morally wrong*. Such examples seem acceptable illustrations of the possibility that moral truth may sometimes *require action in accordance with the (erroneous) moral views* of another...'[174]

This scenario unfolds as follows: *X* defers to *Y*, though *X* believes that *Y*'s opinion is morally wrong, in order to preserve the value of their relationship. This logic is much closer to that of (tolerance) respect than that of estimation respect. The distortion of my account of respect is the paradigm of Soper's. However, deference actually goes beyond the logic of tolerance. Deference does not merely *tolerate* perceived moral wrongs, it *participates* in them. It combines moral opprobrium of a certain view (*Y*'s opinion is 'morally wrong') with joint practical commitment to action upon that view (deference 'requires action in accordance with the (erroneous) moral views of another'). Deference may not seem quite so strange were it to require action upon a slightly misguided opinion (you go with your partner to see a film you know will be awful but which she is keen to see) or a willingness to suspend theoretical disagreement on moral matters (you know that your slightly right-wing friend will not be brought round by already rehearsed arguments on a certain topic, so in the middle of a lovely dinner party, you let the matter go).

On Soper's account, deference is a virtue of relationships, either between oneself and others or a community, or to oneself, in the relationship between one's admitted norms and actions. And yet deference seems a strange ideal. Consider this point in the context of an Aristotelian conception of friendship. In his discussion of the different kinds of friendship (friendships of utility or advantage; perfect friendships 'of people who are good and alike in virtue', and friendships of pleasure), Aristotle notes:

[174] *Deference* 19 (emphasis added).

Perfect friendship is the friendship of men who are good, and alike in virtue; for these wish well alike to each other qua good, and they are good in themselves. Now those who wish well to their friends for their sake are most truly friends . . . therefore their friendship lasts as long as they are good—and goodness is an enduring thing[175] . . . This being so, equals must effect the required equality on a basis of equality in love and in all other respects, while unequals must render what is in proportion to their superiority or inferiority.[176]

In Soper's example, *X* defers to, and acts upon, *Y*'s opinion, which he believes to be morally wrong. He does this through fear of the consequences of any other action for their friendship. In doing so, he undermines both the equality and the goodness of their relationship. By acceding to *Y*'s wishes in this manner, he defers to *Y* while also condescending to him.[177] His beliefs place him in a position of superiority to *Y* which his actions betray. Moreover, he participates in a course of action he considers immoral. In doing so, he diminishes the friendship itself. A good friend counsels his friend towards moral action and does not acquiesce for fear of damage to the relationship. This consequentialist concern is itself troubling. A relationship fragile enough to require acquiescence in immoral opinions may be worth sacrificing to the disputed moral principle. Now, imagine that you are *Y*, and that after the event, *X* tells you that he was happy enough to go along, but that he thought your opinions were morally wrong. Would you be grateful, disappointed, or slightly insulted? Would you wish that *X* had discussed the merits of the point with you, stood upon his principle, and let you act alone? More concerning still, would you wonder that *X* might some day expect similar deference from you?

Deference to law seems similarly unappealing, and for reasons ultimately to do with respect. Even where law purports to act in good faith, and to provide reasons it believes to be justified, issued from procedures that are described as fair, subjects must appraise law to see whether it meets these 'hopes'.[178]

THE UNIVERSALITY OF DEFERENCE

Soper suggests (what I deny) that there is a universal duty to obey the law: 'One will always have at least an intrinsic reason to defer to the state's normative judgments. Instrumental reasons for deference . . . will reach only so far leading to the conclusion that in many cases no such reasons exist'.[179] Intrinsic reasons,

[175] *Nicomachean Ethics* VIII. 3. 1156ᵃ27–1156ᵇ17. See also Cooper 'Aristotle on Friendship'.

[176] ibid. VIII. 13. (1162ᵃ29).

[177] Soper at one point (25) discusses a 'tough-minded sergeant' who 'might believe that friendships are desirable, but they are best understood as requiring one not to defer to super-sensitive friends'. Such a person might, he implies, consider his position 'weakness or . . . toadying or condescension' (26). I suspect it could, on different occasions, be all three. In any circumstance where it combined an attitude of opprobrium with practical commitment to action on that opprobrious principle, I suspect it would be at best misguided.

[178] *Deference* 87.

[179] ibid. 167.

recall, are of two kinds: objective (where deference serves as a sign of respect for a relationship that is in fact valuable) and subjective (where one sincerely, but wrongly, believes that deference is an appropriate sign of respect in a particular relationship, failure to defer would be inconsistent with one's own values). Moreover, reasons for deference arise within relationships. We should, therefore, mark one limit of the duty of deference. In its objective version, it applies only to those who consider themselves in a relationship akin to civic friendship; to self-conscious members of a community governed by law. It does not, ostensibly, apply to the outsider. To this, Soper might reply that the conditions upon intrinsic reasons are doubly objective: they apply not only to relationships with others; but to relationships that are *in fact valuable*. A relationship of civic friendship, it might be argued, simply is valuable. It simply is a human good to identify with a community. Therefore, the outsider remains subject to objective intrinsic reasons. However, while it might always be preferable that one enjoy a sense of belonging, this may not be consistent with self-respect. A black man in the *ante-bellum* US South would have done himself much damage by identifying with his wider community. An outsider to a community might preserve his self-esteem and contribute to change within the community by remaining alienated. Therefore, the theory of respect outlined in this chapter, by explicitly addressing the outsider, reaches deeper than Soper's in the intrinsic/deontological reasons for action it provides.

What of subjective intrinsic reasons? Their nature immediately invokes questions concerning the status of consistency as an independently valuable moral principle. Consider again a black man in the *ante-bellum* South. He believes his relationship with his masters is valuable (they look after him well enough; he is not whipped as are many of his friends) and that deference is not only an appropriate, but a mandatory and conventional, sign of respect in this relationship. These facts may provide subjective reasons for action; but they are bad reasons that snuff out the final flicker of his self-respect. He does not have a universal moral duty to defer to his masters' commands. Ultimately he has a moral duty to rebel. As with deference in close personal relationships, subjective intrinsic reasons seem a shallow ideal. We must first ascertain the appropriateness of deference before consistency to it exercises any moral appeal.

Soper concedes the short span of instrumental reasons to defer. He suggests, as I have done, that (being consequentialist) these reasons are empirically fragile: 'not every act of disobedience will jeopardize the cooperative arrangement'.[180] He considers that they are also endangered by a failure to commit: 'a subject who chooses the competitive relationship over the more fraternal cooperative arrangement will not have instrumental reasons to defer'.[181] However, this is a limitation that my theory does not permit. We will come, in discussion of theories of fair play in Chapter 5, to arguments demarcating the circumstances in which it is morally mandatory, morally permissible, or morally forbidden to

[180] ibid. 161. [181] ibid.

cooperate with others. An independent issue arises as to the circumstances in which it is morally forbidden to interfere with or damage the activities of a morally permissible cooperative group of which one is not a member. Many breaches of the law are of this kind—they do not evidence abstention from cooperation, they damage an existing cooperative venture centrally linked to persons' ability to realize their capacity. Irrespective of whether or not the outsider of my account independently values the state system, where the conditions on the theory of respect for law are satisfied, his duty of respect for persons entails a duty of respect for law which provides instrumental reasons for obedience.

THE IMPLICATIONS OF CONSISTENCY

These conclusions yield a paradox. I have suggested that there is no universal duty to obey, but also that the reasons for action provided by my account extend beyond those provided by Soper's account. One way in which to understand differences between the two accounts, that also partially explains away this paradox, is to attend to the implications of consistency within each. For Soper, the intrinsic reasons flowing from respect include that one must avoid inconsistency between one's actions and one's own admitted norms. Within my account, consistency leads back to the foundation of the duty of respect. Respect for persons is primary. As I noted above, respect for persons sketches a circumference around the conscientious citizen's proper attitude towards law. It requires respect for law where law merits (estimation) respect and proves itself instrumentally vital in protecting and promoting human capacity. But it does not require that all individuals, in identical manner, are subject to an obligation to obey all laws. Respect does not defer; it demurs. However, that respect cannot ground an obligation to obey does not preclude alternative solutions to the problem of conscientious obedience. Historically, the paradigmatic ground for the obligation to obey, and political obligation generally, has been believed to be consent; to which we now turn.

3

Consent, Residence, and the Democratic Voice

> Without a history of choice no dwelling can be a home.
>
> (Berger)[1]

Consent is a peculiarly liberal motif. Axiomatic to the classical liberal tradition is the idea that the individual is free and equal *qua* human being. This leads to respect for the agency of individuals and their capacity to be architects of their own identity. Each is equal and morally significant. As a consequence of this, there is 'nothing more evident, than that Creatures of the same species and rank... born to all the same advantages of Nature, and the use of the same faculties, should also be equal one amongst another without Subordination or Subjection'.[2] This natural condition of freedom and equality requires that no one is obligated to another save where she wills it, and liberalism is, as Waldron notes, insistent in its 'demand for a justification of the social world'.[3] It requires that government be limited, that constitutional safeguards exist, and that individual rights be protected. Consent becomes the means by which authority answers to the individual, and legitimate political authority requires voluntary submission by citizens. The need for consent to authority derives from the natural condition of freedom. Only those restrictions on individual freedom that are voluntarily assumed can be justified. Voluntary consent gives moral significance to obedience; justifying it by reasons relevant to the individual and not to the state. A strong liberal legitimacy thesis therefore claims that the polity is not legitimate unless founded on the consent of the citizenry. This alone makes it morally permissible for government to enforce political power against persons.

This reliance on voluntarily assumed obligations leads to an ideal conception of the polity as a voluntary association. This is a critical evaluative standard for a legitimate state as opposed to a descriptive thesis about the actual functioning of states. The voluntary association model connotes an order to which the individual willingly commits herself, even though this necessarily involves constraints, rules, and structures that limit what she can legitimately will (restrictions on freedom justified by her rational self-interest). Society is manifestly not akin to a voluntary association. Belonging is independent of individual assent to society's

[1] Berger *And Our Faces, My Heart, Brief as Photos* 64.

[2] Locke *Second Treatise* in *Two Treatises on Government* ch. II, sect. 4.

[3] Waldron 'Theoretical Foundations of Liberalism' 135.

basic principles and procedures; 'legitimate' coercion is distinctive of the state's functioning; its claims to authority are comprehensive and its ends more diffuse than the typically determinate ends of such associations.[4] But this does not dull the critical edge of the theory. The state is legitimate in proportion to its approximation to the ideal.

People are social beings. We cannot ask *whether* to be related to other individuals, but consent is fundamental to the *ways* in which we are. By consent we locate ourselves somewhere between the mess of anarchy and the mesh of authority.

Jonathan Wolff has isolated four features of consent theory that make it uniquely suited to liberal accounts.[5] First, 'it is *foundational*'; providing a justification of the state that does not presuppose its existence. Secondly, it is non-consequentialist. The consent of the governed, and not functions or consequences of the state, justifies authority (though these factors may explain *why* people consent). Thirdly, it is an individualistic account, taking as its point of departure individual persons. Finally, it is liberal. It addresses itself to the individual's consent, and not, for example, to optimific happiness.

The classical liberal thinkers, therefore, typically deployed the tools of consent theory. For Locke, morally legitimate state authority is conditional on the free consent of citizens to the exercise of political power in accordance with this consent.[6] The government's legitimacy is then its moral right to impose binding obligations, enforceable by coercion, upon its citizens. Actual personal consent yields legitimacy. Consequently, legitimacy, like authority, is a relational property of states. Legitimacy is grounded in morally significant choices within the interaction between persons and the polity.[7]

It is to these actual personal interactions that this chapter will look for the possibility of obligation.[8] I will not endeavour to characterize (or more likely caricature) the essence of liberal theorizing. Common sentiments more than shared premises unite liberal thinking, and liberal theories are more members of a parish than a family. None the less, I suspect it is uncontroversial to observe that consent is a characteristically liberal motif. Communitarian, consequentialist, and feminist thinkers[9] will not genuflect to consent in the same manner. Such

[4] See also Horton *Political Obligation* 74 and Johnson 'Political Obligation and the Voluntary Association Model of the State'.

[5] Wolff 'What is the Problem of Political Obligation?' 153–4.

[6] Locke *Second Treatise* in *Two Treatises on Government* ch. VIII, sect. 95 and ch. VIII, sect. 99.

[7] See generally, Simmons *Moral Principles* 57–74 and *On the Edge of Anarchy* 59–79 (hereafter, Simmons *Anarchy*).

[8] I will not therefore be looking to hypothetical contract accounts. The enquiry examines the *actual* obligations of *actual* citizens, and, as Dworkin notes in 'The Original Position' 18 'a hypothetical contract is not simply a pale form of an actual contract; it is no contract at all'. On hypothetical contract accounts, see Harris 'From Social Contract to Hypothetical Agreement: Consent and the Obligation to Obey the Law' 679–83; Brudney 'Hypothetical Consent and Moral Force'; Keyt 'The Social Contract as an Analytic, Justificatory, and Polemic Device'; Johnson 'Actual—v. (Rawlsian) Hypothetical Consent'; Wolff 'Anarchism and Skepticism'.

[9] e.g. Hirschmann *Rethinking Obligation: A Feminist Method for Political Theory.*

theories may afford less priority to autonomy, may value community and the common good above atomistic acts of consent, or believe consent chimerical in the context of the state. The *need* for consent flows from the importance of the individual in liberal thinking. Nothing more is claimed. The enquiry here merely concerns whether and how consent is one possible answer to this search for legitimacy—how the liberal consent theorist answers Hume's challenge: 'Where is the mutual agreement or voluntary association so much talked of?'[10]

Consent theory addresses not the justification of government's power and dominion, but its claims to legitimate authority over its citizens. It tries to explain why a state is legitimate—why only a certain body has a right to command other individuals—to show relational state authority over citizens grounded in the citizens' actual consent. I will adopt the traditional analysis of what this consent establishes. If *X* consents to the authority of government, by his undertaking he renders government authority legitimate and promises to obey it. Both government's legitimacy and a citizen's obligation to obey are constituted by consent.

A version of consent theory can make a number of different claims. It can claim that consent is a sufficient condition or ground of legitimate authority, or that consent is a necessary condition of government authority and thus a constraint on legitimacy. It could claim that a legitimate government is one to which one ought to consent, or as Raz suggests, that 'though not a condition of legitimacy itself, those conditions may be such that only a government based on the consent of the governed meets them'.[11] The theory may have different aspirations. A status quo account addresses two questions, the empirical enquiry into whether act-types constituting consent are widely performed by citizens and the normative question as to whether, if they are, they carry the normative significance consent theory claims for them. A reformist or critical account concedes the failure of consent theory as a descriptive thesis of actual states, but argues for the necessity of consent as a condition of legitimacy, while detailing the social reforms necessary to render this critical evaluative standard a reality.[12]

Consent theory must also provide a justification for the binding force of consent and articulate the conditions necessary for a valid consent. Justification is more primitive than validity. A justification must advance reasons relating to the value and rationality of consent-imposed obligations. Instrumental justifications understand consent as a means to achieving beneficial consequences. Non-instrumental justifications feature consent as constitutive of some valuable relationship or project. Secondary justifications might also be advanced in terms of economy of effort and efficiency.[13] Secondary justifications should, however, be marginal in matters as significant as consent to political authority.

[10] Hume 'Of the Original Contract' in *Political Writings* 169.

[11] Raz 'Government by Consent' in *Ethics* 356.

[12] See generally Beran *The Consent Theory of Political Obligation* (hereafter, Beran *Consent Theory*).

[13] Raz *Freedom* 84–8.

The procedural conditions on a valid consent concern status, capacity, voluntariness, and knowledge.[14] Status concerns an agent's normative powers. *X* can only consent to that to which her normative status empowers her. This is a dual demand on qualification. *X* must have a right, as she can only surrender or transfer a right she actually possesses. *X* must also be entitled to waive or transfer the right. Holding a right does not necessarily entail this entitlement. These parameters preserve the condition of freedom, as reflected in Locke's thesis that one cannot consent to enslavement. They also reflect the imperative of justice that one cannot create just any right *de novo*. The will is not infinitely creative. We cannot create or transfer a right to commit injustice since we cannot have such a right; just as we cannot waive our obligation to interfere in the commission of injustices where we have a reasonable opportunity to do so.

Capacity has both internal and external dimensions. Internally, the agent must be mentally *capax* and competent. Insanity, dementia, temporary or permanent mental disability, immaturity, or total intoxication, will, conceptually, prevent an agent from consenting. Neither cognitive nor volitional conditions are satisfied. Externally, consent may be normatively invalidated by the presence of duress, coercion, undue influence, or unconscionability. Voluntarism is here undermined.

Knowledge concerns epistemic conditions on consent. The agent must not be subject to deception, fraud, innocent misrepresentation, or mistake. She must be aware of her actions, of their conventional significance, and others' observation and interpretation of these.

Consent is, broadly, a means by which an individual reorders her normative context, with unilateral, bilateral, or multilateral implications. She may waive or derogate from her rights, creating rights or permissions for another; transfer a right; place a positive obligation upon herself; or create, as the occupant of some role or position, a right or obligation for others not adversely affecting her own situation.[15] Consent may also create rights for the consentor, as in marriage or a contract of employment. Generally, *X* might consent to the imposition or creation of rights and duties, acts done to her, acts done in her name, and as the occupant of a role entailing normative powers. The normative sense of consent is performative. The cognitive, non-normative sense of consent is a psychological sense conveying attitudinal agreement.[16]

CONSENT, INTENTIONS, AND BELIEFS

Before proceeding to the substantive discussion, I will explicate the understanding of 'consent' that will be preferred here. In doing so I will elaborate the accounts advanced by A. John Simmons and Joseph Raz, adopting the latter.

[14] See the related discussions in Bayles 'The Capacity and Power to Consent' 160; Pincoffs 'On Consenting' 108–11, and Raz *Freedom* 83.

[15] For example, the Queen giving royal assent to an Act of Parliament concerning treason.

[16] On 'attitudinal' senses of consent more generally, see Simmons *Moral Principles* 93 and 97.

In *Moral Principles and Political Obligations*, Simmons imposes three procedural constraints on a valid consent. Consent must be given intentionally, knowingly, and voluntarily. This makes it possible for one to consent insincerely but not unintentionally.[17] Simmons distinguishes 'signs of consent' from 'acts implying consent'. A sign of consent is an act that, because of the context in which it is performed (including any appropriate conventions), constitutes an expression of the actor's intention to consent. But acts implying consent entail neither that the actor intended to consent nor that the act would typically be taken as an attempt to do so.[18] Acts implying consent are 'closely related to genuine consent in some way without in fact being consent', ultimately reliant on ideas such as fair play and gratitude.[19] Simmons observes:

> We can describe as acts of consent any acts that deliberately and suitably communicate to others the agent's intention to undertake obligations toward and/or convey rights (or permissions) to others. One can, on this account, consent insincerely (by deliberately communicating to others an intention one in fact lacks)... consent can be defined in terms of the agent's deliberate and effective communication of an intention to bring about this kind of change.[20]

At least two questions can be asked of any act of consent. First, whether it is *factually* an act of consent. Secondly, whether it is a *normatively binding* act of consent. The class of normatively binding acts of consent will be a subset of the class of factual acts of consent. A theory of consent must therefore stipulate what kind of intention, belief, and so on, is necessary for consent to be (prima-facie) normatively binding. This makes it important to understand the sense of intention used in Simmons's account. Consider a simple case. X deliberately conveys, to Y, his intention to undertake to do ϕ. Normative consent may, conceivably, require three alternative types of intention. First, it might involve X's intention to do ϕ (practical intention). Secondly, it may involve X's intention to undertake an obligation to do ϕ (first-order normative intention). Finally, consent need involve only an intention to communicate an intention to undertake to do ϕ (second-order normative intention). Simmons defines consent in terms of the agent's *deliberate* and effective communication of an intention to bring about this kind of change. He also considers that 'an individual cannot become obligated unless he intentionally performs an obligation-generating act with a clear understanding of its significance'.[21] He relies upon a second-order normative intention. Hence consent can be insincere. X may intend to communicate to Y that he intends to undertake an obligation to do ϕ, where he in fact has no intention of doing ϕ. He is bound despite his insincerity. Deliberately communicating an insincere intention will incur obligations. In this regard Simmons's account is

[17] ibid. 77. [18] ibid. 88. [19] ibid. 89.

[20] Simmons *Anarchy* 69–70. This definition arises in an exegetical analysis of Locke, but Simmons also endorses it as a 'quite plausible account in its own right' (69). For a related critique of Simmons, see Boxill 'On Some Criticisms of Consent Theory'.

[21] Simmons *Moral Principles* 64.

objective and not subjective. Insincerity does not rob consent of its voluntariness or normativity.

Consent runs out for Simmons where *X* does an act we might be tempted to call 'consent', but where he does not intend to bind himself. In such a case, the principle under which Simmons argues for holding a person liable is a principle of estoppel, which protects the interests of those who relied on the 'consent'.[22]

In *The Morality of Freedom*, Raz offers a treatment of consent, focusing on an agent's beliefs instead of her intentions. He conceives of consent as an act or omission undertaken by an agent subject to the belief that:

1. it will change another's normative situation;
2. it will do so because undertaken in this belief; and
3. observers will understand it to be of this character.[23]

And so acts of consent are:

> acts believed to change the normative situation because they are performed with that belief. They are performed by people who have certain beliefs about the normative consequences of their acts. In particular they believe that their beliefs make a difference to the consequences of their acts, that their acts impose duties, confer rights, grant permissions, and so on, in part because they believe that their acts do so.[24]

Promise and consent are distinct. Promises are made only by acts whose purpose is to undertake obligations and confer rights. However, acts undertaken in the belief that they will change the normative situation, which have this result because undertaken with this belief, can constitute consent even if undertaken for another purpose.[25]

The most significant distinction between these two accounts lies in the following feature. On Simmons's account, normative consent requires the intention to communicate the intention to undertake an obligation. On Raz's account, consent requires intention, but only the intention to do some act that one believes will incur normative consequences. To speak here of intentionally performing an act detaches intention from intentional communication of obligations. Thus, *X* may intentionally enter a park, without intending to bind himself to anything in particular, and yet consent to the obligations that are entailed by walking in the park, *if* he believes that his act of entering the park has this normative consequence. Simmons too understands this situation as generating obligations. But these are obligations grounded in estoppel and not in consent.

This distinction becomes clearer in *On the Edge of Anarchy*, where Simmons observes that: 'Where intention is absent, we appeal rather to a principle of "estoppel" (to protect the interests of those who relied on the "consent")'.[26] This alludes to Leslie Green's discussion of Simmons's and Raz's respective positions on consent. Green observes that, for Raz, Simmons's reliance on intention excludes cases where intent is absent and having an obligation is consistent

[22] Simmons *Anarchy* 70 n. 31. [23] Raz *Freedom* 81. [24] ibid. 84.
[25] ibid. 83. [26] Simmons *Anarchy* 70 n. 31.

with intending to escape it. He gives two examples of cases we might classify as consent. First, where *X* sits down in a restaurant and orders a meal, he thereby consents to paying the price on the menu, irrespective of any promise to this effect or any intention to leave without paying. Secondly, where *Y* boards a plane, he thereby consents to a security search. 'The structure of these examples is as follows: I freely perform an action, knowing that it is understood to entail some duty, and I am therefore bound by that duty.'[27] However, Green suggests, these are not cases of consent. They are instead cases of estoppel, 'justified as a means of protecting the interests of the parties who might be harmed if the agent later rejected the duty on the ground that he had no intention to assume it'.[28]

However, it seems that just this reliance on intention requires us to consider estoppel obligations, whereas beliefs can mediate the interstices between intention and insincerity. Consider the first example. *X* goes into a restaurant for a purpose other than to consent (to eat a meal) and has no intention of paying. But if he believes, given his understanding of social conventions, that his actions confer rights and impose obligations, there is nothing awkward and there is much common sense in saying that he knowingly (if tacitly) consents to pay.

The second example illustrates this point more clearly. *Y* boards a plane but tries to avoid security checks. But, conventionally, to board is to consent to security checks. Now, will it be possible here to show the reliance or detriment that are constituent elements of estoppel? It may be argued that there is a standing *potential* detriment in allowing passengers to board a plane absent security checks and that each passenger relies upon every other to submit to these checks (and on the airline to enforce them). However, *Y* may be a law-abiding, entirely pacifistic, but severely misanthropic airline passenger. He may pose no actual risk to his fellow passengers. Moreover, at the point of being checked he is not estopped from resiling; he can do so if he wishes. He is simply unable simultaneously to resile *and* board the plane. Ultimately, if *Y* refuses not to board while also refusing to submit to security searches, he must realize (short of irrationality) that while his primary purpose in proceeding through customs is to board the plane, he has intentionally entered a high security area, which he understands entails certain normative consequences. Therefore, though he lacks any explicit intention to submit to checks, if he continues, he has tacitly consented none the less.

Raz's model of consent provides a clearer and more complete ground of obligation, with a more exhaustive explanatory power, not contingent on actual reliance or detriment to be binding. Nor does this model of consent eliminate or unduly limit the scope of estoppel obligations. I have so far discussed only knowing and fraudulent action. But estoppel will cover cases where *X*, by negligent or culpably ignorant conduct, failing the cognitive conditions above, creates a situation where *Y* is entitled to rely on her representations. Nor does this account unduly limit the principle of fair play. Two clear cases remain. First, *X* does ϕ where he is ignorant that (or uncertain whether) it entails π (or β).

[27] Green *Authority* 163–4. [28] ibid. 164.

Here, fairness resolves issues unsettled by convention or in the agent's knowledge.[29] Secondly, there is the case where X knows of the existence of a scheme to which all others in a group contribute. It is of great importance to all, including X. X is asked to contribute, since she voluntarily and happily enjoys the benefits of the scheme, but explicitly declines. She thinks it permissible both to enjoy the benefits, and not to contribute, since her contribution is superfluous to the production of the benefits. Equally, having explicitly declined, she genuinely does not believe that she has undertaken an obligation or generated rights by her actions. This is not an obligation of consent. Considerations of fairness ground any obligations here.

If our concern is to protect an agent from being encumbered by unwitting obligations, we must focus not on intention but knowledge. Neither the innocent nor the insincere consentor has any intention of being bound, but the latter has full knowledge of the significance of her actions. And where X does not want to be bound and is fully aware of social conventions, she knows what she has to do to avoid obligation. In the following therefore, I will treat the clear case of consent as a voluntary, knowing act, performed in the belief that it will in some way alter the normative context.

TACIT CONSENT AND RESIDENCE

> I say, that every Man, that hath any Possession, or Enjoyment, of any part of the Dominions of any Government, doth thereby give his *tacit Consent*, and is as far forth obliged to Obedience to the Laws of that Government, during such Enjoyment, as anyone under it.
>
> (Locke)[30]

> This should always be understood to refer only to free states, for elsewhere family, property, lack of asylum, necessity or violence may keep an inhabitant in the country unwillingly, and then his mere residence no longer implies consent either to the contract or to the violation of the contract.
>
> (Rousseau)[31]

Since Locke,[32] tacit consent has been both the refuge and ridicule of status quo consent theories that seek to insist both that consent is a necessary condition of legitimate government authority and that at least some existing states are legitimate. The tension between the descriptive claim (and its required generality),

[29] See also Brudney 'Hypothetical Consent and Moral Force' 264–70.

[30] Locke *Second Treatise* in *Two Treatises of Government* ch. VIII, sect. 119; emphasis in original.

[31] Rousseau *The Social Contract* book IV, ch. 2 (n. 1).

[32] For discussion of ambiguities in Locke, see: Franklin 'Allegiance and Jurisdiction in Locke's Doctrine of Tacit Consent'; Russell 'Locke on Express and Tacit Consent: Misinterpretations and Inconsistencies'; Farrell 'Coercion, Consent, and the Justification of Political Power: A New Look at Locke's Consent Claim'; MacCormick 'Law, Obligation and Consent: Reflections on Stair and Locke'. Simmons provides a comprehensive and precise discussion in *Anarchy* at 59–79.

and the normative claim, places great strain on the theorist. A dearth of conspicuous performative consensual acts in the personal histories of citizens leads her to look for actions from which consent might be inferred.

Consent takes several forms. Express consent is a written or verbal communication of consent. Explicit consent is expressed tacitly but deliberately. Tacit consent involves conventional acts performed in circumstances that invest the acts with the significance of an expression of consent. Explicit tacit consent is logically equivalent to express consent but lacks written or oral form. It is signified by conventionally understood actions or silence, a raised hand, a nod, or silence where dissent is invited. As Simmons notes, it is given 'by other behaviour that constitutes the making of a morally significant choice in a clear, noncoercive choice situation'.[33] One notable difference is that, while express consent may be a primary act, with creative and expressive potential (where I initiate the consent; for example, by letting my friend know that while I am on holiday she may have access to my library), tacit consent is necessarily a secondary act in response to another's proposal or suggestion (my friend must first ask to have access to my library while I am away).[34]

Implied consent occurs where *X* consents to ϕ and ϕ is conventionally recognized as implying consent to π. An original act of explicit consent entails obligations beyond those explicitly undertaken, but which are reasonably implied by the act. Tacit consent may be implied, where silence constitutes consent to some ϕ conventionally recognized as implying consent to some π.[35] Implied tacit consent occurs, for example, where *X* furnishes *Y* with some unsolicited, perishable goods, in circumstances that make it manifest that this is not a gift. *Y* is delighted and consumes the goods. *Y* now potentially has moral and legal obligations to *X*.[36] This conclusion does not seem to involve improper burdens. *Y* does (or should) understand that her actions create reciprocal obligations towards *X*. Conditions of knowledge, voluntariness, and willingness are satisfied. Moreover, the background circumstances make clear to *Y what* she is undertaking an obligation to do. She must pay for these goods. She is not committed to further receipt of goods, or to discretionary acts of reciprocal goodwill. The context and consequences of obligation are clear.

[33] Simmons *Anarchy* 83.

[34] Contrast this with Pincoffs's 'On Consenting' at 108 who conceives of all consent as necessarily secondary, with the party who enjoys the rights conferred by consent being the primary party. The understanding of primary and secondary status in the text relies on the idea that the party who initiates the relevant relationship invests her acts with creative potential.

[35] This possibility follows from the sense of consent adopted here. Implied consent creates the possibility that *X* is bound by consent though lacking the intention to be bound. Given Simmons's intentionality condition, he must reject that this qualifies as consent. For him, acts implying consent collapse into considerations of fair play: Simmons *Anarchy* 89. Given the sense of consent here, where all epistemic conditions are satisfied, many such acts will be genuine acts of consent. For Simmons's examples of acts implying consent see Simmons *Moral Principles* 88–9.

[36] Harris 'From Social Contract to Hypothetical Agreement: Consent And The Obligation To Obey The Law' 667.

The most discussed recent critique of Locke and the idea of tacit consent by residence is Simmons's treatment of the topic.[37] Here, I will explicate Simmons's position and evaluate different defences, provided by Bernard Boxill[38] and Harry Beran,[39] that attempt to rehabilitate residence as a means of consenting.

Simmons articulates five procedural conditions necessary for silence to constitute a valid *sign* of consent.[40]

1. It must be clear in the context that consent is appropriate, and individuals must be aware of this;
2. There must be a determinate and reasonable period during which expressions of dissent are invited or appropriate, and the acceptable means of expressing this dissent must be understood by the potential consentor;
3. The point after which expressions of dissent are no longer acceptable must be evident to the potential consentor.

Morally meaningful consent requires the possibility of dissent. It also requires satisfaction of epistemic conditions: I must understand that I am consenting. For Simmons, this understanding in the tacit case allows us to know that if *X* does not dissent, he intends to consent. If *X* understands that silence will be construed as consent if he does not dissent, his silence deliberately communicates an intention to be bound.

For Simmons, political applications of the theory of consent require two further conditions.

4. The means for indicating consent must be reasonable and reasonably easily performed (failure to dissent must not arise from an inability to do so);
5. Dissent cannot have extremely detrimental consequences.

The final condition addresses the circumstances of coercion. An act of coerced consent is construed as no act of consent at all (as opposed to a case of non-binding consent), since consent involves a genuine choice freely made. One's capacity to consent must be intact.

Simmons concludes as follows.[41] For residence to constitute genuine consent, it must be in response to a clearly presented choice situation allowing for consent or dissent. No such formal procedure presently exists. But were one instituted and were suitable alterations in political processes effected, could residence be made a genuine sign of tacit consent? Simmons believes that the existence of a formal choice procedure would seem to satisfy demands that consent be knowingly given and voluntary, but doubts whether such a procedure would satisfy

[37] Simmons *Moral Principles* 75–100.

[38] Boxill 'On Some Criticisms of Consent Theory'.

[39] Beran *Consent Theory*; 'What is the Basis of Political Authority?' and 'In Defense of the Consent Theory of Political Obligation and Authority' (thereafter Beran 'In Defense of Consent Theory'). Simmons discusses Beran critically in 'Consent, Free Choice, and Democratic Government' and in *Anarchy*, especially ch. 8.

[40] Simmons *Moral Principles* 80–3.

[41] ibid. 95–100 and 'Consent, Free Choice, and Democratic Government' 802–18 and *Anarchy* 225–48.

conditions 4 and 5. Emigration is a difficult course that could have awful consequences. Conditions 4 and 5 imply that silence or inaction cannot constitute signs of consent if the means by which dissent can be indicated are unreasonable or difficult to perform, or if dissent entails detrimental consequences. Nor is it clear that mere voluntarism transforms such an act into a sign of consent.

Addition of new provisions to the choice procedure—for example, that the poor and oppressed (who may most want, but be least able, to leave) would be given assistance in leaving—will not cure these defects. For many, emigration may constitute a quietly awful event. Accordingly, it may inevitably fail condition 5. Thus, even were reforms made to our present political processes it is hard to conceive of a formal choice procedure that might legitimately establish continued residence as a sign of consent.

Simmons's point is simple. Residence cannot currently constitute tacit consent since it lacks this conventionally understood significance. Cognitive conditions are not satisfied. Nor could it ever become a reality. Were citizens confronted by a formal choice procedure that made the significance of residence common knowledge, consent within this procedure would be non-binding since coercive.

COERCION, UNCONSCIONABILITY, AND THE POSSIBILITY OF CONSENT

Coercion does not simply concern an overborne will. Psychological pressure created by a wholly circumstantial paucity of options does not constitute coercion. This is simply a hard choice.[42] In extreme cases of such pressure, where a party is rendered mentally incompetent, any agreement may be void *ab initio*, since the agent lacks both cognitive capacity and volition. But while such pressure is psychologically and legally relevant, it is morally inert. Where *Y* is in circumstances of innocent misfortune, which negate meaningful choice, there is only metaphorical coercion. The absence of unfairness imposed by an external agency precludes coercion.

In a case of coercion or duress, *Y* is wrongfully placed, by *X*, in a situation where he is compelled to choose between unfairly delimited alternatives in order to avoid a threatened eventuality. As Raz observes, 'duress is always action designed to exert pressure in order to secure the consent'.[43] *Y* must either comply with the demands or pay a deliberately too-high price for defiance. The conditions on cognitive capacity are intact. *Y* rationally maximizes his options. But voluntarism is violated. There is agreement but it is non-binding.[44] Locke aptly asks: 'Should a Robber break into my House and, with a Dagger at my Throat, make me seal Deeds to convey my Estate to him, would this give him any Title?

[42] Murphy 'Consent, Coercion, and Hard Choices'; Becker 'Hard Choices Are Enough'.

[43] Raz *Freedom* 88.

[44] In law, a contract formed under duress is voidable and not void *ab initio*: *Pao On v Lau Yin Long* [1980] AC 614.

Just such a Title by his Sword, has an *unjust Conqueror*, who forces me into Submission.'[45]

For the purposes of the following discussion I will treat coercion as adumbrated by the following. *X* coerces *Y* where:

1. *X* wrongfully applies pressure upon, or threatens *Y* with some wrongful prospect;
2. which is intended to force *Y* or one associated with *Y*, to do something beneficial to *X* or one associated with *X*; and
3. which *Y* does solely or primarily to avoid realization of the threat.

In relation to the first condition, *X* may threaten or apply pressure without justification or which violates *Y*'s rights; may threaten to do a legal wrong or some morally illegitimate action which other reasonable persons in a like situation would find equally compelling. This could be harm to persons, projects, or property valuable to *Y*. Alternatively, *X* may actually do certain damage and promise to repair to the original state of affairs should *Y* agree to terms (for example, kidnapping and hostage situations).[46] As regards the third condition, it is conceivable that *Y* does or could have other reasons for doing the act his coercer requires. However, for coercion to operate, the pressure or threat must at least predominantly motivate the act.

Non-coercive conduct may also be unconscionable. Locke notes such behaviour as one of the circumstances vitiating consent: 'a Man can no more justly make use of another's necessity, to force him to become his Vassal, by withholding that Relief, God requires him to afford to the wants of his Brother, than he that has more strength can seize upon a weaker, master him to his Obedience, and with a Dagger at his Throat offer him Death or Slavery'.[47]

Unconscionability occurs where *X* is in a position to exploit a particular weakness in *Y*. Legally, an unconscionable contract must be both unfair and result from the abuse of power of a stronger party.[48] There is a fine distinction between capitalizing on, and exploiting, another's misfortune. The party who purchases in a quick, cheap sale motivated by the vendor's financial distress does not act wrongfully. One who manufactures or manipulates another's vulnerability wrongfully exploits him.[49]

In brief, coercion is wrongfully to create an unfair situation, while unconscionability is wrongfully to manipulate a weaker party, when in a position of dominance or strength, in each case, to attain a desired end. Having said this, what is the present or prospective status of the idea of tacit consent by continued residence?

Presently, continued residence could only constitute implied tacit consent to political authority since there exists no choice procedure that could set up

[45] Locke *Second Treatise* in *Two Treatises of Government* ch. XVI, sect. 176.

[46] Raz 'Authority and Consent' 126.

[47] Locke *First Treatise* in *Two Treatises of Government* ch. IV, sect. 42.

[48] *Alec Lobb Garages Ltd v Total Oil (GB) Ltd* [1985] 1 WLR 173.

[49] Joel Feinberg understands unconscionability as acts both exploitative and coercive in intent and effect: *Harm to Self* 249–52. Simmons notes that unconscionability is aggravated where contracts concern provision of essential goods: *Anarchy* 238.

explicit tacit consent.[50] However, residence simply lacks this conventional meaning. For tacit consent by residence to become a possibility, it would have to be the case that, in performing certain explicit (though tacit) voluntary actions, each citizen understands that she consents to the state's authority and an obligation to obey its laws. This voluntary action would be continued residence. Residence will serve purposes other than consent. But residence must, among its significations, constitute a silent and consenting response to a choice procedure. Only thus do we avoid fallacious inferences concerning the cognitive conditions on consent. This would be a mandatory choice. But once we introduce a choice procedure, we introduce the possibility of coercion, particularly as regards the necessarily secondary doing of tacit consent. Capacity to consent now seems threatened. Thus we must ask whether government is entitled to create a mandatory choice procedure and whether the terms on which it is offered are fair.

Two alternative types of choice seem possible. First, the binary 'consent or emigrate'. Secondly, a scalar choice among more numerous options, providing mid-states between obligation and exile.

CONSENT OR EMIGRATE

Harry Beran offers a sympathetic rendering of the first alternative:

> In Utopia citizens have the legal right to emigrate and the law requires them to choose, within a specified period of legally coming to age, to accept full adult citizenship or to emigrate ... it is not plausible to claim that citizens of Utopia who continue to live there because of the high cost of emigration are coerced to stay there by their government or anyone else. (Remember, the high cost is loss of homeland, family and friends.) This cost, unlike imprisonment in Dystopia, is neither created by Utopia's government nor removable by it. Nor need it be intended by Utopia's government to contribute towards making people stay rather than leave.[51]

There are two significant features in the example. First, there is a mandatory, binary choice. Secondly, there are the costs entailed by that choice. The government imposes this choice in a context of existing background conditions. It knows the circumstances of most of its citizens and the implications of choice either way for them. It does not, as Beran submits, create the costs of emigration *per se*. These exist independently of the choice and also need not obtain, for example, where X has few emotional ties, little financial stake, or patriotic attachment to his birth nation. But the government does create emigration as a consequence of failure to consent. The government creates emigration *as* a cost

[50] Harry Beran suggests at 'In Defense of Consent Theory' 270 that people do understand that remaining in a state constitutes acceptance of full membership in the state, and that since the state is a rule-governed association analogous to others to which individuals belong, they can, reasonably, grasp the obligations membership entails. Simmons successfully demonstrates the deep errors of this in *Anarchy* 229–32.

[51] Beran 'What is the Basis of Political Authority?' 496.

while not creating the costs *of* emigration. Emigration constitutes a cost only by figuring in a difficult, binary choice. Accordingly, emigration as a cost (as opposed to the costs of emigration) can be removed by government. It is disingenuous to suggest that these costs need not be intended by the government to persuade people to stay. Were government genuinely concerned that the choice rendered citizens psychologically hostage, it would expand the alternatives. By instituting the choice, a government's conduct is at least unconscionable. It capitalizes on its monopoly of power to reduce the choices open to weaker parties and thereby exploits their vulnerability. All of which, of course, is difficult to reconcile with the liberal democratic ideal of the state as the instrument of the people.

Consider an objection to a related point raised by Boxill. He suggests that to think that the high cost of consent, *per se*, could invalidate consent is to suggest that contractarianism is false at its foundations, since inhabitants of the state of nature rationally consent to the institution of a Sovereign precisely because of the detrimental consequences of dissent.[52]

While this is certainly the logic of the state of nature, the analogy is flawed. Consider the nature of the detrimental consequences in each case. In the state of nature, people agree amongst themselves to institute a sovereign. In Hobbes's conception, the Sovereign is not, and cannot be, a party to this contract. The detrimental consequences of dissent are neither created nor exploited by the Sovereign. The people agree independently and are coerced only metaphorically by infelicitous circumstances. Fear of the detrimental consequences of dissent may motivate the consent that founds the commonwealth, but these fears arise from features intrinsic to these circumstances and not by the contrivance of any individual. The circumstances, while compelling, are morally neutral.

This mandatory, binary choice, by contrast, threatens the integrity of citizens' moral and legal right to reside (subject to certain qualifications) in the state of their birth. It threatens to deny them rights of citizenship and civil liberties and also, possibly, certain basic necessities. John Bennett poses an objection.[53] If X designates ϕ a sign of consent, and Y does not want to consent, Y is forced to refrain from doing ϕ. Thus X should have the right to prevent Y from doing ϕ, since this may be the consequence of the choice. Where ϕ signifies residing in one's state of birth, this seems an illegitimate threat.

The oxymoron of a legitimate threat can make sense. Some ostensible threats may be entirely justified. Consider the legal official, tax man, or sheriff officer, who tells X that he must hand over certain monies or he will be fined. This is an authoritative legal command. The sheriff officer has an authority derived from a purportedly legitimate legal system. So the strongest way in which we might dismiss the impression of an unfair choice is to say that the state has a right to put such an option to its citizens.

[52] Boxill 'On Some Criticisms of Consent Theory' 88.

[53] Bennett 'A Note on Locke's Theory of Tacit Consent', cited by Boxill at ibid. 101 n. 15. In some cases, this condition will be too broad, but it seems applicable in the political case.

Some argument of this strength seems necessary to justify such actions. But the state could not possibly argue thus. It is instituting a mandatory choice as a way of eliciting consent from citizens in order to secure legitimate authority correlated to an obligation to obey. If it imposes such a choice it presupposes that it holds rights against citizens, and presupposes its right to issue orders (correlating to an obligation in the citizenry to obey) or at least a moral right to enforce the requirements of justice. The reasoning is circular. The choice presupposes the legitimacy it hopes to establish.

Government might alternatively claim some special justification for having to resort to this course of action. The most obvious candidate would be an instrumental justification claiming that such measures are necessary for social stability.[54] But so egregious a violation of citizens' rights is surely a counter-productive measure. And as Hume asks, in a similar context, 'How chimerical must it be to talk of a choice in such circumstances?'[55]

But Beran has auxiliary conceptual and empirical points. We can only say that a state coerces citizens where the state does want *X* to agree or to leave, it threatens *X* with harm unless she chooses, and *X* agrees to obey the law at least partly because of the sanction for non-agreement. But this will not apply to the majority of citizens in reasonably just and efficient states. Most will be quite happy to consent and obey, in preference to dissenting and leaving, for reasons independent of the choice offered. Consent to the choice need not all (or primarily) flow from the consequences of dissent.[56]

Strictly, if pressure plays no part in *Y*'s consent—even where pressure is present—*Y* is not coerced. None the less, it is still a case of tacit consent given in response to an illegitimately posed choice. There would be a much clearer ground of obligation were *Y* to volunteer an act of unsolicited express consent, or were there to be alternatives to consent. Moreover, the theorist would have to provide a justification for government posing such a choice, and for such tacit consent being binding. As noted above, the obvious candidate is stability. But this seems a dramatic and illiberal overreaction to a need for stability.

The binary choice promises little. We should instead consider briefly a choice involving multiple options.

CONSENT, EMIGRATION, AND RESIDENT DISSIDENTS

For consent to be morally meaningful and for the idea that citizens are obligated by residence to be other than a tautology, there must be the possibility of dissent. For government not to presuppose the legitimacy it tries to secure, options must be provided that do not undermine the unconditional rights of citizens. Government

[54] The circumstances of the choice make it hard to imagine a meaningful non-instrumental justification in terms of a constitutive dimension of some relationship and so on.

[55] Hume 'Of the Original Contract' in *Political Writings* 170.

[56] Beran 'What is the Basis of Political Authority?' 494–6.

is at best free to offer the choice to citizens and thus must provide some acceptable third way for citizens to escape the extremes of obligation and exile.[57] Boxill deploys this strategy. He suggests a weaker condition on tacit consent:

> If my condition is satisfied that a person's sign of consent gives his consent, only if he can freely and easily cancel it with a sign of dissent, anyone can make any state a sign of tacit consent, and there need be no confusion because people in that state will be understood to have consented only if they fail to make a sign of dissent.[58]

Concerns about the ease with which signs of consent are performed, and the costs of dissent, can be mitigated, Boxill suggests, if we stress the importance and nature of available signs of dissent. A person's sign of consent gives his consent only if he can freely and easily cancel it with a sign of dissent. As regards these signs of dissent, it is not necessary that all are easy to perform, or have no detrimental consequences built into them. It is only necessary that some signs of dissent satisfy this condition. We are then free to rebut the presumption that we are consenting. Thus, in a state where tacit consent by residence is possible, many citizens may still withhold their consent to government.

Having established that the options must be wider than mere consent or emigration, we might wonder whether mere silence or inaction will ever be sufficiently clear to signal consent. As options multiply, the citizen may have to indicate exactly what position she prefers, and this may require written or oral express consent. If so, it seems that tacit consent by residence is either practically impossible or very unlikely. To avoid state coercion, we must proliferate options. But once this occurs, express consent will greatly clarify proceedings. We now have not tacit consent by residence but express consent by participation in a formal choice procedure.

The choice could, however, be framed in a manner that leaves a residual role for tacit consent. Continued residence signifies full tacit consent. Emigration signifies complete dissent. Continued residence with performance of a dissenting act signifies qualified dissent. Different dissenting acts corresponding to different qualifications could then be proliferated. Here, simple continued residence without any dissenting acts signifies explicit tacit consent.

The vital enquiry now concerns what rights government could make dependent on consent and how they would structure this. The immediately obvious structure seems to be one of membership packages, corresponding to degrees of agreement.[59] Full consent corresponds to full citizenship rights, qualified consent to a qualified package of burdens and benefits, and dissent to some state-of-nature type existence. What would the content of these latter two packages be? What rights, and beyond rights, what legitimate expectations, could government make contingent on consent? And, would government coercion of those returned to the state of nature by dissent be wrongful?

[57] On exile, dissent, and related topics, see generally Hirschman *Exit, Voice, and Loyalty.*

[58] Boxill 'On Some Criticisms of Consent Theory' 86.

[59] Simmons *Anarchy* 242.

One grave difficulty with the idea of making rights qualified or taking away legitimate expectations following dissent is that many of these rights are no longer strictly the state's to give or to take away. Alongside the already mentioned circularity of the offer, the rights of individuals both as persons and citizens are increasingly creatures of international conventions, European statutes, and transnational organizations, held by individuals as persons and not as citizens. Political evolution has tamed Hobbes's Leviathan.

More fundamentally any choice scenario is undermined by the fact that motivation is opaque. Cowards and saints perform the same acts for different reasons. Government cannot know whether citizens comply with the laws due to moral obligation, fear of sanctions, unreflective habit, or omission. They cannot test the sincerity of consent in ways that avoid deceit. This implies another point. If any number of positive attitudes towards government are sufficient to ensure stability, why would this choice procedure ever be necessary in the first place?

Any choice procedure is likely to achieve too little and request too much. It is disproportionate, counter-productive, and undermines the legitimate expectations and rights of citizens. Democratic theory presumes that government exists to serve the interests of the governed and has no autonomous interests. Even where all cognitive conditions on consent are satisfied, and the possibility of diverse dissents recognizes the importance of capacity, the terms of the justification (instrumental or non-instrumental) for the consent being necessary or binding seem elusive. This kind of solution is also deeply problematic within the liberal theories in which consent is most likely to feature. Given that liberalism favours freedom, not only would this incursion on citizens' liberty require justification (the form of which is not immediately obvious) but any signs of dissent would have to be reasonably easily performed so as not to aggravate the incursion.

Why, finally, would we ever prefer signs of tacit consent to acts of express consent where the latter are at all feasible? It might be argued that tacit consent manifested in conduct over time, though more ambiguous than an act of performative consent, is more sustaining and profound.[60] However, the truth in this observation, where tacit consent is inferred from willing conduct, does not translate into the context of a mandatory choice that purports to yield tacit consent. This context suggests legerdemain as opposed to legitimacy.

[60] Jeremy Waldron's discussion of a Bartolist conception of consent in chapter 3 of *Law and Disagreement* provides one illuminating answer here. The Bartolist argues that an express, performative act of consent at an isolated time may lack the legitimate force of a long and established, tacit pattern of conduct. The only advantage secured by the latter is the linguistic lack of ambiguity in a performative speech act (though we should note that ambiguity may arise within the normative enquiry). For an argument regarding the priority of a silent, attitudinal consent ('a state of acceptance') see Murphy 'Surrender of Judgment and the Consent Theory of Political Authority' and 'Natural Law, Consent and Political Obligation'.

VOTING IN DEMOCRATIC ELECTIONS

> The object is not to have one's way as much as it is to have a way that is one's own.[61]

Democracy is a form of rule in which community members participate equally in the making of decisions relevant to all. Representative democracy is characterized by regularly held elections with (almost) universal suffrage. The moral equality of individuals is thereby preserved. Liberal representative democracy is predicated on collective decision-making which recognizes this equality and respects individual rights; particularly those civil liberties basic to the election process itself (the right to vote; freedom of speech; freedom of association and organization, and so on). Elections aggregate citizens' preferences, translating these through the selection of representatives, accountable to the electorate, who hold office for a defined term, determine national policy, and achieve approval or disapprobation on this basis.

Voting has, historically, assumed an additional ideological significance in liberal political theory, as a possible means by which citizens consent to an obligation to obey government. Three features of such voting make it peculiarly eligible for the consent theorist. Voting, it is claimed, is conceptually linked to consent. Peter Singer suggests that:

> [I]t must be reasonable to assume consent on the part of a person who votes without in any way indicating that his vote is not to be taken as an indication of consent. This must be reasonable, not because people who vote as a matter of fact usually do consent, but because there is a conceptual connection between voting and consenting. What would be the sense of having a vote if no one ever accepted the result of the vote?[62]

Given the additional facts that voting is also the most common and conspicuous political act amongst often otherwise apathetic citizens and that most Western liberal democracies have laws protecting universal suffrage, this argument promises a very broad basis for political obligation. Moreover, it has taken several forms, the first arguing that voting either currently is, or prospectively could be, consent to political authority;[63] the second, that abstention can constitute indirect consent,[64] and the third, that quasi-consensual obligations of estoppel arise from participation within democratic elections and institutions.[65]

These debates have grown tired through repeated treatment.[66] In summary, we can note the following. In evaluating whether there is a conceptual link between

[61] Port Huron Statement by the Students for a Democratic Society 1962; http://coursesa.matrix.msu.edu/~hst306/documents/huron.html. Richard Sennet discusses the social significance of the Port Huron movement in *Respect: The Formation of Character in an Age of Inequality* 256–8, 260.

[62] Singer *Democracy and Disobedience* 50.

[63] e.g. Greenawalt 'Promises, Benefit and Need: Ties that Bind Us to the Law' 754.

[64] e.g. Plamenatz *Man and Society* 240.

[65] e.g. Singer *Democracy and Disobedience* 51–2; on which see Gans *Anarchism* 117–18.

[66] For excellent discussions, see Simmons *Anarchy* 218–24 and 'Consent, Free Choice, and Democratic Government' 798–801; Beran 'Political Obligation and Democracy'; Steinberg *Locke,*

voting and consent we must first look to the current conventional significance of this act. However, the practice of voting is susceptible to multiple interpretations. The individual may construe it merely as a means of expressing a preference, of maximizing a grim situation and retaining some whisper of a voice in her public life, as a way actively to dissent within the bounds of the law, or as a vehicle for identification or expression.[67] Socio-economic features are notoriously significant in party system voting. To cast a vote may be to affiliate oneself with a certain class, group, or cause. One may construe it as a way of making government accountable to the electorate or a way of limiting the legitimate exercise of political power. Singer questions what sense there could be in voting if no one ever accepted the result of the vote. There is a distinction, however, between accepting the result of an election and consenting to obey all of a government's laws by virtue of the act of voting. Two facts aggravate this point. First, circumstances of transnational interdependence. Consider the English legal system. England has an increasingly 'open' legal system, frequently adopting external norms into its law. As a consequence, it is quite impossible for an English citizen to consent to all existing and foreseeable laws that might be enforced against her through voting in a British election. Secondly, legislative survival tells against any clear mapping between democratic voting and consent. New administrations do not start with a *tabula rasa* of laws derived from their election platform. They retain existing laws, repealing some, amending others, and adding new legislation.

Several features of liberal democratic voting argue against its being a case of consent. Democratic voting is majority voting. This severely dilutes any conceptual link between voting and consent. No other consent is given in so collective a manner without some prior unanimous agreement that a particular decision-procedure is binding. Many democratically run associations or organizations may employ majority voting but membership is almost universally the consequence of a voluntary act of joining, the terms of which include agreement, either explicitly or implicitly, to certain decision-making procedures. Agents thus vitally *know* that this is the case when they vote, know that they are committed to this, that other members are committed to this, and that others take them as being so committed. But in voting no individual has either previously agreed to this as a method for reaching decisions nor has she the right or legal power to institute any significant change by this method. As Raz observes: 'I have a legal

Rousseau and the Idea of Consent ch. 6; Gans *Anarchism* ch. 3, and Manin *The Principles of Representative Government*.

[67] Brennan and Lomasky argue to this effect in 'Toward a Democratic Morality'. They suggest that voting allows one to identify oneself with a cause, and express oneself in this way, even in a context in which the impact of one's vote will be nugatory. They suggest that it is satisfying and rational to want to express oneself and it is a morally significant act since a good citizen will engage in politics. Estlund questions both these theses (in 'Introduction' at 19) asking 'what is expressive about voting anonymously in a secluded booth' and whether, even if it is a characteristically good trait to care about politics, it is good to manifest or indicate it. In response to each we might ask; what is expressive about kicking a chair? Though futile (and often counter-productive—frustration is befriended by pain) this is a deeply expressive act. And while kicking a chair in frustration is in a sense more authentic still for being an act done in private, voting is an authentic way to manifest political concern since politics is a necessarily public domain. The real problem with such an understanding of voting is well brought out through analogy with kicking a chair: Pivotal political concerns seem too important to be attended only by the subjective satisfaction of an expressive act.

power only if it is my act which is recognised by law as effecting a legal change'.[68] All power resides in the community as a whole, or a majority thereof.

Abstention too is an ambiguous act. It may signify approval or apathy. One may disapprove but be disaffected and believe, possibly quite correctly, that one's vote is an empty gesture at the polling booth. For consent to be possible and valid one must be able to do something which signifies dissent. Otherwise consent is empty of moral significance. Further, if we do not have an option not to exercise our vote as we choose, it is no longer properly conceived as a democratic *right*. Although abstaining may not be the right thing to do it is a necessarily valid exercise of this liberal political right.[69]

Arguments from quasi-consent based on the legal concept of estoppel by representation suggest that *X* incurs an obligation when he participates in a decision-procedure together with other participants opposed to *X*'s views but prepared to accept and obey the decision the majority favours.[70] The obligation is grounded in *X*'s voluntary participation and is owed to the other participants. The obligation depends on the fact that under certain circumstances, actions and abstentions may justify us in holding a participant to be obligated *as if* he had consented. Thus, *X*, by voluntarily participating in a vote on some matter, understanding that the purpose of the election is to enable the group to reach a decision on the issue, has behaved in such a way as to lead people reasonably to believe that he has accepted the voting process as a suitable means of settling the issue. Others participate in good faith and would have accepted the decision had it gone against them. So too should *X*.

In arguing from estoppel, *Y* will be bound by *X*'s reliance only where *X*'s actions (compliance with the law) are in reasonable reliance upon certain actions by *Y* (*Y*'s compliance). But universal awareness of sanctions argues against this. Many probably believe that others obey laws largely through fear of censure or through independent moral motives, as opposed to reliance on others' compliance. It is very unlikely that the representor (the participant in an election) would intend or foresee reliance. Nor could she, since voting lacks this conventional significance. Further, even though an innocent misrepresentation may be sufficient to ground liability, any reliance by the representee would be quite unreasonable through unilaterally assigning to a social practice a meaning it lacks. Any resulting obligation would also be horizontal (owed amongst members of the state and not from members to the state). There is thus no basis for a vertical obligation to the state, which is one of the great hopes of a consent theory.

[68] Raz 'Voluntary Obligations and Normative Powers' 80.

[69] Posner *Law, Pragmatism, and Democracy* 169: 'The decision not to vote is very much like any other decision not to participate in a particular market... It is one thing to remove artificial barriers to voting; but once they are removed, the choice not to vote is as legitimate an exercise of democratic rights as voting.'

[70] Singer *Democracy and Disobedience* 51–2.

FROM AGGREGATION TO DELIBERATION

JOCASTA. What chiefly galls an exile's heart?
POLYNEICES. The worst is this: right of free speech does not exist.
JOCASTA. That's a slave's life—to be forbidden to speak one's mind.
POLYNEICES. One has to endure the idiocy of those who rule.

(Euripedes)[71]

To speak is to fight.

(Lyotard)[72]

Recent democratic theory has, as Dryzek notes, been characterized by a 'deliberative turn'; an insistence that genuinely democratic decision-making must involve discussion among all potentially affected parties, and must be reached in terms, and on the basis of reasons, acceptable to all.[73] Representative democracy is often depicted as pivoting around the exogenous aggregation of preferences that reflect the private interests of individuals acting strategically. By contrast, models of deliberative democracy typically seek to design discursive political procedures oriented towards the common good, that result in the endogenous transformation of preferences through reflective, public debate. While, in representative democracy, the vote is the equalizing unit of political participation, in deliberative accounts, there is an equivalent notion of discursive equality: All views that may potentially bear upon a debate should, ideally, be admitted. Representative democracy necessarily involves deliberation, at varying political levels, and just as representative democracy relies upon voting, so too, many conceptions of deliberative democracy concede that constraints of time and the impossibility of consensus will demand decisions mediated by voting.[74] The distinctive role of deliberation in accounts of deliberative democracy is normative. It constitutes, or contributes to, the legitimacy of political decision-making; it orients the conditions of reasonable discussion,[75] the object

[71] Quoted in Foucault *Fearless Speech* 29.

[72] Quoted in Benhabib *The Claims of Culture: Equality and Diversity in the Global Era* p. 29.

[73] Dryzek *Deliberative Democracy and Beyond: Liberals, Critics, Contestations* v. The literature is appropriately vast. The leading works include: Benhabib *Situating the Self* and *The Claims of Culture: Equality and Diversity in the Global Era*; Bohman *Public Deliberation: Pluralism, Complexity, and Democracy* and Bohman and Rehg (eds) *Deliberative Democracy: Essays on Reason and Politics*; Chambers *Reasonable Democracy: Jürgen Habermas and the Politics of Discourse*; Cohen 'Deliberation and Democratic Legitimacy'; Elster (ed) *Deliberative Democracy*; Dryzek *Discursive Democracy*; Fishkin *Democracy and Deliberation* and *The Voice of the People: Public Opinion and Democracy*; Gutmann and Thompson *Democracy and Disagreement* discussed in Macedo (ed) *Deliberative Politics: Essays on Democracy and Disagreement*; Habermas *Between Facts and Norms: Contributions to a Discourse Theory of Law and Democracy* and *The Inclusion of the Other: Studies in Political Theory*; Nino *The Constitution of Deliberative Democracy*; Rawls *Political Liberalism* and *The Law of Peoples*; and Sunstein *The Partial Constitution*.

[74] e.g. Cohen 'Deliberation and Democratic Legitimacy' 9. Cf. Dryzek *Deliberative Democracy and Beyond: Liberals, Critics, Contestations* 47.

[75] For Gutmann and Thompson, these include publicity and reciprocity; for Dryzek the slimmer requirements that no communications involving coercion or incapable of extrapolating from the particular to the general be permissible.

of deliberation (the common good), and the reasons and arguments acceptable in political debate.[76]

There are as many variants of deliberative democracy as there might be voices in a political debate, with the result that little meaningful generalization is possible. Accordingly, in the remainder of this section I will first set out a brief exposition of some conceptions of deliberative democracy by discussing internecine disputes among deliberativists. I will then enumerate several concerns about such theories. I finally consider the most recent significant contribution to the debate, Robert Goodin's *Reflective Democracy*,[77] which, crucially, builds upon concession of some of the criticisms I raise below. I conclude that the gulf between ideal deliberative settings and the circumstances of existing democracies is unlikely ever to be bridged, and even if it were, we cannot, in advance, reliably predict the implications of deliberative democracy.

INTERNECINE DELIBERATION

Habermas advances a model of deliberation defined in procedural terms.[78] In his conception, the only legitimate force is that of the stronger argument in a discussion, where discussion is understood as a cooperative, epistemic venture.[79] Deliberation is subject to a principle of discursive validity: 'Just those norms are valid to which all possibly affected persons could agree as participants in rational discourses'.[80] Cohen's model has a substantive dimension.[81] Within his account, decisions are collective (and thereby legitimate) where they emerge from arrangements of binding collective choice that set up conditions of free public reasoning among equals governed by the decisions. Citizens treat each other as equals by offering justifications for the exercise of collective force framed in considerations all can acknowledge as reasons. From ideal deliberative procedures, Cohen attempts to derive substantive egalitarian and liberal political values which are 'elements of democracy rather than constraints upon it'.[82] Beyond procedural and substantive accounts, others define deliberation by its consequences; for example, its success in transforming individuals' preferences.[83]

[76] See generally, Freeman 'Deliberative Democracy: A Sympathetic Comment'.

[77] Goodin *Reflective Democracy*.

[78] For example, Habermas *The Inclusion of the Other: Studies in Political Theory* 137–8 and 264; Baynes, 'Democracy and the Rechtsstaat: Habermas's Faktizitat und Geltung'. See also Maeve Cooke's exposition of Habermas's conception of communicative rationality in *Language and Reason: A Study of Habermas's Pragmatics* especially at 38: 'Communicative rationality is not a substantive conception of reason; it is defined procedurally by way of purely formal characteristics'.

[79] Habermas *Legitimation Crisis* 108.

[80] Habermas *The Inclusion of the Other: Studies in Political Theory* 34 and 41.

[81] Cohen 'Deliberation and Democratic Legitimacy' 87 and 'Democracy and Liberty' 185.

[82] Cohen 'Democracy and Liberty' 187.

[83] Stokes 'Pathologies of Deliberation'.

Theorists diverge on the appropriate fora for deliberation. Some situate deliberation within the institutions of liberal constitutional democracy (Rawls)[84]; others (Habermas, Benhabib)[85] propose 'two-track models' locating deliberation in both state institutions and the civil public sphere. Dryzek is 'insurgent' in relation to existing liberal constitutional institutions and their accompanying political economy. He articulates a critical account that stresses the deliberative importance of maintaining an agonistic civil society and plural public spheres as spaces of democratic critique.[86]

Theorists diverge on the types of discussion admitted to the forum. Some insist that rhetoric, too easily a veil for manipulation, be excluded,[87] while others take a permissive stand, admitting argument, rhetoric, humour, emotion, testimony, storytelling, and gossip.[88] They diverge on the permissible subject-matter of discussion. Rawls takes a narrow view, restricting debate to 'the public good concerning questions of fundamental political justice, which questions are of two kinds, constitutional essentials and matters of basic justice'.[89] He similarly restricts the types of permissible reason that may be advanced in discussion of these matters. Public reason for Rawls[90] must be purely political—we cannot argue from comprehensive doctrines—whereas for Gutmann and Thompson, substantive and controversial moral considerations must be permitted.[91] Some theorists concede the necessity of voting to resolve dissensus, others dispute this.[92] Theorists also differ in their understanding of the conditions necessarily extraneously imposed upon, or endogenous within, democratic deliberation. Gutmann and Thompson impose preconditions on deliberation which include reciprocity and publicity. Cohen imagines that certain formal and substantive equalities are necessary precursors of fair and free deliberation,[93] whereas Dryzek considers that 'deliberation itself possesses substantial endogenous domain restriction mechanisms' and 'the best way for people to learn these values is through the practice of deliberation, rather than being told . . . that they must abide by these principles before they can enter the forum'.[94]

84 Rawls *The Law of Peoples* 133–4: 'The idea of public reason does not apply to the background culture with its many forms of non-public reason nor to media of any kind'. And at 139: 'a framework of constitutional democratic institutions . . . specifies the setting for deliberative legislative bodies'. (See 135 for an outline of the inclusion of citizens within the *ideal* of public reason.).

85 Benhabib *The Claims of Culture: Equality and Diversity in the Global Era* 115.

86 Dryzek *Deliberative Democracy and Beyond: Liberals, Critics, Contestations.*

87 Chambers *Reasonable Democracy: Jürgen Habermas and the Politics of Discourse.*

88 Dryzek *Deliberative Democracy and Beyond: Liberals, Critics, Contestations*; Young 'Communication and the Other: Beyond Deliberative Democracy' and 'Difference as a Resource for Democratic Communication'.

89 Rawls *The Law of Peoples* 133.

90 See Rawls *The Law of Peoples* 137 especially at n. 19.

91 Gutmann and Thompson *Democracy and Disagreement* chs. 1 and 2.

92 Both Cohen and Habermas concede the necessity of a final vote; Dryzek resists this and believes the concession leaves the deliberativist exposed to social choice theory critiques of the aggregation of preferences.

93 Cohen 'Deliberation and Democratic Legitimacy' 93.

94 Dryzek *Deliberative Democracy and Beyond: Liberals, Critics, Contestations* 52, 47.

DELIMITING DELIBERATION

There is a sanguine and counterfactual air to many theories of deliberative democracy that prompts concern as to whether political reality could ever meaningfully approximate the deliberative ideal. Below, I isolate central concerns about the legitimating potential of deliberation.

(*a*) Heroic assumptions mask epistemic and motivational hurdles

As Mill observes:

> Governments must be made for human beings as they are, or as they are capable of speedily becoming... only a disinterested regard for others... ever directs the minds and purposes of classes or bodies of men towards distant or unobvious interests. And it cannot be maintained that any form of government would be rational, which required as a condition that these exalted principles of action should be the guiding and master motives of average human beings.[95]

We need not have surrendered to Schumpeter's scepticism[96] to suspect that citizens within modern societies may be neither (cognitively) able nor (morally) willing to commit the time to political debate that would be necessary to intelligent and reasoned decisions. We live in heterogeneous, multicultural societies.[97] The issues that occupy political agendas are diverse and complex. Some are shaped by transnational interests and actors, many are recondite and require expert knowledge. Some are factual (statistics on crime); others evaluative (the best justificatory rationale for penal policy) or aesthetic/evaluative (the design of inner city housing to inhibit crime). The combination of restricted moral sympathies and sheer epistemic deficit presents hurdles to meaningful democratic deliberation.[98] While communal deliberation may widen the moral horizons of citizens, the opportunity costs of prolonged political discussion and individuals' limited cognitive capacities may render the epistemic deficit ubiquitous.

[95] Mill *On Liberty and Other Essays* 298.

[96] Schumpeter *Capitalism, Socialism and Democracy*. Schumpeter is sympathetically echoed in Richard Posner's recent *Law, Pragmatism and Democracy*.

[97] This is one reason Habermas considers that an actual 'other' is necessary in any discourse that might yield a valid norm: Once we have lost homogeneous conditions of life, 'the moral point of view can only be realized under conditions of communication that ensure that *everyone* tests the acceptability of a norm', from the perspective of her own understanding of herself and the world: *The Inclusion of the Other: Studies in Political Theory* 33.

[98] The fifth formal condition on Cohen's conception of deliberative democracy in 'Deliberation and Democratic Legitimacy' is that the 'members recognise one another as having deliberative capacities, i.e. the capacities required for entering into a public exchange of reasons and for acting on the result of such public reasoning' (92). This could be both a demanding and exclusionary criterion, depending on the issue under discussion.

(*b*) Fragile assumptions regarding the dynamics of deliberation

Argument and reason are primitive.[99] Our decision to resolve a matter by the flip of a coin is a reasoned decision. However, all language is Janus-faced. Deception presupposes, and free-rides upon, truthfulness.[100] This generates problems for theories of deliberative democracy, which often contain dubious conceptual claims about the nature and implications of deliberation, alongside untested empirical hypotheses as to its consequences.

Consider a possible dialogue between the deliberativist and the sceptic.[101] Deliberative democrats often assert the priority of reason; that reasoned deliberation is a universalizable and civilized method of resolving disputes, to be preferred to rhetoric, persuasion, and violence, all of which have coercive potential.[102] In response, the sceptic argues that this conception disenfranchises diversity. Reasoned deliberation privileges a peculiar conception of rationality, that is masculine, detached, and logical. It excludes rhetoric, emotion, narratives, performance, and so on, and may render mute those who do not naturally best express themselves through debate.[103] As Posner notes, one sense in which the vote is potentially fairer than deliberation is that a person cannot be denuded of his vote because he is unable to articulate a defence of his political principles.[104] Alternatively, the sceptic might respond that discussion often simply aggravates difference. And so Shapiro observes: 'People with opposed interests are not always aware of just how opposed these interests actually are'.[105] On certain issues, the promise of shared premises from which to commence discussion may elude us. Difference is inevitable, and often desirable.[106] It may, as Sunstein argues, often be wiser to resort to 'incompletely theorised agreements';

[99] See generally, Johnson 'Arguing for Deliberation: Some Skeptical Considerations'.

[100] For an interesting discussion of the role of deceit in democracy and rhetoric, see Hesk *Deception and Democracy in Classical Athens*. Note also Michel Foucault's comments on the Greek notion of *parrhesia* (free speech) in a democracy: 'Democracy is founded by a *politeia*, a constitution, where the demos, the people, exercise power, and where everyone is equal in front of the law. Such a constitution, however, is condemned to give equal place to all forms of *parrhesia*, even the worst. Because parrhesia is given even to the worst citizens, the overwhelming influence of bad, immoral, or ignorant speakers may lead the citizenry into tyranny or may otherwise endanger the city. Hence *parrhesia* may be dangerous for democracy itself.' Foucault *Fearless Speech* 77.

[101] Much of this debate plays between an ideal (and counterfactual) deliberativist thesis, and the response from non-ideal theory, from existing circumstances of democracy.

[102] Chambers *Reasonable Democracy: Jürgen Habermas and the Politics of Discourse*.

[103] Young 'Communication and the Other: Beyond Deliberative Democracy' and 'Difference as a Resource for Democratic Communication'. These ideas are treated more thoroughly by Dryzek at ch. 3 of *Deliberative Democracy and Beyond: Liberals, Critics, Contestations*.

[104] *Law, Pragmatism, and Democracy* 138. And, as Posner persuasively argues, should the deliberativist suggest that all citizens should always be capable of providing such a defence, she risks an ironic collapse into an elitist democratic vision.

[105] Shapiro 'Enough of Deliberation: Politics is about Interests and Power' 112: 'the problem of democracy, as of government generally, is to manage conflict among persons who, often arguing from incompatible premises, cannot overcome their differences by discussion'.

[106] Mill *On Liberty and Other Essays* 291: 'In all human affairs, conflicting influences are required, to keep one another alive and efficient even for their own proper uses'.

to remain silent on issues of higher level theory, proceeding instead from narrowly circumscribed principles and arguments from analogy, that allow us to agree on a result where we may disagree on reasons.[107] This approach may engage 'the constructive uses of silence': 'Silence—on something that may prove false, obtuse, or excessively contentious—can help minimise conflict, allow the present to learn from the future, and save a great deal of time and expense. In law, as elsewhere, what is said is no more important than what is left unsaid.'[108]

The deliberativist may argue for deliberation from epistemic optimism. Debate allows wider knowledge and perspectives to be brought to an issue and is likely to lead us closer to the truth of the matter (where this exists).[109] In response the sceptic may argue from deliberative delay. Deliberation does not adequately address the exigencies of many political issues, and as a consequence, tends to preserve the status quo.[110] The deliberativist may attempt three related arguments from the transformative potential of deliberation. First, an argument from discursive vanity. Once we must publicly defend a position, we are unlikely to be willing to express it in purely self-interested terms. As Mill observes, 'To be under the eyes of others... is never more important than to those who act in opposition to the opinion of others, for it obliges them to have sure ground of their working against pressure.'[111] In response, the sceptic can note that constraints imposed by the giving of reasons will mediate only public reasons and not private motives; the disingenuous demagogue is a too-familiar political figure. The deliberativist may respond that deliberation may lead to a modification of outcomes. Once speakers are required to defend their positions in terms of the public interest, the claims will be modified as well as disguised. Elster suggests that constraints of imperfection and consistency will modify self-interested claims made within the public domain:

> Because a perfect coincidence between private interest...and impartial argument is suspicious, self-interested... speakers have an incentive to argue for a position that differs somewhat from their ideal point... Once a speaker has adopted an impartial argument because it corresponds to his interest, he will be seen as opportunistic if he deviates from it when it ceases to serve his needs.[112]

However, this argument is vulnerable to the fact that even where these external constraints modify outcomes and yield compromises, they none the less do not attain the purported ends of deliberation. Deliberation is meant to effect a transformation of preferences and generate an expanded moral horizon; it is not meant

[107] Sunstein *Legal Reasoning and Political Conflict* ch. 2 and 'Agreement Without Theory'.

[108] Sunstein *Legal Reasoning and Political Conflict* 37, 38.

[109] Aristotle *The Politics* III. xi. 1281ᵃ39 (at 202) : 'For it is possible that the many, no one of whom, taken singly is a sound man, may yet, taken all together, be better than the few, not individually, but collectively, in the same way that a feast to which all contribute is better than one supplied at one man's expense'. Waldron discusses this and related passages in *The Dignity of Legislation* ch. 5. See also the discussions of Condorcet's jury theorem at Goodin *Reflective Democracy* ch. 5 and Barry 'The Public Interest' and De Tocqueville *Democracy in America* vol. i, part 2, ch. 7, at 288–9.

[110] Sunstein 'Health-Health Trade-offs' 256.

[111] Mill *On Liberty and Other Essays* 360.

[112] Elster 'Deliberation and Constitution Making' 104.

to achieve bargaining, and enforced concession. The deliberativist may go further, arguing from genuine motivational transformation. Benhabib suggests that the 'process of "giving good reasons in public" will... enhance the civil virtues of democratic citizenship by cultivating the habits of mind and public reasoning in exchange'.[113] Not only is this consequence mere conjecture (a clever orator may use interactions to refine his understanding of others' discursive conduct, thereby improving his own strategic manoeuvres) but it will ultimately matter that people actually understand themselves as having reasonably shared interests and objectives.[114] Trust may be compromised where we suspect that motives are only externally constrained.

The deliberativist must ultimately argue from the legitimating potential of deliberative inclusion. If parties who ultimately lose out in a discussion none the less rightly consider that their opinions have been given due respect and consideration, this should both positively and normatively enhance democratic decisions.[115] However, this normative potential is wholly contingent on the institutional realization of deliberation. If deliberative conditions cannot be effected in, or accommodated to, non-ideal political settings, they cannot do the necessary normative work.[116] It is worth noting in this regard that many deliberative accounts are predicated on radically altered political communities. These communities would be characterized by formal and substantive equality, including equality of opportunity, access to resources (including educational), and liberty and so on. Without the satisfaction of these social conditions and of certain political conditions (for example, a ban on the private funding of political parties)[117] deliberation retains coercive potential and preferences may be altered manipulatively. Therefore, not only must we devise meaningful ways of institutionalizing deliberation, we must first make our societies fit for it.

Sceptical of the potential for direct citizen involvement in public discussion on any scale, Dahl noted some time ago that: 'If an association were to make one decision a day, allow ten hours a day for discussion, and permit each member just ten minutes [to speak]... then the association could not have more than sixty members'.[118] Pluralism and globalization have only aggravated the problem. Given constraints of time and cognitive capacity, we must dilute the democratic element of deliberation. Our democratic notions of universality must be compromised along some index: Perhaps we do not all deliberate,[119] or we all deliberate on some but not all issues,[120] or the debates we have are relatively

[113] Benhabib *The Claims of Culture: Equality and Diversity in the Global Era* 115. See also Cohen 'Deliberation and Democratic Legitimacy' 95.

[114] Fearon 'Deliberation as Discussion'.

[115] Gutmann and Thompson *Democracy and Disagreement*.

[116] Bell 'Democratic Deliberation: The Problem of Implementation'.

[117] Rawls *The Law of Peoples* 139.

[118] Quoted in Goodin *Reflective Democracy* 170.

[119] e.g. Fiskin's representative 'deliberative poll': *The Voice of the People: Public Opinion and Democracy* 161–76.

[120] e.g. Cohen and Sabel 'Directly Deliberative Polyarchy'.

superficial.[121] Whatever solution is offered must retain in some meaningful sense a democratic as well as deliberative dimension. Otherwise the ideal atrophies to the reality of elitist representative democracy.

(c) The spectre of self-reference

> Of course, what counts as a good or bad argument can itself become a topic for discussion.
>
> (Habermas)[122]

Discussions about deliberative democracy have a second-order quality that ultimately benefits the sceptic. Once we reach profound disagreement on the nature and possible extent of deliberation, something crucial is conceded. An inability to reach agreement on the method strikes at the feasibility of the method.

THE SILENCE OF REASON

> ... and sometimes even silence/is the trajectory of the first word.
>
> (Someck)[123]

In *Reflective Democracy*, Robert Goodin is awake to the issues of implementation deliberative democracy confronts. He concedes the impossibility of consensus: 'Voting inevitably remains the ultimate act of political legitimation in a democracy'.[124] Indeed, voting is sufficiently crucial to deprive deliberation of independent normative weight: 'none of my mechanisms can claim any democratic legitimacy without' voting.[125] None the less, his challenge—'how can we realistically involve the *entire* community of people affected by a decision in *meaningful* deliberations over that decision?'[126]—is predicated on characteristically deliberative concerns—that inputs, premises, thoughts, and the mute matter alongside outputs, conclusions, actions, and the vocal, and require equal representation in the discussions that eventually inform decisions.

Goodin's solution is the notion of 'democratic deliberation within', an internal dialogue that occurs within each individual's conscience, and not exclusively or even primarily in an interpersonal setting. When an election is called, all within the population need only consider issues from others' perspectives ('imagining yourself into the place of the other')[127] and vote on the basis of this assessment.[128] 'A suitably informed imaginary might serve the same internal-discursive purpose' as do interpretation and imagination in interpersonal discussions.[129] 'Suitably informed' acknowledges the need for appropriate substitute inputs

121 Goodin *Reflective Democracy* 5.
122 Habermas *The Inclusion of the Other: Studies in Political Theory* 44.
123 Someck *The Fire Stays in Red* 11. 124 *Reflective Democracy* 2. 125 ibid. 11.
126 ibid. 4; emphasis in original. 127 ibid. 180. 128 ibid. 230.
129 ibid. 7–8.

for our imaginative dialogues: inputs that operate as a credible proxy for the first-person experience related in conversation. Goodin finds these resources in political arrangements designed to inform the political imagination: cultural institutions and policies; education; policies and institutions that facilitate social mixing; consultative procedures. Literary, visual, and performing arts will be crucial. Through these we will populate our lives vicariously with all types, all narratives, facilitating imaginative projection and a deeper awareness of alterity. These sources will familiarize us with interests that exist but whose voicing is impracticable, alongside interests *incapable* of present articulation (non-human and intergenerational interests). This allows others' preferences and perspectives to influence policy indirectly, through the mediation of imagination.[130] Clearly the monological imagination has no external force correcting its errors.[131] An individual may omit certain interests and parody others;[132] but she must trust herself to correct mistakes by seeking out fresh and better information.[133] Internal-reflective deliberation of this type supplements and does not supplant external-collective deliberation in a democracy. Public validation is necessary to afford internal reflection any genuinely democratic legitimacy.

An empathetic predisposition is essential in our multicultural societies. As I noted above in Chapter 2, a lack of moral imagination, an inability to recognize the humanity and vulnerability of others, can be a terrible moral failing (often with tragic consequences). And where first-hand interaction is impractical or impossible, we must fall back upon imagination informed by indirect sources. Sometimes these will be socially important works of literature with historical impact (*Uncle Tom's Cabin*), sometimes they will be great works that touch people personally in morally important ways.[134] However, a monological conception of discourse carries attendant dangers. Genuine respect sometimes requires that we realize that we cannot authentically stand under another's experience; that we cannot grasp their full otherness without their unmediated contribution. And while narratives are crucial in communicating experience,[135] we do well to recall Iris Murdoch's exposition of a Platonic distrust of art: 'The speaking person is ultimate. A written statement cannot reply but can only say one thing. It is moreover portable and can be handed around among those who

[130] ibid. 61.

[131] This monological conception has Rawlsian and Kantian affiliations, and clashes with a Habermasian dialogue which must involve an actual 'other'.

[132] *Reflective Democracy* 183–4.

[133] ibid. 65.

[134] It is likely that many young children reaching the end of *To Kill a Mockingbird*, have stood with Scout, on Boo Radley's porch, imagined the world that would be mapped out were they walking in Boo Radley's shoes, and fully understood the importance of empathy and imaginative projection into the circumstances of others.

[135] See Benhabib *The Claims of Culture: Equality and Diversity in the Global Era* 14: 'I can become aware of the *otherness of others*, of those aspects of their identity that make them concrete others to me, only through their own narratives'.

do not understand and respect it . . . So it may become a vehicle of falsehood even though it was set down as a memorandum of truth.'[136]

Internal reflective imaginaries may make each of us a better citizen, with a widened moral horizon, but they may also leave us with partially informed, unmediated, understandings. Moral laziness may allow these understandings to settle. 'Truthful imagining requires courage and humility', Murdoch observes.[137] It also demands patience and reliable inputs. And were individuals to engage in genuinely democratic and detailed attempts to understand imagined others, they might discover they have time for little else. Moreover, it is unclear how democratic deliberation within could ever enhance democratic legitimacy. Deliberation can enhance legitimacy epistemically, affectively, or volitionally: Through discussion we reach a superior and better-informed solution; through discussion we comfort the party whose view is ultimately defeated that her comments were considered but did not prevail, and thereby enhance her sense of membership and the respect-worthy nature of our practices. A monological imaginary will struggle to achieve any of these ends.

CONSENT TO POLITICAL AUTHORITY: AN INTERIM CONCLUSION

The discussions above of residence and voting as signs of consent assumed an implicitly defensive stand: If individual consent is the necessary condition of legitimate government, then performative acts of consent must be found amongst the actions of citizens, or the state is not legitimate. And fear of this conclusion, this philosophical anarchism, compels the consent theorist to more and more tenuous claims, which dim the Enlightenment aspirations that authority become answerable to the individual and that consent replace status as the sculptor of society. By contrast, the inexorably counter-factual arguments of deliberative democrats either do not seek to, or fail to, account for the legitimacy of the modern state and its constitutive laws.

Consent is not *necessary* to render a government justified. Government may be very just and efficient even in the absence of citizens' consent. It may help them to act better than they could alone on the reasons that independently apply to them. It may secure worthy goals, coordinate citizens' activities, and maintain peaceful relations with other states. Government may be, on the whole, a very good thing to have.

Nor is it feasible to suggest that consent is *sufficient* for state legitimacy. If the government is not justified, if it commits immoral acts and promotes unworthy ends, then citizens' consent can render it neither just nor legitimate. Justification is more primitive than legitimacy. A state must first be just or nearly just before it can be legitimate. To suggest otherwise is to afford ridiculous creative and

[136] Murdoch *Metaphysics as a Guide to Morals* 19.
[137] ibid. 324.

validating power to the will. Just as limits on normative powers prevent an individual from consenting to injustice, so too, citizens' consenting to the injustices of an evil regime could not increase in any way its justice or legitimacy. It would merely morally implicate the citizens in its unjust acts.

Is consent a necessary condition on government legitimacy and if so, to what does the citizen consent? This essentially comprises two questions. First, is consent *per se* necessary to the relational legitimacy of the state? This enquiry must be deferred until other grounds of obligation have been considered. Secondly, if consent is a sufficient means of meeting this necessary condition, then, to what can we consent?

Most acts of consent are determinate, specific undertakings, defined by the consentor and justified as an act increasing her opportunities, securing benefits to her, or as constitutive of meaningful relationships. Consent to the authority that the modern state claims to itself seems far removed from this conception. As Raz explains: 'Governments typically claim authority to govern any and all aspects of their subjects' lives... Whatever activity you can think of, whether or not it is now forbidden by your law, your government claims the right to forbid it. In just about all states there are legal means to change any law, and to pass any conceivable or inconceivable law.'[138]

As Raz continues, given these claims, it is difficult to imagine what justification one might provide for so open-ended and far-reaching a consent. The state claims to determine all laws and exceptions thereto. The individual simply cannot share this perspective. Nor can one argue from the intrinsic value of an exercise of autonomy. Generally it is true that, while being obliged entails the presence of coercion, voluntary assumption of an obligation presupposes and preserves freedom. By assuming the obligation one does submit future conduct to constraints, but this is reconciled with autonomy since voluntary. However, while a suitably well-defined consent does no violence to autonomy, consent to the complete claims of authority does, being submission to an authority that purports to have the power to diminish or denude one's autonomy. It would be a peculiar moral myopia that misled one to consent to state authority as a means of preserving autonomy.

We can conceptualize this difficulty in a slightly different way. I noted above that the precondition of normative status entails that one can consent only to that to which one's normative powers entitles one to consent. This raises the question as to whether *X* is competent in giving consent so openly. This is a concern about vagueness, which comprises both cognitive and moral aspects. We are not asking merely whether *X* can know what this consent entails, but also whether she can abjure responsibility for the normative consequences of her actions. This is not the too-strong point made by Wolff that individuals have a *duty* to be autonomous. It is the weaker and more plausible claim that the need to maintain moral responsibility for one's actions precludes a consent that may

[138] Raz 'Government by Consent' in *Ethics* 362–63.

involve one in the performance of, or acquiescence in, injustices. There are certain rights an individual should not waive, and there are certain rights an individual does not have to waive. The right to 'do at any time what I think right'[139] may sometimes exemplify the former and the possibility of consent to injustice may exemplify the latter. The citizen could give only a qualified consent. The scope of her consent falls short of law's claims to authority.

CHOICE AND BELONGING

> The choices open to women and men today—even amongst the underprivileged—may be more numerous than in the past, but what has been lost irretrievably is the choice of saying: this is the centre of the world.
>
> (Berger)[140]

Both the argument from tacit consent and voting mistake the real strength of consent theory. Each attempts to ambush some class of persons into obligation. But each is an empty enquiry. Ultimately, a coerced consentor cannot be forced cognitively to accept the authority the state claims for itself. He can be forced to perform a sign of consent and all the indicia of respect may be present—compliance, cooperation, and deference to laws. And yet he will, in his heart, render to the state only the disdain it deserves. This is because, crucially, where the moral imperative is not genuine, it exerts no social or psychological censure. Sanctions are prosaic creatures. Where the consentor violates law L he will be punished for violating his legal obligation to comply with L, not for both this and his consent-based moral obligation to comply. Nor will his 'consent' truly yield additional reasons for action. Consent must be voluntary and informed to be at all meaningful. As Jefferson observes: 'Constraint may make him worse by making him a hypocrite, but it will never make him a truer man'.[141]

A moral obligation to obey, if it is anything, consists in some attitude to a state or society, akin to patriotism and presenting itself *inter alia* in obedience. It is a trust, affection, or respect for those who govern; or solidarity with the community of strangers and friends in which the society consists.

It is here that we should look for the substance and meaning of the obligation—as something that complements and colours an already largely justified state or peaceful community—and not as a state-contrived conning of citizens into extra obligations. Thus construed, it can convert the constraint of obedience into the cooperation of participation, and its presence in a society can tell us something meaningful about the national community as opposed to something disappointing about the sophistry of politicians and philosophers alike.

[139] Thoreau 'Civil Disobedience' 29.
[140] Berger *And Our Faces, My Heart, Brief as Photos* 64.
[141] Jefferson *Political Writings* 394.

Joseph Raz has proposed a theory of respect for law that seeks to apply the reasons that validate consent to political authority in a manner more representative of political phenomenology. This theory issues in a permissible attitude of respect for law that may underpin a general obligation to obey the law. This is a theory of respect that occupies the moral space beyond the theory I advanced in Chapter 2. Whereas my theory of respect requires that agents minimally recognize the value of that which is valuable and react accordingly, Raz's theory addresses those who engage with the value of law and community. Taken together, the theories present respect as a prism through which we can observe the many aspects of the political relationship.

RAZIAN RESPECT FOR LAW

Raz begins from scepticism. He believes that 'there is no general obligation to obey the law, not even the law of a good and just legal system'.[142] One may judge that law is a useful and important institution, or judge that a particular legal system is morally good, and none the less deny the existence of an obligation to obey. It is, consequently, permissible to adopt no general attitude to (even good) law. Equally permissible is the attitude of moral respect for law. Respect for law is an attitude 'such that those who have it have a general reason to obey the law... their reason is their attitude, the fact that they so respect the law'.[143] This attitude is morally permissible in all but iniquitous legal systems.

A patina of paradox covers the thesis from respect. In the absence of obligation, is respect unwarranted? Raz's conception of respect for law consists in both cognitive and practical respect. Primarily cognitive respect comprises cognitions and affective and practical dispositions towards law. These might include belief in the justice of the nation's legal system, affective dispositions such as pride, patriotism, and satisfaction, and practical dispositions such as respect for officials and a willingness to support legal institutions. Primarily practical respect is essentially a disposition to obey the law.

Cognitive respect for law seems unproblematic, since the sceptical conclusion concerning obligation obtains even in reasonably just systems with good law. If law is morally good, cognitive respect is justified. Similarly, one might have cognitive respect for a system of which one is not a member and towards which one, necessarily, has no obligation. But practical respect is largely a reason to obey. The account needs a moral fact, comparable to moral goodness in justifying cognitive respect, to justify this attitude of practical respect. Practical respect for law involves recognizing moral reasons for obedience. The absence of obligation robs practical respect of external foundations. To demonstrate the permissibility of practical respect for law, Raz must invert the order of justification, deriving an obligation to obey from an independently justified attitude of

142 Raz *Authority* 250. 143 ibid.

practical respect. The attitude itself is a reason to obey, and the source of obligation; it is self-referentially justified by its own goodness.

An analogy to friendship underpins the account. Friendship partially rests on the mutual attitudes of the parties to the relationship and is often cited as a reason for action. Citing friendship as the explanation for action contextualizes and provides the background conditions for the reason. Alternatively, the reason may arise out of the patterns of expectation friendship creates.

Participants can model friendship to some extent, but its basic forms are constrained by convention. Valuable activities and relationships alike depend on social factors. Friendship is an intrinsic good with a necessarily normative aspect: We pursue it because it is good. Socialization is necessary to internalize the forms of conduct constitutive of such relationships, and to allow one successfully to pursue them.

However, it is part of the concept of friendship, and not a culturally specific feature, that fitting action is required of a friend regardless of whether she wishes to perform it, and irrespective of whether the friend will discover, or be affected by, the conduct.[144] Due to this conceptually necessary feature of friendship, the relationship provides 'expressive reasons'. Friendship is an expressive reason for actions that conventionally articulate the relationship and against unfitting actions. Expressive reasons can be *welfare reasons* (requiring action beneficial to one's friend), or *symbolic reasons* (requiring action irrespective of any benefit). These reasons require that one act consistent with friendship, independent of one's own interests, or of the knowledge of the other party. Failure to do so is a wrong against the friendship. By implication, it would not be good enough were I to avoid certain actions on account of my desire to avoid later guilt. Where this is my primary motive I reveal myself as having an impoverished conception of friendship. My action is ultimately self-regarding. I act not out of concern for the other for her own sake, but out of concern for my own future psychological well-being. As Blum observes, 'a genuine friend truly cares for the other for his own sake'.[145] To act inconsistently with friendship is, in a possibly minor way, to alter that relationship and the attitudes on which it rests. Irrespective of a friend's knowledge, something of value is lost. Consider an implication. Transplanted to the context of an individual's relationship with the law of her society, a similar observation obtains. If the individual considers herself to be in some form of valuable relationship with her society and the law through which it is regulated, she will have expressive and symbolic reasons for action irrespective of the publicity of her actions. The secret violations that falsify consequentialist accounts due to their lack of adverse results are accommodated by the fact that violation is contrary to a valuable relationship. The integrity of the relationship and the agent's knowledge are sufficient witness to the wrong. This promises much for the theory's potential scope.

[144] Raz *Authority* 255.

[145] Blum *Friendship, Altruism and Morality* 75.

Respect for law, however, is not an instance of friendship. Friendship 'is a reciprocal relation whereas respect for law is not'.[146] Friendship is personal, respect for law, institutional. This is an important qualification. Law is an impersonal phenomenon. Despite this difference, however, Raz suggests four aspects of friendship that find counterparts in an attitude of respect for law.

First, friendship obligations are self-imposed, and depend on a relationship one creates and can terminate. Such relational obligations differ from promissory obligations. They are a constitutive part of a relationship affecting a whole domain of one's life. Obligations are not assumed or terminated in one single act; they derive from the friendship itself. Voluntary obligations are typically undertaken by isolated, deliberate acts or performative utterances. The obligations of friendship, however, are temporally extended by-products of the relationship and not its primary purpose. Similarly, respect for law is a complex phenomenon evolving over time. The attitude is a result of (conditional) choice by the individual. Secondly, our choice of friends reveals our moral character. Given certain information about law, respect for law reveals one's attitude towards matters including socialization, respectable institutions, and authority. It is, however, morally permissible not to have any friends, and not to be friends with any particular person. Thus there is no general obligation to respect the law. 'One may always avoid having any general moral attitude to the law.'[147] Respect and disrespect are, however, asymmetric. One may choose (cognitively) not to respect a just system, but one cannot choose (practically) to disrespect a just system (for example, through public and destructive protest) nor (cognitively or practically) to respect an iniquitous one.[148]

Finally, respect, like friendship, is a reason for action. Those who respect law have reasons others lack. As in friendship, these are expressive reasons to do what is fitting and to avoid what is inappropriate. As in friendship, social conventions partly determine the actions appropriately expressing attitudes. And, 'just as there are qualified or partial friendships, so there are possibilities of qualified respect'.[149]

Friendship obligations are one facet of a complex human relationship. What valuable relationship does the reason to obey provided by respect allow us to express? Raz offers an argument from identification—an internal justification of the intrinsic value of one's identification with society. Respect 'is but one aspect of a complex attitude and style of life, relating not only to the law but to the community whose law it is. Respect for law is an aspect of identification with society (the reverse of alienation).'[150] The relationship of identification is valuable. The attitude of respect derives its value from expressing this relationship.

Respect for law, as a vehicle of identification, furnishes expressive reasons for action. Undertaking an obligation to obey is one such expression.[151] Identification and loyalty are only contingently linked to respect. None the less, practical

[146] Raz *Authority* 258. [147] ibid. [148] ibid. 259 n. 6.
[149] ibid. 259. [150] ibid. [151] Raz *Freedom* 92.

respect is an appropriate expression of loyalty to a society, manifesting trust and confidence in the functioning of law. 'If a person places absolute trust in the law then he will acknowledge the authority of law.'[152] It is also, however, a very specific way of expressing loyalty, through an attitude adopted towards institutionalized forms of the community. Institutions which are unjust (independently, or as an accurate reflection of community values) or which inadequately reflect community values, will not be a fitting object of respect, even where (and sometimes because) the individual remains loyal to her society.

Raz's account from friendship and respect is, therefore, value-dependent.[153] The relationship in question must be (objectively) valuable and not just (subjectively) valued. It is 'the autonomous achievement or pursuit of a goal or an activity of value which makes relationships and personal projects valuable'.[154] The group, association, or geographically bordered group must be morally acceptable. Given this presumption of value-dependence, the stage of the justification of the state is passed, and an attitude of respect comprising an obligation to obey affords relational legitimacy to the authority of the state *vis-à-vis* the respecting citizen.

The surrogate attitude of respect is not consent: 'It is probably not something initiated by any specific act or at any specific time. It is likely to be the product of a gradual process . . . It need not, therefore, be related to any act performed in the belief that it has normative consequences.'[155] Consent in its core sense is performative. It is a performative purporting to change the normative situation, and must thus be public and intentional. To apply this notion to the interaction and identification of citizens with society makes a contortionist of consent. 'Promises and other voluntary commitments are created by an expressed intention to be bound. It is clear that the ordinary life of normal citizens includes nothing amounting to a promise or voluntary undertaking.'[156] Respect for law is argued in order to apply the reasons that validate consent to political authority in a manner more representative of the typical experience of citizens.

In a reasonably just state, the attitude of respect is as valid as an obligation acquired through consent, grounded in the same reasons. Where the attitude of respect is based solely on false assumptions, or does not cohere with the person's other attitudes and beliefs, it cannot be the foundation of authority. However, 'ill-articulated as many people's thoughts sometimes are in substance, they often amount to an assumption of semi-voluntary performative submission to an authority, because it is a morally worthwhile attitude to have'.[157]

152 Raz *Authority* 261.

153 I take the phrase from Simon Caney 'Individuals, Nations and Obligations' 120.

154 Raz *Freedom* 91. 155 ibid. 98. 156 Raz *Authority* 239 and *Ethics* 353.

157 Raz *Freedom* 98. Raz's account is secondary to satisfaction, to a significant degree, of the conditions of the normal justification thesis set out in Chapter 1. Non-instrumentally justified respect can extend the authority of government since it is a constitutive aspect of a valuable relationship, and there is independent value in having such a relationship. Thus, though one cannot consent to the full authority of the state where this consent is instrumentally justified to facilitate better action on right reason, expressive and intrinsically valuable respect can extend the reach of government's authority over the individual. See also Raz *Freedom* 92–4.

Respect for law, however, need not be universal: 'An obligation to obey which is part of a duty of loyalty to the community is a semi-voluntary obligation, because one has no moral duty to identify with this community... Vindicating its existence does not, therefore, establish the existence of a general obligation to obey the law.'[158]

Three questions press upon the account. First, does the analogy between respect and friendship hold? Secondly, does an attitude of respect properly include a disposition towards obedience? Finally, does the sacrifice of consent as a necessary condition on obligation involve any loss?

IN RESPECT OF FRIENDSHIP

> Friendship seems too to hold states together, and lawgivers to care more for it than for justice; for concord seems to be something like friendship, and this they aim at most of all.
>
> (Aristotle)[159]

Friendship is a relationship internally related to duties. Its specification requires reference to duties, which constitute an intrinsically valuable element of the relationship.[160] Friendship involves identification with another, in Blum's phrase, 'the transcendence of self involved in the deep identification with the other's good'.[161] This transcendence of self again entails duties. One who questions the importance of duties to friendship betrays emotional colour-blindness.

Friendship is an uncontroversial locus of value and a fundamental aspect of happiness. Raz justifies the special obligations of friendship on the basis that they are partly constitutive of an intrinsically valuable relationship. The controversial step, of course, occurs in the leap from friendship to other less self-evident objects of identification—ethnic group, nation, race, religion, and so on. Every purported special obligation will have a foundation of particularity. This will sometimes be a twofold specificity; for example, this particular form of relationship (friendship) and this particular friend. The litmus test of legitimacy will be resilience to moral challenge. But the units of identification remain diverse. As Scheffler observes: 'It seems that whenever people value an interpersonal relationship they are apt to see it as a source of special obligations'.[162]

The analogy between friendship and identification with one's society takes the controversial step away from the self-evident. The stability of the analogy rests

[158] Raz *Ethics* 354.

[159] Aristotle *Nicomachean Ethics* VIII. 1. 1155^{a}25 (at 192).

[160] Raz 'Liberating Duties' in *Ethics* 41–2. On Raz, see also Mason 'Special Obligations to Compatriots' 439–45 and Caney 'Individuals, Nations and Obligations' 130–1.

[161] Blum *Friendship, Altruism, and Morality* 75.

[162] Scheffler 'Relationships and Responsibilities' 190. See also 'Individual Responsibility in a Global Age' 225. See also Blum *Friendship, Altruism and Morality* 55–7.

upon its sharing the morally salient features of friendship. Raz refers to identification with, loyalty to, and trust in, all of one's 'community', one's 'society', and one's 'people'. No single locus of identification is specified.

Identification with one's larger community is as much a part of personal well-being as is friendship. It too can encourage a transcendence of the self, and a realization of value. Indifference or alienation directed at any object of potential value typically involves some loss. Understanding and identification are central to belonging, and belonging to personal stillness. With the information given, we have a reasonably just legal system, which is an aspect of the community in which it functions, which is, therefore, also reasonably just. It is valuable, but not morally necessary, for an individual to have a healthy relationship with this group. The controversial residue seems instead to concern the appropriateness of obedience as an expression of respect.

ATTITUDES OF OBEDIENCE

Leslie Green is sceptical of the relationship between identification and obedience. The analogy to friendship exposes the narrow normative scope of the attitude of respect. The many voices through which friendship expresses itself—loyalty, reciprocity, caring—are reduced in the case of law to the monotone of obedience. Respect for law is defined by a duty of obedience. However, this seems not to be 'an appropriate expression of the underlying communal relations of belonging and identification'.[163]

Green compares the thesis from respect to arguments from gratitude. Each, he suggests, assumes that obedience is an appropriate expression of another, non-obligatory, social relationship. But why would obedience ever be an appropriate expression of these relationships? It is not sufficient to reply that it is merely a matter of social convention that obedience expresses these relationships. 'Appropriate' connotes not merely the usual but the desirable and fitting expression of attitudes. A quotation from Locke assists the argument: 'A man may owe *honour* and respect to an ancient, or wise man; defence to his Child or Friend; relief and support to the Distressed; and gratitude to a Benefactor... But all these give no Authority, no right to any one of making Laws over him from whom they are owing.'[164]

Social relationships entail onerous obligations without ever entailing an obligation to obey commands. Until we have independent conditions for legal authority, the appropriateness of obedience as an expression of the communal relationships is doubtful.[165] All legal subjects are to some degree alienated from their legal system, with the result that Razian identification is marginal. 'Whereas one who consented to the rule of a trust-worthy government is bound by that consent, one who respects a trust-worthy government is bound

[163] Green 'Law, Legitimacy, and Consent' 816. [164] ibid. [165] ibid. 817.

by that respect only if the law is also an expression of social convention and outlook.'[166]

However, all the attitudes discussed by Locke are appropriate to the relationship in which they occur. In each society, certain actions will be conventional and appropriate expressions of given attitudes. To analyse the fittingness of obedience within a relationship of identification with one's society, we need fully to characterize that relationship. Raz states that the normative attitudes constituting respect for law include supporting institutions, sharing in communal life, and having trust and confidence in one's government. The question is whether obedience is a performance appropriate to participation in the communal life of one's society as governed by law. If I identify as a member of a group, I will try to promote and not to undermine it. There will be actions appropriate to its promotion and actions from which I must refrain to prevent undermining it. As in friendship, the performances required may often be onerous. But if the relationship is one which is both valuable and valued, I will do as is fitting. In a reasonably just community, run according to reasonably just laws, I will comply with these laws unless unjust. This is both a fitting and desirable reaction to being confronted by just laws which regulate the community with which I identify. Obedience is not appropriate to any of Locke's examples. That is why it does not feature—not because obedience is necessarily an unfitting expression of a non-obligatory social relationship.

CONSENT, RESPECT, SOCIALIZATION, AND DELIBERATION

Respect trades on the same justifications as consent, but surrenders consent as a necessary condition on obligation. Does this descriptive concession forfeit anything of normative importance? In order to assess this I will briefly outline and consider Leslie Green's thesis from consent to the status of citizenship.[167] Green's account is critical and conditional. Consent is a necessary condition of obligation. *If* citizens consent to the status of citizenship they are bound to obey an authority. Consent theory is not 'a failed explanatory hypothesis. It is a critical theory of the conditions under which we would have such an obligation.'[168] The debate has changed. Both thinkers have consciously surrendered universality.[169] The enquiry is more militant. The state must be largely just before we can talk of obligation. Is consent also necessary before we might entertain such talk?

For Green, consent theory should seek to assimilate consent to a kind of voluntary obligation to obey, justified by arguments about the value of this *way* of acquiring obligations. The practice of consent exists in order to express

[166] ibid.

[167] Green *Authority* ch. 7.

[168] Green 'Law, Legitimacy, and Consent' 808.

[169] Green 'Associative Obligations and the State' 117–18 (hereafter, Green 'Associative Obligations').

or secure certain values. 'Consenting is thus a way of intentionally altering a background array of rights and duties, through the beliefs and desires of the parties. The vehicle for the communication of these intentions is a conventional one.'[170] Convention does not justify obligation. Obligations are conventional only in so far as members must invoke certain conventions to be bound, which in turn makes the question of binding consent pivot partly on factual questions relating to an agent's conventional actions.[171]

Within Green's account, consent can be viewed as a mechanism for determining the application for, or varying the content of, existing socially constituted bonds.[172] Marriage instantiates an independently existing institution partly constituted by a set of conventionally recognized rights and duties. The content of the duties is extrinsic to the will of the parties. The will of the parties has applicative and not creative power. Consent, none the less, remains a constitutive aspect of the relationship a couple seeks to establish.

The duties of citizenship are those that constitute the conception of citizenship in a community. Consent theory applies to individuals who willingly assume the role of citizen and requires that political roles, including citizenship, are to be occupied only by consent; with the result that consenting to authority 'concretely instantiates a form of association which may be regarded as a shared good.'[173]

The role of authority relations in this form of association is again demonstrated by analogy to friendship. Friendship is paradigmatic of the sort of commitment shared goods (like citizenship) can generate. A natural expression of such goods is 'to regard the relationship as obligation-imposing, as putting at least certain competing claims out of consideration at all'.[174] Only consent can make the valuable relationship of civic friendship legitimate, since only it can give legitimacy to the authority, that, through its norms, supports and promotes the civic friendship of citizenship. These norms provide a common framework and structure for this shared good. Consent thus gives these norms the authority they claim, and bridges back to authority.

It is not impossible, immoral, or incoherent not to adopt this perspective. Not all individuals do or should consent to the role of citizenship. Not every modern society has this role.[175] But in those that do, consent to the shared good of citizenship is necessary for, and entails, an obligation to obey the law.

RESPECT OR CONSENT?

Green suggests that consensual obligations are preferable to semi-voluntary relational obligations. The obligation to obey the law entails normative burdens. Relational and consensual obligations generally differ not in their ends but in their means. Relational obligations are only semi-voluntary. Typically, we begin

[170] Green *Authority* 166–7. [171] ibid. 167. [172] ibid. 204.
[173] ibid. 208. [174] ibid. 209. [175] Green 'Law, Legitimacy, and Consent' 820.

relationships without believing that we undertake obligations. Consent, on the other hand, always involves, as 'a reflexive but non-redundant element', the fact that certain actions are believed to bring about certain duties since done in that belief: 'one's awareness of the normative consequences of one's actions may be more or less complete, so voluntarism is a matter of degree'.[176] However, in relational contexts, this awareness is either factually absent or normatively redundant. Green's position stresses awareness and deliberation. 'The social role of citizenship can be acquired in various ways ranging from habituation to conscious choice. Role-bound consent restricts its validity to those cases falling well towards the deliberate end of the spectrum.'[177] Consent binds as a constitutive aspect of a valuable relationship.[178] Willing acceptance of the role of citizen is central to transforming a valuable legal system into a legitimate one: 'The normal processes of socialization may provide an explanation of common feelings of loyalty, but they do not justify them, at least not when they have as their object the authority of law.'[179]

The consent theorist must demonstrate that there is special value in empowering one to create duties by agreement, 'not just that it would be valuable to be bound by such duties'.[180] This marks the main conflict between Green and Raz. For Raz, even if not deliberately incurred, obligations entailed by identification are binding if valued and valuable. But for Green, to show that something is valuable 'does not show that it is obligation-imposing'.[181] Political obligation requires consent, not because of anything about the concept of obligation, but because of its particular content. The obligation's structure and content are social, but its incidence is individual and consensual:

> A high degree of awareness is necessary on the part of citizens in order to validate their duties to obey. First, any state is liable to change... Weakly voluntary duties are not sufficiently sensitive... Second, recall again that in the political community the stakes are the highest. Drifting in and out of a association that claims supreme authority... is much more serious here than in the normal ebb and flow of relationships like friendship... the validity of the civic role must rest on consent.[182]

Raz's basic point, and the purpose of the friendship analogy, is that when entering into certain relationships, normative consequences are not at the forefront of our thinking. In this way, the obligations that follow are semi-voluntary. They supervene with the evolution of the relationship. Consent is appropriate when normative consequences are of primary concern, and where we purport publicly to act in the belief that we are altering the normative situation. But at

[176] ibid. 823.

[177] ibid. 824 and Green *Authority* 206: 'political stations, including citizenship, are to be occupied only by consent'.

[178] Green 'Associative Obligations' 111.

[179] Green 'Law, Legitimacy, and Consent' 824–5.

[180] Green 'Associative Obligations' 96.

[181] Green 'Law, Legitimacy, and Consent' 824.

[182] Green 'Associative Obligations' 113.

the incipience of intimacies, we do not think primarily of changes to the normative situation, nor are our actions necessarily public. None the less, and despite this lack of explicit deliberation, the obligations internally related to and entailed by valuable relationships are binding.

Which model is more attractive? Green distinguishes the opposition between deliberation and habituation from that between a single act and a process. Relationships are processes of identification and affection. Consent is inept if restricted to single acts. It is thus vital for Green to be able to maintain that a 'choice-laden process can be consensual provided only that it meets the usual conditions for consent'.[183] Green's sense of consent rests on the idea of certain conventional means of communicating one's intention to alter a background array of rights and duties. There is an implicitly public condition in the idea of communication, and a requirement of conventionally acknowledged ways of consenting.

In describing consensual processes, Green refers to consenting to becoming a lawyer, and of consenting to marriage.[184] Both of these processes involve formal oaths or promises, rituals, uniforms, and patterns of expectation. There is a conventionally recognized point at which *X* becomes a lawyer having previously been only an apprentice, and *X* and *Y* become husband and wife having been engaged. Consent makes all the difference.

Consent is an obvious means through which to express certain bonds, where shared conventions of understanding attend them and social practices buttress its use. We know what it is not to be married, not to be a lawyer. But what it is not to be a citizen? We just *are* citizens, and certain things follow from this, quite irrespective of consent—a (legal) obligation to obey the law; a right to vote; a duty to pay taxes; and, possibly, military requirements. If I am not a citizen, am I a civic spinster or a self-employed public self? Green has a point. Clarity about our obligations is a good thing. But we already have these obligations and rights. Citizenship is a legal status. The concept of citizenship may be a politico-moral one, but citizenship *per se* is a cluster of rights, duties, tokens of membership, and a symbol of dignity and equality. Green's point is surely that through consent we transform a bare legal relationship into a rich moral one. The cluster of legal citizenship rights through consent constitute elements of a valuable moral relationship. However, conventionally recognized means of consenting do not exist, *and are not necessary.* Something not explicitly stated may still have been the subject of much deliberation and this deliberation may entail consequences all but identical to those following upon explicit performative consent. Take the case of marriage. Prior to the typical civil or religious marriage there will be a prelude that moves from tentative flirtation, to intimacy, to commitment. From this interaction, the value of the relationship is born. The relationship is an intrinsic good internally related to its justifying duties. Traditionally oriented couples will proceed through the stages of engagement and marriage, centrally

183 Green 'Law, Legitimacy, and Consent' 823. 184 ibid.

involving a performative consent. Less traditional couples, or those prohibited from marrying, will not do so. But the value of their relationship still resides in the same emotions, attitudes, and responsibilities. Performative consent is not *necessary* to valuable relationships and the obligations they contain.

A human relationship is not a series of consents out of which affection evolves. This is not how we perceive our lives. The voluntary assumption of obligations need not imply an act of consent. Similarly, roles willingly assumed which generate obligations do not thereby become 'consensual processes'. We willingly assume many things to which we do not also consent. We do not consent because we do not undertake public acts in the belief that we alter the normative context, and because convention does not prescribe any acts by which we might do this. There is a difference between becoming a lawyer and a friend. One is a status and one is a relationship. Citizenship too, is a status, but Green construes it as a valuable social relation in order to justify consent as constitutive of a valuable relationship. Green's citizenship is not bare formal citizenship. It is a valuable relationship. However, most valuable relationships culminate and do not begin in performative consents. And some never find or seek consensual expression.

Socialization and choice are placed in too stark opposition. Much socialization and relational development is deliberative to some extent. I typically know that I am becoming someone's friend, falling in love, or forming ties of identification. And many choices are nominal, constrained, or wholly controlled, by environmental, social, economic, or gender-related factors.

Socialization may emanate from an unreflective state. Green's concern here is warranted. We can identify with things in a purely positive, non-critical manner. We might obey unthinkingly due to the manner in which our identification and respect have evolved. But a similar concern could affect the account from consent. Consent, once given, may inculcate a lack of reflection. One has a standing reason to do as the law says. This may truncate deliberation. It may, unwittingly, license immoral obedience. Exactly the same could be said of respect. The point is that we *really* cannot put choice all on one side and socialization on the other.[185] Some people consent without reflection, some form relationships without much reflection. But if the bonds that emanate are valuable, and the agent is aware of the obligations they entail, then these bonds remain valuable. And, if these bonds give rise to an attitude of respect which has amongst its expressive reasons for action an obligation to obey one's community's laws, then an obligation is generated and state legitimacy is no less secured than on the consent account.

Consider a contrast discussed by Scheffler between having a reason to consent to something and being a party to a relationship.[186] This will bring out the superfluity of consent. Imagine I have a reason to consent to Y doing ϕ. If I

[185] ibid.

[186] Scheffler 'Relationships and Responsibilities' 200–2.

consent, I am obligated to allow *Y* to do ϕ. But prior to consenting, I do not have the obligation. I have the obligation only if I consent.

However, for *X* to say that she is party to a valuable relationship is not to say: 'I value my relationship, and therefore have a reason to perform an act, which, if performed, will generate obligations'. If *X* values the relationship, this simply *is* to understand it as generating certain obligations. *X* conceives herself as subject to these obligations by virtue of the valued relationship. The idea is not that one has obligations deriving from a relationship that one *has reason* to value. The idea concerns relationships that parties actually do value. Willingness and voluntary identification are thus maintained.[187]

Given that we consent in the belief that we alter the normative context, what alteration to the role of citizen would be effected by consent? We are born into citizenship. Green's retort is that consent's role is moral. We consent to political obligation, and thereby translate the legally prescribed into the morally binding and the valuable into the obligatory. However, if the relationship is already valuable and valued, we already have moral obligations.

This discussion insinuates that consent theory is underpinned by a voluntarist anxiety. Scheffler suggests that the voluntarist may fear that special, more than general, obligations give others excessive control over one's life. Our central social roles partly determine our social identities. To the extent that we personally determine such factors, we shape our own identities. To the extent that we do not, we are moulded from outside.[188] Green's account mirrors this concern. Consent is subject to the social thesis but still determines the final incidence of obligations, 'not as a device to explain the structure of our moral worlds, but to explain our own positions within them'.[189]

A second concern may underlie voluntarism. Special obligations and relationships, more than general duties or moral requirements, place us under primarily positive and not negative duties. Citizenship is no exception. The emphasis on maximal awareness of obligations in Green's account betrays this concern. This second point also suggests a third, in the idea that moral responsibility requires watchfulness. Consent to citizenship is consent to an association that claims supreme authority and in political community the 'stakes are so very high'.[190]

[187] Scheffler makes the stronger claim that obligations may arise from (objectively) valuable relationships that are not actually (subjectively) valued by the agent. This introduces the possibility that *X* may have obligations of which she is not aware because she mistakenly, or wrongly, fails to recognize the value of a relationship. This seems correct; objective value that is wrongfully neglected may still generate obligations. In the weaker claim, which is more relevant to the two accounts under consideration, the subjective criterion must be satisfied for obligations to arise. The relationship must be valued as well as valuable. Given the value-dependent nature of Raz's account, these two elements are necessary and sufficient conditions of obligation. As a result, a subjectively valued but objectively harmful relationship (one that is demeaning to the agent—slavery—or to others—membership of a white supremacist movement) should not be understood as generating genuine obligations. Similarly, for Green, a valuable relationship becomes obligatory only through an act of consent.

[188] Scheffler 'Relationships and Responsibilities' 192 and 202–3.

[189] Green *Authority* 205.

[190] Green 'Law, Legitimacy, and Consent' 824.

But this only returns us to the point that consent may serve to truncate deliberation.

If *X* is unreflective generally and *Y* is generally conscientious, then the difference between affective identification and deliberative consent for either party may be nugatory. Given the manifest lack of performative acts of consent in our forms of life, and the lack of any ceremony by which this might become feasible, the conflict may reduce to whether deliberative cognitive acceptance constitutes consent, or acceptance of the authority of law flowing from an identification with one's society. If so, and given that both thinkers place purportedly public conditions on performative consent, Raz fights the stronger corner.

Those who behave respectfully towards authority do so intentionally. Respectful behaviour is undertaken within a conception of one's world, and the role of value therein. Though the conduct may rest at any number of points on a continuum of deliberativeness, it remains founded in reasons and intentional. It can reflect an understanding of one's reasons for action as opposed to mere learned responses. It will also be an attitude willingly or voluntarily held. We do not respect things against our will (though we may respect objects grudgingly—essentially a more compelling case of respect) and may behave respectfully through caution, prudence, or coercion. Respect is, therefore, a voluntary and intentional attitude adopted towards objects of perceived value. Extreme voluntarist concern seems misplaced. Consent is not necessary for an obligation to obey.

Nor is consent *sufficient* for valuable relationships and the obligations they contain. Rational consent and deliberation are inadequate for one truly to value something. Certain beliefs, dispositions, attitudes, emotions, and convictions must inform such consent—*if* consent is appropriate. This will include understanding one's attitude and its relationship to its object and to others. As Blum puts it, 'more aspects of a person's being must come into play than merely his will, his capacity for choice, his deliberative reason, in order for us to say that the person holds certain values or attitudes towards others'.[191] A stronger point suggests itself. There is the possibility that excessive deliberation may be counterproductive in relationship formation, or contrary to emotional phenomenology. Raz understands personal relations as capable of being understood only through being lived or experienced emotionally. And of the responses appropriate to these relations he observes that 'even where such responses can be deliberate they should not be. They acquire their significance from the fact that they are not.'[192]

Before leaving this topic, one brief point remains. Green focuses on citizenship, Raz on membership and identification. Identification can hold towards a society, members of which do not identify and who possibly actively do not do so. Green's account concerns only the community of citizens and not society at large. Raz's account is broader. It is also deeper. As I noted above, in Chapter 2,

[191] Blum *Friendship, Altruism and Morality* 177; Williams *Problems of the Self* 227.
[192] Raz *Freedom* 312.

communities increasingly consist in concentric circles of membership and not in the single status of citizenship. Raz's account better accommodates plurality. It requires only that in the society in question, respect for law is recognized as a way of expressing trust and loyalty. The model consequently deals both with more primitive models and with potential models of the future, in which sub-and supra-national allegiances exert significant normative pull. It is both more local and more global than Green's model.

Raz stresses the value of community and qualifies it in a way that preserves some degree of voluntarism in our obligations. Identification and community are central. His theory leaves appropriately vague the boundaries that hem in identification and obedience. It recognizes that our communities do exert some normative pull over us, that perfect voluntarism and deliberation neither do, nor properly should, define many of our important relationships, while also recognizing that bonds must be valuable *and, to some extent*, voluntary. A question remains, however, whether Raz's theory neglects conceptual resources within the notion of community that could underwrite a mandatory and not merely permissible obligation to obey the law.

4

Community, Identity, and Joint Commitment

An other sense tugs at us:
we have lost something,
some key to these things...
identity:
something too huge and simple
for us to see.

(M Atwood)[1]

Some of the ties that bind individuals are felt not as fetters but as freedoms. Membership of communities can introduce individuals to social opportunities and to associations that become central to self-perception. Obligations may be integral to membership. But to members these may be incidental alongside the benefits of belonging. Indeed, they may be important to, and indicative of, the sense of belonging. Obligations may be expressive of commitment and community.

One central paradigm of social association is voluntaristic, the organization one enters and exits at will. Membership is voluntarily assumed, discharged, and, if so wished, discarded. Choice is primary and obligation secondary. The performance of obligations once assumed is not voluntary, but entry is voluntary. The voluntary association model is thus doubly unsuited to political society. Citizenship is not a voluntary status. We are born into, and do not choose, political society. And the obligation to obey the law is not a burden one can discard at will. Law makes demands of its subjects, not requests.

Membership and belonging, however, retain normative force beyond circumstances defined by voluntarism. Our earliest emotional and moral horizons are illuminated by local suns. Before the individual even grasps the concept of belonging she is a member of a family, a town, a nation, a political community, a race, a faith. Concentric circles of pre-existing communities circumscribe her. As Alasdair MacIntyre observes, 'the story of my life is always embedded in the story of those communities from which I derive my identity'.[2] For MacIntyre, one inherits not only identity from communities but also 'a variety of debts,

[1] *Eating Fire: Selected Poems 1965–1995* 25.
[2] MacIntyre *After Virtue* 221.

inheritances, rightful expectations and obligations. These constitute the given of my life, my moral starting point.'[3]

In this chapter I will look to non-voluntary social groupings, membership of which may be thought to ground and generate obligations. I will discuss the theories of John Horton, Ronald Dworkin, and Margaret Gilbert, each of whom attempts to account for non-voluntary political bonds.[4] The chapter's approach will be critical. Though the present theories represent a more realistic accommodation to the circumstances of political society than that provided by the voluntary association model, none the less, each falls short of justifying political obligation.

JOHN HORTON AND COMMUNITARIAN OBLIGATIONS

In *Political Obligation*, John Horton arranges a communitarian defence of political obligation around the axes of community, membership, and identification. Political obligation is conceptually connected to membership of a political community, and like membership, is not typically a matter of voluntary commitment or choice. Neither membership nor its attendant obligations require further moral justification. Obligations of community, like family obligations, are self-justifying. Particularity is thus intrinsic to the account. Individuals are not simply the member of one and not another state, they are members of *a particular* state. The distance between membership and political obligation is mediated by partial identification with the political community. Denial of this identification may involve personal or moral incoherence since certain social roles are non-contingently related to our ends and to our conceptions of who we are. Political obligation requires that members take into account the interests and welfare, variously interpreted, of the polity. Political obligation is also particularly closely linked to acknowledgement of the authority of law since legal regulation constitutes 'the kernel of the terms of political association' (though this is still consistent with particular principled acts of disobedience).

Horton's project is distinctively circumscribed. It is not a strongly normative account. It does not aim to provide any set of necessary and sufficient conditions

[3] ibid. 220. See also Taylor *Philosophy and the Human Sciences: Philosophical Papers 2* 205–6: 'the free individual or autonomous moral agent can only achieve and maintain his identity in a certain type of culture ... the free individual of the West is only what he is by virtue of the whole society and civilization which brought him to be and which nourishes him ... all this creates a significant obligation to belong for whoever would affirm the value of this freedom; this includes all those who want to assert rights either to this freedom or for its sake'. The debate between communitarians and liberals may imply more than it expresses. As Gellner observes at *Language and Solitude: Wittgenstein, Malinowski and the Habsburg Dilemma* 21: 'The traditional organic way of life is probably imperceptible to itself. It is lived, it is danced, it is performed in ritual and celebrated in legend, but it is hardly articulated in theory ... The real traditionalist, al-Ghazzali observed, does not know himself to be such. Community is sung and praised by those who have lost it.'

[4] These three (and other) thinkers are also discussed by Simmons in 'Associative Political Obligations'.

for determining whether, and to what extent, individuals are obligated to obey laws. Nor is it an ethical theory. It does not claim to provide a new truth to replace present error. It does not start from, and structure, a revised framework for our beliefs. It starts instead from our shared beliefs and feelings, from the factors we take for granted, ways we recognize responsibilities, and statements of guilt and shame. Horton hopes only to provide a 'phenomenology of our ethical life'.[5] This may be partly critical, helping to restructure, where disordered, our moral emotions and beliefs. He neither provides, nor thinks it possible to provide, a generalized account of the content of political obligation. This is a necessary consequence of the dual particularity of his approach: Obligations are specific to a particular state and differ between states. This constrains what can be said at the general level.

This observation betrays Horton's qualified affiliation with analytic linguistic accounts of political obligation, advanced, *inter alia*, by Margaret Macdonald[6] and Thomas McPherson.[7] Certain family resemblances unite these writers. Both anchor their theories with the conceptual chain that links social life to concepts such as rules, obligations, authority, and law. These words, in their very *meaning*, cluster in the same conceptual space. Society without rules (of rights, obligations, and so on) is inconceivable. The general enquiry into the existence of some concept of political obligation is absurd and incoherent—to have political obligations is simply what it *means* to be a member of a political society. One might enquire into the particular case—about the merits or applicability of *this* law or *that* statute—but it is a 'point of grammar' that in political society, law, government, and authority all entail obligation at the abstract level.

Horton's approach is anti-voluntaristic.[8] He sets out to provide an account in which obligation does not derive from a voluntary undertaking, the polity is not understood as modelled on a voluntary association, and where persons are understood as more deeply constituted by membership of a polity. Voluntarism assumes a particular conception of persons as atomistic entities only contingently connected to each other and their social context, in a state of natural freedom and minimally reasonable.[9] Voluntarism may acknowledge the importance of communal goods and the necessity of (some) social context for formation of the self, but it neglects the ontological significance of community; the non-contingent way in which social context informs personal development. It

[5] Williams *Ethics and the Limits of Philosophy* 93 and Horton *Political Obligation* 173–4.

[6] Macdonald 'The Language of Political Theory' 183–4.

[7] McPherson *Political Obligation* 59–65. See also the discussions of conceptual linguistic accounts in Simmons *Moral Principles* 38–45; Horton *Political Obligation* 137–45, and throughout Pateman *The Problem of Political Obligation: A Critique of Liberal Theory*.

[8] Simmons discusses 'antivoluntarism' at 'Associative Political Obligations' 66–7.

[9] Horton *Political Obligation* 48. For detailed discussions of the liberal conception of the person, see Gaus *The Modern Liberal Theory of Man* and Donner *The Liberal Self: John Stuart Mill's Moral and Political Philosophy*. For helpful discussions of the theorists and theses of communitarian thinking, see: Mulhall and Swift *Liberals and Communitarians*; Kukathas 'Liberalism, Communitarianism, and Political Community'; and Gutmann 'Communitarian Critics of Liberalism'.

underestimates how profoundly this connection enters into the person, that '*particular* people are in part the products of *particular* societies'.[10] Thus:

> Personal identity, our sense of who we are, is partly constituted by where we are born, resident and educated ... In part, our identity is bound up with the polity of which we are members, and it would not be surprising if this connection between the sense of who we are and the polity of which we are members were reflected in our conception of political obligation.[11]

And later:

> Society and social relations are as much a reality as individuality: we experience life through our living with others and we are unavoidably the product, in part, of the culture, practices and social relations in which we are nurtured ... each of us is born into a complex web of social relations, institutions and practices which contribute to making us what we are, and which cannot all be conceived of as wholly external to a self-sufficient individual with an essence independent of these formative experiences.[12]

Neither society nor the individual has ontological priority. Self and society, and social selves, are interdependent. Society is non-contingently associated with the individual on two levels. First, we are inexorably the product of our culture. This is a conceptual claim about the sources of the person. Secondly, social practices contribute to making us what we are, and cannot all be conceived as external to the self (there are aspects of our identities from which we cannot abstract). This is a substantive claim about the constitution of identity. Individuals are doubly embedded in their community. People 'are necessarily social and as such are partly constituted through a social context which cannot be understood simply as a consequence of their prior choices'.[13]

Horton's analysis proceeds by way of analogy to the family. Family exemplifies a context in which obligations are experienced as genuine and open-ended and do not arise from voluntary undertakings. Membership of a family simply entails certain obligations. The analogy to the family is only partial. Still, obligations are mutual and genuine, though non-voluntary, and need not be accompanied by personal feelings or emotions.

Obligations must be acknowledged before they bind, but caution is necessary in understanding 'acknowledgement': 'Acknowledging or recognising our obligations does not imply that some act of acknowledgement or recognition creates the obligations ... All moral obligations and duties must be acknowledged or recognised if an agent is to act upon them, but this leaves entirely open the question of how any particular obligation is to be explained or justified.'[14]

'Acknowledgement' and 'recognition' can be ambiguous among several senses. I will consider four possible constructions. First, the obligation must be acknowledged for it to obtain at all. The act involved creates obligations anew. This is the *creation* sense of acknowledgement. (This strains 'acknowledged' which seems to imply the pre-existing presence of that which is acknowledged, as

[10] Horton *Political Obligation* 48. [11] ibid. 48–9. [12] ibid. 117.
[13] ibid. 118–19. [14] ibid. 149–50.

opposed to the creation of something anew. I include it to demonstrate the strongest possible role for volition in a political account, and the sense Horton most strongly denies.)

Secondly, a matrix of pre-existing duties attach to a role. An individual, in order to be bound by these obligations, must acknowledge them by entering into the role, or by morally embracing a role non-voluntarily assumed. Acknowledgement entails an institutional bundle of duties the agent now bears. However, acknowledgement does constitute the normative ground of the obligation. This is the *application* sense of acknowledgement.

Thirdly, X is objectively subject to obligation ϕ. He must subjectively acknowledge it in order to fulfil his obligation. Once he has done so, it is binding unless and until he renounces it (which may be morally wrong). This is the *apprehension* sense of acknowledgement. The idea here is this. Being born into certain roles precludes robust choice. Never having been a *tabula rasa,* no choice can return us to that state. If I acknowledge my constitutive roles I do not render them voluntarily entered. However, a logical prerequisite of action following upon the objective fact of obligation is awareness of obligation. Acknowledgement is a cognitive and not a normative condition of my being bound. I recognize obligations I already have, just as, when seeing myself in an old photograph, I recognize the physically continuous self I have always been. If the role is imbricated in a deeply unjust system, its obligations will not bind me. If it is not, it (objectively) binds me in any event. Acknowledgement is neither a necessary nor a sufficient condition of obligation. However, just as the role and its obligations may be acknowledged, they may be rejected. If I am to be an X, I must—logically—acknowledge its attendant obligations, since these are constitutive of my-being-an-X. But I may reject being-an-X, in which case I do not have the obligations of an X. Additionally, I may acknowledge the role not only in the *apprehension*, but also in the *application* sense. I may enthusiastically embrace the role and create a situation in which a set of voluntary obligations of identical content mirror my independent role duties.[15]

The fourth sense involves the same facts as above, but is without the option of rejecting a role and its duties. This is the *academic* sense of acknowledgement. It is purely cognitive, and voluntarism is wholly redundant. Here, what cannot be chosen also cannot be denied. Refusal of acknowledgement cannot render an obligation non-binding. This sense involves the notion that it is logically incoherent to prescind from certain roles (and hence, to deny their attendant responsibilities). This is the continuum of choice against which I will measure Horton' account. Where his ideas finally rest will determine the consistency of his claims.

The ideas of membership, identification, and 'normative independence'[16] play pivotal roles in Horton's account. He contends that certain local practices are so

[15] For a related idea, see Hardimon 'Role Obligations' 351 n. 31.

[16] The phrase is Simmons's—'Associative Political Obligations' 81. He refers to the 'identity thesis' where I have referred to the identification thesis. As I will demonstrate below, the logical and affective gap between identity and identification is a crucial problem for Horton's account.

axiomatic to our sense of self as to be morally primitive. Our very sense of self derives from this social context. Consequently, we need not invoke extrinsic moral principles to justify the obligations these roles entail. However, even if the requirements of family and polity membership seem to stand in no need of justification, do they constitute reasonable expectations or moral obligations?[17] For an answer to this question we must turn to Horton's arguments concerning identification and normative independence. For Horton:

> [S]ome institutional obligations, through their deep-rooted connections with our sense of who we are and our place in the world, have a particularly fundamental role in our moral being. That these kinds of institutional involvement generate moral obligations, and that these obligations rather than standing in need of justification may themselves be justificatory, is only to be expected.[18]

Not all institutional relationships will play this fundamental a role in our lives, but those that do will 'be partly constitutive' of 'our sense of who we are'.[19] Horton believes membership of political community is such a relationship. Obligations are internally related to membership of a polity that is not voluntarily joined. This statement links normative independence to anti-voluntarism and leads into the identification thesis.

Identification entails obligations. Where *X* occupies role ϕ, and ϕ entails attendant obligations, *X*'s denial of these obligations constitutes a denial of his socially informed identity. 'This sense of identity and the corresponding responsibility is part of what it means to be a member of a polity and to recognise one's political obligations.'[20]

Horton proceeds in two stages. First, he argues from phenomenological evidence of the common experience of membership. Secondly, he argues directly for the normative self-sufficiency of role duties. The two are linked. A phenomenological understanding of the polity and membership will reveal the superfluity of further justification.[21]

Political obligation is coextensive with the borders of the political community to which one belongs. Identification with the polity is witnessed in the fact that we view the actions of our polity in distinctive ways. Its actions seem particularly close to us, a connection located in our sense of their authorship, and rendering intelligible feelings of guilt, shame, and pride:

[17] In 'Associative Political Obligations' 76–7, Simmons asks a similar question of Gilbert's thesis of political obligation. It is a question I will also ask of Dworkin below. Note that justifications more primitive than mere family membership can be advanced. Parental responsibilities might be justified (up to a point) in terms of tacit consent or in terms of a natural duty to aid made specific by circumstances or necessity. For examples of the latter see Goodin 'What Is So Special About Our Fellow Countrymen?' See, generally, Friedman 'The Practice of Partiality'.

[18] Horton *Political Obligation* 157.

[19] ibid. 157.

[20] ibid. 154. See also Pitkin *Wittgenstein and Justice* ch. 9 and Simmons 'Associative Political Obligations' 81.

[21] ibid. 155.

such feelings of shame and guilt... logically cannot be experienced in the same way about the actions of other polities... Furthermore, while the extent of one's support for, or active opposition to, the actions of one's polity may modify or qualify these feelings, such opposition or support does not exhaust the sense of an intelligible relationship of responsibility for those actions.[22]

After the Vietnam War, citizens of the USA felt shame, even guilt, for their country's actions. Outsiders felt anger, even outrage. The sense of self and other is clear.[23] Nor is this a simply subjective phenomenon. Outsiders associate individual citizens with their polity and its acts.

Williams contrasts guilt and shame in terms of cause, response, and perceived reparation:

What arouses guilt in an agent is an act or omission of a sort that typically elicits from other people anger, resentment or indignation. What the agent may offer in order to turn this away is reparation; he may also fear punishment or may inflict it on himself. What arouses shame on the other hand, is something that typically elicits from others contempt or derision or avoidance. This may equally be an act or omission, but it need not be: it may be some failing or defect. It will lower the agent's self-respect and diminish him in his own eyes... shame may be expressed in attempts to reconstruct or improve oneself.[24]

'Guilt' refers to an agent's consciousness of having done something wrong, and the occurrent emotional state caused by this awareness. Guilt attaches to acts of the individual where she freely and intentionally does an act she knows or believes to be wrong. It is typically a principle of individual responsibility, but both the moral and legal notions of guilt can have a vicarious aspect. We speak of 'guilt by association', where there exists some real causal and/or moral responsibility between an act and an agent (owners should control their dogs; friends should prevent each other from committing wrongful acts of which they are aware). As Greenspan notes, guilt consists in two perspectives. First, 'a "forward-looking" instrumental assessment in relation to action'.[25] Here guilt motivates towards reparation. Secondly, a backward-looking non-instrumental dimension of negative self-assessment and recognition of wrongdoing. This, in a sense, is alienation from past self and action; creating a moral distance from the self which reparation will close down. Occurrent emotional guilt involves adopting a negative attitude towards the self, and is itself a negative emotional state. It typically involves a disposition to reparative action. Guilt expiates itself only through penance or reparation. The self-punishment of the negative attitude towards oneself is part of this penance.

Shame is the humiliating feeling of having appeared unfavourably in one's own eyes or the eyes of others by offence, deficiency, or exposure, or a similar feeling on behalf of something or someone one associates with oneself. As

[22] ibid. 153–4.

[23] For related theories of group guilt, see Dworkin *Law's Empire* 171–5 and Gilbert *Living Together: Rationality Sociality, and Obligation* ch. 14.

[24] Williams *Shame and Necessity* 89–90.

[25] Greenspan *Practical Guilt: Moral Dilemmas, Emotions, and Social Norms* 120.

Michael Lewis notes: 'Shame is elicited when one experiences failure relative to a standard (one's own or other people's), feels responsible for the failure, and believes that the failure reflects a damaged self'.[26] Shame however, seems less ineliminably personal than guilt. I might feel shame as a human, for the slaughtering of animals every year for nutritional and cosmetic purposes. Alternatively, I might feel a sympathetic shame for one unable to experience an equivalent emotion.[27] Shame, unlike guilt, does not seem to be an essentially moral emotion.[28] Guilt also seems more other-regarding.[29] While guilt tries to heal its object, shame conceals its object. Where guilt or shame would be appropriate reactions to personal actions or traits, anger (or outrage), or disapproval (or disgust) would correspond to the similar actions of others. Much more could and should be said here, but this is enough to facilitate broad analysis.[30]

What would we say of a polity member expressing a sense of collective guilt or shame? As Gilbert notes, two radical critiques would accuse the citizen of confusion. The anti-holist would construe ascriptions of collective guilt as instances of metaphysical holism, implying the existence of the polity as an entity separate and apart from the citizenry, and would deny any separate reality to this entity. The methodological individualist would construe ascriptions of collective guilt as necessarily referring to the aggregate guilt of individual members of a group.[31]

But let us suppose that the individual has a coherent notion of collective guilt whereby she does not believe herself personally guilty of any wrong, but as a member of a group which has committed some wrong, believes she shares in a collective guilt that is not derivative from, or reducible to, individual guilt.[32]

[26] Lewis 'Shame and Stigma' 126.

[27] Smith *The Theory of Moral Sentiments* II. i. 2.5 at 71: (of the dead): 'we feel upon this, as upon many other occasions, an emotion which the person principally concerned is incapable of feeling, and which yet we feel by an illusive sympathy with him'.

[28] Rawls *A Theory of Justice* 440–6, 479–85; Luban 'Intervention and Civilization: Some Unhappy Lessons of the Kosovo War' 99: 'Shame betokens inadequacy, not wrongdoing. We experience shame when we fail (and especially when we are seen by others to fail), and by failing reveal that we are less than we set ourselves up to be . . . even if the failure is not culpable, it diminishes us'.

[29] 'Guilt' may occur in contexts where it refers to an agent's feelings of disappointment in himself. Consider a person who says, after a meal, that he feels guilty for his greed. He realizes that he should have been more restrained and he considers his self-indulgence a shortcoming. This is distinct from feeling shame for having seemed gluttonous in front of others. He believes he has let himself down, and this moral disappointment grounds his feelings of guilt. (This common idea is interesting in so far as it suggests that, in the experience of the everyday, the notion of owing oneself moral duties is intuitively obvious.) On non-moral guilt, see Morris 'Nonmoral Guilt' in *Responsibility, Character, and the Emotions* ch. 9, discussed critically by Deigh in 'All Kinds of Guilt'. There is also Jaspers's related notion of 'metaphysical guilt': 'There exists a solidarity among men as human beings that makes each responsible for every wrong and every injustice in the world, especially for crimes committed in his presence or with his knowledge. If I fail to do whatever I can to prevent them, I too am guilty. . . . That I live after such a thing has happened weighs upon me as indelible guilt.' (Quoted and discussed in Luban 'Intervention and Civilization: Some Unhappy Lessons of the Kosovo War' 96–100.)

[30] Michael Stocker (with Elizabeth Hegeman) provides an excellent analysis of shame in *Valuing Emotions* 217–30.

[31] Gilbert *Sociality and Responsibility: New Essays in Plural Subject Theory* (hereafter, Gilbert, *Sociality and Responsibility*) 142–3.

[32] See Gilbert 'On Feeling Guilt for What One's Group Has Done' in *Living Together: Rationality, Sociality, and Obligation* and 'The Idea of Collective Guilt' in *Sociality and Responsibility*. Burleigh

I noted above that guilt has a vicarious aspect only where we are causally or morally linked to an agent that might be considered an extension of the self. I cannot, intelligibly, feel guilt for something that I perceive as 'other'. Thus, the citizen who genuinely feels guilt for the acts of her nation does identify with it. She perceives it as associated with and not distinct from herself. However, one can identify with something that is neither an aspect, nor (partly) constitutive, of one's identity. Identity and identification are logically separate, though linked concepts. Much identification could occur by default. Excepting the possibility of emigration, I can only identify as a citizen of the state of which I am a member (by territory, birth, or blood). Membership is often this colourless and thin. Just as the individual begins to understand herself in opposition to others, the community member understands herself as part of something distinct from, or in opposition to, others. But distancing from the self and identity may already have occurred. Identification, like membership, often occurs by a blind process of inclusion and exclusion. This fact alone should make us cautious in the face of local affinities. Group sympathies are often birthmarks seen only in the sun of hostile social interactions.

The identification necessary for experiencing intelligible collective guilt need bear no relation to one's sense of identity. Nor need one feel guilt at all. Other emotions are intelligible. In the face of a collective wrong, the self-alienation of personal guilt may become alienation from the group. Anger and resentment will now be felt towards one's own polity. Thomas Nagel refers to one such incident, during the Vietnam War: 'Citizenship is a surprisingly strong bond, even for those of us whose patriotic feelings are weak. We read the newspapers every day with rage and horror, and it was different from reading about the crimes of another country.'[33] Essentially, though guilt and Nagel's outrage are only intelligible if one identifies with a group, one need not identify with the group at all, and one may identify in a way that falls short of this group constituting part of one's identity. Collective guilt tells us something, but not enough, about the implications of membership.[34]

What, then, of the nature of identification? A combination of the claims from normative independence and the identification thesis culminate in a claim concerning the self-justifying nature of certain institutional involvements. Some institutional obligations, through their deep-rooted link to our sense of who we are and our place in the world, have a particularly fundamental role in our moral being. These institutional involvements generate moral obligations and

Wilkins, Jan Narveson, and Virginia Held discuss this and related aspects of Gilbert's work in the dedicated volume of *The Journal of Ethics* 6 (2002) 115–98.

[33] Nagel *Mortal Questions* p. xii. See also Nagel *Equality and Partiality* 84.

[34] Kautz *Liberalism and Community* 142 n. 13 provides an interesting contrast between Alasdair MacIntyre's patriotism which is ineliminably particular, and where the primary object of concern is community and not the ideals it promotes, and the idea of patriotism conveyed in Abraham Lincoln's eulogy for Henry Clay. Lincoln observes: 'He loved his country partly because it was his country, but mostly because it was a free country'. Sometimes, for some people, principles upheld or violated are more significant than the particularity of the party involved.

are self-justifying. This is the channel through which membership flows into political obligation. A member of a community identifies with that community and this leads to political obligation as the institutional obligation binding through membership of a polity.

Identification now seems parasitic on the normative self-sufficiency of social practices. However, as Simmons notes, 'Only if our identities are partly constituted by our roles in local practices that do independently generate moral obligations can the unintelligibility of denying our role responsibilities give us any reason to ascribe moral obligations'.[35] Moreover, identification, alongside recognition, acknowledgement, and cognate concepts, operate within the same logical and normative space which voluntariness fills in individualistic accounts. Identification, however, cannot operate as a surrogate voluntarism without collapsing the account into a diluted individualism.

For Horton, parenthood bears obligation. Citizenship is a morally laden concept and role. Each of these institutionally defined positions can generate obligations for its incumbents. Horton suggests that we do sometimes regard positional duties as morally binding without reference to any further moral principle. Examples from unjust institutional practices and institutions are not counterexamples. Institutional duties do not exist in a vacuum. Moral principles may show a particular institution to be unjust and its obligations non-binding, but they do not ground any obligations that do exist. That an institutional role does not violate any moral principles does not entail that its obligations are justified by these principles.[36] I will first analyse the basic idea of the normative independence of institutional practices and then return to Horton's particular model.

IDENTIFICATION, INSTITUTIONS, AND NORMATIVE INDEPENDENCE

Of institutions and their obligations, Gewirth has observed:'[I]nstitutions are constituted by rules which define what men are required to do if they are to participate in the respective functions or activities [which the institution serves] . . . and these requirements are the obligations which men have qua such participants'.[37]

Rules constitutive of institutions create requirements that impose institutional obligations on participants in institutional activities. Simmons, describing positional duties, observes the following: 'To say of a man that he has a positional duty to do A . . . is to say that because he occupies a certain position, role, or office within some established scheme or institution, he is required (or at least expected) by the scheme or institution to do A, as part of the "job" of a person in that position'.[38]

[35] Simmons 'Associative Political Obligations' 82.
[36] Horton *Political Obligation* 156.
[37] Gewirth 'Obligation: Political, Legal and Moral' 57.
[38] Simmons *Moral Principles* 17.

The only significant distinction between the two duties is that positional duties (PD) are possibly, but not necessarily, institutionally circumscribed, whereas institutional obligations (IO) are so by definition. In discussing IO and PD, I will focus on institutions defined by constitutive, and neither regulative nor instrumental, rules. Only in the former case is the connection between the institution and its requirements logical.

A fusion of the arguments from identification and normative independence triggers the question—can an IO/PD ever constitute the ground of a moral obligation, the latter reflecting the content of the IO/PD? Could one ever say: 'X has an IO/PD to ϕ therefore X has a moral obligation to ϕ?'

This is a central issue. If there is a conceptual connection between IO and moral obligation, the former being capable of grounding and generating the latter, then it could be argued that legal obligation is an IO, and can thus independently morally bind its subjects. This echoes the conceptual linguistic analysis, by suggesting the existence of a conceptual link between legitimate authority/law/government and obligation/obedience. In the present case, a conceptual link is advanced to suggest an analytic link between membership (citizenship) and obligation. What, then, is the nature of the conceptual link between IO/PD and moral obligation?

Following Gewirth and Stocker,[39] we can note the following. Grounds are conceptually linked to obligations. It must be shown that IOs relate to moral obligations as grounds link to obligation for the conceptual link to be made out. Consider the following statements. X, a lawyer, has an IO to be ethical in her dealings with clients, as required by standards of professional responsibility. X also has a moral obligation to deal ethically with her clients. The 'institutionalist' (to use Stocker's phrase) will argue that, if X is morally obligated to deal ethically with his clients where such action is impossible in the absence of the institution of law, the moral obligation to behave in this manner is at least partially attributable to this institution.

We may concede certain weaker claims associated with this very strong claim.[40] First, the professional ethics of legal practice do *logically* presuppose the institution of law. The institution is a necessary precondition of the obligations that follow. Moreover, on entering the institution of law X must, logically, conform to the requirements of the institution in order to consider herself a lawyer. However, while the institution of law is a logical precondition of obligation, it is not a ground of obligation. There is a necessary and non-analytic link between the two. While X must conform by the rules of the practice, this is a merely logical and non-moral must. The obligation to deal ethically with clients is a specification of the duty to act fairly, not to abuse positions of trust and responsibility. From the IO alone we cannot yet draw any moral conclusions

[39] Gewirth 'Obligation: Political, Legal and Moral' and Stocker 'Moral Duties, Institutions, and Natural Facts'. See also Simmons *Moral Principles* 16–24.

[40] Gewirth 'Obligation: Political, Legal and Moral' 57 and Stocker 'Moral Duties, Institutions, and Natural Facts' 604.

regarding action. In the absence of further specification of the content of any requirement, there remain unanswered questions as to whether the relevant institution is justified at all, whether this particular instantiation of the institution and this particular requirement are justified. While an IO/PD may be a necessary logical precondition of a moral obligation it does not constitute the ground of an obligation.

The fact of the existence of an institution may provide ancillary reasons—possibly moral ones, and possibly obligations—for conformity to institutional standards. This is because institutions and the rules that constitute them are common sources of social stability and organization. Expectations and reliance cluster around generally accepted social norms.[41] Thus we might say: '*X* has an IO to ϕ on the grounds of the moral obligation to act justly. But it is also just that he ϕ because *A*, *B* and *C* reasonably expect and rely upon him to do this.' Again, the institution is a precondition of the additional reason (possibly an obligation) but the moral ground remains the duty to act justly and not to frustrate the legitimate expectations of others. Here, the interplay of institutional norms and external social circumstances coalesce to make a moral obligation of the IO still ultimately grounded in the moral obligation to act justly.

Each individual is more than an aggregate of all the roles she occupies, or any particular role. Occupation of a role neither supersedes the self nor suspends responsibility for voluntary acts. The Nuremberg trials underwrote this principle. Justification of illegal and immoral killings in terms of occupation of the role of soldier suggests a deep amorality or irrationality. People do not bifurcate their personalities along the fault lines of different roles. Roles do place demands and institutional obligations on us. But we ultimately act as moral agents, cognizant of all our reasons for action.[42]

Horton combines two theses, one moral and one phenomenological or logical. The moral thesis holds that certain identifications become central to our sense of who we are, 'a self-understanding which characteristically has a fundamentally moral dimension'.[43] The phenomenological thesis suggests that political identity exemplifies one such identification. Does Horton also include the logical thesis that such identification, due to the personal incoherence of denying certain roles non-contingently connected to the self, is necessary? He cannot. For elsewhere he observes that, 'though membership of a particular polity is not usually chosen, it does not follow that it cannot be rejected or renounced'.[44] It is not logically incoherent for an individual not to identify as a member of her polity. It is simply that some appear to do so.

[41] See also Stocker 'Moral Duties, Institutions, and Natural Facts' 612.

[42] For two interesting works around this point, see Cohen 'Beliefs and Roles' and Downie *Roles and Values: An Introduction to Social Ethics*.

[43] Horton *Political Obligation* 157.

[44] ibid. 158. At 159, Horton also notes: 'nothing in what has been said implies that persons *must* think and feel about "their polity" in the manner indicated; only that if they do this is a manifestation of their recognition of themselves as members of a particular polity'.

What is the idea of the moral thesis? Consider the case of some membership that is so basic to my identity as to be self-evidently significant. If I genuinely identify myself as an *X*, I cannot logically deny the responsibilities of an *X*, unless living in bad faith. I have the duties of this role as delineated by local cultural practice. This is a logical and not a moral point about how I understand my world.

Two linked points are now vital. There is no intrinsic moral value in identifying with a morally unworthy object.[45] The white supremacist member of the Ku Klux Klan may have a feeling of Aryan kinship with his fellow members that he will be subjectively gratifying. But this will never sound in moral duties (related to the object of this association). We cannot be morally obligated to perform immoral acts. This links to the idea that self-understanding in respect of certain roles need not be an intrinsically moral notion. Some people engage in deeply harmful practices and institutions. What is self-evident to some people may be opaque and immoral to others. The terms in which I justify my beliefs and actions to others cannot be the subjective dead-end of 'this is simply the way it is'. Justification to others should be in moral terms.

Horton has provided neither a compelling moral nor a deep logical premise. Membership need not be embraced. This has two implications. Horton's model now falls into the second acknowledgement model above, acknowledgement as *application*. Voluntaristic notions re-enter through the door of the implicit voluntariness of identification. Secondly, his thesis is in danger of losing any stretch on the methodological axis of duty–subject universality. Horton seems implicitly aware of this point. He thus asks whether *X* can renounce political obligations while remaining, as against generally accepted criteria, a member of the polity.

For Horton, certain typical patterns of conduct manifest *X*'s recognition of himself as a member of a particular polity. In recognizing himself as a member, *X* also acknowledges the attendant political obligations. *X* may claim to lack such thoughts and feelings, but his actions will often betray otherwise. Political obligation is often implicitly recognized through observance of membership in various ways: participation in political life; observing community rules, and cooperating in a manner appropriate to membership. Lacking these thoughts and feelings attendant on membership is not necessarily evidenced by their explicit denial. Conforming conduct testifies to identification with membership, even where verbally denied.[46]

[45] This is not to preclude the possibility that such organizations have valuable instrumental benefits, for example, that they constrain individuals who would otherwise be dangerous and disaffected loners in a social context that allows for closer supervision of anti-social activities. Questions could also be raised as to whether we should judge associations not by what they do for general social well-being but what they contribute to the lives of their members. (And members could have obligations to each other not related to the object of the association. A promise to baby-sit should be kept amongst members.) Nancy Rosenblum considers these themes in *Membership and Morals: The Personal Uses of Pluralism in America*.

[46] Horton *Political Obligation* 158–67.

This is a bizarre behaviouristic twist to a position so reliant on the affective attitudes of those obligated. The above claims are empirically falsified where *X* participates to overthrow or radically alter the present social order or *X* obeys for reasons of self-interest or prudence, or on account of contingent agreement with the substance of individual directives. Where *X* cooperates in a manner appropriate to a member of the community and yet verbally denies self-conceptualization in these terms, the more obvious inference is that he has reasons of principle for denying such classification.

It is strange to foist obligation on an agent on the basis of what can (questionably) be inferred from his actions when identification with the community bridges from membership to obligation. It is strange because what is essentially an expression of personality transmutes into a behaviouristic interpretation of conduct. Affective attitudes are only valuable where directed at valuable objects and genuinely felt. Otherwise, they are empty of meaning.

The final submission of Horton's account bridges between political obligation and the obligation to obey. He provides only a conceptual foundation for political obligation, allowing local cultures to construct the substantive superstructure. Obedience is distinct from obligation, though obedience is probably the norm. Obligation requires taking into account the welfare and interests of the polity. If law sketches the parameters of association of the polity with which *X* identifies, and of which he is a member, acknowledging the authority of these laws seems a natural consequence of membership and identification.

The difficulty with Horton's suggestion is that there may be smaller sub-state groups with which individuals identify more closely and which are thus more natural means through which to express identity. The relationship between citizenship and identity is ostensibly antonymic. Citizenship is a universal, equalizing status, identification a particular, relational phenomenon.[47] An account defending the centrality of identification with the polity must resolve these tensions. Moreover, in a community in which many of the laws were framed and formalized by a supra-statal group, particularity would be threatened. And in a community where much of social regulation derived from custom or convention, law would not be directly implicated.

Loyalty and identification are not always spatial relationships of shared territory. Identification with other groups may be the catalyst that brings law into question.[48] Above all, identity is a ubiquitous but shifting thing. To attempt to prescribe it is therefore like trying to draw a map of the clouds.

[47] See Isin and Wood (eds) *Citizenship & Identity* 14–24.

[48] See, again, Dunn 'Political Obligation' 71. History is populated with state repression of internal groups seeking to assert an identity distinct from that of the nation or state. Parekh notes in 'Reconstituting the Modern State' 41: 'The state and the citizen represent two interdependent polarities of the political relationship, each defined in formal and abstract terms. Since the two are directly related, the modern state is suspicious of and feels threatened by well-organised ethnic, national and other communities lest they should mediate its relations with its citizens, and set up rival foci of loyalty.'

Horton's account, though flawed, contains a germ of important truth. If I genuinely consider myself a member of *X*, this entails certain responsibilities. Otherwise I live unintelligibly or in bad faith. Social and institutional practices define these responsibilities. However, Horton's errors are also important. He conceives of political obligation as an essential concomitant of membership in a polity. Since membership does not normally result from a voluntary undertaking, neither, *a fortiori*, does political obligation. This necessarily presupposes a biological or territorial sense of membership, and not moral membership. However, the entirely coherent possibility, conceded by Horton, of rejecting membership implies a moral membership that does involve the will and voluntarism. To conceive of oneself as a member will entail certain reasons for action, sources of identification, and so on. However, one must first conceive of oneself as a member. This self-conception may have a voluntary aspect, grounded in acts and choices within an agent's life (choosing to embrace a role or not to reject a locus of identification). Moreover, there is a criterion of value-dependence constraining the act of identification itself. There is just no moral value whatsoever in the Ku Klux Klan association discussed above. As the discussion of Raz's theory of respect in Chapter 2 demonstrated, either value or voluntarism is necessary to convert reasonable amoral expectations into moral requirements. It is permissible for the individual to identify with a just state in a way that generates a robust obligation, but that is all.

RONALD DWORKIN AND COMMUNAL OBLIGATIONS

In *Law's Empire*, Ronald Dworkin justifies political obligation through an account of communal obligation. A complex congeries of theories constitutes the backdrop to this claim, which I will adumbrate before discussing Dworkin's theory.

INTEGRITY, INTERPRETATION, AND LEGITIMACY

Theories of law attempt to account for the nature of law. This requires some minimal consensus on the central concept of law, so that rival theorists can know that they enter combat on the same battlefield and not on a semantic no-man's land. Dworkin's concept of law ascribes to it the following purpose: 'Law insists that force not be used or withheld, no matter how useful that would be to ends in view, no matter how beneficial or noble these ends, except as licensed or required by individual rights and responsibilities flowing from past political decisions about when collective force is justified'.[49] A conception of law must tell us whether the connection between law and coercion is justified at all, whether there is any point in requiring that public force only be used in ways that

[49] Dworkin *Law's Empire* 93.

conform to rights and responsibilities flowing from past political decisions, and how best to account for this notion of 'flow from'.[50]

Dworkin's conception of law, and hence his jurisprudence, revolves around the claim that law consists not merely in the explicit past decisions of a society's political institutions, but incorporates also 'whatever other standards flow from the principles these decisions assume'.[51] Law comprises all principles of personal and public morality presupposed by, or flowing from, the justification for such decisions. The explanatory power of this theory of law rests partially upon success in providing a justification for the use of coercion. For Dworkin, this problem of the legitimacy of the exercise of coercive power runs concurrently with the problem of political obligation. Obligation is not a sufficient condition for justified coercion (since no government should enforce all of its citizens' legal obligations),[52] but it is close to being a necessary condition. Justification of political legitimacy through communal obligation is thus pivotal to Dworkin's jurisprudence.

Within the context of *Law's Empire*, this jurisprudence is articulated as 'law as integrity'. Integrity is advanced, by extrapolation from the personal virtue of integrity, as a distinct ideal in politics, one which may clash with justice or fairness, and which cannot thus be reduced to either. Community or fraternity is the ground on which Dworkin defends integrity as a distinct ideal. A political society accepting integrity as a political virtue becomes a special form of community, in a way that warrants its assumption of a monopoly on coercive force. Integrity hereby links back to the very concept of law that addresses the legitimacy of coercive force.

Political integrity assumes a profound personification of the community. It assumes that the community as a whole can be committed to principles of fairness, justice, and procedural due process. The argument supporting this deep personification assigns no metaphysical priority to community, but rather derives from political morality. Community is characterized as a separate moral agent because social and intellectual practices that so conceptualize community should be promoted.[53]

Dworkin's jurisprudence centrally involves the idea of an interpretive attitude. Law, integrity, and justice are all interpretive concepts. Legal interpretation is constructive interpretation. As noted in Chapter 1, this involves interpreting an object or practice in light of a purpose rendering it the *best possible example* of the genre to which it is believed to belong. The purposes deployed in interpretation are those of the interpreter, not the author. Still, the history and mould of the practice will constrain permissible interpretations. The interpreter proposes a purpose for the practice by articulating a scheme of interests and principles expressed within the practice.[54] If the basic forms of a practice under-determine interpretation—yielding distinct or inconsistent interpret-

[50] Dworkin *Law's Empire*, 94. [51] ibid. 188. [52] ibid. 191.
[53] ibid. 187–8. [54] ibid. 52.

ations—the interpreter must choose the interpretation that frames the practice in its best light.[55] The two essential criteria of constructive interpretation are descriptive fit (a reasonably accurate reflection of actual practices) and normative justification (imputing some defensible normative purpose to the practice).

Dworkin is explicating a conception of law appropriate to a community of communal fraternity. Only this society will adequately meet the normative conditions of communal obligation. Only the satisfaction of these conditions demonstrates the legitimacy of obedience to government. Such a community necessarily instantiates law as integrity. Consequently, the justification of political as communal obligation is a pivotal step in Dworkin's jurisprudence.[56] To whatever extent this thesis is flawed, the general enquiry loses justificatory force.

ASSOCIATIVE OBLIGATIONS

Dworkin refers generically to 'associative or communal obligations' as 'the special responsibilities social practice attaches to membership in some biological or social group, like the responsibilities of family or friends or neighbors'.[57] In establishing political as communal obligation, Dworkin must overcome two acknowledged and likely objections. First, communal obligations are thought to depend upon emotional bonds that presuppose personal acquaintance among members of the group. This is clearly not true of large-scale political societies. Secondly, the idea of special communal obligations uniting such a large group introduces the spectres of nationalism and racism. Dworkin's account must successfully navigate these twin channels.

What, then, is the nature of communal obligations? The history of our social practices defines the communal groups to which we belong and their attendant obligations. Obligation enters by the following route: 'We have a duty to honor our responsibilities under social practices that define groups and attach special responsibilities to membership, but this natural duty holds only when certain other conditions are met or sustained. Reciprocity is prominent among these other conditions.'[58]

This is the first stroke in a complex sketch of communal obligations. Communal obligations are generically grounded in a natural duty to honour the responsibilities social practices define, subject to certain conditions being met. The ground of communal obligation is a conditional natural duty. The first of these general conditions is reciprocity; the practice 'of accepting a kind of responsibility we need the companion ideas of integrity and interpretation to explain'.[59] This reciprocity feeds down into the circumstances in which communal obligations might obtain: 'Associative obligations can be sustained among people who

[55] ibid. 52–3. [56] See also Gans *Anarchism* 86–7 n. 91.
[57] Dworkin *Law's Empire* 196. [58] ibid. 198. [59] ibid. 198–9.

share a general and diffuse sense of members' special rights and responsibilities from or toward one another'.[60]

Dworkin stipulates four conditions necessary for the generation of specifically fraternal political obligations. First, obligations owed within the group are *special* and thus are not owed to non-members. This condition meets the requirement of particularity. Integrity is more particular than universalistic justice. Obligations flow internal to communities. This is buttressed by the fact that integrity 'holds within political communities, not among them'.[61] Particularity is internal to the idea of fidelity to the principles of a particular community. Secondly, they are *personal*—owed from one member to all others individually and not to the group as an abstract entity. This illustrates the strongly individualist and non-communitarian flavour of the account.[62] Community is relational and not an entity *per se*. It is neither ethically nor ontologically prior to the individual. Dworkin thirdly suggests that the responsibilities flow from a more general responsibility of *concern* for the well-being of all others in the group, from which discrete responsibilities derive. Finally this concern is conceptually egalitarian. Practices show *equal* concern for all.

Where satisfied, these conditions convert the responsibilities owed among members of a community into fraternal obligations and transform a bare into a true community. A bare community satisfies the genetic, geographic, and historical conditions social practice prescribes for qualification as a fraternal community. A true community is a bare community instantiating special, personal, and equal concern.

These conditions on obligation are interpretive and not psychological. Dworkin insists that he is making neither an empirical sociological claim about the occurrent attitudes of citizens within a community nor a claim about a psychological property of a determinate number of members. The conditions are interpretive and entail that if the best interpretation of social practices manifests

[60] Dworkin *Law's Empire* 199.

[61] ibid. 185.

[62] Dworkin's agent is a solitary associativist. This individualism similarly informs Dworkin's theory of civil disobedience: 'A citizen's allegiance is to the law, not to any particular person's view of what the law is, and he does not behave unfairly so long as he proceeds on his own considered and reasonable view of what the law requires.' *Taking Rights Seriously* 214; his theory of interpretation: 'Political obligation ... becomes ... fidelity to a scheme of principle each citizen has a responsibility to identify, ultimately for himself, as his community's scheme'. *Law's Empire* 190; and his general conception of the individual within political society: 'Someone who believes in his own responsibility for the central values of his life cannot yield that responsibility to a group, even if he has an equal vote in its deliberations. A genuine political community must therefore be a community of independent moral agents. It must not dictate what its citizens think about matters of political or moral or ethical judgment, but must, on the contrary, provide circumstances that encourage them to arrive at beliefs on these matters through their own reflective and finally individual conviction.' *Freedom's Law: The Moral Reading of the American Constitution* 26. For further articulations of Dworkin's individualism see 'Foundations of Liberal Equality' and 'Liberal Community'. In these works, Dworkin accommodates the notion of the social embeddedness of the self and actual substantive communal goods, while asserting the liberal value of neutrality and the primacy of the individual and her rights. The individual living an integrated communal life realizes the connection between the good of the group and her own well-being.

the necessary concern, we have a sound foundation for communal obligation. However, Dworkin also admits that 'the members of a group must by and large hold certain attitudes about the responsibilities they owe one another if these responsibilities are to count as genuine fraternal obligations'.[63]

Reality must to some extent map onto interpretation. A group will not be maintained as such unless members genuinely feel some emotional bonds to each other. Yet, the conditions, being interpretive, do not demand it.[64] Nor need obligations of fraternity be fully voluntary. 'If the conditions are met, people in the bare community have the obligations of a true community *whether or not they want them*, though of course the conditions will not be met unless most members recognize and honor these obligations'.[65]

Dworkin suggests that we do naturally imagine society as associative when considering the notions of special and personal concern. This is a phenomenological claim about our understanding of our social and political lives: We do suppose that we have special interests in, and that we owe determinate duties towards, members of communal groups to which we belong.[66] Moreover, we treat community as antecedent to justice and fairness in so far as we regard questions concerning each as questions of what constitutes fairness or justice in a particular community (justice has an impliedly geographical element).

In seeking to meet the remaining condition of equal concern, Dworkin offers three models of community. First, *de facto* community. Here members of the community treat their association as a historical and geographic accident; a community of contingency. Secondly, there is rulebook community. Here concern is mandatory but perfunctory. Members obey the rules through a sense of obligation (as opposed to self-interest and so on), but believe that these exhaust their responsibilities. Thirdly, there is the community of principle. This last model renders the requisite concern and reciprocity and is, for Dworkin, the best interpretation of our own political practices. In a community of principle each accepts that she has rights and obligations arising from the scheme, even where these are not formally delineated. Each accepts political integrity as a distinct political ideal and considers general acceptance of the ideal (even amongst those with substantive disagreements) as constitutive of political morality. This community claims the authority of a genuine associative community. The obligations of membership are defined by local and interpretive practices, and the 'central obligation is that of general fidelity to law, the obligation political philosophy has found so problematic'.[67]

One final condition limits the generation of communal obligations: the constraint of justice. A community might perpetrate two kinds of injustice. First, it may, internally, have a defective conception of equal concern for its members. Secondly, it may, externally, perpetrate injustice against non-members. Social practice may define an unjust grouping as associative. However, social practices

[63] Dworkin *Law's Empire* 199. [64] ibid. 201. [65] ibid. 201 (emphasis added).
[66] ibid. 206–8. [67] ibid. 208 (and generally, 208–12).

are subject to interpretation, and justice participates in all interpretations. Justice may allow or require an interpretation that omits unjust aspects of a practice where these are inconsistent with the whole. However, the best interpretation of a practice may sometimes yield the conclusion that it is simply unjust.[68]

It is time to summarize, and to review the manner in which Dworkin has dealt with problems he anticipated in his account. Communal obligations are grounded in a natural duty, subject to general constraints of reciprocity and justice. Political obligations are subject to the four additional constraints that there be special, personal, and equal concern. They are not necessarily voluntary.

The first problem Dworkin anticipated was that associative obligations presuppose personal acquaintance among members of a group. The account from concern as an interpretive practice solves this problem. The second anticipated objection was that communal obligations in a vast political community betray nationalism. Dworkin's introduction of justice within, and as a constraint on, interpretation deals with this problem: 'any conflict between militant nationalism and standards of justice must be resolved in favour of the latter'.[69]

What of objections Dworkin does not anticipate? I will focus on four issues. First, the role of psychological conditions in the community of principle. Secondly, the true nature and grounds of Dworkin's communal obligations. Thirdly, whether Dworkin accounts for the actual obligations of citizens in existing states. Finally, I will articulate some possible counter-attacks by rival theorists.

The discussion of Dworkin's conditions on communal obligation revealed the following. The level of concern required for communal obligations is an interpretive property of the group's practices in acknowledging responsibilities. It is not a psychological property of a determinate number of the members of a community. The claim is neither empirical nor sociological. It is interpretive. However, there is an empirical proviso: 'a group will rarely meet or long sustain... unless its members by and large actually feel some emotional bond with one another'.[70]

This position has attracted criticism.[71] Dworkin seems to intend the following. The theory aims to establish the moral authority of law. It is the legal institutions', and not the citizens', practices that must be justified. The requisite level of concern is established through a moral judgment of the group's actual practices. These practices must exhibit this concern. Actual psychological concern need not be present, though our interpretation must be consistent with the presence of such concern.

The main criticism of Dworkin's thinking here tends to concern the disavowal of psychological factors. Wellman suggests that the specific nature of the disavowal is unclear, and that, in any event, this is inconsistent with an associativist account.[72] I will start with consideration of these two points.

[68] Dworkin *Law's Empire* 202–3. [69] ibid. 206. [70] ibid. 201.

[71] Simmons 'Associative Political Obligations' 77–9; Wellman 'Associative Allegiances and Political Obligations' 190–4.

[72] Wellman 'Associative Allegiances and Political Obligations' 191–2.

There is a distinction between associative bonds between determinate but anonymous others, and associative bonds between intimates. This distinction does not separate the psychological from the non-psychological. Both sets of attitudes (as attitudes necessarily are) are psychological. The idea of associative bonds between determinate but anonymous others, however, calls for no actual knowledge or love of specific persons. Dworkin wants to fend off the associativist's challenge that love and emotion must mediate associative bonds. He need only maintain the possibility of the former type of bond in order to keep descriptive faith to our moral experience of modern community. He does not need to assert absolute purity from psychological factors. Nor does he. Aside from the qualifying provisos above, much of his language has a psychological tint. Dworkin talks of 'our instinct of group responsibility'[73] and of an 'emotional bond'.[74] Given this language, a modified conception of association mediating distant relations, but with minimal psychological content, may aid theoretical consistency. This modified conception is not hard to make out. Associative bonds can be geographical, ideological, or personal. Ties of empathy can transcend specific knowledge of other determinate individuals. What assumes salience is a particular shared cause, culture, or characteristic.[75] However, would adopting this conception create difficulties for Dworkin? In weakening the emotional content of associative bonds in order to accommodate political reality, do we also empty them of necessary normative force? Are these psychological bonds moral, normative, or sentimental? Can these bonds yield obligations and what types of obligations do they yield?

At this point, another distinction is necessary, between the concern instantiated in a community's practices and the concern citizens feel for each other. Even if we believe that the bonds between citizens are associative and can generate obligations (a point I consider in detail below) they would be horizontal obligations. In Chapter 1, I noted the difference between horizontal and vertical accounts of legitimacy. Dworkin's primary concern is the vertical. Horizontal associative bonds are redundant to the main enquiry. This may explain why Dworkin feels able to deny psychological elements as a necessary condition on obligation. But it does raise the question as to why the account is defended in terms of associative bonds. What is presented as the main dish increasingly becomes garnish. Dworkin is not primarily focused on the horizontal but must incorporate it for two reasons. First, the character of a community's practices can only be evidenced in the actual conduct and attitudes of its members. The two cannot coherently be divorced. Secondly, he must maintain an associative veneer.

[73] Dworkin *Law's Empire* 189 and 183 for talk of 'instincts'.

[74] ibid. 201.

[75] On this construction, Dworkin's conception of community is not as rich as MacIntyre's idea that community can be 'composed of a network of small groups of friends, in Aristotle's sense of that word...the sharing of all in the common project of creating and sustaining the life of the city'. MacIntyre *After Virtue* 156. This, descriptively, is a strength.

Perhaps Dworkin is trying, in one very rushed move, to account for both vertical and horizontal obligation (while prioritizing the vertical) because of its importance to the success of his conception of law. The idea may be that in outlining a holistic image of a community of principle, we will have a rich fresco of fraternity justifying both horizontal and vertical obligations. Much of Dworkin's writing suggests that there is merit in this observation. Throughout the discussion of law as integrity, he treats state and community as equivalents: 'Integrity becomes a political ideal when we make the same demand of the state or community taken to be a moral agent';[76] 'Do I really mean to attribute to the state or community principles that are not simply those of most of its members?'[77]

Does Dworkin really mean so wholly to assimilate state and community? If the horizontal and the vertical merge in this manner, attitudes are again important. If state and community form one moral agent, then the coherence of its practices should be pervasive. Dworkin cannot now equivocate over the significance of the horizontal. And he must provide a clear account of why associative bonds, particularly those defined by social practice and holding between relative strangers, will function as obligations in the practical reasoning of citizens.

Associative links may underpin various levels of commitment. They may be understood as a source of simple sentimental bonds. They may be seen as a legitimate source of allegiance and loyalty, upon which the agent morally *may* act.[78] Members of the associative group may understand them as a source of reasonable expectations in their interactions. Members and/or outsiders may perceive them as a source of moral demands and obligations. In order to understand Dworkin's communal obligations, we must analyse the nature of the relationship between social practices and the conditions of reciprocity, justice, and fraternity.

At least two alternative analyses are possible. First, local practices are strongly subject to the necessary conditions on obligation. Prior to satisfying these constraints, practices explicate the internally reasonable expectations of fellow community members: the practices, roles, and expectations social history has shaped. They are not moral obligations until the conditions of reciprocity, and justice and fraternity, have been met. Once these are met, the reasonable expectations are translated into moral obligations.

On the second model, the expectations of local practice have a bi-partite structure. On the first level, the 'duty to honor our responsibilities under social practices that define groups and attach special responsibilities to membership'[79] is a genuine moral duty. On the second level we have associative political obligation. This will only subsist in a community with a legal system

[76] Dworkin *Law's Empire* 166. [77] ibid. 168.
[78] See also Mason 'Special Obligations to Compatriots' 438–9.
[79] Dworkin *Law's Empire* 198.

conforming to law as integrity, satisfying the conditions of fraternity, reciprocity, and justice. This obligation links to the legitimate moral authority of government.

On the first model, when Dworkin observes that 'this natural duty holds only when certain other conditions are met or sustained'[80] we understand 'holds' as connoting that only under these conditions are obligations generated *at all*. On the second model, we understand 'holds' as meaning that obligations already generated are *confirmed* (as opposed to cancelled) by external principles. This understanding ascribes limited normative independence to local practices. The distinction between the two models is that between internally reasonable expectations and externally legitimate moral obligations.

Dworkin does not explicitly address the matter. But he does observe, when discussing a gravely unjust community that 'though the obligations it imposes are prima-facie genuine, the question arises whether the injustice is so severe and deep that these obligations are canceled'.[81] His position seems to be a variant of the second model, and indeed must be in order to be associativist. The obligations of local practice, prior to satisfying the external constraints of justice, constitute prima-facie moral obligations. But failure to satisfy these constraints may result in these prima-facie obligations being *cancelled*. It is significant that Dworkin says 'canceled' and not overridden. This suggests, phenomenologically, that failure to perform the cancelled prima-facie obligation leaves no moral residue.[82]

A promise is *cancelled* when the promisee releases the promisor from the obligation to perform. What was born in agreement ends in agreement. The fact that my friend releases me from the obligation is not a reason for any action, but does cancel my obligation to perform the promise. A promise is *overridden*, when, for example, on my way to perform it, I stumble upon a stranger who needs my urgent help. The fact of the injured man is a reason for contradictory action that overrides my promissory reason to meet my friend.[83] In the former case, no apologies, no residue of guilt remains. In the latter, while no blame or guilt may attend failure, explanations and polite apologies should.

Use of 'canceled' may be a significant slip on Dworkin's part. Consider again the two possible interpretations of obligation considered above. I described the second model as follows. There is a natural moral duty to conform to local practices. Once social practices are subject to, and have passed, the tests of reciprocity and justice, these are confirmed as obligations. If they fail these tests, the obligations they generate may be cancelled. I constructed this model to fit the model Dworkin's comments seem to require. However, the model includes a suspicious intermediate stage that demands analysis. Let us chart the progression of Dworkin's obligation:

[80] ibid. [81] ibid. 204. [82] Williams *Moral Luck* 73–4.
[83] Raz *Practical Reason and Norms* 27, 180–1.

1. Social practices: genuine prima-facie natural (moral) duty to conform.
2. Conditions of reciprocity, justice, and fraternity satisfied: communal (moral) obligation to conform.

Now, these two are counterpoised in a manner that might imply that the first stage is that of prima-facie obligation and the second, that of conclusive obligation. But this is not the case. That we have communal obligations does not let us know that, in any particular case, this will be our conclusive obligation. It may or may not be, depending on countervailing reasons. So the final progression is:

1. (Social practices) genuine prima-facie natural duty;
2. (Conditions of justice and reciprocity satisfied) prima-facie communal obligation;
3. (Assuming certain facts about countervailing operative reasons) conclusive moral obligation.

But now we must ask what strange alchemy occurs between the first and second stages. The conversion from natural duty to communal obligation cannot relate to types of categorical force. Duties and obligations function identically in practical reasoning. Nor is it a mere linguistic shift indicating a difference in content. Both the natural duty and the communal obligation enjoin conformity to local practices. Is the communal obligation merely an instantiation of the natural duty, a species of a genus? But this solution would not yet explain why the genus to which the species belongs is moral as opposed to a locus of reasonable expectations. It would call for still deeper explanation.

Considering this point, we are faced with the prospect that the difference attaches to different senses of 'prima-facie' in the first and second stages. But here we face a Rossian worry.[84] A prima-facie obligation *is* a genuine obligation. It carries categorical force. It is not absolute and may not be judged conclusive, and may thus not be operative. However, if it is overridden, it is not simply eliminated. It remains to be accounted for in some other way. As Leslie Green warns,

> We must take care not to be misled by that fact that associative obligations may only claim prima-facie force. The normative character of an obligation is not identified by whether it is prima-facie or conclusive, but by the function it is meant to play in the practical reason of those whom it binds... the question is not whether, once [the reasons] are in the balance, they will win out against other considerations. The question is how and in what form they get onto the balance in the first place.[85]

The more sensible reading of Dworkin is:

1. Reasonable social expectations;
2. (Conditions of justice and reciprocity satisfied) prima-facie communal obligations;

[84] Ross *The Right and the Good* 20–34. Ross suggests that prima-facie duties are distinct from actual duties in that they are *tendencies to be duties*. For difficulties in this view: Shope 'Prima Facie Duty'; McCloskey 'Ross and the Concept of a Prima Facie Duty'; Simmons *Moral Principles* 24–8.

[85] Green 'Associative Obligations and the State' 103–4.

3. (Assuming certain facts about countervailing operative reasons) *conclusive* communal obligation.

The associative obligation is not grounded solely in social practice or Dworkin's natural duty. The ideas of reciprocity, equality, and justice seem to be shouldering much of the normative load. This can be put more acutely. Dworkin's point can be pared away to: 'We have a natural duty to uphold social practices, including the institutionalized practices of law, subject to the requirement that they be just, and so on. This applies to our local communities, because humans form primary attachments within these communities. This is an associative theory.' But associative obligations now seem no more than a relational mechanism particularizing a natural duty of justice that is a confused cousin of Rawls's related idea.

Perhaps Dworkin has a response. In the case of the cancelled promise, though the obligation is not conclusive (nor absolute, and therefore prima-facie), it is, prior to the issue of the cancelling condition, a genuine moral obligation. It is simply not ultimately binding. This, too, is the structure of associative political obligations. They are natural associative duties. Just as the promisee can cancel the promisor's obligation, so too can justice cancel the community member's obligation.

Does this work? Dworkin has suggested that the associative obligation is grounded in a 'natural duty' to honour our responsibilities under social practices. While promises, and the reasons they provide, may be subject to cancelling conditions, are natural duties similarly subject? We have a natural duty to help the needy stranger whose needs we can feasibly meet. Is this subject to cancelling conditions? Imagine a situation in which this might be thought true. You see an incompetent swimmer drowning in shallow waters. You dive in to rescue him. He urges you to stay away. He explains that this is his fourth suicide attempt, and he neither wants nor needs your help. Perceiving your philosophical pretensions, he shouts, 'I issue a cancelling condition. Your natural duty is cancelled, leave me alone.' Is moral responsibility cancelled? If Dworkin answers that it is, we might respond that this is not an example of a cancelled natural duty to aid. There was never a natural duty to aid the man by saving him, since he subjectively perceives only the need to be left alone.

But this is contrived. It is more fruitful to move inductively from phenomenology. I noted above the appropriateness of guilt in instances of overridden obligations and its absence in cases of cancelling conditions. Would the morally sensitive agent, persuaded by the stranger's hostile desperation, feel a residue of guilt in swimming away from him? It seems very likely that she would, and indeed, should. We do not think of natural duties and the reasons they provide as subject to cancelling conditions. Promises and agreements, as creatures of a single or joint will, seem properly prima-facie moral and subject to cancelling conditions. But natural duties seem to articulate that minimum core of morally decent conduct that could not reasonably be denied, and that the will, not having created, cannot destroy. The contingent world may create circumstances and facts that override natural duties. But we do not typically think of natural duties as subject to a cancelling will. Further, the intervention of a will in promise prima-facie creates an obligation. With regard to the patterns of conduct in a community of place, before we know of the role of value or voluntarism, we have only reasonable expectations.

What are the implications of this for Dworkin's conception of associative obligations? Perhaps he has mistaken their ground. Perhaps they do not reside in a *natural* duty, but in reasons of a different sort. But this suggestion implicitly moves towards a voluntarism Dworkin explicitly rejects. Perhaps they are grounded in something that, though natural, is *amoral*—instinct, affection, or the psychology of human creatures necessarily reared in a local context. But this suggestion robs Dworkin's bonds of obligatory force and emphasizes the challenge for theories of associative duties to explain how association generates obligations without implicating other moral principles within the grounds or necessary conditions of obligation. In Dworkin's structure, however, we are left with a socially defined practice that elaborates the reasonable expectations of participants. Only if the stages of reciprocity, equality, and justice are passed (and true community is instantiated) can we speak of obligation.

In Chapter 1, I noted that the criteria for a successful account require that a theory of obligation explain the *actual* moral obligations of citizens in *actual* societies. Does Dworkin's argument satisfy this methodological requirement?

Dworkin's account is insistently non-ideal. 'I am defending an interpretation of our own political culture, not an abstract and timeless political morality'.[86] However, certain remarks substantiate a reformist construction: 'we should try to conceive our political community as an association of principle'.[87] Dworkin's concluding sentence betrays a similar spirit. 'That is, anyway, what law is for us: for the people we want to be and the community we aim to have.'[88] Dworkin does, however, advance arguments in favour of the reality of integrity, along the dimensions of fit and justification. Dworkin fills out the 'fit' aspect of integrity by reference to the fourteenth amendment to the US constitution and to the official pronouncements of the judiciary. On the dimension of justification he suggests that we do well to interpret our practice this way and that the interpretation offers an attractive basis for claims of political legitimacy.

Constitutional rhetoric and judicial dicta are poor compasses in trying to find critical reflective distance. Judicial opinions are often very far from being 'acts of the community personified'.[89] That Dworkin takes constitutional rhetoric and judicial dicta at face value, as evidence of deep social concern and conceptual equality, is complacent, naïve, or charitable to a dangerous excess. Even if integrity transforms politics into a 'theatre of debate'[90] we should not be blind to the fact that some may live their entire lives in the wings.

[86] Dworkin *Law's Empire* 216. [87] ibid. 411. [88] ibid. 413.
[89] ibid. 248. [90] ibid. 211.

When we consider this descriptive evidence, why does an interpretation of our practices as instantiating integrity seem at all normatively attractive? Dworkin notes that at the post-interpretive stage some reform of the practice we are analysing occurs. But this cannot be excessive. Accurate description is a necessary precursor to moral reform. This could only be a morally attractive interpretation of our practices if they approximate it in reality. If we weight normative appeal to an excessive degree, legitimacy becomes what we see in an institution and not what it presents to us. Our attitudes cease to be the normative consequences of legitimacy, or Weber's descriptive conditions on the subsistence of legitimacy, but become the creators of legitimacy. Now, alarmingly, duty really is in the eye of the beholder.

Dworkin believes that political theory and jurisprudence are necessarily linked. While this is true, they are also distinct. I have stressed the importance of keeping separate the jurisprudential and political enquiries in this regard. Jurisprudence looks to official claims in order to understand the standards law must meet. Political philosophy then adopts the critical stance of evaluation. It should not accept the claims of law at face value. Law may often present itself in a mask. Dworkin's theory cannot simultaneously be 'protestant'[91] and wilfully gullible.

What might Dworkin reply? He might suggest that the balance between fit and justification must be made, and that, even though an imperfect image of our communities, integrity carries enough residual truth to warrant weighting the justification side of the balance. But such an argument would have to be provided, and in so arguing, Dworkin would have to explain how precise balancing between fit and justification occurs, whether the two axes are commensurable, and, if they are, which criterion adjudicates the process of balancing.[92] Much that is important is left silent.

Integrity, Dworkin suggests, translates bare community into a 'theatre of debate'.[93] What might the other players in this theatre, acknowledged and previously silent, reply to Dworkin? The Universalist speaks first: 'It was noted in Chapter 1, that the radical sceptic concerning associative obligation might challenge the very idea of particularistic obligations to compatriots at the most basic level. It was also noted that to assert the possibility of particularistic obligations is not necessarily to assert their priority. Clearly, however, one arguing for the unmediated moral force of local bonds makes himself peculiarly vulnerable to the universalist's challenge. You concede that associative responsibilities are subject to interpretation, and that justice plays a part in this justification.[94] Given the conclusions above on the role of justice as a constraint on

[91] ibid. 190. Alan Hunt also suggests that Dworkin's theory is naïve at 'Law's Empire or Legal Imperialism?' 23 and 25.

[92] Shiell 'Assessing Ronald Dworkin's New Theory of Political Obligations' 30.

[93] Dworkin *Law's Empire* 211. See also Shiell 'Assessing Ronald Dworkin's New Theory of Political Obligations'.

[94] ibid. 203.

interpretation and obligation, we know that, before social practices generate obligations, they must not be gravely unjust. But special associative obligations are *themselves* unjust. Given the external constraint of justice on your internally generated obligations, before you continue with your defence of the particular, you must defend the general project of special obligations. But this is not done. You move inductively by analogy. It is time to make good on your promise to provide "a more abstract interpretation of the yet more general practice of associative obligation itself".[95] Otherwise you assume what you must prove.'

Dworkin might reply that the implication of the criticism of special obligations is that, where 'special' (implying the pronominal adjective), qualifies 'obligation', the partial qualifies the impartial, and the selfish undermines the moral. But Dworkin's special associative obligations are grounded in a natural duty to abide by the responsibilities social practices define, and are supported by phenomenology. What the Universalist misperceives as action on morally irrelevant factors is actually action upon natural duty.[96]

The Universalist reminds Dworkin that, given the above discussion, his idea of natural duty now appears strangely porous. Picking up on this point, the Purist Associativist suggests that Dworkin's theory appropriates the language of associativism while relying heavily on ideas of natural duty, reciprocity, conceptual egalitarianism, and justice. The Voluntarist reminds the Associativist that her own position is deeply flawed, and that Dworkin does well to betray associativism.

'In matters of such personal and political significance, you cannot marginalize the voluntary. That political circumstances do not presently conduce to real conditions for consent does not entail that they do not conduce to change. Change may let in the real possibility of consent.[97] Moreover, the concept of acceptance figures prominently in Dworkin's account of the model of principle: "each accepts political integrity as a distinct political ideal".[98] This claim is strong. Political community is constituted by general acceptance of integrity as a distinct political ideal. This implies some level of consensus clustering around

[95] ibid. 197. Green suggests in 'Associative Obligations and the State' 99 that any such project is not feasible: 'One cannot produce moral reasons for the general act-type doing-what-is-required any more than one can explain the point of being-associated... Any general truths about associative obligations will follow only as generalizations about particular cases, not as deductions from a general theory of association as such.' See also Caney, 'Individuals, Nations and Obligations' 132–3 for the similar point that Dworkin's theory begs the question: 'a Dworkinian defence of national obligations can only work if one asserts (or defends) the claim that the practice of favouring one's fellow nationals is reasonably just. This, however, is partly what is in dispute and it is a large assumption which requires considerable defence.'

[96] For cognate observations, see Jeske 'Associative Obligations, Voluntarism, and Equality' 301.

[97] For examples of an argument from participatory and direct, instead of representative, democracy as reformist ways of realizing consent, see: Pateman *The Problem of Political Obligation: A Critique of Liberal Theory* and *Participation and Democratic Theory* ch. 4; Budge *The New Challenge of Direct Democracy*; Barber *Strong Democracy: Participatory Politics for a New Age* and *The Conquest of Politics*. For a critique of Barber and Pateman see De Lue *Political Obligation in a Liberal State* ch. 6. For discussion of Barber's idea of political community see Kautz *Liberalism and Community* 107–35.

[98] Dworkin *Law's Empire* 211. See e.g. Hunt 'Law's Empire or Legal Imperialism?'.

integrity and contains a whisper of contract theory. To identify oneself as a member of a community is to make a (socially constrained) choice. Voluntarism is limited but not eliminated. And nor would elimination be appropriate. Affective bonds of all kinds are made meaningful by their spontaneity and genuineness. In any event integrity faces the very same problem Dworkin believes undermines consent theory. Just as actual consent theory descriptively fails real politics, so too does integrity.'

Dworkin might take the second point first, observing that integrity does not fail to describe our actual societies. Moreover, even if both fail in descriptive accuracy, consent theory does not simply descriptively fail our moral experience, it also fails our moral hopes. Law as integrity emphasizes rich fraternity instead of bare freedom and is, as a result, normatively more appealing.

The Voluntarist reminds Dworkin that the descriptive concession undermines the relevance of his theory, and that the choice between reformist accounts reduces to one of moral tastes. What of the first point, that Dworkin's linguistic slips betray theoretical leanings? Dworkin's reply is simple: Actual voluntarist notions nowhere do the important normative work. Natural communal duties supported by ideas of equality, justice, and reciprocity exert moral force.

But now the Hypothetical Contractualist can raise an objection. 'Dworkin is correct. Actual consent is quite inert. Hypothetical consent is central. Two ideas distinguish Dworkin's account. First, a natural duty to uphold social practices and institutions constrained by considerations of justice. Secondly, an account of an essentially ideal community in which conceptually egalitarian, reciprocal, and just practices foster communal fraternity, but in which individualism is respected and the distinction between the public and the private is clearly maintained. But the first theory seems to be a modified version of Rawls's natural duty to uphold just institutions, while the second seems a version of a hypothetical reasonable contract. Hence, general acceptance can be constitutive of the community that secures legitimacy. It is the quality of the institutional practices and not citizens' concern that grounds obligation. Associative sentiment does no work. Nor could it. Empirically, the atomism of modernity precludes this. Theoretically, the need for vertical justification precludes it. Actual consent does no work, because it is not a sufficient condition for legitimacy and is chimerical in the circumstances of political society. But where institutions are sufficiently just and egalitarian, legitimacy will be secured. Given your presuppositions about the quality of the institutional practices of law, it would be quite unreasonable to refuse obligations to support this institution. You have the skeleton of a hypothetical reasonable contract.'[99]

As Dworkin gathers breath, a more sympathetic rival speaks up. 'You are looking in the right places, but from the wrong perspective. Membership, social practice, non-voluntariness, obligation, and political community remain the

[99] On the distinction between and features of hypothetical rational and reasonable contracts, see Wolff 'Anarchism and Skepticism' 106–7.

correct axes of an accurate account. But you must understand the real nature of membership, the true nature of the non-voluntariness of political community, the genuine role of psychological factors in obligations of commitment as not supportive but central, and the genuine pre- or a- moral nature of the only obligations this congeries of commitments can generate.' This voice promises an articulate alternative.

MARGARET GILBERT AND ACTUAL OBLIGATIONS

Margaret Gilbert advances a 'plural subject' account of political obligation as a constructive reworking of actual contract theory.[100] Actual contract theory presents a simple answer to the question of political obligation. Members of political society are party to an agreement that makes a country *their* country and creates obligations.[101] But well-rehearsed objections undermine the theory:

1. The 'no agreement' objection. There is no evidence of explicit agreement and the context necessary for tacit consent through silence is absent;
2. The 'not morally binding' objection. Two versions are possible:
   (*a*) a circumstantial objection in terms of coercion or unconscionability; or
   (*b*) a substantial objection in terms of injustice. Consent would involve consenting to obey laws many of which might be unjust. Such consent would not be binding.[102]

By outlining a plural subject account in terms of joint commitment, Gilbert hopes to reshape and rescue contract theory.

A joint commitment comprises two or more people.[103] It is not an aggregate of independent commitments; the obligations of commitment are severally dependent on joint commitment. They cannot exist independently and cannot be unilaterally rescinded. The parties to a joint commitment must jointly rescind the commitment. The crux of joint commitment and the obligations it generates is that 'the relevant expressions of readiness have been made' and that this is '*common knowledge* between the parties'.[104] In a two-person face-to-face model, one party expresses her individual readiness to be committed and the other (explicitly or tacitly) accepts. This is not an agreement but a shared understanding. However, joint commitment requires neither exhaustive face-to-face interaction, nor an explicit moment at which obligations are incurred. Plural subjects can consist in impersonal groups created through non-explicit, temporally extended acts of commitment. For example, in the case of members of a large population, 'members of the population can express their readiness to be jointly committed in a particular way with the other members—*whoever*

[100] Gilbert *Sociality and Responsibility* 97. [101] ibid. 99.
[102] ibid. 100–1. [103] ibid. 101.
[104] ibid. 102. For elaboration of 'common knowledge', see Lewis *Convention: A Philosophical Study*.

precisely these may be. They need not encounter or know of every other member individually to do this. They can openly express their readiness in relation to people they do encounter, perceived not so much as particular individuals but rather as members of the population in question.'[105] A joint commitment is in place once these expressions become common knowledge amongst the relevant population.

Within a society, expressions of readiness are articulated by widespread use of the first person plural pronoun and its corresponding pronominal adjective.[106] In the two-person model, where a closing 'we' complements a tendentious or initiatory 'we', a plural subject is formed. In political community, citizens everywhere speak of 'our constitution', 'our government' and 'our laws'. Use of the plural pronoun acknowledges and constitutes joint commitment; the noun ('government', 'constitution') suggests the subject and content of the commitment.

The bond created between two jointly committed individuals entails that individuals enjoy a 'special standing' in relation to each other.[107] This 'special standing' entails that each is entitled to conforming action on the other's part.[108] He has rights and grounds for complaint in the event of failure to perform. Once two parties are in a joint commitment, one who defaults, betrays the other.[109] A joint commitment can also be understood as a specific kind of order. A plural subject jointly issues an order that constitutes the commitment. This order need only be 'spoken-in-the-heart'. Cognitive commitment, and not verbal consent is necessary. The order is immediately legitimate in the sense of being appropriately constituted as an order (the one who orders is in a position to give orders to the addressee). This sense of legitimacy does not 'concern the content of the order or the consequences of the addressee's conformity'.[110] It is not the last word on the propriety of performance.

Obligations correspond to rights of joint commitment. These are intrinsic to the joint commitment in that, once it exists, so do they. 'Thus neither the circumstances nor the content of a joint commitment, given that it exists, affects the presence of its obligations.'[111] That obligations can exist independently of circumstances and content (connoting coercion and immoral substance) already indicates that Gilbert considers that plural subject theory is capable of rebutting the objections levelled at actual contract theory.

The 'no agreement' objection is rebutted by the widespread use of 'we' talk described above. It is natural to interpret our experience of political life as containing a joint commitment given the fact of plural subject discourse. Gilbert is trying to account for the datum that 'many people take themselves to have certain obligations by virtue of the fact that a given country is *their* country. They believe they are obligated to uphold (as best they can) a certain set of political

[105] ibid. 103. [106] ibid. 108. [107] ibid. 103 (emphasis omitted).
[108] ibid. (emphasis omitted). [109] ibid. 54. [110] ibid. 56.
[111] ibid. 104.

institutions, the institutions of the country they regard as *theirs*.'[112] The content of the joint commitment is taken as a pre-analytic datum, and the search is for evidence of its existence. Gilbert's point is simple. If this is the nature of the commitment, and if promiscuous plural subject language evidences the commitment, then the citizens' understanding of their situation is correct. Is this interpretation reasonable as well as descriptively plausible? If citizens widely use the plural subject about community and state, 'without indicating that they do not wish the plural subject reading to be made'[113] then the plural subject reading is the default interpretation. Iterated use also creates circumstances of common knowledge.

This default reading of the plural subject is substantiated by the fact that members of community express indignation when witnessing others violating laws. This indicates that the speaker considers himself offended against and entitled to intervene. These interactions constitute and confirm a plural subject understanding of political community. Additionally, the 'prevalence of the first person plural in the rhetoric of politicians suggests that this well understood'.[114] (Echoes of Dworkin are audible.) Inculcation of instrumental loyalties is commonplace. But this does not trouble plural subject theory: 'Precisely how people come to refer to a certain country as "ours" is one thing. What they mean when they do so refer is another.'[115] The 'no agreement objection' loses force. The processes and periods of the formation of joint commitment are subtle, constituted, and confirmed in understandings and interactions.

What of the 'not morally binding' objection? For Gilbert, a state of readiness can be created in coercive circumstances. Someone threatened can form and express the intention to be ready to act. 'Mutual expressions of readiness may thus lead to the creation of a joint commitment.' Vitally, it may be the case that 'from the moral point of view a person who has been coerced into entering a joint commitment need not honor the obligations acquired through that commitment'.[116] But that obligations are potentially overridden does not mean they never existed. *Ceteris paribus,* morality requires that we keep our commitments. *Tout court*, it may be the case that one should not keep a commitment. But the obligations of joint commitment remain.

Gilbert's theory is not voluntaristic. Whatever voluntarism the theory contains is compatible with obligations generated under coercion. The theory is 'intentionalist' more than voluntarist. It requires action on an agent's part and requires intention directed at acquiring an obligation.

In analysing Gilbert's theory, I will look to the role of psychological factors in two contexts. The first of these is the definition of political obligation in terms of

[112] Gilbert *Sociality and Responsibility* 109. [113] ibid.
[114] ibid. 110. [115] ibid. 111.
[116] ibid. 105. See also Gilbert 'Agreement, Coercion, and Obligation' 702: 'It may well be that (in some appropriate sense) Ben's coercer is not morally entitled to his performance, does not morally deserve his performance, and will have no basis for complaint against Ben's moral character if he breaks the agreement, given what he himself did to bring the agreement about'.

psychological attitudes and cognitive commitment. Secondly, I will look to the role of psychological factors in the conditions under which commitment can be formed, both from the perspective of the 'intentionality' of which Gilbert speaks, and the possibility of coerced agreements. This will lead on to a fuller analysis of the idea of (potentially) coerced commitments as the basis of political obligation. Gilbert must have a model not vulnerable to the 'not morally binding' objection in order to exhibit priority over actual contract theory. I will analyse the reason-giving nature of coercive threats while considering the nature of the claims of law. Finally, I will look closely at Gilbert's quixotic conception of obligation.

PLURAL SUBJECTION

Psychological factors perforate Gilbert's theory. Political obligation is itself understood as a 'sense of obligation' with a relevant content, 'people *feel* that they are tied, bound or obligated in the relevant ways'.[117] A joint commitment can be a creature of cognitive, non-verbal, non-performative commitment, a shared understanding witnessed in use of the plural subject. Our use of plural language may be the product of insidious influences, but what it expresses is, none the less, a sense of plural subject-hood. Joint commitment requires a voluntarism reduced to intentionality and readiness for action, where the will, even though possibly coerced, none the less chooses among its diminished options, and prepares itself for commitment.

Is a proliferation of plural subject 'speak' within a population sufficient to constitute and confirm a sense of joint commitment? Two polar doubts arise. First, language is often a dull and unthinking tool. This doubt is conceptual. Much usage is lazy and vague and yet intelligible. Secondly, linguistic surfaces may conceal complex subterfuges of inculcated belief. This doubt is normative. One could know the meaning of a word and use the word in a wholly intelligible way without this use necessarily having moral implications. Gilbert leaves dissent without a language. While many words may have normative implications, much language is innocent of moral purposes. And, as discussed above, we do well not to attach too much normative significance to the rhetoric of politicians. Nor should we infer too much from conforming conduct. Ostensibly appropriate action may result from egoistic or prudential motives, unreflective habit and conservatism, or independent approval of laws.

What of the significance of the noun qualified by the pronominal adjective? It is begging the question somewhat to suggest that a 'fairly minimal candidate with respect to the phrase "our government" would presumably be something like this: "we jointly accept that *that* body may make and enforce edicts throughout this country"'.[118] The dissident is again hostage to the limits of language.

[117] Gilbert 'Group Membership and Political Obligation' 127. Emphasis added.

[118] ibid. 127–8.

I am only a citizen of the United Kingdom. I can, due to linguistic, legal, and philosophical conventions, only intelligibly use the plural subject with reference to the state of Great Britain. Once we have the concept of membership, with inclusion and exclusion at each pole, all experience could be reduced to a dualistic either/or with some shades of uncertainty. But there must be more to moral membership than this.

Two concerns might infect the idea of 'coerced agreements'. The first is analytic—is a coerced agreement an 'agreement'? The second is normative—are coerced agreements morally binding? Our focus is the second concern. Gilbert's position here is simple. Even under duress, I exercise my will and rationally choose among options. This is all the voluntariness we need in order to create a readiness to act on intention, and a joint commitment requires only this readiness to act. Once a joint commitment is in place, so too, necessarily, are rights and obligations of joint commitment. Even if later overridden in a moral balance, the obligation does not simply disappear.

The ideas of coerced agreement and obligation require full elaboration. In a Hobbesian spirit, agreement for Gilbert, may be coerced: 'Coercive circumstances need not prevent me from entering into a joint commitment. If I am party to such a commitment I am obligated and that is that. That is not to say that I may not subsequently have good reason to break my commitment and violate my obligation. I may or may not.'[119]

Gilbert is keen to dismiss Simmons's submission that even were consent a viable ground of obligation, the circumstances of modern political societies, in which no true option of state non-membership exists, vitiate consent on the basis of coercion or unconscionable conduct.[120] Commitment must be able to flourish in non-voluntary circumstances for Gilbert's thesis and political obligation to hold.

Ex facie, it seems that the argument would more accurately reflect common linguistic usage if couched in the terminology of 'obliged'. Gilbert's account more approximates Austin's gunman writ large imposing actual and immediate constraints on action, than something we might happily call 'obligation'.[121] Gilbert stresses that the importance of coercion is 'to introduce an extra motivational force into the situation'.[122] This implies 'obliged' more than 'obligation'. Beliefs and motives, and the likelihood that an act *was* done, become central. Gilbert explicitly wishes to de-moralize political obligation, but she cannot wish also simply to demoralize it. This interpretation seems ill-suited to a discussion of political obligation, particularly if we accept the submission of Chapter 1 that law's claims are ineliminably moral and that discussion of political obligation *typically* tries to underwrite the claims of law.

[119] ibid. 129–30.

[120] Gilbert *Sociality and Responsibility* 99–100; Simmons 'Consent, Free Choice and Democratic Government' 812 and 816.

[121] Hart *The Concept of Law* 82–3.

[122] Gilbert 'Agreements, Coercion, and Obligation' 702; Gilbert *Sociality and Responsibility* 105.

Before addressing Gilbert's own conception of obligation, I will analyse the deviant case that Gilbert's analysis takes as paradigmatic—joint commitment reached in circumstances of coercive threats. In order to prevail over actual contract theory, Gilbert's theory must be impervious to the 'not morally binding' objection.

Consider the coercive threat that can nest at the heart of Gilbert's joint commitments: *X* threatens *Y* that, unless she does a certain act, *A*, in circumstances *C*, *X* will bring about a certain eventuality *E*, which is hugely harmful to *Y* or those whom *Y* loves. *Y* agrees to do *A*. What now can we say of 'joint commitment'? I will first consider *commitment*, and in order to do so, will look to the nature of this simple threat.

X intends *Y* to take his threat (assuming it is credible) as a reason to do *A*. This threat is content-independent. Whatever the content of action *A*, *X* would have the same intention. This fits with Gilbert's analysis. She observes that 'neither the circumstances nor the content of a joint commitment ... affects the presence of its obligations'.[123] The obligation is not only content-independent but context and circumstance non-sensitive.

Y has a reason (*X*'s threat) to believe that *E* will occur if she does not do *A*. The conditional occurrence of *E*—not *X*'s threat—provides *Y* with a reason to do *A*. As Raz observes, threats, like offers, are content-independent reasons for *belief*.[124] X need not possess practical authority to issue threats. This distinguishes blackmailers from bailiffs. None the less, the threat provides a very weighty reason for belief and creates a very weighty reason for action. However, if *Y* cleverly evades the choice, or calls *X*'s bluff, *X* will not have grounds for legitimate complaint. He hoped to weight the first order balance of reasons in favour of *Y*'s doing *A*. But he failed. *X* cannot rationally feel aggrieved.[125] Y cannot rationally feel guilty or disloyal. The same would apply were *Y* to verbally submit, and afterwards avoid performing an act scheduled to occur later.

Whatever obligations of joint commitment are, they are not obligations as understood here, and cannot map onto the idea of authoritative commands. Obligations are not simply weighty reasons. Some obligations may be of trivial weight. Obligations have a peculiar categorical structure outlined above, and feature in practical reasoning in a specific way. Massive psychological pressure may also have a very compelling categorical nature. But it operates in practical reason by outweighing all first-order, and possibly second-order, reasons. That this would normally involve the coerced agent in wrongful action explains partly the fact that, morally, coercion operates as a partial or whole justification or excuse. The coerced agent's acts will typically require justification or excuse since ostensibly wrong.

[123] Gilbert *Sociality and Responsibility* 104.

[124] Raz *Freedom* 35–7, 149–51 and 154; *Practical Reason and Norms* 182–4.

[125] Note that in the example *X* acted not out of paternalistic concern but malevolent motives. Were the former the case he might rationally feel aggrieved.

'Joint' seems to imply a union richer than that between victim and perpetrator in a hold-up. Gilbert often distinguishes joint commitment from a decision. A decision I reach alone is a singular achievement. A decision we reach together is 'joint'. What would be the ordinary language way for the victim of the hold-up to describe her quandary? She is unlikely to say, 'so, we agreed that I should hand over my money and not be killed'. She would certainly use both the language of decision and the first person singular.

Gilbert provides a series of clues as to the sense of obligation she intends. First: 'Obligation is a forceful species of reason for action'.[126] Secondly, joint commitments yield an 'actual' obligation: 'what it is *now* incumbent upon *me* to do, all else being equal'.[127] Thirdly, obligation connotes a reason for action that may only be eradicated by both parties in the joint commitment.[128] Fourthly, *S* can have an obligation to ϕ only if *S* has a reason to ϕ which cannot be created and destroyed by *S*'s own arbitrary act.[129] Finally, whether or not political obligations of joint commitment are moral obligations, depends on how we define 'moral obligation'. They are moral obligations if that is defined as, or as including, '"obligation one is, all equal, morally required to fulfill"'.[130] Either way, obligations of joint commitment have implications for motivation and practical reason.

Consider again the threat scenario. It relevantly contains two possible reasons for action, and one reason for belief. *Y*'s reason for belief is *X*'s threat. She has reason to believe that, if she does not do *A*, *X* will cause *E* to happen. Her desire to avoid *E* happening provides a reason for her to do *A*. This is a very weighty reason for action (deriving its weight from the weight of *Y*'s desire to avoid *E*). If *Y* agrees to do *A*, we might also suggest that her agreement provides a reason for action. Gilbert believes this reason exists and is obligatory.

The crucial query is this. Is the agreement a moral reason for action, and if so is it an obligation? *Y*'s desire to avoid *E* happening provides a very *weighty first-order reason for action*. But this reason is independent of the fact of agreement. If the agreement is a reason for action, we have no reason to believe it is weighty, moral, has moral consequences, or is obligatory. Gilbert herself admits that the coercer 'does not morally deserve his performance, and will have no basis for complaint against [his] moral character if he breaks the agreement, given what he himself did to being the agreement about'.[131] But earlier the idea of 'special standing' that conveyed obligation included the idea of unilateral defection as a betrayal, and of the betrayed party having legitimate ground for complaint.

126 'Agreements, Coercion, and Obligation' 679.
127 'Group Membership and Political Obligation' 120.
128 'Agreements, Coercion, and Obligation' 694.
129 ibid. 688.
130 *Sociality and Responsibility* 115.
131 'Agreements, Coercion, and Obligation' 702.

Not only is the reason for action provided by coerced agreement not moral, it is not a weighty reason at all. It is not the reason for action the agent herself is likely cite as her reason for acting as she does. The desire to avoid *E* happening is. In her emphasis on the immediacy of performance of actual obligations, of the exigencies of what it is now incumbent to do, Gilbert trades on the weight of the wrong reason for action. This reason, (the desire to avoid *E* happening) does fulfil Gilbert's finger painting of the main features of obligation. *Y* is beholden to *X* for eradication of that reason; the reason is not a creature of her own will; it is a reason of great weight; and it may dictate what she does both all things equal and all things considered. That this reason satisfies Gilbert's conditions, however, only tells us how incomplete these conditions are.[132]

Gilbert might make two replies. First, even though beliefs in political obligation might initially be formed in coercive or insidious circumstances, over time we willingly embrace them, and better understand their nature.[133] They are then morally binding. But this is not good enough. The theory is no longer immune to the 'not morally binding' objection and requires greater voluntarism in the binding act of tacit commitment. Alternatively she might suggest that the definition of obligation as, or as including, 'obligation one is, all equal, morally required to fulfil', demonstrates her reason as obligation. Often, in circumstances of immediate requirements of action, coercive or otherwise, we perform the action these exigencies require. However, not all obligations are conclusive and not all conclusive reasons are obligations. What one ought to do all things considered may not coincide with any obligation, and may not even invoke moral factors. In coercive circumstances, one is obliged to conform. Though coercion provides one with a reason for action, it creates no obligation. While all obligations provide reason for action, the converse does not hold. Coercion does have normative implications. It will likely guide action, but not in any way we should want to link to obligation.

Much of the problem stems from equivocations in the use of moral terms. Gilbert remains agnostic as to the morality of her reasons, but tries to make suggestive comments as to their potentially moral nature. However, beside this, two other usages sit. First, deeply non-moral uses of normative terms: 'the *legitimacy* of an order in this sense need not be the last word on the question whether to obey it'.[134] Secondly, full-blooded uses of moral terms: 'There is

[132] Rousseau observes at book I, ch. 3 of *The Social Contract*: 'To yield to force is an act of necessity, not of will; it is at best an act of prudence. In what sense can it be a moral duty? . . . once might is made to be right, cause and effect are reversed . . . As soon as man can disobey with impunity, his disobedience becomes legitimate; and as the strongest is always right, the only problem is how to become the strongest. But what can be the validity of a right which perishes with the force on which it rests? If force compels obedience, there is no need to invoke a duty to obey, and if force ceases to compel obedience, there is no longer any obligation.'

[133] For hints at such an understanding see the example in 'Agreements, Coercion and Obligation' at 702–3 of a boy, Ben, coerced by a girl's father to marry his daughter, who despite this coercion later decides that such marriage may not be a wholly bad thing.

[134] *Sociality and Responsibility* 56. Emphasis added.

nothing in what I have said so far that implies that there are any governments or political institutions that *deserve* communal support'.[135]

Can Gilbert account for this equivocation? In discussing coerced agreements, she often stresses the difference between 'all things equal' and 'all things considered' judgments.[136] Perhaps the suggestion is that this marks the distinction between the pre-moral and the moral. But this just seems incorrect. The distinction is between prima-facie and conclusive reasons (moral or prudential) for action. Also, if coercion is deep or systemic, it is present even at the all things equal level. Gilbert seems to be without escape. It seems that only by locating her account in a pre-moral space can she evade the criticisms that trouble actual contract theory. But actual contract theory, too, would avoid these criticisms if located in similar territory.

Gilbert qualifies her account. Many questions sit beyond her enquiry: how important it is from a moral point of view to fulfil these obligations; when and why it is morally permissible to break them; whether or not coerced agreements are morally binding.[137] However, Gilbert's conception of the problem now seems trivial and her solution seems uninteresting since so deeply defeasible. As a vertical justification of obligation, her theory assumes too much in assuming the content of the 'sense of obligation'. Many pro-attitudes to government or community fall short of recognition of the authority of law. Further, the account cannot underwrite the strong moral claims of law. As a horizontal justification, Gilbert paints a thin and oppressive picture of plural subject-hood as plural subjection.

CONCLUSION

Effectively, Gilbert dilutes obligation so that it might have more universal application. Her account does well against the criteria of universality, singularity, and uniformity, but fails the requirements of morality and obligation. She provides a reason of great weight and not an authoritative or morally binding obligation. Weight of moral force is sacrificed to generality of scope. This leaves us with a shell of obligation better conceived as a state of being obliged, and an etiolated image of inherently and deeply defeasible political bonds. Despite this, Gilbert understands the limitations of the conceptual materials she is working with. She grasps that, robbed of strong voluntarism, and prior to exhaustive stipulation of institutional virtues, communal membership need not be a robustly moral phenomenon. She essentially accounts for the low-level psychological self-understanding of citizens of modern states. That this is often infected by false consciousness and unreflective habit renders talk of obligation incongru-

135 'Group Membership and Political Obligation' 128.

136 'Agreements, Coercion, and Obligation' 702 and *Sociality and Responsibility* 105.

137 *Sociality and Responsibility* 115.

ous. Moral standards are not simple inheritances of birth, and obligation is not just another piece of hand-me-down clothing.

But Gilbert was not the last of Dworkin's hypothetical critics. The advocate of Fair Play has listened in silence, as Dworkin's empire, centrally involving reciprocity, has begun its decline. The stage is now hers.

5
The Burdens of Benefit

Qui sentit commodom sentire debet et onus[1]

Reciprocity is a principle ubiquitous in religious, moral, and political philosophy. When Tzu-kung asks Confucius if there is any single saying that one can act upon all and every day, the Master replies: 'Perhaps the saying of consideration: "Never do to others what you would not like them to do to you"'.[2] The idea of reciprocity links to restraint and considerations of fairness. We cannot expect to receive without return. There is a threshold of free-riding beyond which benefits are not produced, and consumption without contribution flaunts both fairness and respect for persons as ends in themselves. Others' efforts become instruments of acquisitiveness. Reciprocity might emanate from concern, from fair-mindedness in the agent, or, more prosaically, from enlightened self-interest. Fairness, in the form of mutual restrictions, may be no more than a quid pro quo. Kant recognizes this when observing that: 'No one is bound to refrain from encroaching on the possession of another man if the latter does not in equal measure guarantee that the same kind of restraint will be exercised with regard to him'.[3]

Whatever the motive, mutual restraint seems the nucleus of all civilized life. It is found in the operation of games, markets, businesses, and relationships. Players on a team cooperate towards the shared goal of victory. Prior to this, opposing teams cooperate towards the goal of organized play.[4] Self-interest is restrained because others too have restrained their interest when required. As Mill observed: 'All that makes existence valuable to any one depends on the enforcement of restraints upon the actions of other people'.[5]

Fairness has also been suggested as a possible ground of the obligation to obey. Since its early discussion by Broad,[6] fairness has been thought to supply the defects of consent theory and better capture the nature of political bonds. This chapter looks to whether such ambitions are warranted.

[1] 'The person who takes the benefit must also take the burden.'

[2] Confucius *The Analects* book 15, verse 23. Christianity replicates the tenet at Matthew 7: 12. See also, Marcus Aurelius *Meditations* book 7 verse 74 and La Rochefoucald *Maxims* maxim 578.

[3] Kant *The Metaphysical Elements of Justice* sect. 42 (at 71).

[4] Plato *The Republic* 351e–352a (at 97): 'Injustice, then, seems to have the following results, whether it occurs in a state or family or army or in anything else: it renders it incapable of any common action because of factions and quarrels, and sets it at variance with itself and with its opponents and with whatever is just.'

[5] Mill *On Liberty and Other Essays* 9.

[6] Broad 'On the Function of False Hypotheses in Ethics'.

MUTUALITY OF RESTRICTIONS AND FAIR PLAY

Hart's initial outline of the principle of fair play, as mutuality of restrictions, provides the skeleton for the corpus that follows:

> when a number of persons conduct any joint enterprise according to rules and thus restrict their liberty, those who have submitted to these restrictions when required have a right to a similar submission from those who have benefited from their submission. The rules may provide that officials should have authority to enforce obedience and make further rules, and this will create a structure of legal rights and duties, but the moral obligation to obey the rules in such circumstances is *due* to the cooperating members of the society, and they have the correlative moral right to obedience. In social circumstances of this sort (of which political society is the most complex example)... the obligation is due to the co-operating members of the society as such and not because they are human beings on whom it would be wrong to inflict suffering.[7]

Benefiting from submission imposes a reciprocal and horizontal obligation to make proportionate return to the cooperating group. This group is made *particular* by its cooperation. We owe restraint to our fellow members *qua* members and not *qua* humans. Not all obligations must be deliberately undertaken, but they do all arise from some previous voluntary act.[8] Finally, 'this claim to interfere with another's freedom is justified because it is fair'.[9]

Hart's formulation is significant also for what it omits. What constitutes a joint enterprise? How is membership of the enterprise decided? What kinds of fairness must the scheme exhibit before fairness can be deployed as an obligating reason without contradiction? Must entry to the scheme, or receipt of benefits, be voluntary? Must one voluntarily receive benefits or must one actively accept them aware of the full normative implications of acceptance? What qualitative and quantitative thresholds are placed upon benefit before it can generate obligation? Must benefits not only exceed costs but also be worth the costs? Is the standard of evaluation for worth subjective or objective?[10]

In 'Legal Obligation and the Duty of Fair Play', Rawls fleshes out Hart's principle:

> Suppose there is a mutually beneficial and just scheme of social cooperation, and the advantages it yields can only be obtained if everyone, or nearly everyone, cooperates. Suppose further that cooperation requires a certain sacrifice from each person, or at least involves a certain restriction of his liberty. Suppose finally that the benefits produced by cooperation are, up to a certain point, free: that is, the scheme of cooperation is unstable in the sense that if any one person knows that all (or nearly all) of the others will continue to do their part, he will still be able to share a gain from the scheme even if he does not do his part. Under these conditions, a person who has accepted the benefits of the scheme is bound by a duty of fair play to do his part and not to take advantage of the free benefit by not cooperating.[11]

[7] Hart 'Are there any Natural Rights?' 85–6. [8] ibid. 85. [9] ibid. 90.
[10] See also Simmons *Moral Principles* 103.
[11] Rawls 'Legal Obligation and the Duty of Fair Play' 9–10.

The obligation depends upon our having *accepted* benefits. It is owed to fellow citizens who cooperate under the constitution, and not to public officials. The scheme must be mutually beneficial and just before obligations are generated. Rawls stresses that any such scheme is immediately vulnerable to the possibility of free-riding, for which fairness is the corrective.

Fair play rests on the mutuality of restrictions, and more broadly on 'the just distribution of burdens and benefits'.[12] If I benefit from the cooperative efforts of others, similar to myself in all morally relevant respects, I too have an obligation to contribute. From the above schematic outlines of the principle of fair play, and the broad literature surrounding the topic,[13] I will set out necessary conditions for the application of the principle of fair play. I will then illustrate the context in which an obligation might arise, explicating its ground and content.

FAIRNESS AND FREE-RIDERS

An obligation of fair play may arise within a political society where:

1. A number of persons are involved in a cooperative practice or scheme which may, but need not, be run according to rules.

This condition, applied to the political case, requires that we are able to conceive of our political society as a scheme of voluntary cooperation. Many theorists consequently restrict the application of the principle to liberal or constitutional democracies, as the closest approximation to such a scheme.[14] I will discuss the role of rules in obligations of fairness below.

2. The scheme actually produces some mutually beneficial good or prevents some evil.

A beneficial scheme is a necessary but not sufficient condition of the application of the principle of fair play. (There are many cooperative associations that, though potentially beneficial, I could never be morally required to join; for example, an Institute of Advanced Italian Language Skills.) Cooperation within certain (subjectively) beneficial cooperative ventures will be morally permissible, within others, morally prohibited, and within some ventures, possibly (the issue under discussion), morally required.

[12] Lyons *Forms and Limits of Utilitarianism* 164.

[13] Arneson 'The Principle of Fairness and Free-Rider Problems'; Samuelson 'The Pure Theory of Public Expenditure'; Frohlich *et al.* 'Individual Contributions for Collective Goods'; Becker 'The Free-Rider Problem'; Hampton 'Free-Rider Problems in the Production of Collective Goods'; Miller and Sartorius 'Population Policy and Public Goods'; Cullity 'Moral Free-Riding'; Lyons *Forms and Limits of Utilitarianism* ch. 5; Taylor *The Possibility of Cooperation*; Pettit 'Free Riding and Foul Dealing'; and Elster 'Rationality, Morality, and Collective Action'.

[14] Rawls *A Theory of Justice* 4 and Klosko *The Principle of Fairness and Political Obligation* 16–26 (hereafter Klosko *Principle of Fairness*).

3. For each individual, the benefits received from others' actions exceed personal contribution costs.[15]

This condition so far is silent as to whether benefit is quantified against a subjective or objective metric.

4. Contribution nonetheless represents a burden for all involved.

Contributions need not be identical though they must be fair. Fairness requires not uniform but proportionate contribution. Note that contributions might be judged unfairly burdensome in two ways. First, *X*'s *absolute* proportion of benefits to burdens may be unfair. This assessment will incorporate objective judgments (for example, 'no man can be made responsible for this many tasks') and inter-systemic evaluations (for example, 'other feasible systems would not create burdens on this scale'). Secondly, *X*'s *relative* ration of benefit to burden may be unfair. This assessment will incorporate intra-systemic comparisons to similarly situated individuals within a group. (As John Broome observes, 'the particular business of fairness is to mediate between the conflicting claims of different people.')[16]

5. The benefit can only be produced through a cooperative effort. Private production or production by only a few individuals is impossible or irrational.

An example of impossible production is the solution of coordination problems such as conventions governing the side of the road on which motorists will drive. An example of an irrational production is the provision of national revenue through taxation, which is only achieved if organized cooperatively.

6. The benefit in question is a public good. There is no necessary correlation between those who create and those who consume. The main characteristics of public goods are:
   (*a*) Non-excludability: If *B*,... *Z* enjoy ϕ, it is either practically impossible or *de facto* infeasible (due to excessive cost), to exclude *A* from enjoying ϕ, even if he does not contribute; and
   (*b*) Joint supply: If ϕ is produced by a group and is a public good, then if it is available to *B*,... Z, it is available to *A* at no cost, even if he is not contributing. (Non-excludability entails joint supply but the converse does not hold.)

The provision of public goods is a factor which, for Adam Smith, necessitates government: 'The third and last duty of the sovereign or commonwealth is that of erecting and maintaining those publick institutions and those public works, which, though they may be in the highest degree advantageous to a great society, are, however, of such a nature, that the profit could never repay the expense to any individual or small number of individuals, and which it, therefore, cannot be

[15] This is the proviso suggested by Nozick in *Anarchy, State, and Utopia* 94.
[16] Broome 'Fairness' 94.

expected that any individual or small number of individuals should erect or maintain'.[17]

7. Non-universal general cooperation with the scheme is a necessary and sufficient condition for the production of the public good.

A combination of 4, 5, 6, and 7 introduce the self-interested rationality of defection. If universal cooperation is necessary, we have a coordination problem and rational agents should (given certain conditions) want to coordinate. But, here, we have a cooperation problem. The *de facto* impossibility of excluding *X* from the consumption of a public good eliminates any direct (self-interested) incentive to contribute. Once a good is available, it is available to *X* free of cost and his added contribution may provide no benefit to himself or others. Where the good is available, net utility is not maximized by cooperation, and it is in *X*'s interest to defect. If it is not available, *X* alone is in no position to provide the good without the others' cooperation and any effort to this end is fruitless.

In stipulating these conditions, I have restricted analysis of the problem of fairness to its application to public goods, those we either cannot avoid or avoid only by undergoing considerable inconvenience. This seems appropriate in discussion of political society. The benefits of living in community include living under the rule of law, national defence, public health and transport systems, protection of the person and property, and, *ex hypothesi*, others' restraint. These benefits simply fall out on all members of a political community. Private benefits are typically sought, accepted, or bought. Consent or acceptance will have more normative play here than with public goods. I will now analyse the content and grounds of the obligation of fairness.

THE NORMATIVE NEXUS OF FAIRNESS OBLIGATIONS

The principle of fair play generates obligations to do one's fair share in a cooperative scheme. In the case of political obedience this will be an obligation to conform to a rule or practice. We must ascertain why the moral requirement is an obligation and why it prescribes conformity to a rule.

At the core of obligations of fairness there is a triadic relationship amongst:

1. The provision of benefits (necessary for an obligation to arise at all);
2. The intentions and actions of others in producing these benefits; and
3. The relationship or attitude of an agent, *X*, to these benefits.

In determining why the moral requirement is an obligation, 3 is relevant. Hart states that obligations originate in the acts of agents, in some species of voluntary act. However, moral obligations and duties can also originate in the needs of others and the independent requirements of morality. There are some goods we

[17] Smith *The Wealth of Nations* V. i. part third (at 413).

should provide to others, irrespective of benefit (and possibly, slight risk) to ourselves, simply because of their overwhelming necessity. The natural duty to save a drowning child exemplifies this kind of requirement. It is important to keep this possibility in mind.

As regards receipt of benefits, there is a continuum of voluntariness running from consent, through acceptance, through knowing receipt, terminating at passive benefaction. The nature of the normative act necessary to generate a genuine obligation in circumstances of fair play is a substantive matter that will be discussed later. Here, it is sufficient to note that obligations must flow from some prior or present voluntary act of the agent or independent moral requirements.

The relationship between the nature of the benefit conferred and the nature and extent of others' intentions and actions in conferring the benefit is relevant to the *content* and *limits* of the reciprocal obligation.

In understanding how rules or practices function in the obligation of fair play, it is crucial to look to the behaviour of others as regards the rule. Following Sullivan[18] and Lyons,[19] we can observe that rules establish the cooperative context in which obligations arise, but need not, *per se*, articulate substantive standards of fairness. They prescribe or proscribe certain actions and therefore create the normative matrix in which obligations arise. Rules establish a cooperative scheme. Individuals then cooperate on the basis of the rule and provide some benefit or prevent some evil. Fairness and distributive justice are critical moral principles made relevant to the rule by others' actions. If the rule is effective and fair, it provides a moral reason to conform. An unfair rule provides no moral reason for action. Fairness applies both to the actions of an agent *X*, guiding what he ought to do, and to the rules themselves, determining which can constitute moral reasons for action according to fairness. The rules only obligate (morally) once the critical standard of fairness, rendered relevant by others' actions, is invoked.

Obligation thus requires the normative nexus of some moral relationship to benefits and the intention and actions of others. Without the former, others could confer a benefit on *X* that holds no subjective value for her. These others may have gone to considerable effort, but it seems unfair to bind *X* through receipt of that which she does not want and does not pursue. Without the latter fairness would be irrelevant. *X* may enjoy looking at the watercolours of the elderly woman who paints for pleasure at the beach, but in doing so, he does not exploit others' efforts directed at conferring such a benefit on him. He fortuitously enjoys a by-product of another's self-interested efforts. Having seen how the principle of fair play can bind, we now turn to when it is able or likely to do so.

[18] Sullivan 'Rules, Fairness and Formal Justice'.

[19] See Lyons *Forms and Limits of Utilitarianism* at 196–7 for comments on the distinction between the rules of a practice and considerations of fairness.

THE STRUCTURE AND LOGIC OF THE PRINCIPLE OF FAIR PLAY

The principle of fair play is a *supervening* ground of obligation, explaining obligations to a scheme only after it exists. I will illustrate this by considering the initiation and maintenance of a voluntary cooperative scheme: Dibbler is a small village in the middle of a dangerous jungle. Neighbouring tribes have sporadically posed a threat to Dibbler, but in recent months the threat has grown acute. The adult members of the community assemble and devise a rotation system of fairly divided half-day patrols. Pre-emptive shooting of arrows will quell any attacks before they begin. All agree on conformity to the plan. Three weeks later, security has returned to Dibbler. At the same point, the village's cartographer Skip, who has been travelling for four months compiling maps of the surrounding area, also returns. He finds Dibbler more peaceful than he ever imagined possible. After two weeks spent resting from his travels, the villagers request that his name be added to the list. Even though he considers the present climate significantly more pleasant than before, and keenly welcomes the scheme, he declines.

The logic of the scheme's obligations traces its chronology. At the point of the meeting, a utilitarian argument justifies instituting the scheme. The overall gain is considerable and for every adult member net total benefit exceeds net personal cost. All those present at the time of agreement consent, either explicitly or tacitly (according to convention) to the terms and content of the scheme. No fairness is yet involved and none can be until benefits are yielded and burdens borne. The intuition that Skip is bound to assist in the scheme is based in considerations of fairness. He did not previously consent to the scheme, and presently declines to do so. His actions are simply unfair. As regards a benefit he values significantly (and considers valuable), and which his community *needs*, he should not free-ride on the efforts of others.

The example teaches us several things. First, the principle of fairness is a ground of obligation independent of consent. However, we cannot apply principles of fairness without the prior application of considerations beyond fairness itself (we need something to be fair *about*). Secondly, the principle of fairness cannot explain the initiation of a scheme of social cooperation though it may well explain obligations to maintain it. The principle of fairness could not justify the *original* establishment of the state. The principle presupposes some other normative or pragmatic act of beginning, some form of social contract, or, 'usurpation or conquest, or both, without any pretence of a fair consent, or voluntary subjection of the people'.[20] It may, however, justify and explain present obligation and obedience. And this is all that is necessary to account for the obligation to obey the law.

The origin or pedigree of practices is no concern of the principle of fairness. Its concern is the efficacy and fairness of the practice. Rules are important as

[20] Hume 'Of the Original Contract' in *Political Writings* 168.

standards regulating social cooperation, which, with the application of principles of fairness, render certain acts or omissions unfair. Strictly, even rules *per se* are not necessary. Rules are necessarily general and the standards that regulate micro-schemes may be both more parochial and less formal than rules. Sullivan illustrates this point.[21] Six men are riding in a car that stalls going uphill. The efforts of five will get the car moving again. But if one exempts himself from, or fakes, this effort, he free-rides on a good that benefits all. No rule applies. The situation lacks the requisite generality for this to be so. But fairness is clearly involved.

Another qualification is implied. The principle applies only to effective rules. Effectiveness is contingent on actual patterns of conformity and not on institutional pedigree. Widely disregarded rules will not generate obligations of fairness and will claim no more influence by virtue of their source (save that which attaches to fear of sanctions). Since ineffective, they yield no benefit and fairness does not apply. Rules of alternative origins, which are effective and beneficial, will also be a locus of fairness. In an Amish community, religious doctrine and Mennonite laws are likely to have much more importance as a locus of fairness obligations than do the Federal laws of the United States or the State laws of Pennsylvania.

Fairness obligations revolve around the normative nexus of benefit, an agent's relationship to benefits received, and the intentions and actions of others. The focus is not rules, but the concerted cooperative action of others around these rules. Fairness is a general, extrinsic moral principle and not a characteristic or necessary feature of laws. The obligations fairness yields are relational among citizens and may vary in weight from one to another. This is not to deny that in a stable, evolved political society, the directives issued by the legal system and schemes of social cooperation will substantially overlap.[22] They may do, and this will testify to the efficacy of the legal system as a solution to problems of cooperation and coordination. But to identify these two too closely obfuscates the proper focus and scope of the principle of fairness. Laws are, generally, reliable indicators of solutions to cooperation problems and of actions fairness requires of an agent. But this may be all and even this need not be the case. The principle of fairness will have many non-legal applications and need not apply to all laws or legal systems. That all laws are rules, and not all laws are effective, emphasizes the contingent role of law in an account from fairness. Our concern remains, however, whether fairness applies sufficiently to all cases of law to yield an obligation to obey.

A DEFENSIBLE CONCEPTION OF FAIRNESS

Several substantive questions were raised when discussing Hart's schematic outline. Three central concerns remain. What sense of voluntariness does the

[21] Sullivan 'Rules, Fairness and Formal Justice' at 329.
[22] See also Greenawalt *Conflicts* 137–8.

account from fairness require: Is receipt or acceptance necessary? How do we evaluate the worth of a scheme and its benefits to members: Is the test subjective and attitudinal or an objective assessment of benefit? How do we properly ascribe membership, participation, or engagement in a scheme to an individual; how do we know the principle's scope? Collectively, these enquiries will let us know how, when, to whom, and to what extent fairness obligations bind.

Scepticism is always a good place to start. Robert Nozick has famously questioned fairness obligations. His objections proceed from examples. 364 adults in your neighbourhood establish a public entertainment service, run on a rotation system for each day of the year. Each individual is assigned a day's responsibility for broadcasting civic wit. Your day comes. Given you have benefited, are you obligated to participate? Nozick suggests a proviso. The benefits to a person from the actions of others must exceed the costs of his share. But this is still insufficient. Benefit is not simply an absolute comparison of burden and benefit, but a relative weighing of different possible benefits. 'For you to be obligated to give up your day to broadcast mustn't it be true, at least, that there is nothing you could do with a day...which you would prefer to hearing the broadcasts for the year?'[23] But fairness is a still more relative notion. For, though you scrape a bare benefit from the scheme, others derive great enjoyment from it. Are you obligated to give an equal share? Nozick's conclusions are twofold. 'One cannot, whatever one's purposes, just act so as to give people benefits and then demand (or seize) payment'.[24] Nor can groups act in this way.[25] Secondly, if the principle is reformulated to avoid these wrinkles, it simply collapses into consent. Fair play, for Nozick, is a deontic dead end.

That fair play does not collapse into consent has been shown above. Recalling the conditions on consent stated above in Chapter 3 compounds this point. Consent is a public performative act, undertaken in the belief that it will change the normative situation, that it will do so because undertaken with such a belief, and will be understood by its observers to be of this character. Fair play obligations may clearly fail these tests. Others may not witness my consumption of benefits. It need not be a public act.

More significant, however, is a diachronic distinction between fairness and consent. Consent paradigmatically looks from the present to the future. I undertake promissory or consensual acts in order to effect immediate or prospective normative changes. The obligation originates in *my* act *now*. 'Fair play looks to the past and present.' (Miller and Sartorius). I may at time t_1 receive a benefit, B, the origin of which I am ignorant. I may welcome that benefit. It may be personally or morally crucial. At time t_2 I understand the origin of B. At this point, I may consider myself obligated by fairness to reciprocate. The obligation originates in a complex relationship between others' previous actions, my own previous willing and happy receipt of B, and my current attitude. Reciprocity inhabits the past and the present, consent inhabits the present

[23] Nozick *Anarchy, State, and Utopia* 94. [24] ibid. 95. [25] ibid.

and the future. Fair play and consent are distinct normative notions. But the first objection remains. I can't willy-nilly foist obligations on you. Something akin to consent must be at play.

Simmons suggests an escape for fairness. We must look to the idea of a 'participant' in the scheme, distinguishing him from an 'innocent bystander'. The innocent bystander to a cooperative scheme finds the scheme 'built up around him in such a way that he could not escape its influence'.[26] He is not bound by these circumstances. Hart's beneficiaries come from among those 'conducting' the joint enterprise. Simmons suggests that only beneficiaries who are also participants in some significant sense are bound under the principle of fair play. Nozick's examples all invoke the figure of the innocent bystander, missing the real target of the participant.

Simmons's account contains one conceptual claim and several empirical claims. The conceptual claim is that participation singles out insiders to cooperative schemes. Participation requires acceptance, not mere receipt, of benefits. Acceptance constitutes both membership and triggers fairness obligations. 'To have accepted a benefit, I think, we would want to say that an individual must either 1) have tried to get (and succeeded in getting) the benefit, or 2) have taken the benefit willingly and knowingly.'[27] The peculiar nature of political benefits again creates difficulties. These benefits are avoided only at great personal inconvenience. Open political benefits include 'the rule of law, protection by armed forces, pollution control, maintenance of highway systems, avenues of political participation, etc.'[28] One can accept such goods by fulfilling criterion (2) above. Acceptance of open benefits requires willing and knowing receipt of the benefits. It requires that benefits be worth their cost to each agent, and that the agent understand the normative context and consequences of acceptance. Only examination of attitudes and beliefs testifies to this.

The empirical claims are that many do not notice benefits, or do not think benefits worth the costs.[29] Many believe that benefits are paid for through (too high) tax payments.[30] Many do not understand the origin of obligations in cooperative schemes.[31] 'We are, after all, born into political communities; and being "dropped into" a cooperative scheme does not seem significantly different from having a scheme "built up around you".'[32] Consequently, very few have fairness obligations. Fair play is an autonomous normative principle, but is, politically, largely inert.

Simmons talks of the benefits typically associated with political society as being the rule of law, protection, pollution control, maintenance of amenities, political participation. These benefits, he suggests, are bought by citizens through tax payments. Consider the rule of law. The broad sense of the term is that people should obey the law and be ruled by it.[33] The technical principles of impartial, prospective, stable, laws, and so on, concern the vertical dimension of

[26] Simmons *Moral Principles* 120. [27] ibid. 129. [28] ibid. 138.
[29] ibid. 132. [30] ibid. 139. [31] ibid. 140.
[32] ibid. 138. [33] Raz *Authority* 216.

the rule of law, how governors must rule in order to secure minimal legitimacy. But this leaves untouched the horizontal dimension, how the governed must behave in order to secure law's proper functioning. Irrespective of government initiatives, citizen compliance is the prerequisite of civilized legal life. Citizens pay taxes to governments to finance welfare schemes, services, public facilities, and so on. Though paid vertically, their fruits (largely) blossom on the horizontal dimension. But what of obedience? Taxes do not finance cooperative restraint. Taxes, if anything, pay for the collapse of cooperative restraint, for the policemen, judges, and wardens who deal with those who disobey. But, as Hart understood, sanctions are required 'not as the normal motive for obedience, but as a *guarantee* that those who would voluntarily obey shall not be sacrificed to those who would not'.[34] Fairness concerns mutual restraint and the horizontal dimension. Obedience and not tax is its focus. A more sympathetic rescue may render more success.

George Klosko constructs an argument in which mere receipt is sufficient to generate obligations.[35] Within his theory, the satisfaction of three necessary conditions will generate obligations to contribute to non-excludable schemes. The goods provided by such schemes must be:

1. worth the recipients' effort in providing them;
2. presumptively beneficial; and
3. overall, fairly distributed.

Presumptively beneficial goods are goods that are indispensable and necessary for an *acceptable* life for a community.[36] If *A* is indispensable, we can assume that *X* benefits from it even if he has not actively sought it. The class of presumptively beneficial goods is restricted to public goods and includes benefits such as physical security, law and order, and national defence.

Klosko observes that identifying whether and how much *X* benefits from certain goods, as a subjective enquiry, requires that *X* evince specific attitudes and beliefs. This creates real difficulties where non-excludable goods are involved (we are unlikely to form explicit attitudes to objects we assume we will receive). However, if the good in question can be identified as presumptively beneficial, then the existence of a substantial degree of benefit can be assumed from rudimentary facts about human nature. Enquiry into individual beliefs is superfluous. If a group wishes to impose obligations on *X*, it must draw up the characteristics of an individual benefiting from the presumptive good in question, and show that *X* has these qualities.[37] This should not be difficult. And, in order to exempt herself, *X* must be able to advance legitimate countervailing considerations, such as self-sufficiency independent of the apparatus of the group.

[34] Hart *The Concept of Law* 198. See also Greenawalt *Conflicts* 135–6.

[35] Klosko *Principle of Fairness* 39–56.

[36] ibid. 39. For a similar account that stresses the importance of the indispensability of benefits, and the mere need for receipt, see Maphai 'The Principle of Fairness' 78.

[37] ibid. 48–9.

Indispensability is intended to render subjective preferences objectively clear and verifiable. Presumptive goods cater to universal needs and not discretionary, personal desires.[38] Indispensability is also meant to demonstrate the legitimacy of coercion. If the good in question is necessary, an unequivocal moral imperative drives its production. For Klosko, coercion is legitimate where *X* must unavoidably profit from the cooperative efforts of others, even where not cooperating himself, and the advantages of non-cooperation cannot be generalized to these others as well.[39]

Finally, indispensability aims to render unimportant the origins of a benefit in a cooperative scheme. Klosko suggests that: 'Because A will receive nonexcludable goods whether or not he pursues them, it is less likely that his not knowing their origin will affect his conduct in their regard. In these cases, it is not clear exactly how his beliefs concerning the origin of various goods are relevant to his obligations to help provide them.'[40]

The possibility of exceptions remains, but is nugatory.[41] The attitudes attendant on participation can be presumed on account of the importance of the benefits. Participation is satisfied without any need to investigate individual attitudes and preferences.

Klosko nowhere directly stipulates a criterion for membership. He does however observe that a community is 'the collection of individuals who receive indispensable benefits from the cooperative scheme in question'.[42] Benefaction alone seems to be the necessary criterion of membership. The parameters of benefit are coextensive with the borders of membership.

Klosko's emphasis on indispensability entails conclusions only as regards the quantity or magnitude of benefit involved. It tells us nothing of the cost or distribution, the quality or relative worth of the benefit. We cannot conclude that presumptive benefits are worth any price, and any distributive unfairness will handicap the argument. Klosko's third condition on obligation is that the benefits of a scheme be fairly distributed, and his first is that the benefits must be worth the recipients' costs in providing them. No obligation will be generated until all three of his conditions are satisfied. But the fairness condition will need to be made out by independent argument (essentially a theory of distributive justice),[43] and it is an appealing aspect of the subjective view that, if an agent does evince all the attitudes of acceptance, we can infer that she considers her share reasonably fair, both in terms of subjective worth and distributive fairness.

How does Klosko cater for subjective worth? The first condition seems to serve this role. The goods must be worth the recipients' efforts in providing them. Jonathan Wolff has suggested that presumptive benefit does not play any independent role in Klosko's argument.[44] He suggests that once we are aware of the work done by the first requirement—that the benefits must be worth the

[38] ibid. 52. [39] ibid. 35. [40] ibid. 51.
[41] ibid. 54. [42] ibid. 62 n. 55. Also Simmons *Anarchy* 259 n. 92.
[43] ibid. Klosko describes his own conception of fair distribution at *Principle of Fairness* 61–84.
[44] Wolff 'Political Obligation, Fairness, and Independence' 95–7.

recipients' efforts in producing them—presumptive benefit is redundant, observing: 'In addition to being presumptively beneficial, the goods must be fairly distributed and *worth the recipients' effort in providing them*. This now turns out to be the crux and forcing unwanted goods on people, or goods they do not think worthwhile, becomes out of the question.'[45]

This, however, seems incorrect (or at least incomplete). The first condition seems designed to cover subjective worth, and the second, objective benefit. We can evaluate benefit from different perspectives. We might say that, objectively, benefit ϕ is reasonably and justifiably priced, for example, a £2 entry fee for a cultural institution. We might also say that benefit ϕ is subjectively worth its cost to *X*, (entry is worth £2 to *X*). Equally, the objective fact might hold while the subjective does not. This may represent a luxury *X* can ill-afford. The benefit is not subjectively worth its cost though it is, objectively, reasonably priced.

Construed subjectively, and in the singular, the first condition (the goods must be worth the recipient's efforts in providing them) reads: ϕ is worth its costs to *X* given her preferences and means. But given the fact that this is merely a subjective preference, she may choose not to pursue this benefit, and invest the equivalent 'costs' in other activities or benefits. Subjective preferences indicate but do not *guarantee* how an agent will invest her efforts.

Construed objectively, the second condition (the goods must be presumptively beneficial) reads: ϕ is objectively beneficial. Presumptive benefit is intended to convey that ϕ is indispensable and so must be obtained. Consequently, if, at the individual level, the first clause is interpreted subjectively and presumptive benefit introduces the objective desirability of these goods, the two clauses do serve different purposes. It is not sufficient to say that the benefits are worth their costs to *X* subjectively; this does not guarantee her pursuit of them, though it makes it more likely. Nor is it sufficient to say that the goods are presumptively beneficial since this only tells us about the quantity and not the quality of the goods. Even indispensable goods may become dispensable due to excessive requirements in the costs for their provision. The combination of the two is sufficient to show that the benefits are justifiably priced and necessary *for X* and will, necessarily, be pursued or welcomed by her.

However, Klosko frames his requirement in the plural, so that the goods supplied must be, 'worth the recipients' effort in providing them'.[46] And he later observes that any problems remaining as regards presumptive benefit will be 'lessened to some extent by the requirement that, in order for (i) to be satisfied, the benefits must obviously outweigh the burdens for *all* individuals'.[47]

The first and second conditions now seem more interdependent. For *anyone* to be bound, condition 1 must be satisfied for *all* individuals. But it is hard to imagine that this will ever be the case unless the goods in question just *are* presumptively beneficial. By making the requirement plural, it loses much of

[45] ibid. 94–5. [46] Klosko *Principle of Fairness* 39. Emphasis added.
[47] ibid. 56. Emphasis added.

its subjectivity. It also creates a very exacting standard to be met before obligations are generated. Only reasonably objectively beneficial goods will now satisfy condition 1. Meeting condition 2 seems to be a way of ensuring satisfaction of condition 1, making condition 2 subordinate, though necessary, to condition 1. On a societal level, it is more important that benefits be worth the *recipients'* costs in providing them, than that the benefits be presumptively beneficial. Presumptive benefit appears to be intended to render subjective desires reasonably objective. But the condition from presumptive benefit still needs support from a subjective criterion. Once phrased in the plural, however, this subjective condition becomes in itself almost a re-rendering of the presumptive benefit condition. And either condition aggregates across typical wants to create grounds of obligation. Hence Klosko must allow that *X* can advance legitimate countervailing reasons to defeat the presumption of fairness obligations.

Klosko believes that presumptive benefit also circumvents the need for *X* to understand the origin of the benefit in a cooperative scheme. But such understanding is relevant because it explains the factual circumstances in which obligation arises. Knowledge implies understanding the significance not only of the value of the goods, but of receipt or acceptance as it relates to the actions of others and to obligation. The reason this knowledge is not important to Klosko as regards presumptively beneficial goods is because he assumes that *X*'s desire and need for these benefits is such that knowing their origin will not affect in the slightest his attitudes or actions in respect of benefits. *X* will want these goods. They are necessary and so their cost, in obligation or obedience, is warranted whatever their origin. However, if *X* does not understand that these goods originate in a cooperative scheme, then he does not understand that he owes obligations of *fairness* to his *fellows*. He knows merely that he is willing to obey or conform wherever this is necessary to keep receiving benefits. Benefit is now primary. If *X*'s lack of understanding is a culpable mistake as to facts, then we might want to say that he lies under some moral requirement independent of his ignorance. If he understands the origins of the goods but makes normative errors as to the implications of these facts, then again we may want to say that he is bound.[48] But we seem to be relying on systemic features and sheer benefit more than fairness.

The fairness theorist faces a dilemma. One version of the principle (Simmons) advances what seems to be a suitably constrained obligating reason, which is clearly too narrow for the political context. The other version (Klosko) provides too broad a reason, which makes mere benefaction sufficient both for obligation and membership. The tyranny of majority tastes seems an inevitable consequence. I will try to sketch a median position that presents fair play obligations in their most defensible light.

[48] Greenawalt *Conflicts* 128–9, 138–40.

REFORMULATING FAIRNESS

The earlier discussion of the tripartite normative nexus at the core of fairness obligations provides the structure for analysing substantive issues. We must look to:

1. benefit (incorporating the idea of fair shares);
2. the actions and efforts of others in producing these benefits; and
3. the relationship or attitude of an agent, *X*, to these benefits.

I will consider the third point first. Klosko describes his presumptively beneficial goods as necessary for any *acceptable* life. This idea of an acceptable life is ambiguous between rational and moral acceptability. Both Simmons and Klosko's discussions focus primarily on what individuals want. This is meant to capture the essence of free-riding. If I would rather have a benefit than not have it, if I prefer benefit and burden to the absence of both, then I should accept the burden with the benefit. Evading the burden is free-riding. This emphasis on desires explains Simmons's stress on subjective attitudes, and Klosko's need to include his first condition. Klosko aggregates across all wants to derive the rational desirability of goods, but this leaves many trapdoors uncovered. *X* may not want benefit ϕ. *X* may ideally want ϕ, though it is not worth the cost to him. *X* may want ϕ but want to provide it himself, or on different terms than are available to him. *X* may value ϕ much less than *Y* does and may prefer Ω (or for that matter, Σ). If *X* genuinely adopts any of these stances, he avoids or diminishes his obligations. Moreover, only personal evaluation gives us access to these fine judgments.

We could divide public goods into three very rough categories:

1. morally necessary goods: schemes concerning public health and safety; coordination schemes necessary to prevent harm to others; a just and efficient legal system;
2. presumptively beneficial goods: protection of persons and property; public amenities and transportation systems;
3. discretionary public goods: national theatres and operas; national sporting and art funds.

Consider a comparison. *G* is an independent, cooperative commune. *G* sets up a mutual book-swapping scheme. All benefits and burdens are shared with perfect fairness. This is a cooperative scheme distributing a discretionary good. Now *G* sets up a water chlorination scheme. Their water carries fatal germs due to a chemical explosion up the river. All must take turns at filtering chlorine through the supply. If anyone forgets or fails to take part, it will not be fatal. A system of checks has been set up. But group confidence will falter and resentments will spread at a time when community concern is already high. *M* is a member of *G*. *M* prefers playing with his Gameboy to reading books and is lazy at the best of times. He shuns all responsibilities. Reading may be edifying and chlorine purifying, but there are checks, so no one is going to die, and *M* can happily thumb away at his game.

As Waldron notes, an 'institution can be just in two ways: (a) it can be just in the way it operates; and (b) it can be just in the sense that it is doing something that justice requires'.[49] Similarly, there is a distinction between a scheme exclusively devoted to morally necessary ends and only partially so committed, or, as Green puts it, 'an institution that does justice and an institution that *only* does justice'.[50] *M* cannot rationally or morally generalize his free-riding in the chlorine case. The benefit is morally required, cooperation is necessary for its production, and any individual who free-rides acts wrongfully.

Once we mention the rational or moral importance of goods, we introduce considerations beyond fairness.[51] We establish coordination schemes around rules of the road in order to prevent harm to individuals. Their imperative lies not in fairness, but in the value of human life and the importance of preventing unnecessary harm. Fairness applies once the scheme exists, is effective, and yields the benefit of coordination. We must thus be careful to keep considerations of fairness and considerations of utility, justice, value, and so on distinct.

The concern of the principle of fair play is primarily distributive: how burdens and benefits are distributed. But are the nature of the scheme and the principle of fairness wholly independent? Consider all the reasons why free-riding within the chlorine scheme seems more unfair than free-riding within the book swapping scheme. We risk greater harm, we impose more onerous burdens on others (when these burdens may already be very onerous), we create instabilities and concern, and we threaten ends of greater value.

Are these concerns of fairness, utility, or an admixture of the two? The fairness theorist might argue thus. These are obligations of fairness since grounded ultimately in others' actions.[52] Simmons replies for the anarchist, to the effect that this condition achieves far too much. Obligations 'to help those in need or promote happiness will *also* be actuated by the cooperative behaviour of others, aimed at achieving these ends'.[53] Imagine I believe I have a duty to contribute to charities. When I make my contribution, my action presupposes the cooperative acts of others aimed at this end. Similarly, is my duty to aid a drowning child actuated by the cooperative behaviour of others aimed at achieving this end? It is if we interpret the act of helping those in need as part of a cooperative practice. This is not ridiculous. We might say that there is a latent cooperative practice justified by the utility of all believing that it is general practice to help those in need, and acting on this practice should occasion arise. However, all these senses seem less internally connected to the practice than in the chlorine case. I can give to those in need—giving money to

[49] Waldron 'Special Ties and Natural Duties' 29.

[50] Green 'Law and Obligations' 539.

[51] See, generally, Simmons *Justification and Legitimacy: Essays on Rights and Obligations* 31–6.

[52] Klosko 'Presumptive Benefit, Fairness, and Political Obligation' 247–8 n. 23.

[53] Simmons 'The Anarchist Position: A Reply to Klosko and Senor' 272. Simmons makes similar points in 'Fair Play and Political Obligation: Twenty Years Later'.

beggars—without going through cooperative organizations. I may save another's life simply through goodness and not through a vested interest in maintaining a utility-promoting scheme. The fairness theorist, however, can reply to Simmons that fairness obligations are partially *grounded* in others' actions, and not merely *actuated* by them. It is part of the normative ground and not a logical or contingent precondition on obligation arising.

Consider the chlorine case. This is a scheme that is not only morally necessary but necessarily involves the cooperative actions of most members of a specific community. This morally necessary end can only be achieved by this cooperative means. (Assume that it has been agreed within G that, though all need not strictly participate at all times, over-determination of tasks helps prevent lapses; communication at certain times during the day within the commune is poor; and comfort will not always be available.) Free-riders therefore know that their unfairness is internally linked to this morally necessary end. Without general cooperation, this end will not be attained. Their unfairness is thereby linked to possible harm, loss of utility, and instability. Unfairness is not contingent on consequences. Free-riding is unfair and exploitative. The necessity of cooperation is a logical and moral point. Attaining this morally necessary goal logically requires a cooperative practice. The question of the link between fairness and bad consequences is an empirical point. If I free-ride I necessarily wrongly exploit others, but whether any other wrong spills out from my actions is a separate empirical question.

What conclusions can we reach on benefits rationally and morally beneficial? I will suggest a rough scheme focusing on the interaction between the nature of benefit and the type of scheme:

1. Morally necessary ends, necessarily attained by cooperative means, with reasonably fair distribution of benefits and burdens. Here there is a strong presumption that all parties have an obligation of fair play to do their fair share. This is just one of the many moral obligations that can arise without the strong involvement of the agent's will. Rebuttal could take the form of claiming that though the end and the cooperative means are necessary, *this* cooperative scheme is flawed or immoral;

2. Morally necessary ends, only contingently attained by cooperative means, with a fair distribution of benefits and burdens. Here, again, there is a presumptive obligation of fair play on all parties. X might query this obligation by illustrating an alternative, morally preferable means (in terms of externalities or fairness). X may also rebut the presumption by showing that, though this benefit is morally vital, it is provided at too high, or an immoral, cost. (An example of the former would be a pacifist who, though assured of the importance of physical security, disowns a state that accumulates nuclear weapons to attain this end.)

3. Presumptively beneficial ends necessarily or contingently attained by cooperative means, with a reasonably fair distribution of benefits and burdens.

Kavka observes that the non-avoidance of morally unnecessary but desirable goods, which are also open benefits, is 'over-determined'.[54] It is difficult to know whether X receives the benefits since difficult to avoid or since desirable (or desired). Without enquiring personally of him, we cannot know his genuine opinion of the objective benefit and subjective worth involved in these benefits. But the benefit is seemingly genuine. If the scheme satisfies relevant requirements of substantive, procedural, and distributive fairness, there is a rebuttable presumption that fairness applies to consumption of goods. Rebuttal takes the form of intra-systemic comparisons from other individuals, from other preferred schemes. If X would genuinely prefer no benefit and no burden to the presence of both, or thinks his burden in some way deeply unfair, he can properly avoid contribution; and

4. Morally permissible ends, yielding discretionarily beneficial goods necessarily or contingently attained by cooperative means. Here there is no presumption of obligation. Instead, only those who clearly evince attitudes of acceptance and enjoyment are obligated by considerations of fair play.[55]

This is impressionistic. However, on the basis of these observations, fairness *potentially* binds participants to cooperative schemes of these kinds. But now, having marginalized acceptance, how do we discern membership? Again, to make fairness feasible, our conditions will have to be relatively neutral.

Jeremy Waldron has suggested a principle by which to determine who constitute 'insiders' to a social scheme.[56] *A* is an insider in respect of a range-limited principle of justice *P1* on the condition that *P1* applies to *A*'s interests, claims, or conduct. Where *L* is an institution administering a range-limited principle in respect which of *A* is an insider, *L* applies to *A*. *A* is an insider to *L* only if part of the point of *L* is to do justice to her claims among all the claims *L* administers. This is morally neutral, but is more sophisticated than merely stipulating citizenship as a criterion of membership. Bare citizenship seems to overlook temporary and permanent residents and guest workers within a country, and hence some of the total of all who benefit and are burdened by a nation's political system. All of these classes may, none the less, make any number of justice claims within their guest state: on courts, welfare, and benefits services, and community members, and so on. Claims of justice will also be made upon them (tax demands, tolls, and so on). Waldron's emphasis on doing justice to an individual's claims is particularly appropriate in the context of fairness. Equally, those who incidentally benefit by provision of goods are excluded. We could therefore adopt Waldron's criterion as capturing a genuine but qualified sense of particularity. However, note that while the range-limited principles exclude from membership those only benefited by chance (or as a by-product of externalities), the spatial dimension of range-limited principles of justice need not and will not

[54] Kavka 'Review of *Moral Principles and Political Obligations*, by A. John Simmons' 228.

[55] Chaim Gans provides a related taxonomy of cases (emphasizing the moral permissibility of certain preference orderings) at *Anarchism* 61–6.

[56] Waldron 'Special Ties and Natural Duties' 19–20.

coincide exactly with state borders. Many transnational norms ultimately operate directly on subjects of otherwise sovereign nation states. Different cooperative schemes will encompass different constituent participants.

Our progress to this point is modest. I have tried to avoid rescuing fairness from scepticism only to hand it over to cynicism. Political society, if conceivable as a cooperative scheme, and if producing morally necessary and rationally desirable goods, satisfying the conditions stipulated above, is susceptible to yielding obligations to contribute one's fair share. The point is deeply conditional. I am not saying that all members have prima-facie obligations. More has to be said before we could reach this conclusion. To decide whether and to what extent fairness obligations can be present, we must establish what kinds of fairness a scheme must manifest, and the nature of others' attitudes within the scheme.

THE RELEVANCE OF OTHERS' ATTITUDES

Attitudes play a dual role in obligations of fairness, implicating the attitude of an agent to the benefits he receives, and others' attitudes to the scheme and their contribution.[57] What attitudes must others in a scheme display before I am properly obligated? Three different suggestions seem plausible. First, all members must participate out of some concern for others. But fairness seems, at its minimum, more impersonal and abstract than this. This idea of special concern seems more appropriate to considerations of gratitude or associative obligations.

Secondly, all must demonstrate fair-mindedness in participating.[58] The idea here is that, while participating, agents have an occurrent sense of acting according to a principle of fairness. Again, this seems too strong. People can act fairly who are not naturally fair-minded. Many who might want to cheat do not, from some sense that it is wrong. Fairness may be a corrective for the instinct towards personal bias. This is, none the less, distinct from the moral agent who would, *ab initio*, be appalled by the idea of cheating.

Finally, members must conceive of their actions as located within and contributing towards a cooperative practice. Here there is only a proper appreciation of the context and consequences of action. This translates the group principle into the first person: Just as there must first be a cooperative enterprise before fairness operates, so too the agent either does, or should, grasp the cooperative nature of the venture before fairness obligations obtain. This, I would suggest, is all that fairness requires. If I understand the context and consequences of my and others' actions, I understand the significance of restraint. I understand that communal actions link up in a network of benefits and burdens. I realize

[57] See also Greenawalt *Conflicts* 133–6.

[58] See, generally, Carr *On Fairness* ch. 6 and Smith *Liberalism and Affirmative Obligation* ch. 8.

that the good is produced only by joint efforts, and (by implication) that free-riding is wrong.

How might this understanding manifest itself? If *X* has ever watched another's actions and inwardly thought or said 'that's not fair', be it of an illegally parked car, an unpaid tax bill, arriving late for a common departing time, driving knowingly down a one-way street, taking more than one's share of the earnings of a joint project, then *X* perceives (or should perceive) the cooperative outline of the practice. The members may be barely known to each other, they may not like each other, they may even secretly want to engage in one-upmanship. But they restrain themselves, because the success of the venture is predicated on this, the benefit is worth the burden, and others are cooperating.

BENEFIT AND FAIR SHARES

Fairness in a legal system has procedural, substantive, and distributive dimensions. Procedural unfairness comprises inequalities before the law.[59] This might be tacit or explicit discrimination, imparity in political influence, or general social or political marginalization. It may be unfair treatment by the general system and operation of laws even prior to the system generating specific benefits. Here the benefit of the system is differentially and unfairly distributed.

Substantive unfairness is actual inequality in the distribution of benefits. This might involve the receipt of fewer amenities, fewer tax benefits, or the investment of less government revenue in a particular area and so on. Here, benefits from the system are unfairly distributed. A procedurally fair system may still yield unfair benefits. Very bad laws are passed by procedurally just legal systems. Where this occurs, the fact of procedural fairness may to some degree ameliorate the wrong. An unfavoured citizen may think that the unfairness perpetrated against him by a particular law represents only a wrinkle and not a feature of the system. There may exist fair procedures that allow substantive unfairness to be altered more easily. These will not make the law *per se* any more fair. But it will place it in a less alarming context.[60]

Both procedural and substantive unfairness may vitiate or reduce an individual's obligations of fair play as regards particular laws. Exploited or marginalized groups such as women, gays, blacks, or the poor should not feel morally bound to obey laws which discriminate against them, either in procedure or substance. Moreover, some forms of discrimination may make individuals question their obedience to other laws related to those that discriminate against them.

[59] For related discussions, see, Greenawalt *Conflicts* 138–40; Gans *Anarchism* 57–66, and Simmons *Moral Principles* 101–42.

[60] See also Greenawalt *Conflicts* 145.

Distributive justice concerns the fair distribution of benefits and burdens. A fair share requires more than that an agent's burdens are proportionate to his benefits.[61] *X*'s evaluation of the ratio of his benefits to burdens is an impressionistic utility function, calculated at the stage of ascertaining whether the benefit justifies participation at all. Fairness is a relative notion, mediating between the claims of different individuals. These considerations will include the ratio of *X*'s benefits and burdens proportionate to A, . . . *V*'s benefits and burdens and the benefits enjoyed, and burdens borne, by class *Z* (to which *X* belongs) relative to those of class *Y*. These are intra-systemic comparisons. As regards significant and wide-ranging injustices, *X* might also employ inter-systemic comparisons between the average benefits and burdens of citizens of his community/state *C* relative to community/state *S*. This comparison has less to do with fairness, as regards the reciprocal restraints between members of a community, and more to do with the question of whether the benefit in question is adequate to activate obligations of fairness at all.

Two comparisons among agents seem important.

1. The *quantity* of others' benefits and burdens. Does *X* receive less protection, does he enjoy fewer social advantages and benefits?
2. The *quality* of others' benefits and burdens. Do others receive benefits more suited to their subjective needs and desires, do they receive fewer impositions on their (legitimate) personal goals and life plans; do they receive more value at less cost from their benefits?

These factors will be relevant for *X* in assessing whether his treatment by his fellows is fair and to what degree unfairness exists.

How will comparative unfairness in allocations alter and affect individual obligations? There appear to be four possibilities. First, there is the case of Tom, who loses out in an unfair scheme. We cannot consistently argue from fairness that he should comply. (Nor should we want to argue this.) He is still obligated to obey all morally imperative individual laws, but he should feel no legal allegiance beyond this. Secondly, there is the case of Dick, who is fairly treated by a fair scheme. He, like his fellows, should obey the rules governing their common scheme. Thirdly, there is Harry, who is preferentially treated by an unfair scheme. Ideally, before he benefits and before accepting the benefits of the scheme, Harry should do all he can to ameliorate this unfairness. But if he does accept the benefits, then he does owe restraints (and possibly beyond what he is requested to provide in order to redress the imbalance which the scheme and his acceptance create). He cannot, without hypocrisy, accept unfair benefits and then refuse restraints because of the unfairness. However, where continued cooperation perpetrates a greater injustice than violation, where obedience harms the general welfare to some great degree, Harry probably ought to refuse to obey. Finally, there is the case of a group *G*, subject to a vertically unjust scheme, where, none the less, their horizontal conduct involves no unfairness.

[61] Simmons seems to suggest the contrary at *Moral Principles* 114.

Consider an occupied state. The invading army make equal but equally unjust demands on all citizens. If all do not tend to their needs in rotation, some among them will be (randomly) killed. The members do have fairness obligations to each other. Vertical injustice does not preclude the possibility of horizontal fairness. This kind of example, however, will obviously not take us very far as regards a domestic political system.[62]

Not all individuals will be equally bound. The idea of a 'fair share' must be responsive to the different benefits and burdens of different individuals and sensitive to discriminations.[63] As Zweibach notes: 'Equality is produced by having equalizing rules to obey rather than being equally obliged to obey inegalitarian ones'.[64] A concern for generality should not distort the enquiry.

SUMMARY

A political society that meets the conditions on fairness obligations within a cooperative scheme may be capable of generating obligations of fair play. In order for this obligation to arise, participants must understand the cooperative nature of the scheme. This understanding proceeds inductively from grasping that micro-and macro-schemes in which one participates depend upon general conformity and restraint from free-riding, and from grasping the interconnectedness of various activities and schemes. As regards morally necessary ends necessarily attained by cooperative means, there is a strong presumption of obligation. The same applies as regards morally necessary goods contingently attained by cooperative ends, save that here the agent may question obligation by illustrating preferable alternative means. As regards rationally desirable benefits, the non-avoidance of which is over-determined by the fact that they are open benefits, there is a rebuttable presumption of willing acceptance. The most compelling rebuttal will take the form of a concession of objective benefit, accompanied by a denial of subjective worth. Where this rebuttal succeeds, the obligations are never generated or are generated in diminished strength or scope (given that fairness is backward looking, some minimal repayment may be warranted before the agent withdraws from the scheme). Discretionary goods create no presumption of obligation. Acceptance and attendant attitudes are vital here.

[62] See also Greenawalt *Conflicts* illustration 7–3 at 129–30. Note that the randomness of possible assassinations renders this a coordination as opposed to a cooperation problem. Each participant has a self-interested reason to conform. Failure to do so is both morally wrong (in-so-far as it may lead to another's death) and irrational (in-so-far as it may lead to the participant's own death).

[63] Nagel *Equality and Partiality* 38: 'What makes it reasonable for someone to reject a system, and therefore makes it illegitimate, is either that it leaves him too badly off by comparison with others (which corresponds to a failure with respect to impartiality), or that it demands too much of him by way of sacrifice of his interests or commitments by comparison with some feasible alternative (which corresponds to a failure with respect to reasonable partiality).'

[64] Zweibach *Civility and Disobedience* 30.

Distributive unfairness, pertaining to relative quality or quantity of benefits, will nullify or diminish obligations. *X*'s fair proportion of the burdens of providing even a morally necessary benefit may, fairly, be negligible. (This benefit may fall out unevenly on him, for example, physical protection in a troubled inner-city area. The benefit may also actually itself perpetrate unfairness against him, for example, a corrupt or racist police force in the same area.) No fairness obligations will arise for those who experience real unfairness. Fairness cannot apply to unfair schemes without contradiction. Underpinning this model, therefore, is a simple idea. Legal systems and their benefits may be appropriate objects of obligations of fair play. In fairness, different participants may have different or no obligations. Only once all considerations relevant to fairness have been evaluated will we be able to know the extent of any agent's obligations.

LEVELS OF GENERALITY: A STRUCTURAL PRELIMINARY

There are different levels at which an argument from fairness can be pitched.[65] We might think of fairness in relation to a particular law *L*, or as regards a class of laws *C*, a branch of laws *B*, or a legal system *X*. From these we would derive arguments from fairness which respectively run: It is fair to obey law *L*; it is fair to obey law *L* because it belongs to class *C*/branch *B*; it is fair to obey law *L* because it belongs to legal system *X*. I will look first at the particular inquiry.

At the lowest level, for *X* to argue to *Y*, 'you have an obligation based in fairness to obey law *L*', it is necessary that the law is both beneficial, and in order to avoid contradiction, that *L* is fair. We might think of unfairness in this context as the wrongful taking advantage or exploiting of others. Now imagine an argument, directed to a 17-year-old gay male, that he should observe age of consent laws (imposing a higher age of consent for homosexual than for heterosexual couples) due to considerations of fairness. This is not a law from which he benefits. It is one that restricts him as others are not restricted. His violation of it in no way unfairly exploits others or takes advantage of their restraint, since for most, non-violation is not a sacrifice but an omission never considered.[66] The law provides no benefit and is unfair in its treatment of him. It is contradictory to argue for its observance from fairness. Or imagine a law prescribing that blacks must sacrifice their seats on public transport for whites, and that whites must accept this sacrifice when offered. As directed at a white male on public transport, this law prefers his convenience to that of his fellows, but on the basis of a morally irrelevant criterion. The white male cannot be urged to comply with this law by arguments from fairness. Neither can the black passenger.

The argument from fairness can only be consistently used as regards individual laws untainted by substantive, procedural, or distributive unfairness. It will

[65] See also Greenawalt *Conflicts* 124.
[66] See also Greenawalt *Conflicts* 138–9.

never be the case that all the laws of a legal system are fair. So the possibility of a general, never mind universal, obligation to obey seems greatly threatened. It is this concern that typically motivates moving the argument to a higher level of abstraction. What might be gained from arguing from law *L* being a member of a certain class or branch of laws?

Reverting to the example of gay consent laws, we might argue that, while *X* does not benefit from this specific law, he does benefit from the general class of laws regarding sexual practices, including laws regarding rape, paedophilia, assault, and so on. The difficulty here, of course, lies in determining the relevant class. *X* may feel that the age of consent law properly belongs, not to the class of laws relating to sexual practices, but to the class of laws concerning informed consent. Also, even if *X* does benefit from a relevantly defined class of laws, fairness concerns not only benefit but also fair distribution of burdens. It will be relevant that this class of laws is more onerous for *X*. Membership of a class of laws consequently seems an intermediate and indeterminate stage of the argument.

At the systemic level, the argument runs that membership of an overall fair system of laws provides a prima-facie reason to obey law *L*, even where the primary legal obligation may involve unfairness. The systemic argument is obviously crucial in an argument for a generic obligation to obey the law *qua* law, as a directive of a legal system. What can be said of the argument at this level of abstraction?

For *X* to be able to argue from fairness that *Y* should obey law *L* because it is unfair to do otherwise, the legal system overall must be reasonably just and fair. The argument here might collapse into the empty analytic point that one ought to obey a legitimate authority, if, as is reasonable, we take legitimacy as implied in describing a system as fair and just.[67] Now, if the system is fair and legitimate, we may well have a prima-facie moral obligation to obey its laws, but it will derive from whatever features or considerations establish its justice and legitimacy and not from the mutuality of restrictions involved in the principle of fair play. It will be a duty owed to the state and not to our fellows. This may then be complemented at the horizontal level by an obligation of fairness. However, an independent theory of justice will then be necessary to flesh out the principle of fair play. Before the theory is provided, therefore, or before any real states are demonstrated as just and fair, the thesis from fairness is an implication of an assumption.

Even where we assume the overall fairness of a system, a question remains. How does the fairness of the system cure the defect of law *L*, or provide external reasons in favour of obedience? For, if we must be fair in a system that is fair and just, why does this logic not flow down to individual laws and require that we must be fair as regards fair laws, and thus not obey unjust laws from considerations of fairness? The argument from fairness can only criticize acts that

[67] See also Pateman *The Problem of Political Obligations: A Critique of Liberal Theory* 113–21.

unfairly exploit or take advantage of one's fellows or acts that have unfair consequences, and thereby exploit or harm others. But as regards the former, even where we view an unfair law through the lens of a fair system, the unfairness of the rule loses none of its focus. It is still the case that law *L* exploits and does not benefit *X*, and obedience seems an act of exploitation by others of *X*. An argument from fairness looks just contradictory. This need not be the case as regards an argument from consequences *and* fairness. Violation may create unfairness which, when combined with systemic fairness, creates a presumption of obedience. We thus need to turn to considerations of consequences and systemic arguments from fairness.

CONSEQUENTIALISM AND THE FIRST PREMISE OF FAIR PLAY

In the Dibbler example, the initial rationale supporting the scheme is consequentialist. Group cooperation is a necessary and sufficient condition for establishing a scheme that produces some good or prevents some evil. So, too, liberal political theory traditionally conceives of the state as a utilitarian association, established to serve and promote the common good.[68]

Arguments from utilitarian generalization, serving the same end as arguments from fairness, attempt to show the moral imperative of universal compliance where only general compliance is necessary, by generalizing the consequences of violation.[69] But as Broad stresses, the argument from generalization generally relies on counter-factual assumptions about the actions of others.[70] The appeal of fairness is that it is actually unfair to exploit others, and fairness thereby supplies some of the defects of utilitarian theory. However, while fairness seems a compelling ground for obedience at the particular level, it seems to falter at the systemic level and, as we saw above, some resort to consideration of consequences seems necessary to make out the argument.

The consequentialist argument relevant in the present context is the argument from bad consequences, which attempts to show that the fact that a government is beneficial to society entails that individuals have obligations of support and obedience. The argument from bad example rests on three premises. First, the legal system and the benefits it yields are preferable to the absence of any legal system. Secondly, no legal system can sustain pervasive violations, therefore, thirdly, one has a prima-facie obligation to obey all laws. Between the second and third stages there is a suppressed and fallacious premise that there exists an empirical link between a single violation and systemic collapse. To support the

[68] A similar understanding is also found in Aristotle *The Nicomachean Ethics* VIII. 9. 1160^{a}6–30 (at 208); especially: 'and it is for the sake of advantage that the political community too seems both to have come together originally and to endure'.

[69] Ewing 'What Would Happen If Everyone Acted Like Me?'

[70] Broad 'On the Function of False Hypotheses in Ethics' 377.

thesis, it is necessary that every act of defiance in some way snags the fabric of society.[71] This cannot account for secret violations (which most violations *strive* to be). Nor does it account for laws broken by *X*, where he rightly believes that the law *per se* is antithetical to the spirit or stability of the legal system, and where obedience will possibly entail consequences worse than violation. The argument from bad example implies a dually corrosive effect—that violation gives a bad example to others, and that it encourages *X* himself to violate more frequently. Both claims can be rebutted by empirical evidence. Others may not act as *X* does, and even if they do the actions may not have the predicted consequences. None the less, can arguments combining consequentialism and fairness achieve together what individually they cannot?

GREENAWALT AND INDIRECT GENERAL OBLIGATION

In 'Promises, Benefit and Need'[72] Kent Greenawalt makes the following submission:

> Since all citizens generally benefit from a decent legal order, part of the duty of fair play is to help maintain its viability. The duty of fair play thus reaches violations of law that could, if multiplied, undermine law observance, *whether or not the duty reaches the particular law involved*. This aspect of the duty may usually be much weaker than the requirement not to "take advantage" of one's fellows in some more direct way, but it does count.

While direct fairness obligations pertain to benefits produced *by* the system, indirect fairness concerns attach to the benefit *of* the system. This indirect fairness generates a general but weak duty of obedience. This duty may reach laws the direct theory of fairness does not. The argument will cover two cases. First, there is a law ϕ. It is directly covered by considerations of fairness, and buttressed by this concern of systemic fairness. Secondly, and more interestingly, there is a law λ. Arguments of fair play do not argue directly for conformity to λ. But the system overall is decent. And *X* should not disobey λ if widespread disobedience of λ would undermine the system. The primary fairness rationale has fallen through, but the secondary, systemic rationale may apply. Two claims are combined. First, an empirical claim about the consequences of the effects of multiplied violations. Secondly, a normative claim about the unfairness of jeopardizing a decent system, the benefit of which is shared with others. Both the argument from fairness and consequences necessarily presuppose an already effective scheme. The thesis from consequences must link empirically to actual harm. According to the principle of fairness, however, the actual consequences of an individual's behaviour are not necessarily at issue. If *A* disobeys, he does wrong because the benefits of disobedience cannot be extended to those whose sacrifices make the rule of law possible.

[71] See also Soper *A Theory of Law* 60.

[72] Greenawalt 'Promises, Benefit, and Need: Ties That Bind Us To The Law' 763. Emphasis added.

Consider again the case of unfair law λ in overall decent system. The primary rationale for obligation has failed. Therefore, we already know one of the following. First, X's violation involves no unfair exploitation of his fellows, for example, a law which when violated neither has adverse consequences, nor involves any unfairness, since *X* does not accord himself a privilege he would not extend to others (for example, running the 4 a.m. red light). Alternatively, the law in question treats *X* unfairly. To supply this defect, Greenawalt's argument partially adopts the structure of the consequentialist argument from bad example: 'the duty of fair play thus reaches violations that could, if multiplied, undermine law observance, whether or not the duty reaches the particular law involved'. But the argument still ultimately rests on causal propositions, and the fallacious premise that individual violations might undermine systemic stability or viability. If *X* has no primary reason of fairness to obey λ, fairness can only pertain to systemic concerns if his violation actually *does* damage the system or spread violation from one domain to another, only if his actions actually have unfair consequences. Therefore, either the indirect argument is secondary because the direct duty of fair play exists, or the latter has failed and an empirical case must be made out for the former. In many cases this will be falsified (for example, where *X* can be quite sure that his violation will not have adverse consequences).

It is telling that Greenawalt omits this argument in *Conflicts of Law and Morality*. Here, where discussing fairness from the perspective of maintenance of law in general, Greenawalt introduces a modified and muted version of the argument:

> All citizens benefit from the observance of law by other citizens, and one aspect of the duty of fair play may be to do one's share to maintain an overall fair system of law observance. Viewed in this way, the duty may seem to reach all the laws of a society and to be a potential source of a general obligation to obey. In a small group setting, at least, such an argument would have considerable force . . . The fairness duty to maintain the legal order overall will apply only if the system overall is reasonably just.[73]

The emphasis on the small group setting here is probably meant to suggest the greater likelihood of some infectious effect of violation. If the organization of the group is fair overall, non-compliance with rules in one domain could reasonably be viewed as unfair to those who observe the rules in other domains. This both provides implicit support for an argument from adverse consequences and suggests the inappropriateness of such a rationale in large-scale society. Greenawalt's final point, that a system must be just overall for this reasoning to hold, supports the earlier submission that general fairness is a prerequisite for the application of this argument. This, however, leaves the point strangely empty. If the legal system is decent or just, any duty linked to this fact seems more likely to be some variant of Rawls's natural duty of justice to support and uphold just institutions, in turn buttressed by consequentialist premises. It will be a vertical

[73] Greenawalt *Conflicts* 146–7.

duty owed to the system, and not a horizontal one owed to fellow citizens. And we will need to argue for the justice of the system.[74]

RAWLS'S SYSTEMIC ARGUMENT

John Rawls advances two arguments based on fairness, the obligation owed to fellow citizens outlined above and a second, systemic argument.

> If one thinks of the constitution as a fundamental part of the scheme of social cooperation, then one can say that if the constitution is just, and if the rule enacted is within certain limits, and if one has accepted the benefits of its working and intends to continue doing so, then one has an obligation based on the principle of fair play, to obey when it comes one's turn. In accepting the benefits of a just constitution one becomes bound to it, and in particular one becomes bound to one of its fundamental rules: given a majority vote in behalf of a statute, it is to be enacted and properly implemented.[75]

This final statement stems from Rawls's consideration of the apparent paradox involved in an individual accepting a procedure (majoritarian democracy) which he knows will sometimes place him in a minority and will therefore potentially commit him to obedience of laws he thinks unjust.

Rawls talks of the 'acceptance of constitutional procedure',[76] demonstrating equivocation between acceptance of the terms of a constitutional democracy and acceptance of benefits produced by others' cooperative efforts within a constitutional democracy. If *X* accepts the terms of a democracy this acceptance suggests implied or tacit consent, or more fundamental approval, and not fairness as the basis of obligation. Even consent may be otiose within Rawls's argument since he stipulates in advance exhaustive necessary features of justice for the system.[77] The justice of the constitution is a necessary condition of obligation.[78] This borders on being little more than the point of grammar that we ought to obey a legitimate authority or support a just government,[79] the province finally ceded to the natural duty of justice in *A Theory of Justice*.

Rawls implicitly assumes that the citizen in question is a supporter of democracy, agreeing with the majoritarian decision-mechanism, and cites as numbering amongst his beliefs that, 'given that a majority will vote for *B*, *B* should be enacted and implemented'.[80] For *X*, a reflective democrat believing in the majority voting system, it is not the principle of fairness that binds him to obey when in a minority. These are simply the logical implications of his political commitments.[81]

[74] For an argument similar to Greenawalt's, see Klosko *Principle of Fairness* 101–7.
[75] Rawls 'Legal Obligation and the Duty of Fair Play' 9.
[76] ibid. 9. [77] ibid. 5. [78] ibid. 11.
[79] Pateman *The Problem of Political Obligation: A Critique of Liberal Theory* 113–21.
[80] Rawls 'Legal Obligation and the Duty of Fair Play' 7.
[81] See also Hook 'Law, Justice and Obedience' 58.

Consider Y, a non-democrat or a democrat believing in universal direct democracy. *Y* may not accept the terms of the constitution, he may work from within to alter its composition, but he may still owe obligations based on the principle of fair play to his fellows for their cooperative efforts without which he would lose many important social benefits. Nor need this bifurcation alarm him. The only laws likely to cause him real moral dilemmas are substantively institutional laws, pertaining to the make-up or support of the political system. As regards these he may be able to make a supportable moral case that he receives insufficient benefit for obligations to arise.

SUMMARY

Given requirements of logical consistency, we can only argue for a systemic obligation of fair play if the system overall is just and fair. This may explain Rawls's inclusion of the justice condition. Now, if this is so, citizens very possibly have an obligation to obey or political obligations or a natural duty of justice. All of these will be based on whatever features of the system make it fair and just. The obligation of fair play will be a secondary, horizontal obligation owed to one's fellow citizens—if the mutuality of restrictions properly applies. It could apply at the systemic level by virtue of two arguments. First, if violations of even unfair laws have (more) unfair consequences for other cooperators. The difficulties with this argument have been detailed above. Secondly, one might argue that in violating, one takes unfair advantage of the benefit of the system *per se*, which remains viable only on account of others' cooperation. As regards a fair law, one should already have primary obligations to obey, based on independent considerations, the natural duty, or fair play. As regards an unfair law, where the obligation of fair play is used as a port manteau obligation, it is inconsistent to argue for obedience from fairness unless adding considerations of consequences, or relative weightings of unfairness (the unfairness of *X* violating law λ is greater than the unfairness of requiring obedience). This argument will not obviously apply to laws not directly related to the idea of a beneficial system. Of more importance is the fact that the relevant comparison as regards the unfairness and exploitation involved in disobedience is *other citizens*. As a result, if *X* breaks one law λ, he is only unfairly taking advantage of his fellows if they disobey no laws. If they also disobey some laws—as all people do—then overall, they may treat each other fairly. The standard is not absolute obedience of all laws, but a degree of obedience that is fair relative to the conduct of others.[82]

There is something insidious in arguing from a tolerably just society to the requirement to obey all individual laws regardless of content. A just society has little to fear from occasional, morally justified violations of legal norms. And the

[82] See also Greenawalt *Conflicts* 143.

argument from fairness flirts with logical inconsistency where relying on reasonable systemic fairness to obligate citizens to individually unfair rules.

FINNIS'S FINESSE

> He compared laws to spiders' webs, which stand firm when any light and yielding object falls upon them, while a larger thing breaks through them and makes off.
>
> (Diogenes Laertius)[83]

John Finnis defends the moral authority of law from the perspective of fairness.[84] He builds from a criticism of Raz's suggestion that where the law secures a coordinative practice, the moral reasons affecting the agent's reasoning derive entirely from the factual existence of the social practice of cooperation, and not from the fact that law is instrumental in its institution or maintenance.[85] The origin of the practice is unimportant. Finnis has two replies. First, what is instrumental in securing a morally obligatory goal must itself be morally obligatory, unless there is some instrumentality as or more effective. Secondly, where a practice is secured by law, and not by other means, the practical reasoning of the agent should change. This change is effected by considerations of fairness that legal prescription entails.

The agent now reasons thus.[86] 'Though I do not like or approve of law λ, I should comply because of the many benefits I receive from the legal system. My person and property are protected, markets are regulated, and tax laws are enforced. Given that I accept these benefits from law, I ought to accept its burdens. Violation may benefit me, but I want to be fair to others and for others to be fair to me.' This is an argument from cooperative fair play. The agent also reasons: 'I think the votes of elected representatives are a useful and fair method of resolving national issues. In this case, my view lost out. But sometimes it wins and I expect others to abide. So too should I now.' This is an argument from fair political procedures.

For Finnis, law specifically invokes considerations of fairness. Law, unlike custom, yields innumerable benefits to the citizen. And law presents itself to the citizen as 'a seamless web', from which she cannot pick and choose. Law links together, in a unique and privileged way, all persons and all temporal periods. Not all aspects of the common good are identified and protected by law. Fairness and community pursue avenues other than law. However, 'to trace out the seamless web of the law is to gain a singularly adequate view of the breadth and *complexity* of the common good, of fairness, and of what may be involved in

[83] Diogenes Laertius *Lives of Eminent Philosophers* book 1, ch. 58 (describing Solon).

[84] Finnis 'The Authority of Law in the Predicament of Contemporary Social Theory', 'Law as Co-ordination', and generally, *Natural Law and Natural Rights*.

[85] Raz *Authority* 249.

[86] Finnis 'The Authority of Law in the Predicament of Contemporary Social Theory' 119.

an appropriate *philia politike*'.[87] Once law makes demands of me, I must be aware of the reciprocity through which benefits are born and burdens are borne.

Wherein, however, lies the moral authority of law? Law is one paradigm of political authority. Political authority is best explained by reference to the solution of coordination problems (CP). Finnis does not deploy a game-theoretic notion, using an intuitively more appealing sense of coordination. A CP is any situation where, if 'there were a coordination of action, significantly beneficial payoffs otherwise practically unattainable, would be attained by significant numbers of persons, where there is sufficient shared interest to make some such coordination attractive, and where the problem is to select some appropriate pattern of coordination in such a way that coordination will actually occur'. The question for law concerns how action is to be coordinated (how to select a solution, how a solution attains this status, and how to maintain the solution).[88]

Group action, Finnis suggests, is only susceptible to coordination through unanimity or authority. Either option must select and implement a pattern of coordination. Authority may either exist in the form of a process that is quasi-unanimously acknowledged, or in some authoritative figure who enforces a particular scheme. The viability of political solutions relies on the cooperation of a vast number of people. For Finnis, those who participate in the polity must daily acknowledge that the selection of a scheme did authoritatively settle the question.[89] The selection *must* be treated as authoritative. This 'must' imports rational necessity (and would also connote moral necessity were obligatory ends able to be pursued only by this means). There is no unanimity concerning the solution of any particular coordination problem. Any unanimity therefore *must* result from quasi-unanimity regarding the desirability of conforming to the authoritative scheme.

Two points require final clarification. Why must we treat law as authoritative, and what sense of 'sharing of aim' does Finnis postulate for political community? Legal systems, being supreme and comprehensive, are salient in the communities in which they rule. They hold themselves out as public and privileged sources of solutions for social problems. If accorded this status, law offers the prospect of speedy and salient solutions. Moreover, legal institutions for devising and maintaining solutions secure fairness by the stability, generality and non-discriminatory character of their solutions. Finally, law imposes solutions on free-riders by a process minimizing arbitrariness and self-interest. In summary, the virtues of the rule of law give legal systems their distinctive entitlement to be treated as an authoritative source of solutions.

The shared interest that Finnis believes gels together members of community is the interest in maintaining a fair method of interrelating benefits, burdens, and persons, over a complex set of aspirations and transactions. Only a legal order promises such a method.

[87] ibid. 120. [88] ibid. 133. [89] ibid. 135.

Finnis's first thesis, therefore, is that what is instrumental in securing a morally obligatory goal must itself be morally obligatory, unless there is some equally or more serviceable means. However, law is only a sufficient and not a necessary condition for the solution of individual coordination problems. Other possibilities exist, with different and sometimes preferable externalities. Our moral obligation is to do that which is necessary to secure coordination, and to follow practices already achieved which secure coordination. Law is only contingently connected to coordination. This point is particularly strong in an account from fairness since, as noted above, fairness pays no cognizance to the origin of rules. It looks only to efficacy and procedural and substantive fairness.

Finnis's response here might be twofold. First, this point ignores the fair and uniquely efficient democratic mechanism at the heart of legal decision-making. Secondly, though there may be other logical possibilities for the solution of individual CP, they are simply not practicable, or are inferior to law. Moreover, this ignores that legal systems are, *per se*, a solution to a large-scale, second-order CP.

Let us look to the first point. The idea is that those subject to representative democracy accept that this is a fair decision-procedure for the resolution of disputes. Those who happily conform when in the majority are required by fairness to conform when in the minority. Otherwise, the system and coordination are infeasible. This point returns us to the discussion of Rawls above. If *X* accepts majority representative democracy, then this commits him to abiding by its rules. This is both a logical and a moral point. Not to abide is inconsistent with his deeper commitment, and is also unfair, given his and others' commitments. However, his commitment, and the application of fairness, is grounded in his acceptance of this method. What of a direct democrat, one who believes in proportional representation, or one who seeks greater local devolution? If he genuinely believes the present system is unfair and does not and would not reasonably accept it, is he bound by fairness? He may seldom be in the majority and may lose out on all those matters most important to him. (Consider, for example, the situation of Socialists in Scotland during the 1980s. Despite overwhelming votes in favour of the Labour Party, the Westminster Parliament, with a significant Conservative majority, governed, and often ignored, Scottish interests.) Fairness seems unconvincing. If *Y* does not accept the system as fair, he must be persuaded of its procedural and substantive fairness.

Further, is no systemic or particular alternative to law ever available or preferable? The systemic concern is more a concern of utility or justice and is not immediately relevant here. Fairness applies only to actually existing operative schemes and the relative claims of parties. What then of the particular case? The deep difficulty in Finnis's account seems to be the way he wholly adopts and presumes the perspective of authority. He, like law, privileges, law.[90] Even if unanimity and authority are exhaustive of the options, is law exhaustive of the

[90] See also Raz 'The Obligation to Obey: Revision and Tradition' in *Ethics* 350–2.

possible authorities? Is coercive law necessary? Could other sets of arrangements be justified to all reasonable people? Finnis's approach helps only the descriptive and not the critical enquiry. The origin of rules is incidental to fairness. Rules matter as a source of expectations and a locus for fairness considerations. Other sources of solutions are possible and must be considered.

Where the obligation of obedience is an obligation owed to fellow citizens, we can, at the general level or at the level of the distribution of particular goods, consider alternatives to the state. As regards a micro-scheme, a free-rider problem may blossom on account of production of a public good, such as clean air and an unpolluted environment. The state, with its coercive apparatus of sanctions and incentives, now appears as just one amongst several possible solutions to a social problem. And once it is conceived in these terms, alternative solution strategies, centring on cooperation and coordination concepts, are opened up.[91] The externality costs involved may be preferable. Thus we might consider the possibilities of non-state agencies coordinating social schemes, or order achieved cooperatively over time.[92] Recent work within socio-biology and evolutionary theory regarding the naturally cooperative instincts of humans within certain circumstances is suggestive here.[93]

It is not enough to say that law is uniquely broad in the benefits it confers. Comprehensiveness and supremity simply entail a certain impressive scope. The functioning of the rule of law should also secure procedural fairness, and provide some check against arbitrary and biased interests. But these features alone, should the rule of law be disappointed in performance, also create the potential for great harm. Seamless webs are spun to catch small insects. We should take seriously the claims of those whom legal authority disadvantages.

The fairness thesis again seems flawed. Can the auxiliary principle of coordination provide any additional strength? Finnis does not tell us how coordination requires a general obligation to obey the law. He may imply, but does not explicitly argue for, a thesis from adverse consequences. This has been dealt with above. A further point is relevant. Though law does coordinate action by the provision of information, not all laws are coordinative. Law is only trivially a coordinative authority. Consider some clear examples—murder, assault, rape, contract law, and tort law. None of these seems specifically coordinative in function. George Christie has questioned this.[94] Take homicide laws:

[91] Hampton 'Free-Rider Problems in the Production of Collective Goods' and *Hobbes and the Social Contract Tradition*; Taylor *The Possibility of Cooperation*; Hargreaves-Heap and Varoufakis *Game Theory: A Critical Introduction* and Varoufakis *Foundations of Economics: A Beginner's Companion* ch. 9.

[92] See also Green 'Authority and Convention' and 'Law, Co-ordination and the Common Good'; on the latter of which, see Finnis 'Law as Co-ordination' 100 n. 4; and see further Coleman 'On the Relationship between Law and Morality' 77.

[93] See, amongst many others, Ridley *The Origins of Virtue: Human Instincts and the Evolution of Cooperation*; Wright *Non-Zero: The Logic of Human Destiny*; Pinker *The Blank Slate: The Modern Denial of Human Nature*; Hinde *Why Good is Good: The Sources of Morality*; and Midgeley *Beast and Man: The Roots of Human Nature*.

[94] Christie 'On the Moral Obligation to Obey the Law'.

I would submit that it is not absurd to look at the law concerning murder and manslaughter as serving the purpose of providing the social coordination for the practice of killing... What constitutes murder or manslaughter, what counts as self-defense or unavoidable accident, are all notions of considerable complexity in which legal analysis informs our notions of what is morally permissible perhaps as much as our notions of morality dictate what should be the content of law.[95]

Christie rejects the counter-argument that while talk of coordination may be appropriate as regards morally indifferent matters, it is not so as concerns morally charged matters. Law informs morality at the edges in these matters. Gaps within moral principles require further determination by legal norms.[96] Law fills in these holes and serves a coordinative function.

Again, this seems wrong. At most these little known and technical rules coordinate the actions of legal officials, lawyers, policemen, judges, and so on. Ordinary people do not typically know the fine points of provocation law, the precedents on reasonable force in self-defence, or the limits of necessity. If we were to learn that *X*, an ordinary citizen, was looking into the fine detail of these matters in order to coordinate his actions, we would have cause, not to celebrate law as a coordinative authority, but for alarm as to *X*'s intentions. Raw morality may not suffice for the courts, but in these matters it should suffice for citizens acting in good faith. Neither coordination nor cooperation ultimately persuades.

THE LIMITS OF FAIRNESS

Certain fundamental aspects of the account from fairness ultimately count against it. Most significantly, fairness has no concern for the origin of rules. Its concern is the action of others around these rules and the expectations and claims this generates. Law, custom, practice, or habit can all be the focus of fairness. Now, so long as people take legal rules as definitive of appropriate behaviour, and comply with these laws, this concern is, as Greenawalt notes, little more than a 'quibble'.[97] But ineffective laws are not covered and other, non-legal, effective practices are covered. This strongly suggests that for fairness the moral reason for action is generated by the fact of a practice in combination with the actions of others, and that law as such provides no moral reason to conform. The comments concerning Finnis's ideas on coordination should support this conclusion. There may sometimes be a high degree of coincidence between the claims of law and settled practice, but that is all.

This normative nexus of effective practices, others' actions, and the good faith attitude of the agent, suggests numerous qualifications to the scope and strength of fairness obligations. Others' actions are both part of the ground and limits of the obligation. Fairness requires a fitting and proportionate return. Only if

95 ibid. 1321.
96 Honoré 'The Dependence of Morality on Law' 1.
97 Greenawalt *Conflicts* 137.

I genuinely believe in, or witness, the exhaustive conscientiousness of others, will I feel obligated to reciprocate with obedience to all duty-tokens. Only if all others commit to exhaustive obedience is there universality of duty-subjects. But people are not this conscientious. The horizontal return is often a fine judgment made almost intuitively, and falls short of universality on all its axes. Most importantly, the obligation to obey the law on this account is not an obligation to obey the law *qua* law, but *qua* contingently salient identifier of a fair and efficient practice. Not only law, and not all laws, fill this role. Law loses its privileged status.

Paradoxically, this is part of the appeal of fairness. It looks first to our fellows and moral reasons for action. It approximates an answer to the weaker enquiry. In a reasonably fair state in which our fellows seem intelligibly engaged in a mutually beneficial cooperative enterprise with us, and where laws and effective practices largely coincide, the fact that something is a law will usually indicate a moral reason for obedience (the effective and fair practice which law has established or secured). Legally prescribed practices will have some presumptive force. And from the perspective of community, this is to be welcomed. We are social creatures. Our selves, our beliefs, our upbringing, and even our autonomy, are socially crafted strengths.[98] By understanding this, our interdependence grows defined.

But fairness fails because the benefits it focuses on rest in the efforts of our fellows, and because fairness itself imposes certain conditions on schemes in order to avoid contradiction. Perhaps then, a notion of reciprocity that ties benefits more directly to the state, and looks less to horizontal variables will satisfy the main enquiry. And so it is to gratitude that we now turn.

[98] MacIntyre *Dependent Rational Animals: Why Human Beings Need the Virtues* 74: 'to learn how to become an independent practical reasoner is to learn how to cooperate with others in forming and sustaining those same relationships that make possible the achievement of common goods by independent practical reasoners'. Richard Dagger makes a related observation in a fairness account at *Civic Virtues: Rights Citizenship, and Republican Liberalism* 66: 'no one becomes or remains autonomous without the assistance and cooperation of other people'.

6

Benevolence and Gratitude

> Whatever conduct promotes the good of the community, is loved, praised and esteemed by the community, on account of that utility and interest, of which every one partakes;... this affection and regard be, in reality, gratitude.'
>
> Hume[1]

Moral fashions have not favoured the duty of gratitude. Where Kant once identified obloquy: '*ingratitude*... is... publicly judged to be one of the most detestable vices',[2] Kagan now identifies obsolescence: 'previously, gratitude might have been prominent on a list of normative factors, today its status is at best peripheral and many, I think, would be skeptical of the existence of any such requirement at all'.[3] Arguments grounding an obligation to obey the law on gratitude may therefore seem the rather sad marriage of two tired ideas. Yet, originating in Socrates' impassioned pleas of the personified laws of Athens, gratitude has, in various voices, spoken in defence of obligation.

Like fair play obligations, obligations of gratitude are reciprocal, reactive obligations. However, whereas fair play consists in the requital of benefits produced within a cooperative effort, gratitude consists in a response to benevolence. Gratitude is an affective and sometimes active response to the goodwill of another.

There is a gallery of conceptions of gratitude in the history of philosophy. A detailed early study occurs in Seneca's *De Beneficiis*, a work explicating acts of kindness between individuals and focusing on the motives and activity of favour.[4] In this conception, favour is a knowing and ineliminably particular[5] kindness,

[1] Hume *Enquiries Concerning Human Understanding and Concerning the Principles of Morals* sect. VI, part 1 (at 243). Hume also observes: 'Of all the crimes that human creatures are capable of, the most horrid and unnatural is ingratitude, especially when it is committed against parents'. Hume *A Treatise of Human Nature* III. 1. 1 (at 466).

[2] Kant *The Metaphysics of Morals* 'The Doctrine of Virtue' sect. 36, 6: 459 (at 206).

[3] Kagan *Normative Ethics* 136. For notable exceptions to this waning interest, see: Godbout and Caille *The World of the Gift*; Amato *Guilt and Gratitude*; McConnell *Gratitude*; Buckley Jr *Gratitude: Reflections on What we Owe our Country*; Viroli *For Love of Country: An Essay on Patriotism and Nationality*; Camenish 'Gift and Gratitude in Ethics'; Card 'Gratitude and Obligation'; Martin 'Good Fortune Obligates: Gratitude, Philanthropy, and Colonialism'; Berger 'Gratitude'.

[4] Seneca *Moral and Political Essays* 181. At I. 6. 1: Seneca describes an act of favour as '[A]n act of benevolence bestowing joy and deriving joy from bestowing it, with an inclination and spontaneous readiness to do so. Thus what matters most is not the deed or the gift but the mentality behind them: the kindness lies not in the deed or the gift but in the mind itself of the person responsible for the deed or gift.'

[5] ibid. I. 2. 1.; I. 14. 1.

motivated by unselfish concern for the other.[6] The kindness consists in the act of favour, and not the vehicle of its expression.[7] Favour should act according to the interests and not the wishes of the beneficiary: True friendship frustrates and does not facilitate destructive desires. The beneficiary must accept the gift and not merely have it thrust upon him. (That which we cannot decline does not bind us.) The essence of favour resides in the intention of the giver. Its special feature is not to think of return but to look to helping and pleasing the recipient. The benefactor who looks to return no longer confers a favour but does a deal. Given this, if the beneficiary accepts the benefit in the state of mind in which the benefit was given, he has repaid the true essence of favour.[8] He has held a moral mirror up to the benefactor's kindness. It may be the case that the beneficiary should still strive to make an appropriate active or material return. There may still be something missing, something that would restore symmetry to the dual dimensions of thought and action. But it remains important to keep the two separate.[9] Material return is a duty distinct from affective response.[10] An object in kind will return the gift, just as gracious acceptance returns the favour. But material return is not mandatory, for, 'favours would be in a poor way were gratitude never allowed to be empty-handed'.[11] Similarly, gratitude must be spontaneous and cannot be enforced. Legal regulation would transform favour into a loan, providing self-interested reasons and motives for compliance. Performance would no longer be predicated on goodwill and affection, and there 'can be no glory in gratitude if you cannot be ungrateful without impunity'.[12] The benefactor's gain is moral and self-referential: 'Things that are honourable contain their own reward'.[13]

Aristotle touches briefly upon favour and gratitude in both *The Nicomachean Ethics* and *The Art of Rhetoric*. In the latter, he discusses favour directly, the Greek equivalent, 'kharis' encompassing favour, gratitude, charm, grace, and general agreeability. It is defined as 'that by which he that has it is said to do a good turn—a service to the asker in return for nothing else—to the advantage not of the server himself but of the beneficiary'.[14] The authenticity of favour and the appropriateness of gratitude can be forfeited in several ways. One can show that the service was done for the doer's benefit, that it was done by chance or compulsion, or that it was a return as opposed to a gift.[15] In the first two cases,

[6] Seneca *Moral and Political Essays* 181. At I. 6. 1: Seneca describes an act of favour as '[A]n act of benevolence bestowing joy and deriving joy from bestowing it, with an inclination and spontaneous readiness to do so. Thus what matters most is not the deed or the gift but the mentality behind them: the kindness lies not in the deed or the gift but in the mind itself of the person responsible for the deed or gift.' I. 2. 3.

[7] ibid. I. 5. 1.; I. 7. 1.

[8] ibid. II. 22. 1; II. 31. 4.

[9] ibid. II. 34. 5; II. 35. 1.

[10] ibid. II. 33. 1.

[11] ibid. II. 31. 4.

[12] ibid. III. 7. 3.

[13] ibid. IV. 1. 3; IV. 9. 1.

[14] Aristotle *The Art of Rhetoric* sect. 6, ch. 2.7 (1385^{a}) (at 161). Emphasis omitted.

[15] ibid., ch. 2.7 (1385^{b}) (at 162). See also Aristotle *The Nicomachean Ethics* IX. 7 (1167^{b}21–1168^{a}33) (at 233).

inappropriate motives, or the absence thereof, preclude favour. In the last, the element of repayment prevents an act of favour. Two final categories are excluded. First, any actions the benefactor would do for one's enemies. Here, the required particularity is absent. Secondly, a favour the benefactor knows to be negligible.

For Kant, gratitude consists in, 'honouring a person because of a benefit he has rendered us'.[16] The beneficiary respects the benefactor, who is in a relation of love to the beneficiary. Beneficence (active gratitude) and benevolence (affective gratitude) are distinct. However, heartfelt benevolence without any active beneficence, the mere disposition of goodwill, can itself ground an obligation of gratitude. Gratitude is a sacred duty. The obligation it creates cannot be completely discharged in a single act. The party under obligation remains so. Moreover, violation of this duty can destroy the essential moral incentive to beneficence. The duty reaches to contemporaries, predecessors, and even to those one cannot with certainty identify.[17] Gratitude for a beneficiary is not love but respect (a notion later echoed in the writings of Sidgwick). Universal love of neighbours is necessarily based on equality of duties. In gratitude, the obligee stands below the benefactor. Thus, some resile from the relationship of gratitude, fearing that by the display of gratitude they assume an inferior, dependent position, contrary to self-esteem. But such ingratitude is 'a vice shocking to humanity'. The harm of such an example deters others from further beneficence. Proper affection is inverted. Absence of love authorizes hatred of the one who loves.[18]

In his *Enquiries* Hume describes the 'crime of ingratitude' as found, 'wherever we observe good-will, expressed and known, together with good-offices performed, on one side, and a return of ill-will or indifference, with ill-offences or neglect on the other'.[19] In examining wherein lies that 'matter of fact which we call crime' he suggests: 'It resides in the mind of the person who is ungrateful. He must, therefore, feel it and be conscious of it. But nothing is there, except the passion of ill-will or absolute indifference.'[20] The crime of ingratitude arises from the congeries of circumstances that excites blame in the spectator.

Hobbes ultimately disputes the altruistic basis of beneficence. In setting out the fourth law of nature, he observes that he who receives a gift through the grace of another should ensure that the benefactor never has reasonable cause to regret doing so: 'For no man giveth but with intention of good to himself; because gift is voluntary; and of all voluntary acts, the object is to every man his own good; of which if men see they shall be frustrated, there will be no

[16] Kant *The Metaphysics of Morals* 'The Doctrine of Virtue' sect. 31, 6: 455 (at 203).
[17] ibid., sect. 33, 6: 455–6 (at 204).
[18] ibid., sect. 36, 6: 459 (at 207).
[19] Hume *Enquiries Concerning Human Understanding and Concerning the Principles of Morals* app. I 'Concerning Moral Sentiment' sect. 236 (at 287).
[20] ibid., sect. 237 (at 287).

beginning of benevolence, or trust; nor consequently of mutual help; nor of reconciliation of one man to another'.[21] Were this to be so, men would remain in the state of war, contrary to the first and fundamental law of nature, that men should pursue peace. The act of giving need not be for its own sake. Enlightened self-interest brings the source of all kindnesses back to benefit to the giver. And the preservation of the practice of gratitude is fundamental where, without the advantage to the benefactor that gratitude constitutes, the practices of benevolence and trust would destabilize.

Sidgwick mediates between Seneca and Hobbes by stressing both the crucial affective dimension of benefaction—'the affection, if practical and steady, seems a higher excellence than the mere beneficent disposition of the will, as resulting in more excellent acts'[22]—and its utilitarian justification. No onerous service will be adequately rendered unless there is a general disposition to reciprocity: 'A general understanding that all services which it is expedient that A should render to B will be in some way repaid by B, is a natural supplement of the more definite contracts by which the main part of the great social interchange of services is arranged'.[23]

W. D. Ross advances a quite contrasting conception of gratitude.[24] Gratitude is, for Ross, a special obligation arising incidentally as a result of another conferring benefits upon us. This original act may not have been intended to create obligations, but it does so.[25] Fidelity and gratitude strictly connote 'certain states of motivation'.[26] However, 'it is not our duty to have certain motives, but to do certain acts'. 'Gratitude' is used to denote the returning of services irrespective of motive. And beneficence is used in preference to benevolence throughout, again to denote that we can speak only of the duty to do certain acts and not to have certain motivations or dispositions.

The insistence that moral requirements range over actions and not feelings returns in the context of political obligation, in Simmons's work,[27] where he suggests that it is inappropriate to make the having of certain feelings the substance of a moral requirement:

> We are presumed to have a kind of control over our actions that we do not have over our feelings; we can at least normally, *try* to act in specified ways, where we cannot try to have certain emotions or feelings (in the same way). And surely part of the point of a moral requirement is that its content be the sort of thing which we can, at least normally, *try* to accomplish.[28]

[21] Hobbes *Leviathan* ch. VX (at 162).
[22] Sidgwick *The Methods of Ethics* 223; 259–61, 279, 437–8.
[23] ibid. 437.
[24] Ross *The Right and the Good* 22–3, 27.
[25] ibid. 27.
[26] ibid. 22.
[27] Simmons *Moral Principles* 167.
[28] ibid.

GRATITUDE AND GRATEFULNESS

These different conceptions simultaneously evidence diversity and unity, and raise many topics central to later discussion. I will now structure a conception of gratitude around the following enquiries.

1. What is the appropriate object of gratitude?
2. What are the conditions and background circumstances under which gratitude is appropriate or due?
3. What is the nature of gratitude and gratefulness, and their characteristic composition and role in our reasoning?
4. As regards performances motivated by gratitude, what factors are relevant to the:
   (*a*) Nature and content; and
   (*b*) Extent and degree, of performance?
5. Are acts grounded in duties appropriate objects of gratitude?
6. Is gratitude obligatory?

I will then proceed to analyse the suitability of gratitude as a, or the, ground of the obligation to obey the law, with particular focus on the theory advanced by A. D. M. Walker.

THE APPROPRIATE OBJECT OF GRATITUDE

The appropriate object of gratitude is favour.[29] Favour is a kindness or concern that the benefactor is not required to confer, and that finds its particular focus in the beneficiary. It is supererogatory and specific. What the beneficiary is entitled to demand will not be typically an object of gratitude. Nor will a benefit conferred widely and without discernment. The favour, *per se*, resides in the attitude or disposition of kindness or goodwill. But favour may also manifest in action or take material form. The former is a disposition of benevolence, the latter an act of beneficence. In each, the benefactor demonstrates an attitude of goodwill to the beneficiary. It is this goodwill, this common core of benevolence, that distinguishes favour from other attitudes and motives that may also result in one party conferring benefits upon another. Favour also involves giving without expectation of return.

That the essence of favour is goodwill entails that it is not fungible in the way many good deeds or benefits may be. Once conferred, the kindness is intact. Again, the magnitude of the favour resides in the magnitude of the spirit of the giving and not the material benefit. (Hence the parable of the widow's mite.)

The dual features of a kindness done specifically for the beneficiary and a giving without asking for return, looking only to the beneficiary's advantage,

[29] See also Berger 'Gratitude' and Walker 'Gratefulness and Gratitude' for related 'affective' accounts of gratitude.

bring the notion of favour close to that of friendship. In *The Art of Rhetoric* Aristotle observes that friendship is 'wishing for someone what one thinks to be good things, for his sake and not for oneself, and being productive of these up to one's capacity'.[30] The factors productive of friendship are 'the favour and acting without being asked and not revealing that one has acted'.[31] In these circumstances, motivation is pure. The action seems most clearly to be for the friend's sake and no other reason.

The emotional element is fundamental to favour and thus to gratitude. But it is important to note that gratitude is neither friendship nor love. It is appreciativeness, combined with goodwill, possibly respect, and the desire to make some affective or active return. Gratitude will often feature in loving relationships and will strengthen claims formerly resting only on love, where not only love, but also beneficence, has been received. Claims may then become imbricated, with love, gratitude, goodwill, and duty all inclining towards the same action.

CONDITIONS UNDER WHICH GRATITUDE IS APPROPRIATE OR DUE

The following are advanced as necessary and sufficient conditions for appropriate instances of gratitude. Focus will fall not upon benefit but favour. This focus narrows the enquiry. Motivation is central. The bare category of benefit leaves scope for ambiguity in a way favour does not. The conditions build around the scaffolding of Simmons's conditions.[32] The emphasis on favour over benefit distinguishes the two accounts. Therefore, some of Simmons's conditions are retained, some are altered and some new conditions are added. I will indicate any interesting overlaps and divergences where they occur.

1. The favour must not be too trivial.

Too trivial an act of goodwill may prevent both the appropriateness of gratitude and of obligation. Seneca observes that 'there are things which do not measure up to the standards for this name'.[33] Ordinary kindnesses should not burden us. Rules of etiquette are obvious examples here. A thankfulness that expresses itself sufficiently in a perfunctory 'thanks'—for example, to the 'chivalrous' door opener—is a requirement of etiquette and not an obligation of gratitude. There is nothing peculiar to you that makes the door opener open the door. Something peculiar to him does. Both this lack of a personal focus and the triviality of the performance preclude favour. We acknowledge the kind thought and a failure to do so would be impolite. But it would not be immoral. Rudeness is not wrongfulness.[34] Both the kindness and the requital are trivial

[30] Aristotle *The Art of Rhetoric* sect. 6, ch. 2.4 (1381ᵃ) (at 150).

[31] ibid., sect. 6, ch. 2.4 (1381ᵇ) (at 152).

[32] Simmons *Moral Principles* 170–8.

[33] Seneca *De Beneficiis* IV. 29. 2 in *Moral and Political Essays.*

[34] Save possibly for grave acts of rudeness with very hurtful or harmful consequences. See also Lyons 'The Odd Debt of Gratitude'.

and routinized. Gratitude is thus out of place. Triviality also precludes actions involving nugatory or minimal effort. Thus:

2. The favour must involve some degree of special effort.

This does not entail that the favour must take material or tangible form. Two cases suggest themselves. The benefactor hopes to confer material benefit upon the beneficiary, but his attempts are frustrated. The beneficiary is deeply touched by the benefactor's efforts, and has a disposition of gratitude towards him. This may express itself only in verbal thanks. But it may mean that, on a later occasion, when the beneficiary has an opportunity to invest approximate effort in the benefactor's welfare, he does so. And he may even succeed in his efforts, in a way the original beneficiary failed to do. Secondly, the benefactor may seek to confer favour on the beneficiary in a manner never intended to take material, permanent form, for example, by composing a song for his fiftieth birthday celebrations which he plays only once on the night of the party.

Favour need not be a success concept. Someone might try very hard to help us and yet, blamelessly, fail. Gratitude may be appropriate here. A relative may be deeply grateful to the brave swimmer who nearly loses his own life struggling to save a loved one, but who fails due to the tide. There is no benefit. But gratitude remains appropriate. Effort can be independent of benefit as a sufficient condition for gratefulness and gratitude.

Simmons's equivalent condition states that the benefit must be granted by means of some special effort or sacrifice.[35] We should, however, keep the criteria of effort and sacrifice separate. Some special effort is essential to favour, but this need not involve special sacrifice. A millionaire philanthropist can confer favour without any great sacrifice, but this will not exclude it from the categories of gratitude. Sacrifice is a factor relevant to the *degree* and not to the *fact* of favour and gratitude. Effort and goodwill are essential to favour. To make sacrifice essential is to inflate the condition.

3. The benefactor must choose the beneficiary as the exclusive or at least selective focus of favour.

At Book IV. 26. 5 of *De Beneficiis*, Seneca observes that 'there is a great difference between not excluding someone and actually choosing him. Some things could not fall to particular people without being given to everyone.' Favour is a particular and not a promiscuous phenomenon. What is given to all is no special kindness to any one person, and while he may feel glad to receive it, gratitude is out of place. The personal dimension is lacking. The analogy with friendship holds here. It would seem that there is some upper limit to the number of persons with whom one can be a good friend before one risks being a poor friend to too many.[36]

[35] Simmons *Moral Principles* 178.
[36] Aristotle *The Nicomachean Ethics* IX. 10 (1170^b20) (at 242).

4. The benefactor must confer favour on the beneficiary voluntarily and intentionally:
   (*a*) Having as one of his significant motives for doing so a feeling of goodwill towards the beneficiary; and
   (*b*) Not having as one of his significant motives for doing so, a feeling of ill-will towards some other party.

One action can serve many ends. Promoting *X* may be deliberately to overlook *Y*. Where unprincipled ill-will towards *Y* combines with favour towards *X* in motivating the benefactor's actions, it may evidence immoral reasons for deciding. Whether or not immoral, it will diminish the degree to which the action is a product of special favour.

There are two ways of looking at this, just as there are two ways of looking at the question of whether immoral promises are binding. As regards the latter we can say either that they do bind, but are deeply defeasible, and will thus be overridden. Or we can say that, being inherently immoral, they never generate moral obligations. Here, exactly the same could be said. Either that the dubiously, but partly favour-motivated, acts do generate a deeply defeasible obligation of gratitude; or, that they generate no obligations *ab initio*.

In so far as favour is an instantiation of goodwill, and in so far as ill-will (or culpable lack of regard) towards another features heavily within the benefactor's reasoning, I would be inclined to say that no obligation is generated. The kindness and particularity of the act are lost. This is especially so where the other motivations are actually immoral, for example, racial prejudice against another. Other mixed motives can be accommodated—for example, kindness combined with some incidental self-interest. The bare fact of having acted on duty will not preclude obligations of gratitude. I will discuss this point in detail below.

5. The favour must be conferred with advantage to the beneficiary as the primary concern and not in expectation of return.

There is a difference between deliberately conferring a benefit in expectation of requital, and having once conferred a benefit without any immediate thought of return, and later, when needy, asking for something by way of repayment. Assume that a benefactor has, some time ago, done the beneficiary some kindnesses. He is now in a state of need the beneficiary can ameliorate. The beneficiary makes no offer. The benefactor makes a request referring to these past actions. What is ugly here is not that the benefactor makes the request, but that he is required to. The beneficiary may not have offered for any number of reasons. He may have perceived the benefits very differently. He may feel that, though the kindness was appreciated, he cannot or should not meet the present demands. It may be that, alongside the many benefits conferred, many harms were occasioned. Each situation, like every personal relationship, is *sui generis*. But mere later mention of benefits conferred does not affect their genuineness at the time of the giving if, at the time, the expectation of return did not factor significantly in the reasons for giving.

6. The beneficiary must not actively not want the favour/benefit and it must not be forced upon the beneficiary against her will.

In such a case we will not even feel thankful for the state of affairs that transpires, never mind have a standing inclination towards return. Coercively to force a benefit on another is wholly antithetical to the nature of favour. It is a deficient advantage that the recipient does not want.

Within his equivalent requirement, Simmons makes allowance for the possible case of *real* benefits that may have to be forced upon one.[37] For example, a friend may forcibly prevent her friend from drinking, fearing that she is an alcoholic and trying to correct this. This is the basic distinction between one's immediate wishes and one's genuine interests, which may often conflict, particularly where rational capacity is diminished. As Seneca notes, any compliance 'that ruins the petitioner is a cruel sort of kindness. The finest of actions is to save people even against their wills, even if they refuse.'[38]

7. The beneficiary must be, on balance, happy to receive the favour, or alternatively, it must be the case that the beneficiary would be, on balance, happy to receive the favour were certain impairing conditions corrected.[39]

There are two possible background circumstances in which attitudes or obligations of gratitude might occur. First, *X* asks *Y* to do him a particular favour and *Y* does so. This grounds a special positive obligation of gratitude. The obligation is grounded in *X*'s voluntary request. Secondly, *X* makes no such request, and *Y*, believing genuinely that he acts to *X*'s advantage performs a particular favour for him. If there is a duty in this case, it is a pure special positive duty. *X*'s volition is less central. Condition 6 prevents abuse of this lack of voluntarism and places brakes on unbridled obligations.

We should not overstate the condition. We must not actively not want a benefit, either for its content or its source. But we need not actively want it either. The comparison to the state without benefit and debt may sometimes be opaque and the kindness involved, even in misguided attempts to help, may sometimes be quite touching. Too strict a language of benefit and degree of reciprocity resonates of fair play and justice and not the more subtle and affective matter of gratitude.

In describing the intrinsic beauty of favour, Seneca draws an analogy to the Three Graces. He pictures a fluid dance going back upon itself.[40] While often not this poetic, personal relationships are almost always this finely balanced and it is futile to prescribe too exactly the categories of appropriate conduct. In a happily functioning relationship, this will be obvious above all to the actor.

[37] Simmons *Moral Principles* 177–8. Simmons notes, however, that the mere fact that the use of force is legitimate will not establish that granting the benefit generates an obligation. The additional conditions stated must also be fulfilled.

[38] *De Beneficiis* II. 14. 1; II. 14. 4.

[39] Simmons *Moral Principles* 178.

[40] *De Beneficiis* I. 3. 4.

The rider for diminished capacity allows for cases where a benefactor's actions serve one's genuine interests and not one's immediate wants.

8. The beneficiary must not want the benefit not to be provided by the benefactor; or alternatively, it must not be the case that the beneficiary would not want the benefit to be provided by the benefactor if certain impairing conditions were corrected.[41]

This condition implies two possible restrictions on scope. First, *X* may not want a benefit to be provided *by Y*, because of *Y*'s identity. This could be because *X* does not want to owe any debt to *Y*, or because he knows that *Y* can ill afford to confer this benefit. Secondly, *X* may not want to be *provided* with this benefit at all. He may want to earn it, or he may believe it is more than he deserves or will ever deserve. Again the rider for diminished capacity applies.

THE NATURE OF GRATEFULNESS AND GRATITUDE

Gratefulness is thankfulness or happiness for a benefit received or an advantageous state of affairs. It does not presuppose the intentional kindness of a human or divine agent. Its focus is essentially benefit. It is not nonsense to feel grateful for the birdsong that fills a spring garden.[42]

Gratitude is a reactive attitude to favour conferred on one by another.[43] It demands some agent as its object. Its object is favour that is predicated on intention. Ungratefulness is thus different from ingratitude. We are ungrateful when we are not happy to have received this benefit or to have received it from this benefactor and so on.[44] Ungratefulness can be wrong: What we ought to accept it is ungrateful (and possibly hurtful) to refuse. But if such refusal is motivated by a sense of independence or self-sufficiency, then the agent is entitled to his decision. Gratitude, on the other hand, already presupposes gratefulness, a happiness at the state of affairs which transpires. Ingratitude is therefore the absence of any wish to make a return to one's benefactor despite the fact that one has gladly accepted the benefit.

Gratitude on the part of the beneficiary will usually be attended by respect and goodwill: respect for the benefactor as one who has assisted us, and goodwill in the desire to make a return. Respect generally connotes that one would treat another with consideration and, minimally, that one would refrain from violating his interests. Goodwill may translate into a standing disposition to protect

[41] Simmons *Moral Principles* 178–9.

[42] See Walker 'Gratefulness and Gratitude' 45–47 for discussion of circumstances in which gratefulness need not involve a triadic relation involving 'someone to whom' as alongside 'something for which' one is grateful.

[43] On 'reactive attitudes' see generally, Strawson 'Freedom and Resentment'. See Walker 'Gratefulness and Gratitude' 48 for a similar focus on 'favour' (which crucially, is substituted by a notion of 'benefit' in his account of gratitude and political obligation).

[44] See also Walker 'Gratefulness and Gratitude' 49.

and promote the benefactor's interests where appropriate—a general feeling of affection, falling short of, but similar to, friendship. (These indications are only typical.)

In fully comprehending what is distinctive to gratitude it is important to systematize the distinction between gratitude and fair play. In fair play accounts of obligation, the ground of obligation is the acceptance of benefits as a result of the sacrifices of other participants in a cooperative scheme. It is an obligation of reciprocity. Acceptance of benefits is thus a/the ground or a necessary condition of being obligated. Considerations of utility justify instituting the scheme. Benefits received must outweigh actual losses incurred by any obligated agents. It is presumed, and the benefit proviso confirms, that all agents (while they may hope also to further the common good) participate on the condition that doing so advances personal ends. Self-interested motives on the part of other participants do not preclude *X* being obligated.[45] Part of the reason fairness obligates us is that these benefits are not intended as a gift. Free-riding is not ingratitude. It is exploitation.

Appropriate affective attitudes are fundamental to gratitude and irrelevant to fair play. The former dwells on internal states, the latter on external acts. Gratitude and fair play are different, both in their foci and in what they may demand. Where necessary conditions are met, fair play will require cooperation with the same rules that have constrained others. Gratitude is seldom this simple.

Some of the writers discussed above do suggest that utility is part of the justifying rationale for gratitude, that without its practice, favour would diminish. There may be some truth in this, but while knowledge of non-reciprocity in a scheme of fair play would certainly inhibit one from participating, the same is not likely to be as true of favour. Many favours are conferred without an immediate hope of return—certainly not of a like return—and verbal thanks may often be sufficient acknowledgement of the goodwill. Utility is not so obvious a concern. And this is because the benefactor will often be in a relationship of goodwill or love to her beneficiary.

That which we requite without affection to the giver, and in equal measure, we return through considerations of fairness. Metrics of fairness seem more natural because to measure return does not violate the spirit of the gift. Genuine gratitude would blush at weighing its return too precisely. Too exact a return of gifts given lovingly may betray an etiolated understanding of the spirit of the gift, or a different understanding of the relationship involved.

Aristotle, in his treatment of friendship in *The Nicomachean Ethics*, includes a discussion that is a happy analogy to the point made here.[46] He distinguishes friendships of utility and friendships of virtue. In a friendship of utility, each uses the other for his own interests, and thus always wants to get the better of the bargain. The friendship of utility can be legal, on fixed terms (contract), or

[45] See also Simmons *Moral Principles* 172–4.

[46] *The Nicomachean Ethics* ch. VIII. 13 (1162^{a}29) (at 215).

moral. This is not on fixed terms. It makes a gift as if to a friend, but expects to receive as much or more in return, 'as having not given but lent'. In such a relationship, he continues, the question may arise as to how to measure the appropriate return to an act of beneficence. Two different criteria suggest themselves: to measure a service by its utility to the recipient, or to measure it by the beneficence of the giver. In a friendship of utility the former is more apt. The receiver asks for the assistance, and thus the assistance is precisely as great as the advantage to the receiver and he must return proportionate to his receipt.

In a friendship of virtue, the latter is a sort of measure, though measure is less relevant since complaints do not arise. Purpose is the measure, 'for in purpose lies the essential element of virtue and character'.

Similarly, in fair play (friendship of utility), utility justifies the relationship. We look to the benefits of the recipient before we calibrate obligation. In gratitude (friendship of virtue), we look to the beneficiary's purpose to measure the act and the relationship receives justification through the goodwill and respect that the parties feel towards each other.

THE NATURE OF THE GRATEFUL RETURN

Correlating to the margin of individuality and discretion in the benefactor's goodwill, is a discretion in the beneficiary's return. This is the personal dimension expressive and demonstrative of goodwill. It distinguishes gratitude from both contract and conventionally bound actions. There is a vital residue of meaning in gratitude, as a subjective reactive attitude, which is not easily converted into a metric of required action. As Sidgwick notes, 'as in other affectionate services, we do not like too exact a measure of duty'.[47]

When Lear wrongly confronts Cordelia on the measure of her debt to him, her reply reflects her awkwardness at having to try to articulate what is 'right fit':

> I love your Majesty
> According to my bond; nor more nor less...
> You have begot me, bred me, lov'd me: I
> return those duties back as are right fit,
> Obey you, love you, and most honour you.[48]

Cordelia is bonded to her father through love. His demand, however, invokes a bond of duty. Her understatement captures well the ineffable quality of a loving return. In knowing itself well, it knows how to respond. Forced into expression it becomes formal and aloof.

In so far as it is possible to prescribe appropriate returns, the following factors may be relevant. The favour must first have *some* value for the recipient. This need not be material value. It may be emotional. Effort expended or sacrifice

[47] Sidgwick *The Methods of Ethics* 260.

[48] Shakespeare *King Lear* I. i. 91–2 and 95–7; see p. 29 and accompanying notes.

incurred will then be relevant to the degree of debt owed. Benefit and effort will meet in different ratios. Some negligible efforts yield vast rewards. Consider an adult picking a drowning infant out of a shallow pool. By implication, there will typically be some correlation between the effort required and the degree of blame and censure failure to help provokes. Sometimes too, the effort will be huge and the benefit tiny. The quietest acts are often the most affecting. In the context of an institutional practice based on fair play and mutual restraints, great effort with little result will quickly meet with impatience.

Sensitivity to the benefactor's needs seems fundamental to any grateful return. Goodwill and respect refrain from hurt and seek to help. Just as the benefactor sought to attend to the beneficiary's particular needs, so too should the beneficiary look to this factor.

GRATITUDE FOR ACTS FULFILLING DUTY

One difficulty that troubles many discussions of gratitude is the question of the relationship between gratitude and acts of ostensible favour that are based upon the benefactor's prior duties. Providing a benefit because one has a duty to provide it may be viewed as a reason vitiating obligation.

Seneca observes that a 'favour is something done by someone in a position not to do it'.[49] What the beneficiary is entitled to demand is not an appropriate object of favour. I am not, all things equal, in a position not to perform my duties. Nor, it would seem, should I feel gratitude for that to which I am entitled. Simmons notes, that, paradoxically, it is often just in cases where we believe parties owe us a certain duty that we feel gratitude for actions fulfilling those duties, and discusses several examples to illustrate this point.[50] First there is the example of a philanthropic friend (Jones) who promises to give his somewhat more parasitic friend $10,000 a year for the rest of his life. Jones, having promised, has an obligation to pay this money to his friend. But Jones's friend seems to owe him a debt of gratitude for this payment. Simmons first suggests that the gratitude is due not for the obligatory payment but for the making of the promise. However, making the promise provides no direct benefit in itself. Only keeping the promise does so. So, instead, Simmons suggests that the promise confers a right on the friend, and for this he is grateful. But what if the friend, in a qualm of conscience, chooses not to exercise the right? Simmons resigns himself to the conclusion that, 'it is the payment itself for which I owe a debt of gratitude, and . . . this payment is obligatory'.[51]

Simmons's second example is the case of a parent's duties to care for his child. Here, he concludes, 'there are . . . reasons to believe that this particular duty-meeting conduct does *not* generate an obligation of gratitude on the child'.[52]

[49] *De Beneficiis* III. 19. 1 [50] Simmons *Moral Principles* 179–83.
[51] ibid. 181. [52] ibid. 182.

Simmons suggests that we have duties only to perform certain actions. Parental duties can only be duties to care well for children. It cannot be a duty to love, or to provide goods dependent on such feelings: 'Yet when parents do not do these things, when they do not provide the benefits of warm and affectionate care which are only possible when the parent *feels* in certain ways we believe, I think, that *no* gratitude is owed them for the care they give their children'.[53]

Love establishes ties of filial gratitude. We cannot routinely assume that children, even the ostensibly fortunate, have obligations of gratitude to their parents. Simmons concludes with a question mark: 'I am unable to concoct any clear principle distinguishing cases in which duty-meeting conduct (which satisfies our five conditions) does generate a debt, from those in which it does not'.[54]

Simmons's difficulties stem from an anaemic conception of gratitude. Concentration on benefits and losses is a poor index of intention. Intention distinguishes favour from chance, contract, institutional practices sustained with a certain understanding and expectation of reciprocity, and gifts given from ulterior motives. It is not action on duty or obligation that is antithetical to gratitude, but action based in self-interested motives. Considering various examples provided by Simmons—a natural moral duty to aid, a positional duty to perform the requirements of one's job, and of parental duties to care for children—allows us to see this point.

The natural duty to aid one in obvious danger is an aspect of natural, non-institutional morality. It does not typically correlate to an enforceable (legal) right to be saved (France is an exception here). Consequently, it is not something to which we are strictly entitled. By contrast, 'positional'[55] duties are an aspect of institutional morality. They occur in a framework of roles, contractual duties, rights, and responsibilities. The nature of each of these duties leads to certain presumptions concerning motive. The natural duty is not correlated to a right and is neither contractual nor institutional. We can assume that the major (though not necessarily sole) motivation for action is other-regarding concern. But we cannot assume this as regards positional or institutional duties.

Thus as regards the natural, but not positional, duties we can infer other-regarding motives. This is merely presumptive. The presumption is weightier where the natural duty's performance involves risk to the helper. Similarly, with a positional or a contractual duty there is a presumption of self-regarding or commercial motivation for action. But context will sometimes rebut presumptions of form. The vital factor is action springing from benevolent, other-regarding motives.[56] Entitlement to benefits often indicates that the benefactor's discretion is not in play. But entitlement, be it moral or legal, does not wholly preclude the possibility and appropriateness of gratitude. Duty and desire to act can sometimes overlap. Mixed motives do not preclude gratitude where

[53] ibid. 183.
[54] ibid. 181. Though Simmons does follow this confession with helpful suggestive principles.
[55] Simmons *Moral Principles* 4.
[56] See also Gans *Anarchism* 44 n. 6.

goodwill is significant amongst these motives. This observation leads to the issue of parental duties.

Some preliminary points should be noted. Filial analogies have shadowed gratitude accounts of the obligation to obey law. The manifest points of disanalogy can be quickly rehearsed. The child, unlike the citizen, lacks full capacity and rationality. The child's duty to obey ceases on majority or before, citizens' duties to obey continue until death. Additionally, the fact that children may have obligations of gratitude to parents, and the possibility that they also (up to a certain age) have an obligation to obey, does not entail that the latter instantiates the former.[57]

The analogy displays an obvious appeal to the theorist of political obligation. The sheer diversity of the parent–child relationship, the potentially uneasy mix of ineffable debt and ineffable disappointment, and the vast scope of influence exerted, is nowhere mirrored in quite the same manner as in the state–citizen relationship. The analogy also flatters the latter. Excepting cases of abuse and neglect, we unreflectively assume that filial debts are considerable. It also suggests a conception of gratitude more aligned to Kant's idea of a sacred duty, which sustains, and cannot be discharged by a one-off payment. This is obviously important in discussion of the obligation to obey. No one-off performance fulfils the obligation. The following discussion is an attempt to use the difficult topic of filial duty to illuminate the equally difficult topic of gratitude for actions performed through duty.

Simmons's essential contention is that, in the parent-child relationship, it is just what we cannot sensibly require—love, concern, care—that nurtures the germ of gratitude. This is not an uncommon position amongst modern thinkers. In *Liberalism and Affirmative Obligation*, Patricia Smith observes: 'Duties of children to parents . . . cannot . . . be accounted for by debts of gratitude, for good favours done by parents, since that would undermine the idea of parental duty. (Parents presumably are not doing their children a favour to raise them; they are doing their duty.)'[58] These arguments, however, seem to involve a crudely dualistic view of duty and love—that duty cannot be a vehicle of love or love an actor also on duty.

As Goodin observes, 'the discharge of a duty is a binary variable, whereas the discharge of a responsibility is a scalar one'.[59] We either do our duty or we fail to do our duty. I either stop at the red light or I drive on. Some other duties and obligations, though relatively simple actions, have qualities of performance. I promise to meet you for supper and we arrange a time of 8 p.m. I either meet you or I do not. But this obligation to meet you can be performed poorly. I can arrive at 8:15. Punctuality is a means of performing the obligation well. Some

[57] For a defence of this analogy, see Kraut *Socrates and the State* 145. For related criticisms, see Simmons *Moral Principles* 161–3.

[58] Smith *Liberalism and Political Obligation* 92.

[59] Goodin 'Responsibilities' 53.

duties have a component of responsibility, of discretionary performance. It allows for a duty performed thoughtfully, lovingly, with concern.

We fulfil or fail in our duties, but responsibilities are measured on a scalar metric. It matters *how* one does what one ought to do. This margin of discretion and judgment is the domain of benevolence. Law stipulates general requirements but leaves the details of performance to the parent. There are clearly some duties that the law neither could nor would seek to regulate. Stair marked this distinction as that between natural and civil obligations; those 'obligations that stand, and are acted in the mind and affections' which law does not enforce and duties to educate and maintain one's children which law does require.[60] Parents have a legal and moral duty to provide an education for their child. This, ex facie, entails that a child should not be grateful merely for being educated. Now, imagine a parent who becomes aware that the school within her catchment area achieves very poor results. She works long hours to secure an education for her child at the nearest independent school. The child receives an excellent education. All this time a trade-off occurs. Time that might have been spent in 'obvious' loving contact, playing in parks, going to pantomimes, is sometimes sacrificed to work. But the child owes much gratitude to the parent, and *just for* the performance of a duty to the sacrifice of other time lovingly spent together. Life is littered with imperfect trade-offs in which a gain in resources is a loss in relationships, and vice versa. Parents cannot always be Solomonic. Some love is necessarily communicated at a distance, and concentrates on what is basic to the child's welfare and future happiness.

Certain actions may be over-determined by reasons. Many parental actions may be mandated both by love and duty. As Frankfurt has noted, the necessities of love are not rational but volitional, 'love constrains the will rather than the understanding'.[61] This over-determination suggests that gratitude might be directed at right motives as well as actions. To have been loved where one might merely have been reared may appropriately ground gratitude. Similarly, to have received a kindness through friendship even if articulated as a promise is an appropriate ground of gratitude.

Gratitude to the parent requires only goodwill coupled with a desire to make an appropriate return. If goodwill is present, a certain self-defining symmetry will occur. A moral mirror will be placed before the parents' kindnesses. The grateful response may be infused with love, and may never be felt by the child as obligations. But even in the presence of goodwill and love, these responsibilities

[60] Viscount Stair, *The Institutions of the Law of Scotland* I. v. 6; I. iii. 5; I. v. 1, quoted in Jamieson *Parental Responsibilities and Rights* 2.

[61] Frankfurt *Necessity, Volition, and Love* 141. Frankfurt earlier observes that: 'Moral obligation is really not what counts here. Even if parents are somehow morally obligated to love or to care about their children, it is not normally on account of any such obligation that they do love them. Parents are generally not concerned for their children out of duty, but simply out of love; and the love, needless to say, is not a love of duty but a love of the children. To account for the necessities and the authority of parental love, there is no reason to invoke the moral law.'

may sometimes be felt as obligations, as exclusionary reasons conflicting with immediate self-interest. And this is likely to occur in cases of conflict—either conflict of obligations or conflict of this responsibility with things which the child herself strongly wishes to do, things fundamental to her own goals. Here, the amount and quality of kindnesses, alongside any hurts and failings, will be a factor in resolving the conflict.

Where goodwill is, without adequate reason, absent, we sometimes still seem to want to say that a duty of gratitude exists. Imagine the case of a child brought up with care and concern, whose parent, later in life, is severely ill and needs care. The child feels no gratitude towards his parent. He does not feel animosity, simply an absence of love or gratitude. He does not want to care for his parent.

Something in this emotional flatness is disturbing. But is the child morally culpable? Simmons and Ross alike would observe that we cannot have obligations to feel. The child has not failed in a moral requirement since affection is not something morality could or should prescribe. However, that we cannot have duties to feel does not mean that we are not responsible for our characters, that it is not within our moral capacities to cultivate appropriate reactions to circumstances and to persons. We can reach our emotions by evaluating our reactive attitudes. This allows us some control over the ultimate actions in which our character expresses itself, even if in the initial stages of its reactive response it is spontaneous and ungoverned by the will. Desires too can seem to hijack us. But where we perceive desires as unhealthy or immoral we strive to control or eliminate them.[62] Proper feeling is fundamental to gratitude, and in so far as we cannot have obligations to feel, we cannot speak externally of obligations of gratitude. But we can speak of duties to try to cultivate appropriate moral attitudes.

What then of the child who honestly feels neither love nor gratitude? Here we might speak instead of obligations of reciprocity and fairness. The basis of the obligation will be participation, with some voluntary acquiescence or acceptance, in the institution of the family, from which the child has benefited and to which it is now fair that he make some return.[63] A combination of roles, conventions, and expectations, alongside benefits accepted, generates a positive special obligation of fair play. This is more likely to be felt as an obligation.

Attitude defines gratitude but is less relevant to fairness. This fact explains the felt incongruity of the idiom of 'obligation'. We cannot demand states of the mind or the heart. But in gratitude properly so called, desire will often trace duty in the agent's actions.

[62] See generally, Blum *Friendship, Altruism and Morality* ch. 8 and Baron 'The Alleged Moral Repugnance of Acting from Duty'.

[63] Excluded from obligation here, therefore, is an adult child who does not and never truly has valued the institution of the family, and thus has not voluntarily participated in it; or who has genuinely not benefited from it—either through neglect or abuse, be it psychological or physical.

IS GRATITUDE OBLIGATORY?[64]

Language creates ambiguities here. Gratitude is often what we 'owe' another. It is often what we 'ought' to demonstrate. It is wrong not to do so. But just as 'owe' can connote mandatory realization of a right, it can also indicate what it is merely right to do. And just as 'ought' can connote obligation, it can imply only prudential, ideal, or evaluative guidance. It can be guidance for the virtuous agent and not an imperative indicating the obligatory act. Some performances we are owed are more sensitive than debts. They are not the sort of things that can be enforced, and enforcement would change their nature. Gratitude seems to be a thing of this sort.

The essence of favour and of the grateful return resides in mental states. Consequently, gratitude, as with other attitudes, is peculiarly unsusceptible to external regulation. It is not something about which we would expect to make 'demands' without undermining sincerity.

The above discussion suggests a framework. We cannot have an obligation to feel and gratitude is a fundamentally affective concept. We can however have duties to try to cultivate appropriate moral responses to situations and persons. Should both of these fail, and given other conditions, concerning the voluntary receipt of benefits within institutional practices, one may have an obligation of fair play.

One who feels genuine gratitude may, under ordinary circumstances, not experience her attitude as an obligation. The desire to make appropriate return will be a first-order reason for action. The attitude may be a 'burden' only in the sense that the beneficiary never feels capable of an adequate return. However, in cases of conflict with other strong first- or second-order reasons for action, gratitude may be experienced as a strong exclusionary reason. Gratitude will also exclude certain actions on the part of the beneficiary. She should not speak ill of, hurt, damage, or undermine her benefactor, unless a material change in circumstances occurs. Many of the excluded actions may already independently be morally proscribed. This proscription gains strength where a benefactor is concerned.

WALKER, WELL-BEING, AND OBLIGATION

In 'Political Obligation and the Argument from Gratitude' Walker develops a conception of gratitude applicable to the relationship of a citizen to her state. He suggests that the traditional gratitude account of obligation does not focus unambiguously on any genuine obligation of gratitude. The grateful response comprises a number of different obligations. And, while we cannot base political obligation on an obligation to requite a benefactor, arguments based on other *obligations of gratitude* have a better prospect of success.[65]

[64] See generally, Card 'Gratitude and Obligation'.

[65] 'Political Obligation and the Argument from Gratitude' 195.

Walker submits that the core of the grateful response is a set of attitudes, and that we must look to these attitudes to understand what actions gratitude requires. Gratitude requires that we properly appreciate the benefit, and it requires an attitude of goodwill and respect towards the benefactor. These attitudes place two constraints on the beneficiary's actions:

1 *X* must make it clear to *Y* that he possesses such attitudes. This is essentially declarative and symbolic: *X* communicates to the benefactor that he is grateful because he is grateful; and
2 *X* must not act in ways incompatible with these attitudes. This is not essentially declarative. It is a substantial benefit. *X* is committed to this requirement by his genuine goodwill. Unlike a symbolic demonstration, which may be a one-off, this is likely to be recurring.[66]

As an aside, it should be clear that the second of these is more fundamental. Basic to the grateful response is sensitivity to the needs of the benefactor. This will not always be compatible with the first proposition. As we noted above, secrecy may be vital in the return. But sensitivity to the benefactor's needs will, it seems, always be consistent with the second proposition.

The second proposition excludes not only ill will in the attitude of a beneficiary but also indifference, callousness. On this basis, Walker argues that there exist different *kinds* of obligation of gratitude: 'We have distinguished obligations to demonstrate our gratitude from obligations not to act in ways incompatible with the attitudes which make up the core of the grateful response. But we can also distinguish obligations of gratitude in terms of the different attitudes underlying them: some arise out of good will, others out of respect, and so on.'[67]

He distinguishes his thesis from an argument that appeals to an obligation to demonstrate our gratitude, constructing instead an obligation not to act in ways incompatible with the attitudes that constitute the core of a grateful response.

Walker chooses to focus on goodwill. Goodwill as the basis of obligation, he suggests, may recommend additional possible constraints. We have an obligation of gratitude to be mindful of the benefactor's interests.[68] We must not damage his interests and must weigh his interests specially in our consideration.[69] And the obligatoriness of the actions does not seem generally to depend on their being obligatory for any other reasons.

66 ibid. 200–1.

67 ibid. 201.

68 ibid. 203–4.

69 Note that these are all distinct. To be mindful of X's interests simply entails that we must not ignore them in our decisions. To weigh these interests specially means that we have to give them special regard when deciding. But not to damage his interests can mean two different things. It could mean a minimal sense of avoiding damage through inattention or indifference. But it could also be a proscription on ever damaging his interests in any way, even after weighting specially his interests in our decision-making process. This second interpretation seems to give undue absoluteness to his claims. This suggests that the first interpretation is preferable. Unless Walker intends that prima-facie we are to assume that we are not to damage his interests. Irrespective, note that interests and wishes may diverge. Sometimes we might genuinely believe, either as benefactor or beneficiary, that the best way to advance the other's interests is not to comply with or facilitate his wishes.

We can argue that non-compliance violates the principle of obligation on the proviso that the citizen in question actually does benefit from the state. In general, non-compliance with law damages the state's interests. It is, in general, in the state's interests for citizens to be law-abiding. The state will not survive without a reasonably fair measure of compliance with law. Citizens need not comply universally with every law no matter how misled or unjust. The gratitude thesis demands non-compliance where it might advance the state's interests to disregard bad legislation. It is interesting to note that this observation is usually found in consequentialist views. One should disobey if the good consequences of this, all things considered, outweigh the bad. But the point can also be deontological. It is based on the importance to gratitude of respect. I fail to respect my benefactor if I mollify him with compliance. None the less, it is generally in the state's interests for citizens to respect law and respect entails general compliance.[70] Walker's thesis thus states:

1. one who benefits from *X* has an obligation of gratitude not to act contrary to *X*'s interests;
2. every citizen has received benefits from the state;
3. every citizen has an obligation of gratitude not to act in ways contrary to the state's interests;
4. non-compliance with the law is contrary to the state's interests; therefore
5. every citizen has an obligation to comply with the law.[71]

I will argue that, while points 3 to 5 hold, they are wrongly premised on points 1 and 2.

DOES GOVERNMENT BENEFIT CITIZENS?

Given the above conception of gratitude, it is clear that I would suggest reformulating the first premise in terms of a person who 'receives favour from *X*'. The implications of this point will be addressed later in discussing the particularity of favour. However, as phrased, the first premise begs the question of whether and how much citizens receive benefits from the state.

Much traditional political theory does not question that citizens are beneficiaries of the state. The state is the contractual solution to the state of nature. It protects us from outsiders and from each other, educates us, treats us when ill, and maintains our public facilities.

A distinctive feature of the modern state, however, in industrialized Western nations, is the extent to which it contracts out, privatizes, and deregulates services previously provided directly by government agencies.[72] Even where

[70] 'Political Obligation and the Argument from Gratitude' at 204.

[71] ibid. 205.

[72] See generally: Feigenbaum *et al. Shrinking the State: The Political Underpinnings of Privatisation*; Sassen *Losing Control: Sovereignty in an Age of Globalization*; Elfstrom *New Challenges for Political Philosophy* ch. 5.

regulation is increased following privatization, the service is often no longer directly provided by government. It is provided by private profit-making agencies. This is increasingly the case in even that most central domain of state activity, law and order. But we would be very uncomfortable to talk of obligations of gratitude owed to Group 4. This is a microcosm of the deeper point that traditional state-conferred benefits are not now always provided directly by the state, being assumed instead by transnational institutions or devolved to private enterprise. This observation is specifically troublesome to a benefits account based upon gratitude. Fair play accounts are not similarly troubled. The relevant benefits in that case are those provided by the mutual restraints of our fellow citizens. The benefits of obedience and tax payment are unaffected by who provides the services the taxes fund. Even where the state is characterized as the collective of our citizens, the gratitude account is affected. We need to show the goodwill, respect, or kindly benefaction that unites citizens. Fairness places fewer constraints on intention and understanding in the provision of benefit. In addition, benefits fall out differentially as between different states and different classes within one state. The strength and scope of obligations will vary.

Moreover, the thesis provides no mechanism to discriminate between conflicting obligations of gratitude. Walker does not suggest that the state is the source of all or necessarily most of the benefits we enjoy. This concession increases the possible sources of obligations of gratitude owed to groups from which we receive properly motivated benefits. There is the real possibility of conflicting obligations of gratitude owed to other horizontal social organizations. Delicate counter-weighting or principles beyond gratitude will be necessary to adjudicate this conflict.

The typical rebuttal of gratitude theory argues that payment of taxes changes the nature of the relationship involved. The paradigm of a commercial transaction, and not personal affective relations, now seems more apt.[73] Walker denies that the citizens' payment of tax undermines the account in any fundamental way. The state is a redistributive agency. There is no direct relationship between taxes paid and benefits received. Many benefits are available to those not paying taxes. McConnell correctly points out that this fact seems only to limit the argument's potential: 'Since those who pay the most are presumably subsidising others, they seem to be untouched by the gratitude argument'.[74]

Taxes do give a contractual veneer to the citizen–state relationship. This creates a presumption of self-interested motives on both sides of the transaction. As noted above, this is a presumption of form which substance can rebut. However, only gullibility could allow us to believe that citizens pay taxes out of mutual concern. Some may see the justice in redistributive and welfare states. By no means all will.

[73] Simmons *Moral Principles* 189.

[74] McConnell *Gratitude* 192.

Walker concludes that his model suggests a view of political community in which members are or should be bound to one another by ties of goodwill or respect.[75] But the converse seems more accurate. Such a view of political community suggests the possibility of appropriately felt obligations of gratitude among the citizenry. And even were this view of community accurate, gratitude may be simply part or a consequence of these relations, as opposed to a, or the, ground of them. This picture of society is a noble normative thesis, but gratitude does not seem to be the principle we are looking for. The fair play picture is unquestionably absent the kindness and concern that colour gratitude. But it is just this dullness that renders it realistic in faceless bureaucratic as opposed to face-to-face *polis* society.

GRATITUDE TO INSTITUTIONS

Gratitude centrally involves the intentions of a benefactor. The gratitude theorist of political obligation thus faces two hurdles. First, he must provide a characterization of the benefactor. Secondly, he must demonstrate the sense in which this benefactor forms and conveys the intentions central to gratitude, and distinguish this corporate intention from the intentions of individual members of the institution.

Many different conceptions of the relevant benefactor are available: the personified Laws of the *Crito*; the state *qua* abstract entity; the state *qua* government, either as a collegiate body or as the individuals who comprise it; the state *qua* the citizen body; or the state *qua* personified sovereign of the Austinian and Benthamite models of law.[76]

Walker characterizes the state as the collective of our fellow citizens.[77] This group is not, strictly, an institution. Difficulties do however attach to the idea of obligations of gratitude directed towards institutions. Walker believes his account will be stronger if he can accommodate these. Thus, even if we conceive of the state as a collective of citizens, 'the state' remains an institution and two difficulties attach to the idea of gratitude to an institution.

Walker questions whether we are grateful to institutions that benefit us or to individuals within that institution. Consider the case of an ex-pupil hearing of her school being in dire financial need who contributes through feelings of 'gratitude'. Is she necessarily grateful to specific teachers? Walker retorts that she donates money not to the individual but to the institution. Nor *need* she feel any particular fondness for specific individuals.

Walker willingly concedes that gratitude to institutions is always derivative from gratitude to individuals. But to concede this is already to concede the

[75] 'Political Obligation and the Argument from Gratitude' 210–11.

[76] This last is suggested by Gans *Anarchism* 44.

[77] 'Political Obligation and the Argument from Gratitude' 195–9.

genuineness of gratitude to institutions. Moreover, while gratefulness to an institution may necessarily presuppose *activity* by some person(s) associated with the institution, it does not necessarily presuppose *gratitude* to a person associated with the institution.

Walker's second difficulty resides in the fact that to speak of gratitude is only appropriate with regard to benefits conferred through a certain motive. Can we speak of institutions, whether conceived as institutional entities or as collective groups of individuals, as having motives?[78] While we may not directly use the language of intention, two things can be said to be true. Institutions do have policies and functions. They have reasons for producing certain benefits. Secondly:

> We can distinguish between the *intended* and the *unintended* benefits that result from the operations of an institution, and draw distinctions, similar to those we draw in the case of benefits conferred by individuals, between someone's benefiting from an institution which exists to benefit him, his benefiting incidentally from the operation of an institution, his receiving benefits which are intended ultimately to further the interests of the institution, and so on.[79]

This, he suggests, is more than sufficient to legitimize use of the language of gratitude.

Kraut makes additional suggestions. In other contexts (financial, business) we intelligibly talk of being indebted to institutions. We owe debts to companies and not to the individuals constituting the company.[80] We can quickly retort that what is fitting in an arm's length transaction is out of place in an affective personal context. The requisite intention is clearly lacking (McConnell also equivocates between legal and moral notions of indebtedness). Anticipating this objection, McConnell suggests that, given that it is intelligible to talk of institutions owing gratitude to individuals, the converse may also be plausible.[81] One mistake in this idea is that the dynamic is asymmetric. While the benefactor must show love and particularity in giving, the beneficiary in responding need show only respect and goodwill. Objections from methodological individualism and anti-holism would similarly not be dismissed by McConnell's point.

Simmons wholly doubts the possibility of owing gratitude to institutions. Group and institutional intention may not be uniform and may be opaque. We might owe gratitude to particular individuals. However, even this is unlikely. Those holding institutional roles perform actions that are essentially positional duties, and hence unfitting objects of gratitude. Sacrifices beyond positional

[78] See here Hart's discussion of attributing motives to corporations in *Essays in Jurisprudence and Philosophy* 43–7, where he observes that groups are aggregates of individuals in which we use unifying phrases extended by analogy from individuals. 'But these are just what these are. Analogy is not identity, so though we can now (as lawyers) say that a company has intended to deceive, this has no theoretical consequences.'

[79] 'Political Obligation and the Argument from Gratitude' 199.

[80] Kraut *Socrates and the State* 148.

[81] McConnell *Gratitude* 198.

duties do deserve gratitude, but this is owed to the individual. Ultimately the ascription of intentions to government may be impossible or incoherent. Even if anthropomorphized, governments do not provide benefits for other-regarding reasons. Acquisitiveness is more typical than altruism.[82]

I will briefly suggest an alternative way of understanding this problem. Consider an ex-pupil donating funds to her struggling school. She may not feel particular fondness for any one person. Or she may feel fondness for many individuals. Her affections may be directed beyond specific individuals at a collective ethos. On Walker's own account, *X* can feel gratitude only towards some agent. But *X* can clearly feel *goodwill* towards agents, institutions, and collective groups. A man may feel goodwill towards the French, maybe because he is a lover of Bordeaux wines, maybe because he adores the French dialect. This goodwill is not gratitude. Bordeaux vintners make wine for profit and the French have a dialect born of convention and accident. Goodwill may itself be a reason for action. It predisposes one to help when one can, and possibly in preference to helping another. This will depend on the help required and the stakes involved. The lack of particular benefit or affective motive will be relevant here. But its absence will not preclude the possibility of a kindly disposition that manifests in action.

What of the idea of feeling gratitude to an ex-teacher? I suggest that we feel gratitude to the teacher in a very specific way. We feel grateful with regard to a combination of individual and institutionally defined role. We are grateful to *this* individual in *this* role. These are two necessary components. The former is personal. The latter is institutional. I am grateful to Mrs Long as *my teacher.* It is because of what *I* received educationally from her. But it is directed at her only *qua* teacher.[83] Gratitude to Mrs Long in this institutional role may however transfer goodwill to the institution. Goodwill and gratitude are distinct. Sincere gratitude may, *inter alia*, include goodwill, but goodwill can exist independently of gratitude. I can feel both goodwill and respect towards entities, individuals, or ideas that have never directly benefited me.

The language of gratitude is often used analogically. A scientist might say, 'I am so grateful to Einstein'. He does not assume that Einstein comprehended relativity with him in mind. He does not think himself peculiar in enjoying this benefit. Nor can he desire to make some return to Einstein. He may want to make a similar contribution to science. But this is different. He speaks of a collective intellectual debt and not of a specific affective debt. He uses 'gratitude' metaphorically. He exaggerates the relationship to reflect the depth of his appre-

[82] Simmons *Moral Principles* 187–90. Stuart Hampshire observes: 'I have difficulty imagining that purity of intention and undivided purpose can be the normal case in politics'. *Innocence and Experience* 5.

[83] I am assuming here an ordinary pupil–teacher relationship with no deeper personal attachment. It stretches to include the case where one might say of a teacher that she was a mentor, but not to anything more significant.

ciation. He is, properly, thankful. His intellectual life is richer for Einstein's genius and he is thankful for that state of affairs.

Returning to the generous pupil, she may be grateful to have received a good education.[84] She may feel gratitude towards particular teachers for kindnesses beyond the requirements of their jobs, but it seems incorrect and unnecessary to explain her generosity in terms of gratitude. She feels goodwill towards the school. This may be a logically necessary attendant of feelings of gratitude, but it also functions quite independently of gratitude, particularly in cases where this concept seems incongruous.

'Benefit' is neutral as to intention. To say that something has benefited me is not necessarily to speak of gratitude. Gratefulness does not require a subject. Any student may say that her university experience benefited her. But she could not say that the university favoured her. It did not specially select her on personal qualities, but on standardized grade requirements. She was not particular in any meaningful way to the university. And towards those teachers to whom she was, she may feel gratitude. But again, there is no requirement of this. Favour is particular. Benefit can be promiscuous and multi-purposive. Goodwill more than adequately accounts for the desire to help when the institution is in financial need.

We are grateful for kindnesses exceeding our entitlements. Beyond entitlement, people behave more kindly than we might reasonably expect. Institutions cannot be kind in this way. Institutions, for example, charities and trusts, can be kind in their basic purposes. But they cannot go beyond their purposes in this way. Individuals do this.

Could we, however, say that a charity already goes beyond what we might expect, and that while its principles and purposes might be those of its original founder, it is the institution and its practices that keep these purposes alive? The function of charities generally is to promote and preserve a minimum of human dignity or health, or to preserve a minimum of essential environmental or animal integrity. Charities tend to scrape the surface of sufficiency. The recipients of the benefits of charities are typically entitled to these as human beings deserving of dignity and help. Something of value would be lost if an emaciated victim airlifted from a famine expressed a felt need to make some return to Oxfam. He is very likely to feel thankful. But gratitude seems to debase his humanity in some way because of the basic inequality and lack of entitlement it implies. In relationships of gratitude, the benefactor feels love or goodwill and the beneficiary feels respect and goodwill. But in this instance we would think that it is respect that motivates the original aid. Much the same applies to government institutions carrying out the more mundane tasks of redistributing wealth, establishing protection and control, organizing local services and maintenance.

[84] Note that 'generous' seems appropriate here. We would praise the ex-pupil helping the school and understand if one of her contemporaries could not prioritize in this way. This is the language of the morally praiseworthy and not the morally obligatory.

The citizen can reply that this is the least he deserves given the authority the state claims for itself, the liberties it infringes, and the taxes he pays.

THE CONTENT OF THE GRATEFUL RETURN

Simmons has questioned whether the gratitude theorist can insist on obedience as the appropriate means of expressing gratitude. While obedience might be one means of discharging an obligation of gratitude it will not be the only one. Unless we can show that obedience is a uniquely suitable return, it lies within the agent's discretion to determine alternative forms of requital.[85]

The grateful response should be sensitive to the benefactor's needs. Is obedience not an obvious candidate action for requital? Simmons replies that even if gratitude requires us to work for the fulfilment of a particular need of a former beneficiary, we need not do everything within our power to fulfil that need. Thus, from the fact that a government requires obedience in order to subsist, it does not follow that any debt of gratitude to a government can be discharged only by obedience.

Despite the general difficulty of defining the content of an obligation of gratitude, were such owed to the state or the laws, obedience would be a very eligible candidate. It would be an almost minimal return. It is equivalent to refraining from kicking our benefactor in the street when we see him. Many laws consist in negative duties. Gratitude may not underwrite a duty to obey every law. But there seems no difficulty, *in principle*, of obedience being an active return for benevolence.[86]

IS WALKER'S GRATITUDE OBLIGATORY?

Walker's account provides the following picture. Gratitude is proper treatment of one's benefactor. It comprises grateful acceptance, the desire to make a return, and a goodwill vital to sincerity, which precludes action inconsistent with the benefactor's interests. But gratitude is not in itself obligatory. It is doubly supererogatory. The grateful return is not already obligatory on some other ground, and no particular action (in fact, no action at all) is required by gratitude. This supererogatory character entails the impossibility of gratitude being demanded of an agent. However, certain attitudes, such as respect and goodwill, necessarily accompany gratitude. Gratitude incorporates a number of obligations including obligations of respect and goodwill.

Translated into a political thesis, the obligation of gratitude grounded in goodwill prohibits disobedience to law and makes obedience to law generally obligatory. This is a negative restraint of goodwill and not a positive return of

[85] Simmons *Moral Principles* 187.

[86] See also Gans *Anarchism* 46 n. 12.

gratitude. These are, essentially, requirements of respect and goodwill characterized as obligations of gratitude.

His account is therefore conditional. *If* one has an attitude of gratitude, one also has these obligations. But gratitude *per se* is supererogatory. However, internal states are not our only concern. A discussion of love could look only to the internal. But gratitude allows the external to be smuggled back in via the vehicle of benefits. It is not entirely up to the individual as to whether or not to feel gratitude. But it does remain supererogatory. Walker's picture suggests that gratitude is multifaceted and has constituent obligations grounded in attitudes such as respect and goodwill (both alike in requiring a certain minimum standard of treatment of those to whom they are directed). Certain conduct will be logically and morally incompatible with a sincere attitude of respect or goodwill.

However, I suggest that these are not *obligations of gratitude*. They are attitudes and obligations that are, at best, necessary presuppositions or consequences of gratitude. They can exist quite independently of gratitude. Gratitude is necessarily linked to respect and goodwill but these are not necessarily linked to gratitude.

The account remains conditional. If we feel genuine gratitude, certain obligations, appropriate feelings, and attitudes follow. But the attitude of gratitude is supererogatory. Gratitude seems too humble an attitude on which to base the obligation to obey.

PARTICULARITY AND IMPARTIALITY

I suggested above that instead of referring to benefits, Walker's first premise should have reduced ambiguity by referring to favour. This entails a very important feature of both favour and gratitude that seems manifestly missing in the citizen–state relationship. It fundamentally lacks any particularity. Public goods are not private kindnesses. They fall out as indiscriminately as rain and show no preference. Seneca observes: 'The laws extend their protection to those who break them the most. Some things could not fall to particular people without being given to everyone. You cannot argue about things that are offered to us *en masse*.'[87] By implication he denies the possibility of gratitude to the law.

An obvious rejoinder to this point suggests itself. The state does specifically benefit its citizens. It prefers them to the citizens of other states. It may not confer private benefits but it does show particularity to its citizens. We might wonder whether the classes of favour are not already too wide. Aside from this, however, another reply is available. The state's law and order protection is extended to aliens and tourists alike. Further, as traditional conceptions of citizenship shift and change, as evidenced most clearly in the European Union, and as increasing

[87] *De Beneficiis* IV. 29. 2.

numbers of migrant populations reside and work abroad,[88] the classes of protection and 'benefits' extended not only to nationals and indigenous peoples, widens. Labour mobility has greatly affected the way in which states operate. The laws also extend their protection to anarchists, terrorists, and criminals. Aristotle notes in *The Art of Rhetoric* that one of the factors destructive of favour is, 'they did the same or equal or more for one's enemies; for it is clear that these things are also not for one's own sake'.[89] Now we might say that the laws do not equally extend their protections to these classes. Less protection is promised to the criminal. If caught his freedom will be taken from him. He lacks the security in planning of the obedient. But it is not the state that diminishes the protection available to him, but his actions. The state merely warns him of the sanctions in event of breach.

This leads on to a most fundamental criticism of a gratitude account of obligations to law. Favour is particular. A clear case of gratitude involves giving motives in the benefactor, corresponding to gratefulness and the desire to make a return, coupled with goodwill and respect in the beneficiary. But laws are (typically) general rules addressed to general classes of people. Norms can be particular in nature. Courts make orders applicable often to one or several individuals. But in order to conform to the rule of law these should be guided by open, stable, clear, and general rules. Only bad laws could pass condition 3 above. Further, laws generally have the common good as their concern and thus would also fail condition 5.[90] As Rousseau observes, law 'may establish several classes of citizen, and even specify the qualifications which shall give access to those several classes, but it may not say that this man or that shall be admitted ... in a word, no function which deals with the individual falls within the province of the legislative power'.[91]

Laws can clearly focus upon and benefit a particular class of people—anti-discrimination laws, laws providing additional benefits for the blind and disabled, laws promoting tax advantages for the married, and laws regarding age of consent. Many different specific criteria are employed—gender, race, disability, status, or age. However, the brocard 'government by laws and not by men' is meant to capture the basic fact that the discretion, the genuine spontaneous affection that manifests in action, and which is definitive of favour, is antithetical to the nature of laws functioning well.

One final objection from analogy might be suggested. Were a philanthropist to donate a vast sum of money to a struggling community *X*, all the members of *X* might intelligibly express deep gratitude to him. He has favoured the community

[88] Soysal *Limits of Citizenship: Migrants and Postnational Membership in Europe*.

[89] *The Art of Rhetoric* sect. 6, ch. 2.7 (1385^b) (at 162).

[90] The problem here does not relate to the fact that laws *demand* obedience. The example of the frustrated benefactor illustrates that one who later asks for help by referring to past kindnesses need not detract at all from the initial kindness. McConnell discusses the relationship between demands and gratitude in *Gratitude* 201–2.

[91] Rousseau *The Social Contract* book II, ch. 6.

en masse, and not any particular individual. So too with the state: it favours this group, and this is sufficient. Partiality need not be personal, and it need not be discriminatory. It need only be discriminating.

However, a coalescence of factors relevant to the state undermine this analogy. The philanthropist chose this group and could have chosen another group, or none at all, as the object of his generosity. The government has no such choice. The combination of institutional impartiality and governmental duty is fatal. Consider Aristotle's exception from gratitude when we can say of an act 'that it was a return and not a gift'.[92] In representative democracies, governments have electoral platforms and promises on the strength of which they are elected. Not only do governments have positional duties and responsibilities to govern well, but they have obligations to perform grounded in their electoral promises. Keeping to their promises and governing well is the proper return for their election. This is all that they can and should do.

CONCLUSION

Ultimately, the political context cannot accommodate the specialness, discretion, and motivation necessary for gratitude. Gift relationships are creatures of subtle shifts and meaningful, discreet (and discrete) kindnesses. Love's singular voice is unrequested consideration. Personality itself may be enriched in this context. Political relationships in vast nation states, on the other hand, are creatures of crude power and impartial benefaction. Receipt of political and legal benefits often defines an instrumentally and not intrinsically rewarding relationship. What is valuable in the account from gratitude is the affective core that is suitably directed at institutional practices. This element of the account is retained and better captured by the theory of respect.

[92] *The Art of Rhetoric* sect. 6, ch. 2.7 (1385^{b}) (at 162).

7
The Implications of Respect

Although obedience is an education as basic as language, unlike language, the limits of obedience do not mean the limits of our world.[1] Obedience to law is circumscribed by its object. Law is both instrumental and jurisdictional. Values are ultimately neither. And in a world of increasing interdependence, our moral and political duties to others do not trace out the juridical lines of national borders, but the causal and moral lines that define this dependence.

In this book I have suggested a theory of conscientious obedience that accommodates this interdependence without neglecting the pragmatic particularity of our political relationships. I have taken as my starting point the traditional discourse of political obligation, articulating versions of that tradition of varying degrees of stringency, and evaluating the strongest advocates of obligation. None of these theories has successfully yielded a universal obligation of obedience. The distance between theoretical goals and achievements may seem to testify primarily to a problematically phrased problem. However, as Chapter 1 demonstrated, the problem is not semantic but substantive, residing in the nature and extent of the claims of law. Scepticism therefore terminates in the conclusion that subject and authority necessarily occupy different perspectives when evaluating law's claims. But while the law retains its moral mask, the moral problem remains.

DEGREES OF SCEPTICISM

In addressing this moral problem, theories fall to rest somewhere between the poles of autonomy/conscience, and authority/conscientiousness. In recent debate, scepticism has typically been characterized as philosophical anarchism. This involves 'the removal of any moral presumption in favor of compliance with and support for the state'.[2] But not all denials of the full claims of authority are equivalent. Having denied authority's comprehensive claims, I have attempted to view the residual value in both law and community through the prism of respect.

To recap. Where law is an instrument presently necessary for, or vital to, preventing harm, and preserving the well-being of members of a community, and is integral in creating opportunities for the realization of human capacity,

[1] See Wittgenstein *Tractatus Logico-Philosophicus* sect. 5.6 (at 68).

[2] Simmons 'Philosophical Anarchism' in Sanders and Narveson *For and Against the State: New Philosophical Readings* 23–4.

our duty of respect for persons extends to a duty of respect for law. Respectful behaviour towards law, or an attitude of respect, is necessary to respect for persons because, where law functions well, and given its supremacy and comprehensiveness, people organize their expectations around legal directives. The attitude of respect is necessarily required by the grounds of the duty and is obligatory. Since it is directed at an instrument, that instrument must first satisfy the demands of (estimation) respect and demonstrate its centrality to the realization of human value. However, this obligatory respect, given the substantively self-limiting nature of an attitude of (estimation) respect, does not lead to an obligation to obey. The theory of respect distinguishes the object of respect from the characteristic in virtue of which it is respected. The adjectival status of 'legal' mirrors the distinction between object and grounds and the contingency of the link. But the link, though contingent, is real and pervasive. When one knowingly undermines law, one knowingly undermines the most comprehensive normative system in a society, and confidence therein. The requirements of respect are less extensive than an obligation to obey but remain categorical. We must refrain from damaging or diminishing what is of value.

My conclusion, therefore, essentially issues in respect for law conditioned by respect for persons and guided by conscience. Mention of conscience, like autonomy, inspires some and inspires only alarm in others. Thus Whitman celebrates as 'the great city' that city:

> Where the men and women think lightly of the laws...
> Where the populace rise at once against the never-ending audacity of the elected persons...
> Where outside authority enters always after the precedence of inside authority[3]

By contrast, Auden mocks the ubiquitous (and myopic) arrogance of conscience:

> And always the loud angry crowd
> Very angry and very loud,
> Law is We;
> And always the soft idiot, softly, Me.[4]

Both sides seem to have a case, and this is hardly surprising. The truth lies between. The etymology of 'conscience' lies in the Latin *con scientia* meaning 'joint knowledge'.[5] This notion returns us to the opening quotation from Camus; that rebellion must recognize its internal limits, 'where minds meet, and, in meeting, begin to exist'.[6] The individual who first understands herself in opposition to the 'other', ultimately flourishes only amongst others. Each individual achieves moral orientation only by engaging with, and acknowledging the equal

[3] Walt Whitman *Selected Poems* 120.
[4] W. H. Auden *Collected Shorter Poems 1927–1957* 155.
[5] See Sibley 'Conscience, Law, and the Obligation to Obey' for an illuminating discussion of the notion of 'conscience'.
[6] Camus *The Rebel* 27.

demands of, others; by rigorously testing her own intuitions against conflicting conceptions, and by renewing this process continually throughout her life. This moral conversation presupposes some sense of community. It should be clear that legal norms, as a more or less faithful articulation of community standards, have a peculiar force in this conversation. This is the force not only of the coercive mechanisms of the state but of the moral implications of normative claims that are as comprehensive and supreme as the claims of law. If we are to challenge law, we arrogate to ourselves the last word in the moral (though not the legal) conversation, and our reasons should be robust. If we are to comply with law, we must be sure that more basic values are not jeopardized or transgressed by its norms; that we have not stayed silent when we should have spoken out.

DEGREES OF CONCERN

The theory of respect, I have suggested, is the ineliminable core of a theory of conscientious obedience. It is only pragmatically relativized to the parochial and is at all times capable of extension where our legal or moral duties transcend territorial boundaries. Being the core of any such theory, it may be complemented by arguments that emphasize the value of community (such as Raz's argument from respect) and thereby gain a more 'particularized' aspect. It is important to remember, however, that all preference of the near over the distant requires a justification grounded in principles that do not assume the moral significance of ex facie morally arbitrary facts such as national borders.

Our fellow legal subjects, as people, deserve our most basic respect. This generates a duty not to damage legal systems meriting (estimation) respect, in so far as its institutions protect and extend human possibilities and capacities. As citizens, our fellows deserve a proper reciprocity. As members in a community of identification, our fellows and our laws may receive a commitment deeper than this. Belonging may issue in obedience and service. Outsiders to a community owe it only a good effort at respect. Even those in the margins of membership should, for the sake both of themselves and others, look for what is valuable in the world around them. What they find they should not damage or demean.

DEGREES OF DISPUTE

The theory of respect need not significantly intrude on related debates within jurisprudence such as those between legal positivists and natural lawyers briefly discussed in Chapter 1. As I noted there, adopting the sources thesis is not *necessarily* inconsistent with a belief in obligation and many possible links between law and morality will not argue for the existence of an obligation to obey the law. Advocates of each school *could* embrace the conclusions reached in this work without compromising other doctrinal commitments. This likelihood is increased by the two-stage structure of the theory—the core theory of respect can be complemented by additional arguments otherwise consistent with its premises. Moreover, I would urge that the theorist should wish to reach conclusions consistent with these premises, thereby keeping analytic focus on issues of intrinsic and not merely instrumental importance. As Perry has noted: 'is illegality per se a reason for doing what the law requires or not doing what it forbids? To answer affirmatively is to claim that obedience to law is intrinsically and not merely instrumentally good. Surely on reflection no one would accept that claim, except someone who fetishizes obedience to law.'[7] This is not to suggest that all behaviour towards law is of merely instrumental significance. Where law operates well, promoting conditions conducive to realized potential, each has an obligation to treat it with the requisite respect, and just because of the intrinsic values it protects. But this respect is necessarily derivative and conditional.

The implications for political theory are again qualified. The theory of respect answers, both descriptively and normatively, to the increasing interdependence of our communities and urges a more cosmopolitan conception of political responsibility. None the less, its two-stage structure allows for an accretion of reasons building to accommodate local, moral concerns. This is to limit but not eliminate the criterion of particularity. We can, I would suggest, attend to particularity only against a backdrop that acknowledges the increasingly global nature of moral concerns.[8] Similarly, while the needs of intimates may sometimes properly prevail over the needs of strangers, our moral theories should be sensitive to the possibility that often the needs of strangers should prevail over the preferences and wants of intimates and fellow citizens.[9] The theory of respect accommodates this concern by conceiving of agents first as persons and then as citizens.

Being a profoundly cognitive attitude, respect also encourages an active and politically awake conception of the citizen's role in public life. Just as a government's respect-worthiness is partly predicated on it facilitating, in so far as possible, its subjects' self-respect, these subjects must preserve self-respect by being watchful of law. A watchful citizenry is arguably as important to the rule of law as is a compliant one. Citizens must keep their governments to account to avoid official complacency, secrecy, and corruption. Our modern cultures, with their narrow specializations, infinite divisions of labour, and proliferating conveniences, tend to dull the questioning edge within civil society. Kant's sarcasm again seems apt:

> It is so convenient to be immature! If I have a book to have understanding in place of me, a spiritual adviser to have a conscience for me, a doctor to judge my diet for me, and so on, I

[7] Perry *Morality, Politics and Law: A Bicentennial Essay* 110 (on which see Gaus *Justificatory Liberalism: An Essay on Epistemology and Political Theory* 286–8).

[8] Cf. Simmons 'Political Obligation and Authority' 29.

[9] See generally Jeske 'Associative Obligations, Voluntarism, and Equality' and Scheffler 'Families, Nations, and Strangers'.

need not make any efforts at all. I need not think, so long as I can pay; others will soon enough take the tiresome job over for me.[10]

This moral laziness is of particular concern in current Western democracies characterized by heightened security and reduced civil liberties, following the 11 September 2001 attacks on America. The partial suspension of civil liberties and human rights increases the degree to which we must be able (intelligently) to trust our leaders to act wisely and justly, or instead, believe that the citizenry will ensure, through scrutiny and peaceful protest, that abuse of power by officials is prevented. Taken seriously, an attitude of respect for law is a crucial corrective to this moral laziness.

DEGREES OF LEGITIMACY

One further implication that must be considered relates to the residue of legitimacy left where obligation is surrendered. I noted in Chapter 1, that where legitimate authority is understood as a right to command correlated to an obligation to obey, the failure to ground an obligation to obey frustrates this model of legitimacy. However, it need not frustrate all models of legitimacy. Even in the absence of an obligation to obey strictly understood, a state may be a largely justified type of institution and any particular instantiation of the state may be largely legitimate as measured against other indices (for example, the indices of respect-worthiness discussed in Chapter 2). Here, an asymmetry obtains. For while the legitimacy of the state may in some respects survive scepticism regarding obligation, the converse is more difficult to imagine. If a state is simply not legitimate, not even a weakened obligation to obey the law *qua* law will survive. None the less, a sceptical conclusion regarding obligation does not preclude legitimacy under some model. It suggests instead that legitimacy will not be demonstrated through a clean logical correlation. This should not trouble us too much. It seems only right that the project of political legitimacy should be a messier affair than this. Law may overstate its claims, and there may be good instrumental justifications for this; but that does not prevent a good legal system from nearly measuring up to its claims. No absolute legitimacy may ever be possible, but we will remain sensitive to relative degrees of legitimacy and justification. And law, like the individual, will each day face the challenge of meriting the (estimation) respect it demands.

[10] Kant *Political Writings* 54.

Bibliography

Alabaster, Anthony and Lukes, Steven *The Good Society* (London: Methuen & Company, 1971)

Alexy, Robert 'On Necessary Relations between Law and Morality' *Ratio Juris* 2/2 (1989) 167

Alston, William 'Moral Attitudes and Moral Judgments' *Nous* 2 (1968) 1

Amato, Joseph A. *Guilt and Gratitude* (London: Greenwood Press, 1982)

Anderson, Benedict *Imagined Communities* (London: Verso, 1983)

Anscombe, Elizabeth 'On the Source of the Authority of the State' *Ethics* 20/1 (1978) 1

Arendt, Hannah *On Revolution* (London: Penguin, 1965)

Aristotle, *Nicomachean Ethics* trans. Ross, D. (Oxford: Oxford University Press, 1980)

—— *The Art of Rhetoric* trans. Lawson-Tancred, H. C. (London: Penguin, 1991)

—— *The Politics* trans. Sinclair, T. A. (London: Penguin, 1992)

Arneson, Richard J. 'The Principle of Fairness and Free-Rider Problems' *Ethics* 92 (1982) 616

Atiyah, Peter S. *Essays in Contract* (Oxford: Oxford University Press, 1986)

Atwood, Margaret *Eating Fire: Selected Poems 1965–1995* (London: Virago, 1999)

Auden, W. H. *Collected Shorter Poems 1927–1957* (London: Faber and Faber, 1996)

—— (ed) *The Living Thoughts of Kierkegaard* (New York: New York Review Books, 1999)

Audi, Robert 'Intrinsic Value and Moral Obligation' *Southern Journal of Philosophy* 35 (1997) 135

Aurelius, Marcus *Meditations* trans. Staniforth, M. (London: Penguin, 1964)

Austin, John L. *How to Do Things with Words* (2nd edn) Urmson, J. O. and Sbisa, M. (eds) (Cambridge Mass.: Harvard University Press, 1975)

Baier, Kurt 'Moral Obligation' *American Philosophical Quarterly* 3/3 (1966) 210

—— 'Obligation: Political and Moral' in Pennock, J. R. and Chapman, J. W. (eds) *Nomos XII: Political and Legal Obligation* (New York: Atherton, 1970)

—— 'Maximization and Fairness' *Ethics* 96 (1985) 119

Barber, Benjamin *Strong Democracy: Participatory Politics for a New Age* (Berkeley: University of California Press, 1984)

—— *The Conquest of Politics* (Princeton: Princeton University Press, 1988)

Baron, Marcia 'The Alleged Moral Repugnance of Acting from Duty' *Journal of Philosophy* 81/4 (1984) 197

Barry, Brian 'The Public Interest' *Proceedings of the Aristotelian Society* (Supplement) 38 (1964) 1, reprinted in Quinton, A. (ed) *Political Philosophy* (Oxford: Oxford University Press, 1967)

Batnitzky, Leora 'A Seamless Web? John Finnis and Joseph Raz on Practical Reason and the Obligation to Obey the Law' *Oxford Journal of Legal Studies* 15/2 (1995) 153

Bayles, Michael D. 'The Capacity and Power to Consent' *Archiv für Rechts-und Sozialphilosophie* 12 (1980) 159

Baynes, Kenneth 'Democracy and the Rechtsstaat: Habermas's Faktizitat und Geltung' in White, Stephen K. (ed) *Cambridge Companion to Habermas* (Cambridge: Cambridge University Press, 1995)

Beck, Ulrich *Risk Society: Towards a New Modernity* (London: Sage, 1992)
—— *World Risk Society* (Cambridge: Polity, 1999)
—— Giddens, Anthony and Lash, Scott *Reflexive Modernisation: Politics, Tradition and Aesthetics in the Modern Social Order* (Cambridge: Polity, 1994)
Becker, Lawrence C. 'Reciprocity and Social Obligation' *Pacific Philosophy Quarterly* 61 (1980) 411
—— 'Hard Choices Are Enough' *Virginia Law Review* 67 (1981) 97
—— 'The Free-Rider Problem' in Miller, H. B. and Williams, W. H. (eds) *The Limits of Utilitarianism* (Minneapolis: University of Minnesota Press, 1982) 217
—— *Reciprocity* (London: Routledge & Kegan Paul, 1986)
Beckett, Samuel *Endgame* (New York: Grove Press, 1958)
Bedau, Hugo A. (ed) *Civil Disobedience in Focus* (London: Routledge, 1991)
Bell, Daniel A. 'Democratic Deliberation: The Problem of Implementation' in Macedo, Stephen (ed) *Deliberative Politics: Essays on Democracy and Disagreement* (New York: Oxford University Press, 1999) 70
Benhabib, Seyla *Situating the Self: Gender, Community, and Postmodernism in Contemporary Ethics* (London: Routledge, 1992)
—— *The Claims of Culture: Equality and Diversity in the Global Era* (New Haven: Yale University Press, 2002)
Beran, Harry 'Ought, Obligation and Duty' *Australasian Journal of Philosophy* 50/3 (1972) 207
—— 'Political Obligation and Democracy' *Australasian Journal of Philosophy* 54/3 (1976) 250
—— 'In Defense of the Consent Theory of Political Obligation and Authority' *Ethics* 87 (1977) 260
—— 'What is the Basis of Political Authority?' *Monist* 66 (1981) 487
—— *The Consent Theory of Political Obligation* (London: Croom Helm, 1987)
Berger, Fred 'Gratitude' *Ethics* 85 (1974–5) 298
Berger, John *And Our Faces, My Heart, Brief as Photos* (New York: Vintage, 1984)
Bickel, Alexander M. *The Morality of Consent* (New Haven: Yale University Press, 1975)
Black, Anthony 'The Juristic Origins of Social Contract Theory' *History of Political Thought* 14/1 (1993) 57
Blum, Lawrence A. *Friendship, Altruism and Morality* (London: Routledge & Kegan Paul, 1980)
Boardman, William 'Coordination and the Moral Obligation to Obey the Law' *Ethics* 97 (1987) 546
Bogg, Alan 'In Defence of Correlativity: Authority, Autonomy and Mistaken Legal Directives' *Ratio Juris* 15/1 (2002) 84
Bohman, James *Public Deliberation: Pluralism, Complexity, and Democracy* (Cambridge Mass.: MIT Press, 1996)
Bohman, James and Rehg, William (eds) *Deliberative Democracy: Essays on Reason and Politics* (Cambridge Mass.: MIT Press, 1997)
Booth, Ken, Dunne, Tim and Cox, Michael *How Might We Live? Global Ethics in the New Century* (Cambridge: Cambridge University Press, 2001)
Boxill, Bernard R. 'On Some Criticisms of Consent Theory' *Journal of Social Philosophy* 4 (1993) 81
Brandt, Richard. B. *Ethical Theory* (Englewood Cliffs NJ: Prentice Hall, 1959)

——'The Concepts of Obligation and Duty' *Mind* 73 (1965) 374

Brennan, Geoffrey and Lomasky, Loren 'Toward a Democratic Morality' in Estlund, D. (ed) *Democracy* (Oxford: Blackwell, 2002) 237

Broad, Charlie D. 'On the Function of False Hypotheses in Ethics' *International Journal of Ethics* 26 (1915–16) 377

——'Conscience and Conscientious Action' in Feinberg, Joel (ed) *Moral Concepts* (Oxford: Oxford University Press, 1969)

Broome, John 'Fairness' *Proceedings of the Aristotelian Society* 91 (1990–1) 87, repr. in Broome, John *Ethics out of Economics* (Cambridge: Cambridge University Press, 1999) 111

Brudney, Daniel 'Hypothetical Consent and Moral Force' *Law & Philosophy* 10 (1991) 235

Buchanan, Allen 'Recognitional Legitimacy and the State System' *Philosophy and Public Affairs* 28/1 (1999) 246

——'Rule Governed Institutions versus Act-Consequentialism: A Rejoinder to Naticchia' *Philosophy and Public Affairs* 28/3 (1999) 258

Buckley Jr, William F. *Gratitude: Reflections on What we Owe our Country* (New York: Random House, 1990)

Budge, Ian *The New Challenge of Direct Democracy* (Oxford: Polity, 1996)

Calabresi, Guido and Melamed, A. Douglas 'Property Rules, Liability Rules, and Inalienability: One View of the Cathedral' *Harvard Law Review* 85 (1972) 1089

Camenish, Paul F. 'Gift and Gratitude in Ethics' *The Journal of Religious Ethics* 9 (1981) 23

Camus, Albert *The Rebel* trans. Bower, A. (London: Penguin, 1971)

——*The Outsider* trans. Laredo, J. (London: Penguin, 1983)

Caney, Simon 'Individuals, Nations and Obligations' in Caney, Simon, George, David and Jones, Peter (eds) *National Rights and International Obligations* (Boulder Colo.: Westview, 1996) 119

——George, David and Jones, Peter (eds) *National Rights and International Obligations* (Boulder Colo.: Westview, 1996)

Card, Claudia 'Gratitude and Obligation' *American Philosophical Quarterly* 25/2 (1988) 115

Carr, Craig L. *On Fairness* (Aldershot: Ashgate Publishing Ltd, 2000)

Chambers, Simone *Reasonable Democracy: Jürgen Habermas and the Politics of Discourse* (Ithaca NY: Cornell University Press, 1996)

Christiano, Thomas 'Justice and Disagreement at the Foundations of Political Authority' *Ethics* 110 (1999) 165

——'Democracy as Equality' in Estlund, David (ed) *Democracy* (Oxford: Blackwell, 2002) 31

Christie, George C. 'Dworkin's Empire' *Duke Law Journal* (1987) 157

——'On the Moral Obligation to Obey the Law' *Duke Law Review* (1990) 1311

Clarke, Paul B. (ed) *Citizenship* (London: Pluto Press, 1994)

Cohen, Gerry A. 'Beliefs and Roles' in Glover, Jonathan (ed) *The Philosophy of Mind* (Oxford: Oxford University Press, 1980) 53

Cohen, Joshua 'Deliberation and Democratic Legitimacy' in Hamlin, Alan and Pettit, Philip (eds) *The Good Polity: Normative Analysis of the State* (Oxford: Basil Blackwell, 1989) repr. in Estlund, David (ed) *Democracy* (Oxford: Basil Blackwell, 2002)

Cohen, Joshua 'Democracy and Liberty' in Elster, Jon (ed) *Deliberative Democracy* (Cambridge: Cambridge University Press, 1998) 185

——and Sabel, Charles 'Directly Deliberative Polyarchy' *European Law Journal* 3 (1997) 313

Coleman, Jules 'Negative and Positive Positivism' *Journal of Legal Studies* 11 (1982) 139

——'On the Relationship between Law and Morality' *Ratio Juris* 2/1 (1989) 66

——'Authority and Reason' in George, Robert P. *The Autonomy of Law: Essays on Legal Positivism* (Oxford: Clarendon Press, 1996) 287

——*The Practice of Principle: In Defence of a Pragmatist Approach to Legal Theory* (Oxford: Oxford University Press, 2001)

Confucius *The Analects* trans. Waley, A. (Hertfordshire: Wordsworth Classics, 1996)

Cooke, Maeve *Language and Reason: A Study of Habermas's Pragmatics* (Cambridge Mass.: MIT Press, 1994)

Cooper, John M. 'Aristotle on Friendship' in Rorty, Amelie O. (ed) *Essays on Aristotle's Ethics* (London: University of California Press, 1980) 301

Copp, David, Hampton, Jean and Roemer, John E. (eds) *The Idea of Democracy* (Cambridge: Cambridge University Press, 1995)

Cottingham, John 'Partiality, Favouritism and Morality' *Philosophical Quarterly* 36 (1986) 357

Cranor, Carl F. 'Respect for the Law: An Evaluation' *Philosophy Research Archives* 2 (1975) 522

——'Toward a Theory of Respect for Persons' *American Philosophical Quarterly* 12/4 (1975) 309

——'Justice, Respect and Self-Respect' *Philosophy Research Archives* 2 (1976) 89

Cullity, Garrett 'Moral Free-Riding' *Philosophy & Public Affairs* 24/1 (1995) 3

D'Entreves, Alexander P. *Natural Law* (London: Hutchinson, 1970)

Dagger, Richard 'What is Political Obligation?' *American Political Science Review* 71 (1977) 86

——'Rights, Boundaries and the Bonds of Community: A Qualified Defence of Moral Parochialism' *American Political Science Review* 79 (1985) 436

——*Civic Virtues: Rights Citizenship, and Republican Liberalism* (New York: Oxford University Press, 1996)

Dan-Cohen, Meir in 'In Defense of Defiance' *Philosophy & Public Affairs* 23 (1994) 24, reprinted in *Harmful Thoughts: Essays on Law, Self, and Morality* (Princeton: Princeton University Press, 2002) 94

Dancy, Jonathan *Practical Reality* (Oxford: Oxford University Press, 2000)

Darwall, Stephen L. 'Two Kinds of Respect' in Dillon, Robin S. (ed) *Dignity, Character, and Self-Respect* (London: Routledge, 1995)

——(ed) *Equal Freedom* (Ann Arbor: University of Michigan Press, 2000)

Davidson, Donald *Subjective, Intersubjective, Objective* (Oxford: Clarendon Press, 2001)

Davidson, Donald *Inquiries into Truth and Interpretation* (Oxford: Clarendon Press, 2001)

DeGeorge, Robert T. 'Consent and Obedience' *Archiv für Rechts-und Sozialphilosophie* 12 (1980) 49

Deigh, John 'All Kinds of Guilt' *Law & Philosophy* 18/4 (1999) 313–25

DeLue, Steven M. *Political Obligation in a Liberal State* (New York: State University of New York Press, 1989)

De Tocqueville, Alexis *Democracy in America* trans. Bevan, G. (London: Penguin, 2003)
Dickson, Julie *Evaluation and Legal Theory* (Oxford: Hart Publishing, 2001)
Dillon, Robin S. (ed) *Dignity, Character and Self-Respect* (London: Routledge, 1995)
——'Introduction' in Dillon, Robin S. (ed) *Dignity, Character and Self-Respect* (London: Routledge, 1995) 1
Donner, Wendy *The Liberal Self: John Stuart Mill's Moral and Political Philosophy* (Ithaca NY: Cornell University Press, 1991)
Downie, Robert S. *Roles and Values: An Introduction to Social Ethics* (London: Methuen, 1971)
——and Telfer, Elizabeth *Respect for Persons* (Glasgow: George Allen & Unwin, 1971)
Dryzek, John S. *Discursive Democracy* (Cambridge: Cambridge University Press, 1990)
——*Deliberative Democracy and Beyond: Liberals, Critics, Contestations* (Oxford: Oxford University Press, 2000)
Dummett, Michael *On Immigration and Refugees* (London: Routledge, 2001)
Dunn, John *Political Obligation in its Historical Context* (Cambridge: Cambridge University Press, 1980)
——'Political Obligation' in *The History of Political Theory and Other Essays* (Cambridge: Cambridge University Press, 1996) 66
——'Trust' in *The History of Political Theory and Other Essays* (Cambridge: Cambridge University Press, 1996) 91
Dworkin, Ronald 'The Original Position' in Daniels, Norman (ed) *Reading Rawls* (Oxford: Blackwell, 1975)
——*A Matter of Principle* (Cambridge Mass.: Harvard University Press, 1985)
——*Law's Empire* (London: Fontana Press, 1986)
——'Liberal Community' *California Law Review* 77/3 (1989) 479, repr. in Dworkin, Ronald *Sovereign Virtue: The Theory and Practice of Equality* (Cambridge Mass.: Harvard University Press, 2000) ch. 5
——*Freedom's Law: The Moral Reading of the American Constitution* (Oxford: Oxford University Press, 1996)
——'Foundations of Liberal Equality' in Darwall, Stephen (ed) *Equal Freedom* (Ann Arbor: University Of Michigan Press, 2000) 190
——*Taking Rights Seriously* (Cambridge Mass.: Harvard University Press, 2001)
Edmundson, William A. *Three Anarchical Fallacies* (Cambridge: Cambridge University Press, 1998)
——(ed) *The Duty to Obey the Law: Selected Philosophical Essays* (Lanham, Md.: Rowman & Littlefield, 1999)
Elfstrom, Gerard *New Challenges for Political Philosophy* (London: Macmillan, 1997)
Elliott, Gregory and Osborne, Peter 'Community as Compulsion?' *Radical Philosophy* 58 (1991) 14
Elster, Jon 'Rationality, Morality, and Collective Action' *Ethics* 96 (1985) 136
——(ed) *Deliberative Democracy* (Cambridge: Cambridge University Press, 1998)
——'Deliberation and Constitution Making' in Elster, Jon (ed) *Deliberative Democracy* (Cambridge: Cambridge University Press, 1998) 104
——'Introduction' in Elster, J. (ed) *Deliberative Democracy* (Cambridge: Cambridge University Press, 1998) 1
——*Ulysses Unbound* (Cambridge: Cambridge University Press, 2000)
Estlund, David 'Introduction' in Estlund, David *Democracy* (Oxford: Blackwell, 2002) 1

Estlund, David *Democracy* (Oxford: Blackwell, 2002)

Ewing, Alfred F. 'What Would Happen If Everyone Acted Like Me?' *Philosophy* 28 (1953) 16

Fain, Haskell 'The Idea of the State' *Nous* 6 (1972) 15

Farrell, Daniel M. 'Coercion, Consent, and the Justification of Political Power: A New Look at Locke's Consent Claim' *Archiv für Rechts-und Sozialphilosophie* 65/4 (1979) 521

Fearon, James D. 'Deliberation as Discussion' in Elster, Jon (ed) *Deliberative Democracy* (Cambridge: Cambridge University Press, 1998) 44

Feigenbaum, Harvey, Henig, Jeffrey and Hamnett, Chris *Shrinking the State: The Political Underpinnings of Privatisation* (Cambridge: Cambridge University Press, 1999)

Feinberg, Joel 'Duties, Rights and Claims' *American Philosophical Quarterly* 3/2 (1966) 137

——'The Nature and Value of Rights' *The Journal of Value Inquiry* (Winter 1970) 243

——*Harm to Others* (New York: Oxford University Press, 1984)

——*Harm to Self* (New York: Oxford University Press, 1986)

Ferejohn, John 'Accountability and Authority: Toward a Theory of Political Accountability' in Przeworski, A. Stokes, S. C. and Manin, B. *Democracy, Accountability, and Representation* (Cambridge: Cambridge University Press, 1999) 131

Findlay, John N. 'The Justification of Attitudes' *Mind* 63 (1954) 145

Finnis, John M. *Natural Law and Natural Rights* (Oxford: Clarendon Press, 1980)

——'The Authority of Law in the Predicament of Contemporary Social Theory' *Notre Dame Journal of Law, Ethics and Public Policy* 1 (1984) 115

——'Law as Co-ordination' *Ratio Juris* 2/1 (1989) 97

Fishkin, James S. *The Limits of Obligation* (New Haven: Yale University Press, 1982)

——*Democracy and Deliberation* (New Haven: Yale University Press, 1991)

——*The Voice of the People: Public Opinion and Democracy* (New Haven: Yale University Press, 1995)

Flatham, Richard E. *Political Obligation* (London: Croom Helm, 1973)

Fletcher, George P. *Loyalty: An Essay on the Morality of Relationships* (New York: Oxford University Press, 1993)

Flew, Anthony G. N. (ed) *Logic and Language* (1st series) (Oxford: Blackwell, 1963)

Foot, Philippa 'Utilitarianism and the Virtues' in Scheffler, Samuel *Consequentialism and its Critics* (Oxford: Oxford University Press, 1988) 224

Forrester, James W. 'Conflicts of Obligation' *American Philosophical Quarterly* 32/1 (1995) 31

Foucault, Michel *Fearless Speech* Pearson, J. (ed) (Los Angeles: Semiotext(e), 2001)

Frankena, William K. 'The Ethics of Respect for Persons' *Philosophical Topics* 14/2 (1986) 149

Frankfurt, Harry *Necessity, Volition, and Love* (Cambridge: Cambridge University Press, 1999)

Franklin, Julian H. 'Allegiance and Jurisdiction in Locke's Doctrine of Tacit Consent' *Political Theory* 24/3 (1996) 407

Frazer, Elizabeth *The Problems of Communitarian Politics: Unity and Conflict* (Oxford: Oxford University Press, 1999)

Freeman, Samuel 'Deliberative Democracy: A Sympathetic Comment' *Philosophy & Public Affairs* 29/4 (2000) 371

Friedman, Marilyn 'Feminism and Modern Friendship: Dislocating the Community' *Ethics* 99 (1989) 275

——'The Practice of Partiality' *Ethics* 101 (1991) 818

Frohlich, Norman, Hunt, Thomas, Oppenheimer, Joe, and Wagner R. Harrison 'Individual Contributions for Collective Goods' *Journal of Conflict Resolution* 19/2 (1975) 310

Fuller, Lon L. 'Positivism and Fidelity to Law: A Reply to Professor Hart' *Harvard Law Review* 71 (1958) 630

Gaita, Raimond *A Common Humanity: Thinking About Love & Truth & Justice* (Melbourne: Text Publishing Company, 1999)

Gallie, W. B. 'Essentially Contested Concepts' *Proceedings of the Aristotelian Society* 56 (1955–6) 167

Gans, Chaim 'The Normativity of Law and its Coordinative Function' 16 (1981) *Israeli Law Review* 333

——'Mandatory Rules and Exclusionary Reasons' *Philosophica* 15 (1985–6) 373

——'The Obligation to Obey the Law: Comment' in Gavison, Ruth (ed) *Issues in Contemporary Legal Philosophy: The Influence of H. L. A. Hart* (Oxford: Oxford University Press, 1986) 180, 184

——*Philosophical Anarchism and Political Disobedience* (Cambridge: Cambridge University Press, 1992)

Gaus, Gerald F. *The Modern Liberal Theory of Man* (London: Croom Helm, 1983)

——*Justificatory Liberalism: An Essay on Epistemology and Political Theory* (New York: Oxford University Press, 1996)

Gellner, Ernest *Language and Solitude: Wittgenstein, Malinowski and the Habsburg Dilemma* (Cambridge: Cambridge University Press, 1998)

Geuss, Raymond *History and Illusion in Politics* (Cambridge: Cambridge University Press, 2001)

Gewirth, Alan 'Obligation: Political, Legal and Moral' in Pennock, J. R. and Chapman, J. W. (eds) *Nomos XII: Political and Legal Obligation* (New York: Atherton Press, 1970) 55

——'Ethical Universalism and Particularism' *Journal of Philosophy* 85 (1988) 283

——'"Ought" and Reasons for Action' *Southern Journal of Philosophy* 35 (1997) 171

Giddens, Anthony *The Runaway World: How Globalization is Re-shaping our Lives* (London: Routledge, 2000)

Gilbert, Margaret *On Social Facts* (London: Routledge, 1989)

——'Rationality, Coordination, and Convention' *Synthese* 84 (1990) 1

——'Agreement, Coercion, and Obligation' *Ethics* 103 (1993) 679

——'Group Membership and Political Obligation' *Monist* 76 (1993) 119

——*Living Together: Rationality, Sociality, and Obligation* (Lanham Md.: Rowman & Littlefield, 1996)

——*Sociality and Responsibility: New Essays in Plural Subject Theory* (Lanham Md.: Rowman & Littlefield, 2000)

Gilbert, Paul and Andrews, Bernie *Shame* (New York: Oxford University Press, 1998)

Godbout, Jacques T. and Caillé, Alain *The World of the Gift* trans. Winkler, D. (Montreal: McGill-Queen's University Press, 1998)

Goldman, Holly S. 'David Lyons on Utilitarian Generalisation' *Philosophical Studies* 26 (1974) 72

Goodin, Robert E. *Protecting the Vulnerable* (Chicago: University of Chicago Press, 1985)

Goodin, Robert E. 'Responsibilities' *Philosophical Quarterly* 36 (1987) 50
——'What is so Special about our Fellow Countrymen?' *Ethics* 98 (1988) 663
——*Reflective Democracy* (Oxford: Oxford University Press, 2003)
Grant, A. Campbell 'Conscience and Conscientiousness' in Feinberg, Joel (ed) *Moral Concepts* (Oxford: Oxford University Press, 1969)
Green, Leslie 'Law, Co-ordination and the Common Good' *Oxford Journal of Legal Studies* 3/3 (1983) 299
——'Authority and Convention' *Philosophy Quarterly* 35 (1986) 329
——*The Authority of the State* (Oxford: Clarendon Press, 1988)
——'Law, Legitimacy, and Consent' *Southern California Law Review* 62 (1989) 795
——'Associative Obligations and the State' in Hutchinson, A. and Green, Leslie (eds) *Law and the Community: The End of Individualism?* (Toronto: Carswell, 1989) 93
——'Who Believes in Political Obligation?' in Sanders, John T. and Narveson, Jan (eds) *For and Against the State: New Philosophical Readings* (Lanham Md.: Rowman & Littlefield, 1996) 1
——'Law and Obligations' in Coleman, Jules and Shapiro, Scott (eds) *The Oxford Handbook of Jurisprudence and Philosophy of Law* (New York: Oxford University Press, 2002) 514
Green, Thomas H. *Lectures on the Principles of Political Obligation* (Ann Arbor: University of Michigan Press, 1967)
Greenawalt, Kent 'Promises, Benefit, and Need: Ties That Bind Us To The Law' *Georgia Law Review* 18 (1984) 727
——*Conflicts of Law and Morality* (Oxford: Clarendon Press, 1987)
Greenspan, Patricia *Practical Guilt: Moral Dilemmas, Emotions, and Social Norms* (New York: Oxford University, Press, 1995)
Griffin, James 'Some Problems of Fairness' *Ethics* 96 (1985) 100
——*Value Judgment: Improving our Ethical Beliefs* (Oxford: Oxford University Press, 1996)
Gutmann, Amy 'Communitarian Critics of Liberalism' *Philosophy and Public Affairs* 14/3 (1985) 308
——and Taylor, Charles *Multiculturalism: Examining the Politics of Recognition* (Princeton: Princeton University Press, 1994)
——and Thompson, Dennis *Democracy and Disagreement* (Cambridge Mass.: Belknap Press of Harvard University Press, 1996)
Habermas, Jürgen *Legitimation Crisis* trans. Thomas McCarthy (Boston: Beacon Press, 1975)
——*Between Facts and Norms: Contributions to a Discourse Theory of Law and Democracy* trans. Rehg, W. (Cambridge Mass.: Harvard University Press, 1996)
——'The European Nation State and the Pressures of Globalisation' in De Greiff, Pablo and Cronin, Ciaran *Global Justice and Transnational Politics* (Cambridge Mass.: MIT Press, 2002) 217
——*The Inclusion of the Other: Studies in Political Theory* De Greiff, Pablo and Cronin, Ciaran (eds) (Cambridge: Polity Press, 2002)
Hacker, Peter M. S. and Raz, Joseph (eds) *Law, Morality and Society* (Oxford: Oxford University Press, 1977)
Hall, John A. (ed) *Civil Society: Theory, History, Comparison* (Oxford: Polity, 1996)

Hall, Mark and Klosko, George 'Political Obligation and the US Supreme Court' *Journal of Politics* 60/2 (1998) 462

Hampshire, Stuart *Innocence and Experience* (London: Allen Lane, 1989)

——*Justice is Conflict* (London: Duckworth, 1999)

Hampton, Jean *Hobbes and the Social Contract Tradition* (New York: Cambridge University Press, 1986)

——'Free-Rider Problems in the Production of Collective Goods' *Economics and Philosophy* 3 (1987) 245

——*Political Philosophy* (Oxford: Westview, 1997)

Hardimon, Michael O. 'Role Obligations' *Journal of Philosophy* 91/7 (1994) 333

Hardin, Russell 'Do We Want Trust in Government?' in Warren, M. E. (ed) *Democracy and Trust* (Cambridge: Cambridge University Press, 1999) 22

——'Group Boundaries, Individual Barriers' in Miller, D. and Hashmi, S. H. (eds) *Boundaries and Justice: Diverse Ethical Perspectives* (Princeton: Princeton University Press, 2001)

Hare, Richard M. *Freedom and Reason* (Oxford: Oxford University Press, 1963)

——'Political Obligation' in *Essays in Political Morality* (Oxford: Oxford University Press, 1989)

Hargreaves-Heap, Shaun P. and Varoufakis, Yanis *Game Theory: A Critical Introduction* (London: Routledge, 1995)

Harris, Edward A. 'From Social Contract to Hypothetical Agreement: Consent and the Obligation to Obey the Law' *Columbia Law Review* 92 (1992) 651

Harris, Paul (ed) *Political Obligation* (London: Routledge & Kegan Paul, 1990)

Hart, Herbert, L. A. 'Positivism and the Separation of Law and Morals' *Harvard Law Review* 71 (1958) 593

——*Essays in Jurisprudence and Philosophy* (Oxford: Oxford University Press, 1980)

——*Essays on Bentham* (Oxford: Clarendon Press, 1982)

——*The Concept of Law* (2nd edn with postscript) Bullock, Penny and Raz, Joseph (eds) (Oxford: Oxford University Press, 1994)

——'Are There Any Natural Rights?' in Waldron, J. (ed) *Theories of Rights* (New York: Oxford University Press, 1995) 77

Havel, Vaklav *Open Letters* (selected and ed by Paul Wilson) (London: Faber & Faber, 1991)

Hegel, Georg W. *Philosophy of Right* trans. with notes by Knox, T. M. (Oxford: Oxford University Press, 1967)

Helton, Arthur C. *The Price of Indifference: Refugees and Humanitarian Action in the New Century* (New York: Oxford University Press for the Council on Foreign Relations, 2002)

Hershowitz, Scott 'Wittgenstein on Rules: The Phantom Menace' *Oxford Journal of Legal Studies* 22/4 (2002) 619–40.

Hesk, Jon *Deception and Democracy in Classical Athens* (Cambridge: Cambridge University Press, 2000)

Hill, Jr, Thomas E. *Autonomy and Self-Respect* (New York: Cambridge University Press, 1991)

——*Respect, Pluralism and Justice: Kantian Perspectives* (Oxford: Oxford University Press, 2000)

Hill, Roscoe 'Legal Validity and Legal Obligation' *Yale Law Journal* 80 (1970) 47

Himma, Kenneth E. 'Positivism, Naturalism, and the Obligation to Obey Law' *The Southern Journal of Philosophy* 36 (1998) 145

——'Law's Claim of Legitimate Authority' in Coleman, J. (ed) *Hart's Postscript: Essays on the Postscript to 'The Concept of Law'* (New York: Oxford University Press, 2001) 271

Hinde, Robert A. *Why Good is Good: The Sources of Morality* (London: Routledge, 2002)

Hinton, J. M. 'Knowing and Valuing Fairness' (1990) 65 *Philosophy* 271

Hirschleifer, Jack 'From Weakest-Link to Best Shot: The Voluntary Provision of Public Goods' *Public Choice* 41 (1983) 371

Hirschman, Albert O. *Exit, Voice, and Loyalty* (Cambridge Mass.: Harvard University Press, 1970)

Hirschmann, Nancy J. *Rethinking Obligation: A Feminist Method for Political Theory* (Ithaca NY: Cornell University Press, 1992)

Hobbes, Thomas *Leviathan* Plamenatz, J. (ed) (London: Fontana, 1962)

——*Elements of Law* Ferdinand Tommies (ed) (London: Frank Cass and Company, 1969)

——*Human Nature and De Corpore Politico* (Oxford: Oxford University Press, 1994)

Hohfeld, Wesley N. *Fundamental Legal Conceptions* (New Haven: Yale University Press, 1923)

Hollis, Martin *Trust within Reason* (Cambridge: Cambridge University Press, 1998)

Holmes, Oliver W. 'The Path of the Law' *Harvard Law Review* 10 (1897) 457

Holmes, Stephen and Sunstein, Cass *The Cost of Rights: Why Liberty Depends on Taxes* (New York: Norton, 2000)

Holton, Robert J. *Globalization and the Nation-State* (London: Macmillan, 1998)

Honderich, Ted *Violence for Equality* (London: Penguin, 1980)

Honoré, Anthony M. 'Must We Obey? Necessity as a Ground of Obligation' *Virginia Law Review* 67 (1981) 39

——'The Dependence of Morality on Law' *Oxford Journal of Legal Studies* 13 (1993) 1

Hook, Sidney 'Law, Justice and Obedience' in Hook, Sidney (ed) *Law and Philosophy* (New York: New York University Press, 1964) 56

Horton, John *Political Obligation* (Atlantic Highlands NJ: Humanities Press, 1992)

Hume, David *A Treatise of Human Nature* (2nd edn) Selby-Bigge, L. A. and Nidditch, P. H. (eds) (Oxford: Clarendon Press, 1978)

——*Enquiries Concerning Human Understanding and Concerning the Principles of Morals* (3rd edn) with text and notes by Nidditch, P. H. (Oxford: Clarendon Press, 1995)

——*Political Writings* Warner, Stuart D. and Livingston, Donald W. (eds) (Indianapolis: Hackett Publishing, 1994)

Hunt, Alan 'Law's Empire or Legal Imperialism?' in Hunt, Alan (ed) *Reading Dworkin Critically* (New York: Berg, 1992)

Hurd, Heidi 'Challenging Authority' *Yale Law Journal* 100 (1991) 1611

Hurley, Susan *Natural Reasons: Personality and Polity* (New York: Oxford University Press, 1989)

Ignatieff, Michael *The Needs of Strangers* (London: Vintage, 1984)

Isin, Engin F. and Wood, Patricia K. (eds) *Citizenship & Identity* (London: Sage Publications, 1999)

Jackson, Frank *From Metaphysics to Ethics: A Defence of Conceptual Analysis* (Oxford: Clarendon, 2000)

Jamieson, George *Parental Responsibilities and Rights* (Edinburgh: W. Green Sweet & Maxwell, 1995)

Jefferson, Thomas *Political Writings* Appelby, Joyce and Ball, Terence (eds) (Cambridge: Cambridge University Press, 1999)

Jeske, Diane 'Associative Obligations, Voluntarism, and Equality' *Pacific Philosophical Quarterly* 77 (1996) 289

Joffe, Hélène *Risk and 'the Other'* (Cambridge: Cambridge University Press, 1999)

Johnson, Conrad D. 'Actual—v. (Rawlsian) Hypothetical Consent' *Philosophical Studies* 28 (1975) 41

——'Moral and Legal Obligation' 72 (1975) *Journal of Philosophy* 315

Johnson, James 'Arguing for Deliberation: Some Skeptical Considerations' in Elster, J. (ed) *Deliberative Democracy* (Cambridge: Cambridge University Press, 1998) 161

Johnson, Karen 'Political Obligation and the Voluntary Association Model of the State' *Ethics* 86 (1976) 17

Johnson, Mark *Moral Imagination: Implications of Cognitive Science for Ethics* (Chicago: University of Chicago Press, 1993)

Kaase, Max and Norton, Kenneth *Beliefs in Government* (Oxford: Oxford University Press, 1998)

Kagan, Shelly 'Rethinking Intrinsic Value' *The Journal of Ethics* 2 (1998) 277

——*Normative Ethics* (Boulder Colo.: Westview, 1998)

Kahn, Paul W. 'Community in Contemporary Constitutional Theory' *Yale Law Journal* 99/1 (1989) 1

——*The Reign of Law: Marbury v Madison and the Construction of America* (New Haven: Yale University Press, 1997)

Kamm, Francis, M. 'Non-consequentialism, the Person as an End-in-Itself, and the Significance of Status' *Philosophy & Public Affairs* 21 (1992) 354

Kant, Immanuel *The Metaphysical Elements of Justice* trans. Ladd, John (Indianapolis: Bobbs-Merrill, 1965)

——*Political Writings* Reiss, H. S. (ed) (Cambridge: Cambridge University Press, 1991)

——*Groundwork of the Metaphysics of Morals* trans. Paton, H. J. (London: Routledge, 1995)

——*The Metaphysics of Morals* trans. and ed by Gregor, Mary (Cambridge: Cambridge University Press, 1998)

Kautz, Steven *Liberalism and Community* (Ithaca NY: Cornell University Press, 1995)

Kavka, Gregory 'Review of *Moral Principles and Political Obligations*, by A. John Simmons' *Topoi* 2 (1983) 227

Kekes, John 'Morality and Partiality' *American Philosophical Quarterly* 18 (1981) 295

——*Moral Wisdom and Good Lives* (Ithaca NY: Cornell University Press, 1995)

Keyt, David 'The Social Contract as an Analytic, Justificatory, and Polemic Device' *Canadian Journal of Philosophy* 4/2 (1974) 241

King, Jr., Martin L. 'Letter from Birmingham City Jail' in Bedau, H. A. (ed) *Civil Disobedience in Focus* (London: Routledge, 1995) 68

Klosko, George 'Presumptive Benefit, Fairness, and Political Obligation' *Philosophy & Public Affairs* 16 (1987) 241

Klosko, George 'The Moral Force of Political Obligations' *American Political Science Review* 84 (1990) 1237

——*The Principle of Fairness and Political Obligation* (Lanham Md.: Rowman & Littlefield, 1992)

Korsgaard, Christine 'Two Distinctions in Goodness' in Carson, T. L. and Moser, P. K. (eds) *Morality and the Good Life* (New York: Oxford University Press, 1997) ch. 9 (initially published in *Philosophical Review* 92 (1983) 169)

Kramer, Matthew H. 'Requirements, Reasons, and Raz: Legal Positivism and Duties' *Ethics* 109 (1999) 375

——and Simmonds, Nigel E. 'No Better Reasons: A Reply to Alan Gewirth' 36 *Southern Journal of Philosophy* (1998) 131

——and Simmonds, Nigel E. 'Reason without Reason: A Critique of Alan Gewirth's Moral Philosophy' *Southern Journal of Philosophy* 34 (1996) 301

Kraut, Richard *Socrates and the State* (Princeton: Princeton University Press, 1984)

Kukathas, Chandran 'Liberalism, Communitarianism, and Political Community' (1996) *Social Philosophy and Policy* 80

Kung, Hans and Schmidt, Helmut *A Global Ethic and Global Responsibilities* (London: SCM Press, 1998)

Kymlika, Will 'Territorial Boundaries: A Liberal Egalitarian Perspective' in Miller, David and Hashmi, Sohail H. (eds) *Boundaries and Justice: Diverse Ethical Perspectives* (Princeton: Princeton University Press, 2001) 249

La Rochefoucald *Maxims* trans. Humphreys, A. L. (Hertfordshire: Wordsworth Classics, 1997)

Ladd, John 'The Grounds of Obligation' *Journal of Philosophy* 53 (1956) 653

——'Legal and Moral Obligation' in Pennock, J. R. and Chapman, J. W. (eds) *Nomos XII: Political and Legal Obligation* (New York: Atherton, 1970) 27

Ladenson, Robert 'In Defense of a Hobbesian Conception of Law' *Philosophy and Public Affairs* 9/2 (1980) 139, repr. in Raz, Joseph (ed) *Authority* (New York: New York University Press, 1990) 32

Laertius, Diogenes *Lives of Eminent Philosophers* (vol i) trans. Hicks, R. D. (London: Loeb Classical Library William Heinemann Ltd, 1966)

Lardy, Heather 'Citizenship and the Right to Vote' *Oxford Journal of Legal Studies* 17 (1997) 75

Larmore, Charles *Patterns of Moral Complexity* (Cambridge: Cambridge University Press, 1987)

——*The Morals of Modernity* (New York: Cambridge University Press, 1996)

Lemmon, E. J. 'Moral Dilemmas' *Philosophical Review* 71 (1962) 141

Lessnoff, Michael *Social Contract Theory* (New York: New York University Press, 1990)

Letwin, Shirley R. 'Morality and Law' (1989) 2/1 *Ratio Juris* 55

Levmore, Saul (ed) *Foundations of Tort Law* (New York: Oxford University Press, 1994)

Lewis, David *Convention: A Philosophical Study* (Cambridge Mass.: Harvard University Press, 1969)

Lewis, Michael 'Shame and Stigma' in Gilbert, Paul and Andrews, Bernie (eds) *Shame: Interpersonal Behavior, Psychopathology, and Culture* (New York: Oxford University Press, 1998) 126

Locke, John *Two Treatises of Government* Laslett, P. (ed) (Cambridge: Cambridge University Press, 1988)

Lomasky, Loren 'Toward a Liberal Theory of National Boundaries' in Miller, David and Hashmi, Sohail H. (ed) *Boundaries and Justice: Diverse Ethical Perspectives* (Princeton: Princeton University Press, 2001) 55

Lowe, Scott C. 'Free Riders, "Fair Share" and the Principle of Fairness' *Public Affairs Quarterly* 10/1 (1996) 49

Luban, David 'Intervention and Civilization: Some Unhappy Lessons of the Kosovo War' in De Greiff, Pablo and Cronin, Ciaran (eds) *Global Justice and Transnational Politics* (Cambridge Mass.: MIT Press, 2002) 79

Lupia, Arthur and McCubbins, Matthew D. *The Democratic Dilemma: Can Citizens Learn What they Need to Know?* (New York: Cambridge University Press, 1998)

Lyons, Daniel 'The Odd Debt of Gratitude' *Analysis* 29 (1969) 92

Lyons, David *Forms and Limits of Utilitarianism* (London: Oxford University Press, 1965)

——'The Correlativity of Rights and Duties' *Nous* 4 (1970) 45

——'Moral Aspects of Legal Theory' in French, P. A., Uehling, T. E., Jr., and Wettstein, H. K. (eds) *Midwest Studies in Philosophy Volume 7: Studies in Social and Political Philosophy* (Minneapolis: University of Minnesota Press, 1982) 223

——*Ethics and the Rule of Law* (Cambridge: Cambridge University Press, 1984)

Maaloof, Amin *On Identity* (London: Harvill Press, 2000)

McCloskey, H. G. 'Ross and the Concept of a Prima Facie Duty' *Australasian Journal of Philosophy* 41 (1963) 336

McConnell, Terrence *Gratitude* (Philadelphia: Temple University Press, 1993)

MacCormick, Neil 'Law, Obligation and Consent: Reflections on Stair and Locke *Archiv für Rechts-und Sozialphilosophie* 65/3 (1979) 387

——*Legal Rights and Social Democracy: Essays in Legal and Political Philosophy* (Oxford: Clarendon Press, 1982)

——'Of Self-Determination and Other Things' *Bulletin of the Australian Society of Legal Philosophy* (1990) 15

——'Is Nationalism Philosophically Credible?' in Twining, W. (ed) *Issues in Self-Determination* (Aberdeen: Aberdeen University Press, 1991)

——'What Place for Nationalism in the Modern World?' in Caney, Simon, George, David and Jones, Peter *National Rights and International Obligations* (Boulder Colo.: Westview, 1996) 34

——*Questioning Sovereignty* (Oxford: Oxford University Press, 1999)

McCorquondale, Robert 'International Law, Boundaries, and Imagination' in Miller, David and Hashmi, Sohail H. (eds) *Boundaries and Justice: Diverse Ethical Perspectives* (Princeton: Princeton University Press, 2001) 136

Macdonald, Margaret 'The Language of Political Theory' in Flew, A. G. N. (ed) *Logic and Language* (1st series) (Oxford: Basil Blackwell, 1963) 167

Macedo, Stephen (ed) *Deliberative Politics: Essays on Democracy and Disagreement* (New York: Oxford University Press, 1999)

MacIntyre, Alasdair *After Virtue* (London: Duckworth, 1985)

——*Dependent Rational Animals: Why Human Beings Need the Virtues* (Duckworth: London, 1999)

McMahon, Christopher 'Autonomy and Authority' *Philosophy and Public Affairs* 16 (1987) 303

McPherson, Thomas *Political Obligation* (London: Routledge & Kegan Paul, 1967)

Mandelbaum, Maurice 'On Grounds' *Journal of Philosophy* 53 (1956) 662

Manin, Bernard *The Principles of Representative Government* (Cambridge: Cambridge University Press, 1997)

Maphai, Vincent 'The Principle of Fairness' *South African Journal of Philosophy* 6/3 (1987) 73

Margalit, Avisahi *The Decent Society* (Cambridge Mass.: Harvard University Press, 1998)

——*The Ethics of Memory* (Cambridge Mass.: Harvard University Press, 2002)

——and Raz, Joseph 'National Self-Determination' in Raz, Joseph *Ethics in the Public Domain* (rev edn) (Oxford: Clarendon Press, 1996)

Margolis, Joseph 'The Analysis of Ought' *Australasian Journal of Philosophy* 48/1 (1970) 44

Marmor, Andrei (ed) *Law and Interpretation: Essays in Legal Philosophy* (New York: Oxford University Press, 1995)

——*Positive Law and Objective Value* (Oxford: Clarendon Press, 2001)

Martin, Mike W. 'Good Fortune Obligates: Gratitude, Philanthropy, and Colonialism' *Southern Journal of Philosophy* 37 (1999) 57

Martin, Rex 'Wolff's Defence of Philosophical Anarchism' *Philosophical Quarterly* 24 (1974) 140

Mason, Andrew 'Special Obligations to Compatriots' *Ethics* 107 (1997) 427

Massey, Stephen J. 'Is Self-Respect a Moral or a Psychological Concept?' in Dillon, R. S. *Dignity, Character, and Self-Respect* (London: Routledge, 1995) 198

Midgeley, Mary *Beast and Man: The Roots of Human Nature* (rev edn). (London: Routledge, 1995)

Mill, John S. *On Liberty and Other Essays* (Oxford: Oxford University Press, 1991)

Miller, David 'The Ethical Significance of Nationality' *Ethics* 98 (1988) 647

——'Community and Citizenship' in Avineri, Shlomo and de Shalit, Avner (eds) *Communitarianism and Individualism* (Oxford: Oxford University Press, 1992) 85

——and Hashmi, Sohail H. *Boundaries and Justice: Diverse Ethical Perspectives* (Princeton: Princeton University Press, 2001)

Miller, Frank and Sartorius, Rolf 'Population Policy and Public Goods' *Philosophy & Public Affairs* 8/2 (1979) 148

Miller, Richard 'Cosmopolitan Respect and Patriotic Concern' *Philosophy and Public Affairs* 27/3 (1998) 202

Miller, Seamus 'Rationalising Conventions' *Synthese* 84 (1990) 23

Mish'Alani, James K. '"Duty", "Obligation" and "Ought"' *Analysis* 30 (1969) 33

Moellendorf, David *Cosmopolitan Justice* (Boulder Colo.: Westview, 2002)

Moffat, Robert 'Obligation to Obey the Law: Substance and Procedure in the Thought of Lon Fuller' *International Journal of Applied Philosophy* 1 (1983) 33

Moore, Michael 'Authority, Law, and Razian Reasons' *Southern California Law Review* 62 (1989) 827

——'Interpreting Interpretation' in Marmor, Andrei (ed) *Law and Interpretation: Essays in Legal Philosophy* (New York: Oxford University Press, 1995) 1

Moran, Richard *Authority and Estrangement: An Essay on Self-Knowledge* (Princeton: Princeton University Press, 2001)

Morris, Christopher *An Essay on the Modern State* (Cambridge: Cambridge University Press, 1998)

Morrison, Ken *Marx, Durkheim, Weber: Foundations of Modern Social Thought* (London: Sage, 1997)

Mulhall, Stephen 'Promising, Consent and Citizenship' *Political Theory* 25/2 (1997) 171
——*Stanley Cavell: Philosophy's Recounting of the Ordinary* (Oxford: Clarendon Press, 1998)
——and Swift, Adam *Liberals and Communitarians* (2nd edn) (Oxford: Basil Blackwell 1997)
Murdoch, Iris *Metaphysics as a Guide to Morals* (London: Penguin, 1993)
——*Existentialists and Mystics: Writings on Philosophy and Literature* (Middlesex: Penguin, 1999)
Murphy, Jeffrie G. 'Hume and Kant on the Social Contract' *Philosophical Studies* 33 (1978) 65
——'Consent, Coercion, and Hard Choices' *Virginia Law Review* 67 (1981) 79
Murphy, Mark C. 'Acceptance of Authority and the Duty to Comply with Just Institutions: A Comment on Waldron' *Philosophy & Public Affairs* 23 (1994) 271
——'Surrender of Judgment and the Consent Theory of Political Authority' *Law & Philosophy* 16 (1997) 115
——'Natural Law, Consent and Political Obligation' in Paul, Ellen F., Miller, Fred D. and Paul, Jeffrey (eds) *Natural Law and Modern Moral Philosophy* (Cambridge: Cambridge University Press, 2001) 70
Nagel, Thomas *The Possibility of Altruism* (Oxford: Clarendon Press, 1975)
——*Equality and Partiality* (New York: Oxford University Press, 1991)
——*Mortal Questions* (Cambridge: Cambridge University Press, 1992)
Narayan, Uma 'Towards a Feminist Vision of Citizenship: Rethinking the Implications of Dignity, Political Participation and Nationality' in Shanley, Mary L. and Narayan, Uma (eds) *Reconstructing Political Theory: Feminist Perspectives* (Oxford: Polity, 1997) 48
Nathanson, Stephen 'In Defense of Moderate Patriotism' *Ethics* 99 (1989) 535
Naticchia, Chris 'Recognition and Legitimacy: A Reply to Buchanan' *Philosophy & Public Affairs* 28/3 (1999) 242
Newey, Glen 'Reason beyond Reason? "Political Obligation" Reconsidered' *Philosophical Papers* 25/1 (1996) 21
Nickel, James W. 'Does Basing Rights on Autonomy Imply Obligations of Political Allegiance?' *Dialogue* 28 (1989) 531
Nielsen, Kai 'Why is there a Problem about Political Obligation?' *Journal of Value Enquiry* 24 (1990) 235
Nino, Carlos *The Constitution of Deliberative Democracy* (New Haven: Yale University Press, 1996)
Nozick, Robert *Anarchy, State, and Utopia* (Oxford: Blackwell, 1974)
Nussbaum, Martha C. *The Fragility of Goodness: Luck and Ethics in Greek Tragedy and Philosophy* (Cambridge: Cambridge University Press, 1986)
——*Love's Knowledge: Essays on Philosophy and Literature* (Oxford: Oxford University Press, 1990)
——*Upheavals of Thought: The Intelligence of Emotions* (Cambridge: Cambridge University Press, 2001)
——'Capabilities and Human Rights' in De Greiff, Pablo and Cronin, Ciaran *Global Justice and Transnational Politics* (Cambridge Mass.: MIT Press, 2002) 117
Oakley, Francis 'Disobedience, Consent, Political Obligation: The Witness of Wessel Gansfort (c.1419–1489)' *History of Political Thought* 9/2 (1988) 211

Offe, Claus 'How Can We Trust our Fellow Citizens?' in Warren, Mark E. (ed) *Democracy and Trust* (Cambridge: Cambridge University Press, 1999) 42

Ohlsson, Ragnar 'Who Can Accept Moral Dilemmas?' *Journal of Philosophy* 90 (1993) 405

Oldenquist, Andrew 'Loyalties' *Journal of Philosophy* 4/79 (1982) 173

Oliver, Dawn and Heater, Derek *The Foundations of Citizenship* (Hertfordshire: Harvester Wheatsheaf, 1994)

Olson, Mancur *The Logic of Collective Action* (Cambridge Mass.: Harvard University Press, 1971)

O'Neill, Onora *Bounds of Justice* (Cambridge: Cambridge University Press, 2000)

——*A Question of Trust* (Cambridge: Cambridge University Press, 2002)

Owen, David *Philosophical Foundations of Tort Law* (Oxford: Clarendon Press, 1997)

Parekh, Bhiku 'A Misconceived Discourse on Political Obligation' *Political Studies* 41 (1993) 236

——'Reconstituting the Modern State' in Anderson, J. (ed) *Transnational Democracy: Political Spaces and Border Crossings* (London: Routledge, 2002) 39

Parfit, Derek *Reasons and Persons* (Oxford: Clarendon, 1984)

Pateman, Carole *Participation and Democratic Theory* (Cambridge: Cambridge University Press, 1970)

——'Political Obligation and Conceptual Analysis' *Political Studies* 21 (1973) 199

——*The Problem of Political Obligations: A Critique of Liberal Theory* (Cambridge: Polity, 1985)

Patterson, Orolando 'Liberty against the Democratic State: On the Historical and Contemporary Sources of American Distrust' in Warren, Mark E. (ed) *Democracy and Trust* (Cambridge: Cambridge University Press, 1999) 151

Pennock, J. Roland and Chapman, John W. (eds) *Nomos XII: Political and Legal Obligation* (New York: Atherton, 1970)

Perry, Michael J., *Morality, Politics and Law: A Bicentennial Essay* (New York: Oxford University Press, 1988)

Perry, Stephen 'Judicial Precedent and the Common Law' *Oxford Journal of Legal Studies* 7 (1987) 213, 239–43

——'Second Order Reasons, Uncertainty and Legal Theory' *Southern California Law Review* 62 (1989) 913

——'Interpretation and Methodology in Legal Theory' in Marmor, Andrei (ed) *Law and Interpretation: Essays in Legal Philosophy* (New York: Oxford University Press, 1995)

Pettit, Philip 'Free Riding and Foul Dealing' *The Journal of Philosophy* 83/7 (1986) 361

——'The Paradox of Loyalty' *American Philosophical Quarterly* 25/2 (1988) 163

——'Consequentialism' in Singer, P. (ed) *A Companion to Ethics* (Oxford: Basil Blackwell, 1997) 230

——and Goodin, Robert E. 'The Possibility of Special Duties' *Canadian Journal of Philosophy* 16 (1986) 651

Pierson, Christopher *The Modern State* (London: Routledge, 1996)

Pincoffs, Edmund L. 'On Consenting' *Archiv für Rechts-und Sozialphilosophie* 12 (1980) 107

Pinker, Steven *The Blank Slate: The Modern Denial of Human Nature* (London: Penguin Allen Lane, 2002)

Pitcher, George 'On Approval' *The Philosophical Review* 67 (1958) 198

Pitkin, Hannah F. *Wittgenstein and Justice* (Berkeley: University of California Press, 1973)
Plamenatz, John P. *Man and Society* (London: Longmans Green and Company, 1963)
—— *Consent, Freedom and Political Obligation* (2nd edn) (Oxford: Oxford University Press, 1968)
Plato *The Last Days of Socrates* trans. Tredennick, H. (London: Penguin, 1969)
—— *The Republic* trans. Lee, D. (London: Penguin, 1987)
Pogge, Thomas *World Poverty and Human Rights* (Cambridge: Polity, 2002)
—— 'Human Rights and Human Responsibilities' in De Greiff, P. and Cronin, C. *Global Justice and Transnational Politics* (Cambridge Mass.: MIT Press, 2002) 151
Posner, Richard A. *Law, Pragmatism, and Democracy* (Cambridge Mass.: Harvard University Press, 2003)
Postema, Gerald 'Coordination and Convention at the Foundations of Law' *The Journal of Legal Studies* 9 (1982) 165
Powell, Douglas and Leiss, William *Mad Cows and Mother's Milk: The Perils of Poor Risk Communication* (Montreal: McGill-Queen's University Press, 1997)
Powers, Madison 'Rule Consequentialism and the Value of Friendship' in Hooker, Brad, Mason, Elinor and Miller, Dale E. (eds) *Morality, Rules and Consequences* (Edinburgh: Edinburgh University Press, 2000) 239
Putnam, Hilary *Mind, Language and Reality: Philosophical Papers Volume 2* (Cambridge: Cambridge University Press, 1975)
Quinton, Anthony *Utilitarian Ethics* (London: Duckworth, 1989)
Raphael, David D. *Problems of Political Philosophy* (London: Macmillan, 1976)
Rawls, John 'Legal Obligation and the Duty of Fair Play' in Hook, S. (ed) *Law and Philosophy* (New York: New York University Press, 1964) 3
—— *A Theory of Justice* (Oxford: Oxford University Press, 1973)
—— *Political Liberalism* (New York: Columbia University Press, 1993)
—— *The Law of Peoples* (Cambridge Mass.: Harvard University Press, 1999)
Raz, Joseph, 'On Lawful Governments' *Ethics* 80 (1970) 296
—— 'Voluntary Obligations and Normative Powers' *Aristotelian Society Supplementary Volume* 46 (1972) 79
—— *Practical Reason and Norms* (London: Hutchinson, 1975)
—— 'Promises and Obligations' in Hacker, P. M. S. and Raz, J. (eds) *Law, Morality and Society* (Oxford: Oxford University Press, 1977) 210
—— (ed) *Practical Reasoning* (Oxford: Oxford University Press, 1978)
—— *The Authority of Law: Essays on Law and Morality* (Oxford: Clarendon, 1979)
—— *The Concept of a Legal System* (2nd edn) (Oxford: Oxford University Press, 1980)
—— 'Authority and Consent' *Virginia Law Review* 67 (1981) 103
—— 'Hart on Moral Rights and Legal Duties' *Oxford Journal of Legal Studies* 4 (1984) 123
—— 'Authority, Law and Morality' *Monist* 68 (1985) 295, repr. in *Ethics in the Public Domain* (revised edn) (Oxford: Clarendon, 1996) 210
—— *The Morality of Freedom* (Oxford: Clarendon Press, 1986)
—— 'Liberating Duties' in Raz, Joseph *Ethics in the Public Domain* (rev edn) (Oxford: Clarendon Press, 1996), originally printed in *Law and Philosophy* 8 (1989) 3
—— 'Facing Up: A Reply' *Southern California Law Review* 62 (1989) 1153
—— (ed) *Authority* (New York: New York University Press, 1990)

Raz, Joseph 'Authority and Justification' in Raz, Joseph (ed) *Authority* (New York: New York University Press, 1990) 115

——*Ethics in the Public Domain* (rev edn). (Oxford: Clarendon Press, 1996)

——'Interpretation without Retrieval' in Marmor, A. *Law and Interpretation* (Oxford: Clarendon, 1996) 163

——*Engaging Reason: On the Theory of Value and Action* (Oxford: Oxford University Press, 1999)

——*Value, Respect and Attachment* (Cambridge: Cambridge University Press, 2001)

Regan, Donald *Utilitarianism and Co-operation* (Oxford: Oxford University Press, 1980)

——'Law's Halo' *Social Philosophy and Policy* 4 (1986) 15

——'Authority and Value: Reflections on Raz's *Morality of Freedom*' *South Californian Law Review* 62 (1989) 995

Rescher, Nicholas 'Rationality and Moral Obligation' *Synthese* 72 (1987) 29

Reynolds, Noel B. 'Law as Convention' *Ratio Juris* 2/1 (1989) 105

Richards, David A. J. 'Conscience, Human Rights, and the Anarchist Challenge to the Obligation to Obey the Law' *Georgia Law Review* 18 (1984) 771

Ridley, Matt *The Origins of Virtue: Human Instincts and the Evolution of Cooperation* (London: Penguin, 1997)

Robinson, Richard 'Ought and Ought Not' *Philosophy* 46 (1971) 193

Rogowski, Ronald 'The Obligations of Liberalism: Pateman on Participation and Promising' *Ethics* 91 (1981) 296

Rorty, Richard *Contingency, Irony, Solidarity* (Cambridge: Cambridge University Press, 1989)

——*Philosophy and Social Hope* (London: Penguin, 1999)

Rosen, Allen D. *Kant's Theory of Justice* (Ithaca NY: Cornell University Press 1993)

Rosenblum, Nancy *Membership and Morals: The Personal Uses of Pluralism in America* (Princeton: Princeton University Press, 1998)

Ross, David *The Right and the Good* (Oxford: Oxford University Press, 1932)

Rousseau, Jean Jacques *The Social Contract* trans. Cranston, M. (London: Penguin, 1968)

——*A Discourse on Inequality* trans. Cranston, M. (London: Penguin, 1984)

Rubio-Marin, Ruth *Immigration as a Democratic Challenge: Citizenship and Inclusion in Germany and the United States* (Cambridge: Cambridge University Press, 2000)

Russell, Bertrand *Authority and the Individual* (London: Routledge, 1995)

Russell, Paul 'Locke on Express and Tacit Consent: Misinterpretations and Inconsistencies' *Political Theory* 14/2 (1986) 291

Samuelson, Paul A. 'The Pure Theory of Public Expenditure' *The Review of Economics and Statistics* 36 (1954) 387

Sandel, Michael *Liberalism and the Limits of Justice* (Cambridge: Cambridge University Press, 1982)

——*Democracy's Discontent: America in Search of a Public Philosophy* (Cambridge Mass.: Harvard University Press, 1996)

Sanders, John T. and Narveson, Jan (eds) *For and Against the State* (London: Rowman & Littlefield, 1996)

Sartorius, Rolf *Individual Conduct and Social Norms* (California: Dickenson Encino, 1975)

——'Political Authority and Political Obligation' *Virginia Law Review* 67 (1981) 3

——'Positivism at the Foundations of Legal Authority' in Gavison, Ruth (ed) *Issues in Contemporary Legal Philosophy: The Influence of H. L. A. Hart* (Oxford: Oxford University Press, 1986)

Sassen, Saskia *Losing Control: Sovereignty in an Age of Globalization* (New York: Columbia University Press, 1996)

Scanlon, Thomas 'Promises and Practices' *Philosophy and Public Affairs* 19 (1990) 199

——*What we Owe to Each Other* (Cambridge Mass.: Belknap Press of Harvard University, 2000)

Schauer, Frederick 'Positivism as Pariah' in George, R. P. (ed) *The Autonomy of Law: Essays on Legal Positivism* (Oxford: Clarendon, 1996)

Scheffler, Samuel 'Ethics, Personal Identity, and Ideals of the Person' *Canadian Journal of Philosophy* 12/2 (1982) 229

——*The Rejection of Consequentialism* (Oxford: Clarendon Press, 1984)

——*Consequentialism and its Critics* (Oxford: Oxford University Press, 1988)

——*Human Morality* (New York: Oxford University Press, 1992)

——'Individual Responsibility in a Global Age' *Social Philosophy and Policy* 13 (1995) 219, repr. in Scheffler, Samuel *Boundaries and Allegiances: Problems of Justice and Responsibility in Liberal Thought* (Oxford: Oxford University Press, 2001) 32

——'Relationships and Responsibilities' *Philosophy & Public Affairs* 26/3 (1997) 189, repr. in Scheffler, Samuel *Boundaries and Allegiances: Problems of Justice and Responsibility in Liberal Thought* (Oxford: Oxford University Press, 2001) 97

——'Families, Nations, and Strangers' in Scheffler, Samuel *Boundaries and Allegiances: Problems of Justice and Responsibility in Liberal Thought* (Oxford: Oxford University Press, 2001) 48

Schmidtz, David 'Justifying the State' *Ethics* 101 (1990) 89

Schroeder, Christopher H. 'Causation, Compensation, and Moral Responsibility' in Owen, D. G. *Philosophical Foundations of Tort Law* (Oxford: Clarendon 1997) 347

Schumpeter, Joseph *Capitalism, Socialism and Democracy* (New York: Harper & Row, 1950)

Searle, John 'Prima Facie Obligations' in Raz, Joseph (ed) *Practical Reasoning* (Oxford: Oxford University Press, 1978)

Seidler, Victor J. *Kant, Respect and Injustice: The Limits of Liberal Moral Theory* (London, Routledge & Kegan Paul, 1986)

Seligman, Adam B. *The Idea of Civil Society* (Princeton: Princeton University Press, 1992)

——*The Problem of Trust* (Princeton: Princeton University Press, 2000)

Sen, Amartya and Williams, Bernard (eds) *Utilitarianism and Beyond* (Cambridge: Cambridge University Press, 1982)

Seneca *Moral and Political Essays* trans. and ed. by Cooper, J. M. and Procope, J. F. (Cambridge: Cambridge University Press, 1998)

Sennet, Richard *Authority* (London: Secher & Warburg, 1980)

——*Respect: The Formation of Character in an Age of Inequality* (London: Penguin Allen Lane, 2002)

Senor, Thomas 'What if There are No Political Obligations?' *Philosophy & Public Affairs* 16 (1987) 260

Sesonske, Alexander *Value and Obligation* (New York: Oxford University Press, 1964)

Shafir, Gershon (ed) *The Citizenship Debates* (Minneapolis: University of Minnesota Press, 1998)

Shakespeare, William *King Lear* (Oxford: The New Clarendon Shakespeare, 1967)

Shapiro, Ian 'Enough of Deliberation: Politics is about Interests and Power' in Macedo, Stephen (ed) *Deliberative Politics: Essays on Democracy and Disagreement* (New York: Oxford University Press, 1999) 28

Shapiro, Scott 'Authority' in Coleman, James and Shapiro, Scott (eds) *The Oxford Handbook of Jurisprudence and Philosophy of Law* (New York: Oxford University Press, 2002) 382

Shiell, Timothy 'Assessing Ronald Dworkin's New Theory of Political Obligations' *Proceedings of the Hericlatean Society* 15 (1990) 23

Shklar, Judith N. 'Obligation, Loyalty, Exile' *Political Theory* 21/2 (1993) 181

Shope, Robert K. 'Prima Facie Duty' *Journal of Philosophy* 62 (1965) 279

Sibley, Mulford Q. 'Conscience, Law, and the Obligation to Obey' *Monist* 54 (1970) 556

Sidgwick, Henry *The Methods of Ethics* (London: Macmillan, 1963)

Simmonds, Nigel E. 'Normativity and Norms' *Ratio Juris* 13/2 (2000) 219

Simmons, A. John *Moral Principles and Political Obligations* (Princeton: Princeton University Press, 1979)

—— 'Consent, Free Choice, and Democratic Government' *Georgia Law Review* 18 (1984) 791

—— 'The Anarchist Position: A Reply to Klosko and Senor' *Philosophy & Public Affairs* 16 (1987) 269

—— *On the Edge of Anarchy: Locke, Consent, and the Limits of Society* (Princeton: Princeton University Press, 1993)

—— 'Associative Political Obligations' in *Justification and Legitimacy: Essays on Rights and Obligations* (Cambridge: Cambridge University Press, 2001) 65 (originally published in *Ethics* 106/2 (1996) 247)

—— 'Justification and Legitimacy' in *Justification and Legitimacy: Essays on Rights and Obligations* (Cambridge: Cambridge University Press, 2001) 122 (originally published in *Ethics* 109 (1999) 739)

—— '"Denisons" and "Aliens": Locke's Problem of Political Consent' in *Justification and Legitimacy: Essays on Rights and obligations* (Cambridge: Cambridge University Press, 2001) 158

—— 'Fair Play and Political Obligation: Twenty Years Later' in *Justification and Legitimacy: Essays on Rights and Obligations* (Cambridge: Cambridge University Press, 2001) 27

—— 'Political Obligation and Authority' in Simon, Robert L. (ed) *The Blackwell Guide to Social and Political Philosophy* (Oxford: Blackwell, 2002) 17

Simon, Yves R. *A General Theory of Authority* (Indiana: University of Notre Dame Press, 1980)

Singer, Peter *Democracy and Disobedience* (New York: Oxford University Press, 1974)

—— *One World: The Ethics of Globalisation* (Melbourne: Text Publishing Company, 2002)

Skillon, Tony 'Active Citizenship as Political Obligation' *Radical Philosophy* 58 (1991) 10

Skyrms, Brian *Evolution of the Social Contract* (New York: Cambridge University Press, 1996)

Smart, J. J. C. 'An Outline of a System of Utilitarian Ethics' in Smart, J. J. C and Williams, B. *Utilitarianism For and Against* (Cambridge: Cambridge University Press, 1993) 1

Smith, Adam *The Theory of Moral Sentiments* Raphael, D. D. and Macfie, A. L. (eds) (Indianapolis: Liberty Fund, 1984)

——*The Wealth of Nations* (Oxford: Oxford University Press, 1998)

Smith, Anthony D. *National Identity* (London: Penguin, 1991)

Smith, Malcolm B. E. 'Is there a Prima Facie Obligation to Obey the Law?' *Yale Law Journal* 82 (1973) 950

Smith, Patricia *Liberalism and Affirmative Obligation* (New York: Oxford University Press, 1998)

Snare, Francis *Morals, Motivation and Convention* (New York: Cambridge University Press, 1991)

Someck, Ronny *The Fire Stays in Red* trans. from the Hebrew by Dor, Moshe and Goldberg, Barbara (Takoma Park Md.: University of Wisconsin Press, 2002)

Sommers, Christina H. 'Filial Morality' *Journal of Philosophy* 83 (1986) 441

Soper, Phillip 'Legal Theory and the Obligation of a Judge: The Hart Dworkin Dispute' *Michigan Law Review* 75 (1977) 511

——*A Theory of Law* (Cambridge Mass.: Harvard University Press, 1984)

——'The Obligation to Obey the Law' in Gavison, R. (ed) *Issues in Contemporary Legal Philosophy: The Influence of H. L. A. Hart* (Oxford: Oxford University Press, 1986)

——'Legal Theory and the Claim of Authority' *Philosophy and Public Affairs* 18 (1989) 209, repr. in Edmundson, W. (ed) *The Duty to Obey the Law: Selected Philosophical Readings* (Lanham Md.: Rowman & Littlefield, 1999) 213

——'Law's Normative Claims' in George, R. P. *The Autonomy of Law: Essays on Legal Positivism* (Oxford: Clarendon Press, 1996)

——*The Ethics of Deference: Learning from Law's Morals* (New York: Cambridge University Press, 2002)

Soysal, Yasemin N. *Limits of Citizenship: Migrants and Postnational Membership in Europe* (Chicago: University of Chicago Press, 1994)

Spelman, Elizabeth 'On Treating Persons as Persons' *Ethics* 88 (1978) 150

Steinberg, Jules *Locke, Rousseau and the Idea of Consent* (London: Greenwood Press, 1978)

Steiner, Hillel 'Hard Boundaries, Compensation, and Classical Liberalism' in Miller, D. and Hashmi, S. H. (eds) *Boundaries and Justice: Diverse Ethical Perspectives* (Princeton: Princeton University Press, 2001) 79

Stevens, Jacqueline *Reproducing the State* (Princeton: Princeton University Press, 1999)

Stiglitz, Joseph E. *Globalization and its Discontents* (London: Penguin, Allen Lane, 2002)

——'On Liberty, the Right to Know, and Public Discourse: The Role of Transparency in Public Life' in Gibney, M. J. (ed) *Globalizing Rights* (Oxford: Oxford University Press, 2003) 115

Stocker, Michael 'Moral Duties, Institutions, and Natural Facts' *Monist* 54 (1970) 602

——'Moral Conflicts: What They Are and What They Show' *Pacific Philosophy Quarterly* 68 (1987) 104

——with Hegeman, Elizabeth *Valuing Emotions* (Cambridge: Cambridge University Press, 1996)

Stokes, Susan 'Pathologies of Deliberation' in Elster, Jon (ed) *Deliberative Democracy* (Cambridge: Cambridge University Press, 1998) 123

Stokes, Susan 'What do Policy Switches Tell us about Democracy?' in Przeworski, Adam, Stokes, Susan C., and Manin, Bernard (eds) *Democracy, Accountability, and Representation* (New York: Cambridge University Press, 1999)

Strawson, Peter F. 'Freedom and Resentment' in Strawson, P. F. (ed) *Studies in the Philosophy of Thought and Action* (Oxford: Oxford University Press, 1968)

Sugden, Robert 'Reciprocity: The Supply of Public Goods through Voluntary Contributions' *The Economic Journal* 94 (1984) 772

Sullivan, Daniel 'Rules, Fairness and Formal Justice' *Ethics* 85 (1975) 322

Sunstein, Cass R. *The Partial Constitution* (Cambridge Mass.: Harvard University Press, 1993)

——'Incompletely Theorised Agreements' *Harvard Law Review* 108 (1995) 1733

——*Legal Reasoning and Political Conflict* (New York: Oxford University Press, 1996)

——*Free Markets and Social Justice* (New York: Oxford University Press, 1997)

——'Health-Health Trade-offs' in Elster, J. (ed) *Deliberative Democracy* (New York: Cambridge University Press, 1998) 232

——'Agreement without Theory' in Macedo, Stephen (ed) *Deliberative Politics: Essays on Democracy and Disagreement* (New York: Oxford University Press, 1999) 1123

——*Risk and Reason: Safety, Law, and the Environment* (Cambridge: Cambridge University Press, 2002)

Sztompka, Piotr *Trust: A Sociological Theory* (Cambridge: Cambridge University Press, 1999)

Tamir, Yael *Liberal Nationalism* (Princeton: Princeton University Press, 1993)

Taylor, Charles *Philosophy and the Human Sciences: Philosophical Papers 2* (Cambridge: Cambridge University Press, 1985)

——*Sources of the Self: The Making of the Modern Identity* (Cambridge: Cambridge University Press, 1989)

——'The Politics of Recognition' in *Multiculturalism: Examining the Politics of Recognition* (Princeton: Princeton University Press, 1994)

Taylor, Michael *The Possibility of Cooperation* (Cambridge: Cambridge University Press, 1987)

Thomas, Laurence 'Self-Respect: Theory and Practice' in Dillon, Robin S. (ed) *Dignity, Character and Self-Respect* (London: Routledge, 1995) 251

Thoreau, Henry D. 'Civil Disobedience' in Bedau, H. A. (ed) *Civil Disobedience in Focus* (London: Routledge, 1991) 28

Tolstoy, Leo *The Slavery of Our Times* trans. Maude, A. (Maldon, Essex: The Free Age Press, 1900)

Tussman, Joseph *Obligation and the Body Politic* (New York: Oxford University Press, 1970)

——*The Burden of Office* (Vancouver: Talonbooks, 1989)

Ullmann-Margalit, Edna *The Emergence of Norms* (Oxford: Oxford University Press, 1977)

Uslaner, Eric M. *The Moral Foundations of Trust* (New York: Cambridge University Press, 2002)

Van Creveld, Martin *The Rise and Decline of the State* (Cambridge: Cambridge University Press 1999)

Varoufakis, Yanis *Foundations of Economics: A Beginner's Companion* (London: Routledge, 1998)

Vincent, Andrew *Nationalism and Particularity* (Cambridge: Cambridge University Press, 2002)

Viroli, Maurizio *For Love of Country: An Essay on Patriotism and Nationality* (Oxford: Clarendon Press, 1997)

Waldron, Jeremy 'Theoretical Foundations of Liberalism' *Philosophical Quarterly* 37 (1987) 127

——'Special Ties and Natural Duties' *Philosophy & Public Affairs* 22/1 (1993) 3, reprinted in Edmundson, William A. *The Duty to Obey the Law: Selected Philosophical Writings* (Lanham Md.: Rowman & Littlefield, 1999) 271

——'Legislation, Authority and Voting' *Georgetown Law Journal* 84 (1996) 2185

——*Law and Disagreement* (Oxford: Oxford University Press, 1999)

——*The Dignity of Legislation* (Cambridge: Cambridge University Press, 1999)

——'Legal and Political Philosophy' in Coleman, Jules and Shapiro, Scott (eds) *The Oxford Handbook of Jurisprudence and Philosophy of Law* (New York: Oxford University Press, 2002) 352

Walker, A. D. M. 'Gratefulness and Gratitude' *Proceedings of the Aristotelian Society* 81 (1980–1) 40

——'Political Obligation and the Argument from Gratitude' *Philosophy & Public Affairs* 17/3 (1988) 191

Walter, E. 'Personal Consent and Moral Obligation' *Journal of Value Enquiry* 15/1 (1981) 19

Waluchow, Wilfred *Inclusive Legal Positivism* (Oxford: Clarendon, 1993)

Walzer, Michael *Obligations: Essays on War, Disobedience and Citizenship* (Cambridge Mass.: Harvard University Press, 1970)

——*Spheres of Justice*: A *Defense of Pluralism and Equality* (London: Basic Books, 1983)

Warnock, Mary *Imagination* (Berkeley: University of California Press, 1978)

Warren, Mark E. (ed) *Democracy and Trust* (Cambridge: Cambridge University Press, 1999)

——'Democratic Theory and Trust' in Mark E. Warren (ed) *Democracy and Trust* (Cambridge: Cambridge University Press, 1999)

——'Conclusion' in Warren, Mark E. (ed) *Democracy and Trust* (Cambridge: Cambridge University Press, 1999) 346

Wasserstrom, Richard 'The Obligation to Obey the Law' *University California at Los Angeles Law Review* 10 (1963) 780

Weil, Simone *The Need For Roots* (London: Routledge Classics, 2002)

Weinrib, Ernest J. *The Idea of Private Law* (Cambridge Mass.: Harvard University Press, 1995)

Wellman, Carl H. 'Associative Allegiances and Political Obligations' *Social Theory and Practice* 23 (1997) 181, 190–4

Whitely, C. H. 'On Duties' *Proceedings of the Aristotelian Society* 53 (1952–3) 97

Whitman, Walt *Selected Poems* (London: Penguin, 1973)

Williams, Bernard 'The Idea of Equality' in Feinberg, J. (ed) *Moral Concepts* (London: Oxford University Press, 1969)

——*Morality* (Cambridge: Cambridge University Press, 1972)

——*Problems of the Self* (Cambridge: Cambridge University Press, 1973)

——*Moral Luck* (Cambridge: Cambridge University Press, 1981)

——*Ethics and the Limits of Philosophy* (London: Fontana, 1985)

Williams, Bernard 'A Critique of Utilitarianism' in Smart, J. J. C and Williams, Bernard *Utilitarianism For and Against* (Cambridge: Cambridge University Press, 1993)

——*Shame and Necessity* (Berkeley: University of California Press, 1994)

Wittgenstein, Ludwig *Philosophical Investigations* trans. Anscombe, G. E. M. (Blackwell: Oxford, 1997)

——*Tractatus Logico-Philosophicus* (London: Routledge Classics, 2001)

Wolff, Jonathan 'What is the Problem of Political Obligation?' *Proceedings of the Aristotelian Society* 91 (1991–2) 153

——'Hume, Bentham, and the Social Contract' *Utilitas* 5/1 (1993) 87

——'Pluralistic Models of Political Obligation' 56/2 (1995) *Philosophica* 7

——'Political Obligation, Fairness, and Independence' *Ratio* (New Series) 8 (1995) 87

——*An Introduction to Political Philosophy* (Oxford: Oxford University Press, 1996)

——'Anarchism and Skepticism' in Narveson, Jan and Sanders, John T. (eds) *For and Against the State: New Philosophical Readings* (Lanham Md.: Rowman & Littlefield, 1996) 99

——'Fairness, Respect, and the Egalitarian Ethos' *Philosophy and Public Affairs* 27/2 (1998) 97

Wolff, Robert Paul (ed) *The Rule of Law* (New York: Simon & Schuster, 1971)

——*In Defense of Anarchism* (Berkeley: University of California Press, 1998)

Woozley, Anthony D. *Law and Disobedience: The Arguments of Plato's Crito* (London: Drickworth, 1979)

Wright, Robert *Non-Zero: The Logic of Human Destiny* (London: Little Brown and Company, 2000)

Young, Iris Marion 'Polity and Group Difference: A Critique of the Ideal of Universal Citizenship' *Ethics* 99 (1989) 250

——'Communication and the Other: Beyond Deliberative Democracy' in Benhabib, S. *Democracy and Difference: Contesting the Boundaries of the Political* (Princeton: Princeton University Press, 1996)

——'Difference as a Resource for Democratic Communication' in Estlund, David (ed) *Democracy* (Oxford: Blackwell, 2002) 213

Zimmerman, Michael J. 'Intrinsic vs. Extrinsic Value' http://plato.stanford.edu/entries/value-intrinsic-extrinsic/

——'Subsidiary Obligation' *Philosophical Studies* 50 (1986) 65

——'Remote Obligation' *American Philosophical Quarterly* 24/2 (1987) 199

——'Prima Facie Obligation and Doing the Best One Can' *Philosophical Studies* 78 (1995) 87

Zinn, Howard 'Law, Justice and Disobedience' *Notre Dame Journal of Law, Ethics and Public Policy* 5 (1991) 899

Zweibach, Burton *Civility and Disobedience* (Cambridge: Cambridge University Press, 1975)

Index

The manufacturer's authorised representative in the EU for product safety is Oxford University Press España S.A. of el Parque Empresarial San Fernando de Henares, Avenida de Castilla, 2 – 28830 Madrid (www.oup.es/en or product.safety@oup.com). OUP España S.A. also acts as importer into Spain of products made by the manufacturer.

www.ingramcontent.com/pod-product-compliance
Lightning Source LLC
LaVergne TN
LVHW011749200926
848484LV00003B/658
9780199265671